CHILDREN OF HOPE

Children of

The Odyssey of the Oromo Slaves
from Ethiopia to South Africa

HOPE

SANDRA ROWOLDT SHELL

Ohio University Press

Athens

Ohio University Press, Athens, Ohio 45701

ohioswallow.com

© 2018 by Ohio University Press

To obtain permission to quote, reprint, or otherwise reproduce or distribute material from Ohio University Press publications, please contact our rights and permissions department at (740) 593-1154 or (740) 593-4536 (fax).

Printed in the United States of America

Ohio University Press books are printed on acid-free paper ⊗ ™

28 27 26 25 24 23 22 21 20 19 18   5 4 3 2 1

Library of Congress Cataloging-in-Publication Data

Names: Shell, Sandra Rowoldt, author.
Title: Children of hope : the odyssey of the Oromo slaves from Ethiopia to
  South Africa / Sandra Rowoldt Shell.
Description: Athens, Ohio : Ohio University Press, 2018. | Includes
  bibliographical references and index.
Identifiers: LCCN 2018025973| ISBN 9780821423189 (hc : alk. paper) | ISBN
  9780821446324 (pdf)
Subjects: LCSH: Child slaves--Ethiopia--Biography. | Slave
  trade--Ethiopia--History. | Oromo (African people)--South
  Africa--Lovedale--History.
Classification: LCC HT869 .S54 2018 | DDC 306.3/62092393550963 [B] --dc23
LC record available at https://lccn.loc.gov/2018025973

To the memory of Robert Shell

and the courage and
resilience of the Oromo children

Contents

List of Illustrations   ix

Acknowledgments   xv

Introductory Ruminations   1

PART I

Roots: Memories of Home   13

    CHAPTER 1   *Ethiopia: The Lie of the Land*   15

    CHAPTER 2   *The Family Structure of the Oromo Captives*   29

    CHAPTER 3   *Wealth and Status of the Oromo Captives' Families*   42

    CHAPTER 4   *Topography, Domicile, and Ethnicity of the Oromo Captives*   52

PART II

Routes: From Capture to the Coast   61

    CHAPTER 5   *The Moment of Capture*   63

    CHAPTER 6   *On the Road*   73

PART III

Revival: From *Osprey* to Lovedale   95

    CHAPTER 7   *Interception to Aden*   97

    CHAPTER 8   *Sojourn in the Desert and the Onward Voyage*   111

    CHAPTER 9   *By Sea and Land to Lovedale*   122

    CHAPTER 10   *Education at Lovedale*   131

PART IV

Return: Forging a Future   155

    CHAPTER 11 *Going Home*   157

PART V

Reflections   185

Appendices   201

    APPENDIX A   *The Variables and Authentication of the Data*   203

    APPENDIX B   *The Oromo Narratives*   213

    APPENDIX C   *Gazetteer of Place-Names in the Narratives*   257

    APPENDIX D   *"My Essay Is upon Gallaland," by Gutama Tarafo*   261

    APPENDIX E   *Repatriation Questionnaire, 1903*   263

Notes   265

Selected Bibliography   307

Index   323

Illustrations

Figures

1.1.	Mountainous terrain between Axum and Lalibela in Ethiopia	17
1.2.	Holy tree festooned with cloth and votive offerings for Oromo worship	20
1.3.	Ancient walled city of Harar	25
2.1.	Oromo children shortly after their arrival at the Keith-Falconer Mission	34
3.1.	Oromo oxen	48
3.2.	Cavalry on the Wadela plateau in Ethiopia	50
6.1.	Billy King's descent from highlands to coast	75
7.1.	Cross section of a two-masted slave dhow	98
7.2.	Gardner gun	100
7.3.	Tadjoura in the mid-nineteenth century	102
7.4.	Modern Rahayta/Raheita/Araito	104
7.5.	Slave ship captured by HMS *Osprey*, ca. 1885	106
8.1.	Aden in 1882	112
8.2.	Oromo children on arrival at Sheikh Othman, September 1888	114
8.3.	Reverend William Gardner at Sheikh Othman	115
8.4.	Keith-Falconer School: boys on ground floor; girls on upper floor, 1889	117
8.5.	Keith-Falconer Mission: Oromo children and missionaries	118
8.6.	Berille Boko at Lovedale, ca. 1899	119
8.7.	Oromo children at Sheikh Othman, 1890	120
9.1.	*Conway Castle*, 1880	123
9.2.	Fillis Circus poster for World's Fair, Chicago, 1893	124
10.1.	Oromo boys at Lovedale shortly after their arrival, ca. 1890	136
10.2.	Oromo boys at Lovedale shortly after their arrival, ca. 1890 (same photo as 10.1, with Lochhead replaced by Alexander Geddes)	138
10.3.	Oromo girls in their Sunday best at Lovedale, ca. 1892	143
10.4.	Samuel Edward Krune Mqhayi	144

10.5. Berille Boko at Lovedale, ca. 1898   151

10.6. Bisho Jarsa at Lovedale, ca. 1898   152

10.7. Dr. Neville Alexander in 2008   153

11.1. Wreck of the *König*, East Africa, 1914   158

11.2. Ethiopian delegation at the coronation of Edward VII, 1902   160

11.3. Tolassa Wayessa at Lovedale   161

11.4. *Kronprinz*   175

11.5. Deck plan of the *Kronprinz*   176

A.1.   Extract from Aguchello Chabani's personal narrative   204

A.2.   Extract from Aguchello Chabani's entry in SPSS data form   204

Graphs

2.1.   Ages of boys and girls when interviewed   33

2.2.   Years of capture showing onset of drought, famine, and rinderpest   35

2.3.   Family sizes of boys and girls   37

2.4.   Orphanhood of the Oromo children vs. children in
       South Africa, Ethiopia, and Oromia   39

3.1.   Parental occupation by gender of child   43

3.2.   Relative sizes of land occupied by Oromo families   45

3.3.   Family livestock ownership by gender of child   47

4.1.   Altitude at which each child was captured   54

4.2.   Altitudes of places of origin by gender of child   56

4.3.   Home countries of the Oromo children   57

4.4.   Ethnicities of the children   58

5.1.   Places of origin of the children's captors   65

5.2.   Places of origin of raiders and of children   66

5.3.   Modes of capture by gender of child   67

5.4.   Domestic and external slave trade networks   69

5.5.   Occupations of captors   71

6.1.   Final legs to entrepôts   77

6.2.   Distances (km) from capture to coast: boys and girls   80

6.3.   Distances (km) from capture to coast: boys   82

6.4.   Distances (km) from capture to coast: girls   83

6.5.   Travel times on the road: boys and girls   84

6.6.   Years in domestic enslavement by gender of child   86

6.7.   Total first-passage time in years from home to dhow   88

6.8.   Ethnic identities of slave traders and owners   89

6.9.   Changing hands   90

6.10.   Attempted escapes by gender of child   92

10.1.   Ages of Oromo children on arrival at Lovedale, 1890   132

10.2.   Class marks in percentages at Lovedale, 1880–1890   139

10.3.   Distribution of class marks for Oromo and non-Oromo
         scholars by gender   140

10.4.   Marks of Oromo and other Lovedale scholars by gender   141

10.5.   Oromo class positions   142

10.6.   Mortality of the Oromo boys   145

10.7.   Mortality of the Oromo girls   145

10.8.   Mortality rates of Oromo and non-Oromo students, 1891–1899   149

11.1.   Results of Lovedale's 1903 repatriation poll   166

A.1.   Bird's-eye view of the classification of variables   206

Maps

1.1.   Modern Ethiopian administrative regions   16

1.2.   Reclus's population figures overlaid on a modern outline
         map of Ethiopia   19

4.1.   Places of domicile of the Oromo captives   55

6.1.   Two entrepôts and penultimate points of call   78

6.2.   Crisscrossed journeys of the sixty-four Oromo children   79

7.1.   Perim Island in the Strait of Mandeb   103

9.1.   Sea voyage from Aden, Yemen, to East London, South Africa   122

9.2.   Route from East London to Lovedale   127

11.1.   Arena of Buller's forces in Natal, January–July 1900   161

11.2.   Bismarck's dream of a German Mittelafrika   170

11.3.   Domiciles of the Oromo in South Africa by 1909   181

Maps of Oromo Children's Slave Routes
Males

B.1.   Aguchello Chabani   213

B.2.   Amanu Bulcha   214

B.3.   Amanu Figgo   214

B.4.   Amaye Tiksa   215

B.5.   Badassa Nonno   216

B.6.	Badassa Wulli	216
B.7.	Baki Malakka	217
B.8.	Balcha Billo	218
B.9.	Bayan Liliso	218
B.10.	Daba Tobo	219
B.11.	Faraja Lalego	220
B.12.	Faraja Jimma	220
B.13.	Fayissa Hora	221
B.14.	Fayissa Murki	222
B.15.	Fayissa Umbe	222
B.16.	Gaite Goshe	223
B.17.	Galgal Dikko	224
B.18.	Gamaches Garba	224
B.19.	Gilo Kashe	225
B.20.	Gutama Tarafo	226
B.21.	Guyo Tiki	226
B.22.	Hora Bulcha	227
B.23.	Isho Karabe	228
B.24.	Katshi Wolamo	228
B.25.	Kintiso Bulcha	229
B.26.	Komo Gonda	230
B.27.	Liban Bultum	230
B.28.	Milko Guyo	231
B.29.	Mulatta Billi	232
B.30.	Nagaro Chali	232
B.31.	Nuro Chabse	233
B.32.	Rufo Gangila	234
B.33.	Sego Oria	234
B.34.	Shamo Ayanso	235
B.35.	Tola Abaye	236
B.36.	Tola Lual	236
B.37.	Tola Urgessa	237
B.38.	Tolassa Wayessa	238
B.39.	Wakinne Nagesso	238
B.40.	Wayessa Gudru	239
B.41.	Wayessa Tikse	240
B.42.	Wayessa Tonki	240

Females

B.43. Agude Bulcha 242

B.44. Asho Sayo 243

B.45. Ayantu Said 243

B.46. Berille Boko 244

B.47. Berille Nehor 245

B.48. Bisho Jarsa 245

B.49. Damuli Diso 246

B.50. Damuli Dunge 247

B.51. Dinkitu Boensa 247

B.52. Fayissi Gemo 248

B.53. Galani Warabu 249

B.54. Galgalli Shangalla 249

B.55. Halko Danko 250

B.56. Hawe Sukute 251

B.57. Jifari Roba 251

B.58. Kanatu Danke 252

B.59. Meshinge Salban 253

B.60. Soye Sanyacha 253

B.61. Turungo Gudda 254

B.62. Turungo Tinno 255

B.63. Wakinni Ugga 255

B.64. Warkitu Galatu 256

Tables

7.1. Details of three dhows intercepted by HMS *Osprey* 99

10.1. Comparative crude death rates, 1891–1901 150

11.1. Confirmed independent and *Kronprinz* repatriates 179

A.1. Changing sex ratios 210

C.1. Place-names and alternatives mentioned by Oromo children 257

Acknowledgments

This book has been several years in the making, and along the way there have been countless people who have offered valuable help and encouragement. The topic intrigued and enticed many, and I have appreciated their interest and enthusiasm. The staff of the Cory Library at Rhodes University have always evinced a special interest in the project, knowing that it was there it all began. After all, my first inkling of the existence of these Oromo children came in the form of brief entries on cards in the Cory Library's manuscript catalog. I am grateful to Dr. Cornelius Thomas, Liz de Wet, Zweli Vena, Sally Poole, Louisa Verwey, and all the Cory Library staff, past and present, who went the extra mile with their professional assistance. Thank you for your encouragement, kindness, friendship, and laughter over the years.

In Cape Town, I thank all the staff, past and present, in Special Collections at University of Cape Town (hereafter UCT) Libraries, particularly Bev Angus, Busi Khangala, Allegra Louw, Sue Ogterop, and Belinda Southgate. Thank you for your professionalism, encouragement, and humor in equal measures. Thank you to Dr. Colin Darch for his personal insights into past and present Ethiopia and for the loan of precious items from his personal library. I am grateful to the staff in Manuscripts and Archives for access to the James Stewart Papers and the Monica and Godfrey Wilson Papers, particularly Lesley Hart, Clive Kirkwood, and Isaac Ntabankulu. That the James Stewart Papers were deposited in Manuscripts and Archives at the University of Cape Town instead of in the Lovedale Archives in the Cory Library has been, for the purposes of this study, a most useful anomaly. I applaud the unfailing efficiency of all those in UCT Libraries' Inter Library Loans section who speedily located countless obscure sources for me over the years. My warm thanks to them for their efficient, friendly, and enthusiastic support.

I am profoundly grateful to Nicholas Lindenberg and Thomas Slingsby of the GIS lab at the UCT for their interest in and assistance with this project. I thank them for their patience, the many afternoons spent in their lab, for the generation of countless maps from my data, and for their unflagging enthusiasm. I am similarly grateful to Professor Roddy Fox of the Department of Geography at Rhodes University in Grahamstown, who skillfully created an additional map from a subset of data.

The National Library of South Africa has been a favorite haunt since the early 1970s, so spending much time in the Reading Room and Special Collections was, as ever, a pleasurable and fruitful experience. My special thanks go to Melanie Geustyn and her staff in Special Collections for helping in innumerable ways, as well as to the ever-helpful and cheery Reading Room staff.

Similarly, the staff of the Western Cape Archives and Records Service—particularly Thembile Ndabeni, Jaco van der Merwe, and Erika le Roux—have offered strong support and assistance. I remain ever grateful for their knowledge and expertise, equaled only by their friendly helpfulness. I thank, too, all the tireless stack attendants who endlessly retrieved box after box and volume after volume.

In the Library of Parliament, Lila Komnick kindly supplied me with Lovedale and Oromo photographs from their collection. She also gave generously of her time and I am grateful to her. I am beholden to the staff of the Kimberley Africana Museum for locating details in their collections on some of the Oromo who settled in their city. Cecilia Blight, formerly an archivist in the National English Literary Museum (NELM) in Grahamstown, expressed strong interest in this project. I would like to thank her most warmly for that interest, in particular for discovering and sending valuable information relating to Gilo Kashe, one of the Oromo boys.

Alison Metcalfe in the National Library of Scotland went way beyond the call of duty with all her help and support. Thank you, Alison, for your friendly, professional expertise and for easing the way over the years. I am ever grateful. My warm thanks also go to Dr. Sheila Brock—also in Edinburgh—for her generous help in acquiring copies of material and for her collegiality and friendship. Captain Eberhard Stoetzner, archivist of the Deutsche Ost-Afrika Linie in Hamburg, Germany, graciously responded to my requests for information about the *Kronprinz* and the Deutsche Ost-Afrika Linie in general, and supplied photographs. Similarly, I am grateful to Philip Short and George Hendrie of the Cape Town branch of the Ship Society of South Africa for sharing their knowledge of shipping around the South African coast. Professor William Patch of Princeton University gave generously of his time and expertise and I extend my sincere gratitude to him. The staff of the National Maritime Museum and the Victoria and Albert Museum, both in London, earned my deep respect and gratitude for their efficient, friendly assistance.

Over the years, I have been overwhelmed by the professionalism, skill, commitment, empathy and outreach of each member of staff of Ohio University Press and their typesetting designer colleagues with whom I have worked and corresponded. I have been grateful for the humour laced through many of their messages as well as their unfailing willingness to help and encourage. Thank you, primarily, to Gillian Berchowitz, Nancy Basmajian, Beth Pratt, Deborah Wiseman, Charles Sutherland and all those at the Press who helped bring this book into existence.

I am profoundly grateful to my longtime friend Brian Willan for his constant encouragement over the years and for his ever-generous assistance in retrieving material and securing copies of significant documents for me at Kew and in the British Library. Similarly, I am grateful to Matthew Hopper, who was able to supply copies of material he had located for his own research among the India Office records that he believed might be of interest in relation to the Oromo children after landing at Aden. When all my appeals for travel and research funding were turned down time and again, I was gratified that so many professionals, scholars, and friends in distant parts were willing to help.

I am grateful to several medical doctors who advised on various illnesses and conditions the Oromo children experienced, in particular Dr. Andrew McKenzie, Dr. Stephen Craven, and Dr. Louis Botha for their observations on the illnesses assailing the Oromo children. Professor Chris van der Merwe helped with insights into trauma experienced by children through the course of history, and offered suggestions for further reading. Special thanks go to Professor Howard Phillips for his unfailing encouragement, which helped me through some of the darkest moments.

I am deeply indebted to Professor Mekuria Bulcha, a leading Oromo scholar and professor emeritus of Mälardalen University, Uppsala, Sweden. I thank him for his elucidations about the Oromo people and their past and for his constant support. I thank the many Oromo people in Oromia and in the diaspora for responding to a BBC web posting about my research, initiated by Martin Plaut in London—who has given generously of his steadfast support, advice, and friendship over the years—and three Voice of America broadcast interviews with Jalene Gemeda in Washington. Similarly, I have valued the unwavering encouragement and friendship of international journalist and author Bryan Rostron. I am indebted to each of these respected journalists for their interest in the Oromo children, for their enthusiasm and support, and for spreading the word. In response, e-mails and social media messages of support have flooded in from all over the world, from Cambodia to Canada. I thank, in particular, the descendants of one of the Oromo boys, Tolassa Wayessa: grandson Berouk Terefe in Canada, his niece Rediet Feleke Wiebel in England, and cousin Doe-e Berhanu in Ethiopia. I thank them and all the descendants of Tolassa Wayessa for sharing their memories, family documents, and genealogical tracings.

In particular, I wish to express my gratitude and to pay tribute to the late Dr. Neville Alexander, who, with patience and grace, gave many hours of his time to share his memories and family links back to his Oromo grandmother, Bisho Jarsa. I was privileged to have known him and to have had the opportunity for these interactions. We are the poorer for his death in August 2012.

Professor Christopher Saunders has been a skilled, intuitive reader and valued mentor for many years. I am supremely grateful for his knowledgeable, careful, and thoughtful reading of my texts, for his sage advice, and for his steadfast support and friendship across the decades.

Finally, my most profound thanks go to the late Robert Shell, my husband, soul mate, and life partner, who inducted me into the realms of African history and put my feet firmly on the quantitative path. He was simultaneously my most rigorous critic and my strongest supporter. My gratitude to him knows no bounds. Requiescat in pace.

Introductory Ruminations

In the summer of 2007, thirty-five years after I had come across an obscure reference to a group of liberated Oromo slave children at Lovedale Institution in the Eastern Cape, I sat spellbound in the University of Cape Town's African Studies Library as Neville Alexander, the grandson of one of those children, recounted what he remembered of a woman named Bisho Jarsa and her remarkable story. The children had been enslaved in their lands located to the south, southwest, and southeast of Abyssinia (old Ethiopia) in the late 1880s.[1] They were taken to the coast and crammed into dhows that were to ferry them across the Red Sea to further bondage in Arabia. British naval gunships intercepted the dhows, rescued and liberated the children, and took them to Aden in today's Yemen, where a Free Church of Scotland mission station at a nearby oasis, Sheikh Othman, took them in. Eventually, a group of sixty-four of these Oromo children were transported thousands of kilometers away and entrusted to the care of Scottish missionaries at the Lovedale Institution in South Africa.

Dr. Neville Alexander was a man of towering intellect and firm convictions. He was also an intrepid campaigner for justice who had spent ten years as a political prisoner on Robben Island and subsequently became one of South Africa's most distinguished educationalists. There we were, sitting side by side near the library window, bathed in late afternoon sunlight, as Neville recalled his frail, old Oromo grandmother, a former slave girl named Bisho Jarsa. Neville remembered Bisho when he was a young boy in Cradock, a small town in the Eastern Cape, South Africa. He remembered his grandmother murmuring to herself in an incomprehensible language. His younger siblings would run to their mother, Dimbiti, asking, "What's wrong with Ma? Why is she talking in that strange language?" Dimbiti, Bisho's daughter, would respond soothingly, "Don't worry about Ma. She's talking to God."

But who were these Oromo children and why were they here in South Africa? In February 1972, I began working for Rhodes University's Cory Library for Historical Research[2] in the Eastern Cape. Within weeks, while familiarizing myself with the library's manuscripts and the various card catalogs, I came across several entries reading "Galla slaves."[3]

I was baffled. Who were these "Galla" slaves and what was their link with the Eastern Cape? As I asked questions of then head of the Cory Library Michael Berning and explored further, I discovered that the cards referred to a cluster of documents in the archives of Lovedale Institution relating to a group of sixty-four Oromo children who had been enslaved in the Horn of Africa during 1888 and 1889. These children had different experiences of enslavement, but all were eventually put aboard dhows headed for the Arabian slave markets on the opposite shores of the Red Sea. One set of dhows was intercepted and their cargoes of slave children liberated by a British warship in September 1888. However, as Bisho Jarsa's story related, a further group of dhows was similarly intercepted by the Royal Navy, and a smaller group of Oromo slave children were liberated in August 1899. Both groups of children were transported to Aden in Yemen, where they were taken in by a Free Church of Scotland mission at Sheikh Othman, just north of the city. Two of the missionaries applied themselves to learning the children's language, and, with the assistance of three fluent Afaan Oromoo speakers, they interviewed each child, asking for details of their experiences effectively from their earliest memories to the moment they reached the Red Sea coast.

It was soon obvious that the children, weakened by their experiences, had severely compromised immune systems and were therefore easy targets for disease. When a number of the children died within a short space of time, the missionaries decided to find a healthier institution for their care. After medical treatment and a further year of recuperation and elementary schooling, the missionaries shipped these sixty-four Oromo children to Lovedale Institution in the Eastern Cape, South Africa.

Despite the wealth of documentation on these children in the Cory Library and other South African libraries and archives, the story of the liberated Oromo children of Lovedale had lain virtually unexamined for more than a century. As I probed deeper, I felt a frisson of speculative anticipation. Here was evidence and documentation of an unprecedented nature. Here were potentially important personal narratives of slavery and the slave trade, overlooked for far too long. The flame of what would prove to be a lifetime interest in and fascination with these Oromo children—their origins and their outcomes—was ignited deep within me there in the Cory Library over forty years ago.

However, my passion was tempered by pragmatism and life circumstances that intervened. At the time, I was busy with my part-time professional studies at Rhodes as well as working at the Cory Library. In addition, I was a social science graduate without a history major. It took years to acquire the essential grounding in history master's-level study, first at Rhodes and later at the University of Cape Town, always driven by that unquenchable flame.

What I could do immediately was to make photocopies of the children's narratives to take home. Many years later, I showed them to my husband, the late Robert Shell, a leading historian of Cape slavery. As one of the few cliometricians in the history profession, he was proficient in the use of quantitative methodology. Robert read the stories through with gathering enthusiasm. He pointed out that these stories, besides being a set of rare individual mini-biographies of slave children, were clearly the result of consistent interviewing and lent themselves readily to systematic analysis. He told me that if I encoded these narratives, translating them into numbers, the children's stories would allow for, at the very least, an opportunity to glimpse trends in the patterns of slavery and the slave trade in the Horn of Africa—in addition to enabling the individual children to tell their own stories. Theirs were authentic African voices relating their first-passage experiences within weeks of their liberation.

Analysis at a group level meant mastering the methodology of quantitative history (cliometry). Further, the nature of the documents suggested the development of a cohort-based, longitudinal prosopography, based on the core documentation of the Oromo children's own first-passage accounts. While biography is familiar as a tool by which we examine the lives of individuals, prosopography is a collection of biographies that allows for the study of groups of people through systematic analysis of their collective characteristics. Prosopography hands the historian a tool with which to discover common attributes within a group as well as to highlight any variation. From that variation, historical knowledge is generated.

In looking at the history of prosopography, we discern three distinct phases. In the first phase, prosopographers focused on studies of elites, mostly in the classical era, producing static, paper-based texts in the precomputer era. Almost without exception, the earliest applications of prosopography were within the context of studies of classical, Byzantine, and medieval nobility.[4] In 1929, Lewis Namier, an influential historian, launched his lifelong prosopography of eighteenth-century British parliamentarians. His work dominated British historiography during the 1930s.[5] In response, the British Parliament commissioned the Houses of Parliament Trust, which, in 1951 and under Namier's oversight, began the monumental project of documenting the biographies of all British members of Parliament.

Static text prosopographies were not the preserve of the precomputer era alone. In 2005, Ghada Osman, an Arabic scholar and linguist, published a rare slave prosopography—a bottom-up rather than top-down study—examining the position of foreign slaves in Mecca and Medina during the sixth century.[6] To do this, the author looked at Christian slaves used as "teachers" of the Prophet and slaves used as builders of the Ka'aba, as well as a selection of Byzantine, Abyssinian, Egyptian, Persian, and Mesopotamian slaves in Mecca and Medina during the same period. She listed the names of slaves and as much biographical information as she was able to glean from the available sources.

Prosopographers of the second phase also engaged in top-down studies of elites but had moved into the age of the mainframe computer. Lawrence Stone, an influential historian of the Tudor period, kept the spotlight on elites in 1966 when he published his studies of the British aristocracy.[7] In 1971, Stone defined *prosopography* as "the investigation of the common background characteristics of a group of actors in history by means of a collective study of their lives."[8] Stone used the mainframe computer to process machine-readable texts so that he could maximize the application of the techniques of prosopography.[9] However, Stone conducted his study nine years before the advent of the personal computer in 1980. Stone had to query or process everything in terms of the hierarchy of operators and programmers who were largely insensitive to the needs of the historian. These interlocutors came between Stone and his data.[10] Nevertheless, scholars acknowledge Stone as the pioneer of modern prosopography in the premodern era, although he never used the computer again.

In 1981, Bruce M. Haight, using an IBM 134, contributed one of the few African prosopographies with his study of the rulers of the Gonja of West Africa.[11] Four years later, in 1985, he and William R. Pfeiffer II, the president of a Michigan-based computer service bureau, published a methodological account of their "pilot study in the use of the computer to handle information for the writing of African oral history."[12] The mainframe computer enabled them to test hypotheses that would have been too complex and impractical to test manually.

The third and present phase began with the advent of the personal computer in 1980. This not only democratized the approach to prosopography but coincided with the inclusion of bottom-up analyses, which, under the influence of the Annales school, were becoming popular. A persistent feature of prosopography was that it remained a methodology applied largely to top-down studies of society. However, following the introduction of the personal computer, prosopographers used the collective biography approach with great effect for bottom-up as well as top-down analyses. For example, Katharine Keats-Rohan, a pioneer prosopographer, lauded the technological advances, pointing out the suitability of the relational database to prosopographical research.[13] Her work, widely regarded as seminal in the field of modern prosopography, and her prosopography portal resource site,[14] have provided an invaluable stimulus to such research. Since the 1990s, with the escalating sophistication and accessibility of technology and the ever-increasing capabilities of the PC, the popularity of historical quantitative methodology—including prosopography—has experienced a flourishing resurgence.

While the children's narratives provided the core set of unique documents distinguishing this episode of postemancipation slavery, the Royal Navy (which liberated this group of children in the Red Sea) kept excellent records of the events, and fortunately the Scottish missionaries at the Keith-Falconer Mission in Sheikh Othman maintained full records. The prosopography also links with information gleaned from various external sources, including school records, the responses to a repatriation poll taken by the Lovedale Institution in 1903, death registers, street directories, census data, official documentation, and the personal correspondence of the children themselves. Such documents transformed the core prosopography from a synchronic to a longitudinal or diachronic database.[15]

The use of the prosopographical technique allows for a flexible analysis that goes far beyond anecdotal methods. Encoding the narratives enables the researcher to move from the realms of narrative, social history to an empirical, systematic analysis and creates the potential for generating new insights into one of the least researched areas of African slavery: the first passage.[16] Robert was right: this prosopographic technique yielded a profoundly different and more complex picture of the children's first passage, which emerged as a far longer, more intricate, and more varied ordeal than generally recognized.

Exploring the historiography of the slave trade and slavery in the Horn of Africa region, I soon discovered for myself the scarcity of personal slave accounts of that "first passage" (i.e., contemporary accounts of captives' experiences from capture to the coast). As sources in the historiography of slavery and the slave trade, a large clutch of contemporary and systematic child slave narratives such as this is virtually unknown.[17]

Three discrete traditions impinge on this book: first, the study of the slave trade, namely the first and middle passages, which includes the phenomenon of prize slaves;[18] second, the study of missions in the nineteenth century; and third, the study of the histories of Ethiopia and of the Oromo people.

In the course of exploring slavery and the slave trade, I have long been curious about the identity and experiences of the slaves themselves: Who were they? What was their status within their own societies? What were their lives like? How and why and by whom were they enslaved? In the majority of accounts of the slave trade, answers to these questions do not emerge, simply because of the dearth of information about the identity of the slaves themselves. There have, however, been several first-person slave accounts—single biographies—and the vast majority of those have emanated from West Africa. Those studies have contributed considerably to our knowledge of the lives of specific individuals such as the celebrated Nigerian Olaudah Equiano (or Gustavus Vassa, as he was known throughout his life, dubbed "the father of African literature" by Chinua Achebe)[19] and Mahommah Gardo Baquaqua.[20] Crossing to the other side of the African continent, the leading Oromo sociologist and scholar Mekuria Bulcha included "four biographical vignettes" in his study of the Oromo in the diaspora, which offered examples of "the different ways of wresting honour from the dishonour of slavery."[21]

In recent years, clusters of scholars have gone beyond the standard Western sources and instead have searched for authentic African voices within the African communities themselves: oral traditions and testimonies, life histories gleaned from interviews with missionaries and colonial authorities, as well as folktales, songs, and other African sources. This ongoing drive, led by Alice Bellagamba, Sandra Greene, and Martin Klein, seeks to illuminate African perspectives.[22] Still, their focus remains largely on the slave trade of West and North Africa, with only a relative nod toward personal slave accounts drawn from the Horn or East Africa. They have aimed, primarily, to bring the essential human perspective into play through seeking qualitative interpretations to supplement the purely numeric quantitative assessments offered by, for example, Abdul Sheriff's statistical work on the slave trade of Zanzibar.[23]

With this study it has been possible to offer both, pulling the quantitative and the qualitative together in a unique and unified set of insights. On the one hand, the prosopography (or, loosely, group biography) presents group analyses suggesting trends and practices in the slave trade of the Horn of Africa; and on the other, it presents the personal accounts of each of the sixty-four children, tracking them not only during their period of enslavement but from cradle to grave.

We need to bear in mind that these accounts were almost exclusively penned as memoirs years after enslavement. The genre of the memoir is essentially one of reconstruction of an elusive past, informed in part by the inevitable interventions of experience and learned knowledge. We all experience this in recalling events from our own childhoods—how much of what we "remember" is what really happened, and how much has been suggested by and inextricably interwoven with our conversations and readings, with the natural subliminal adjustment born of the knowledge of hindsight, and with our own experiences and interpretations across the intervening years?

For example, the East/Central African life histories assembled by Marcia Wright were part biography and part autobiography, compiled by a female Moravian missionary in Tanzania "when the women were grandmothers" at the turn of the twentieth century.[24] By contrast, the immediacy of the children's narratives analyzed in this study adds a significant new dimension to our knowledge and understanding of child slave experiences. Interviewed within weeks of their liberation, each Oromo child answered the same series of questions, presenting the reader with freshly minted, systematic detail without the filter of hindsight, learned experience, or suggestion.

First-person slave accounts have, for the most part, been retrospective records of stand-alone experiences, snapshots of individual lives situated in differing times and places. These certainly provide valuable insights into individual experiences, but the historian would be on shaky ground in any attempt to draw inferences from these specifics to define a general first-passage reality. However, caches of small groups of child slave narratives do exist in East and Central Africa. Missionaries played an important role in encouraging the recording and preservation of slave biographies at their stations in Kenya in East Africa. Significant studies based on these and other missionary collections include the early work of Arthur C. Madan, in which he used narratives from the collections of the Universities' Mission to Central Africa (UMCA); followed more recently by Ned Alpers (who regarded the UMCA accounts as representing "a genuine African voice"); Margery Perham; and Fred Morton, who explored narratives held in the archives of the Church Missionary Society (CMS).[25] The groups are small—those in the UMCA archives number only twelve, with thirty-nine in the collections of the CMS. Nonetheless, these have extended our knowledge of the slave experience on the eastern side of the continent and would suggest that the discovery is possible of further caches of records in the missionary archives of East and Central Africa.

Despite this scholarly interest, no one has yet attempted a systematic group analysis of these pluralities of narratives. Should the Kenyan narratives lend themselves to group analysis, the results could provide a useful comparative study with the Oromo children's experiences. Of course, the accounts of the Oromo children have the advantage of greater numbers (N = 64), allowing for more effective group analyses and the possibility of determining trends and representivity more accurately. Data quality permitting, there would also be virtue in amalgamating the Kenyan and Oromo data to generate fresh results from the augmented sample. These are enticing possibilities for what the consolidated data might reveal, and for the potential of extending the pioneering findings detailed in this study.

The sensitive topic of African domestic slavery—that is, the enslavement of Africans by Africans as opposed to the raiding for slaves to supply the external, oceanic slave trade—has engaged the minds of many historians of slavery, particularly those who have interpreted the phenomenon as a degree of kinship, and their interpretations have frequently produced vastly different conclusions. Anthropologists have suggested that rather than participating in the commercial trade in slaves, precolonial African slave owners exchanged rather than sold their slaves.[26] Suzanne Miers and Igor Kopytoff counterposed the Western notion of slavery as a fixed status of chattel, permanently at the bottom of the social ladder, with a need to consider the influence of rights-in-persons and a slavery-to-kinship continuum within an African model of social and kinship relationships.[27] Others noted the incidences of male relatives selling their children in East Central Africa, and there are comparative examples of kin selling their children in southern Asia, where this was apparently common practice.[28] Among the Oromo, slave ownership was common.[29] Interestingly, the Borana Oromo, living in the southern regions of today's Oromia as well as across the border in Kenya, practiced a system of adoption, or *guddifachaa*, by which, for example, child war captives were adopted rather than enslaved. This practice would conform to the Miers and Kopytoff model but takes it further to include those children's incorporation into the community and ultimately into the national Oromo stream.[30]

The level of detail of the Oromo children's data informing this study included the identity of their captors and, subsequently, their successive purchasers and sellers. The children also gave details of the prices paid or commodities bartered for them—for example, "a handful of peppers"—at capture and when they changed hands. These data offered the unique opportunity to explore the nature of the moment of capture and the frequently contested question of agency. They also produced incontrovertible evidence of commodity trading rather than kinship absorption at the time of capture and later during the children's often long periods of domestic servitude.

The social status of slaves prior to capture has long been an arena of speculation rather than empirical analysis. The rare commentaries on slave status invariably focus on postcapture and postemancipation mobility. However, the eyewitness accounts of two English army officers contributed useful insights into social conditions among the Oromo at the end of Emperor Menelik II's reign and directly after World War I.[31] And Philip Curtin contributed a useful perspective in his study of the social structure of Senegambia, in which he concluded that the slaves who fell within the Senegambian social strata were foreigners or *captifs* who were later integrated into Senegambian society.[32] This study elucidates this generally opaque feature and period of the slave trade and pushes our knowledge forward with intricate details of parental occupation, measures of immovable and movable property (including slave ownership), the species and numbers of livestock, and other measures of relative wealth of the slave children's families—including evidence that four of the Oromo girls sprang from princely families.

The reasons for targeting particular individuals for captivity and the methods used during capture have been largely broadbrushed in the literature. Those brushstrokes were informed primarily by the third-person accounts of travelers, missionaries, military, and other observers; reasons for capture ranged from spoils of war and housebreaking to debt redemption and retribution; and the modes of capture were largely kidnapping, ambush, or negotiation.[33] Whatever else, the moment of capture was indubitably the most traumatic point of a slave child's life, prompting Fred Morton to write with graphic insight that for children, "life's memory was anchored in that place and moment."[34] The memories of the Oromo children were indeed firmly "anchored in that place and moment," and, as demonstrated in this study, they were able to give detailed evidence about the moments when they lost their freedom. They were able to tell us who enslaved them and where their captors came from. They were able to tell us if they were seized by force, if their seizure was negotiated with their parents, if they were sold or bartered, or if they were they stolen by stealth. These are detailed insights from a sizable group of children that no external-observer account could possibly reveal.

Invaluable quantitative analyses have provided innovative models and base grids not only for our better understanding of the middle passages in both the Atlantic Ocean and the Indian Ocean slave trades, but also in elucidating the first passage of the Horn of Africa and Red Sea slave enterprise. Philip Curtin broke new ground with his quantification of the Atlantic slave trade as well as his attempt to create a first census. However, he also provided an invaluable model for the calculation of the time slaves spent on the first passage—the journey from capture to the coast—which helps illuminate that recondite and underresearched slave experience.[35] Fred Cooper, Jon R. Edwards, Abdussamad H. Ahmad, W. G. Clarence-Smith, Timothy Fernyhough, Ralph Austen, and Patrick Manning have all contributed informed analyses that have advanced our empirical knowledge of the first passage as experienced by captives entrapped in the slave trade of the Horn of Africa, Red Sea, and Indian Ocean regions.[36] These studies have, variously, modeled the slave trade, estimated slave numbers, analyzed prices paid, compared routes taken from the scant data available, and also calculated the slave sex ratio on the Indian Ocean side of the African continent.

This study demonstrates the considerable divergence in the Horn of Africa from the Atlantic slave trade norm, not only because of the starkly different target population for slave traders (the trade of the Horn of Africa was a trade primarily of children rather than strong young men to work the transatlantic plantations), but also because the middle passage, which primarily informs our knowledge of the Atlantic trade, was virtually absent in the Red Sea trade. The Oromo children endured no middle passage of any duration. The period they were held aboard the dhows amounted to a matter of a few hours before they were liberated. What this study uniquely contributes in the literature is the probability that deaths on board the slave ships of the Atlantic were not the result of the harsh middle-passage experience alone but primarily the consequence of the lengthy and grueling first-passage ordeal.

When the Oromo children were liberated in the Red Sea through the interventions of the Royal Navy, they technically became "prize slaves." The British Admiralty instituted a reward system after the abolition of the slave trade in 1807 that called for the Royal Navy to intercept vessels believed to be carrying slaves, seize the vessels, capture the slavers, and liberate the slaves. The Admiralty paid "prize" money for every slave liberated, and, all too often, the crews aboard Britain's naval vessels regarded slave dhow hunting and the liberating of "prize slaves" as something of a sport. As Lindsay Doulton has pointed out, the prize money, which was distributed among the crew proportionately to rank, was an incentive not only to sign up for naval service but also to track and secure as many slave vessels and their slave cargo as possible, regardless of the levels of violence used in their apprehension. Prize money, albeit at a lower rate, was paid out on the corpses of slaves as well, victims of "collateral damage" in the inevitable skirmishes between navy and slavers.[37] Fortunately, British naval officials were required to document their activities minutely, so the primary documentation of the naval interventions during which the Oromo children were liberated is substantial.[38] Christopher Saunders, Richard Watson, and Patrick Harries are among those who have contributed substantially to what we know about the impact of "prize slaves" at the Cape of Good Hope.[39]

This study takes its place within the literature as a unique, comprehensive analysis shining twin spotlights on two issues for which scholarly sources of information are woefully scarce. The first shines further light on the history of an underresearched geographic area of Africa. The second spotlight, most significantly, illuminates the scarcely documented first-passage experience through analyses of experiential narratives of the period not only from capture, but from cradle to the coast, told by a group of enslaved children themselves.

South African Missionary Efforts

Nineteenth-century missionary education at the Cape has long been the subject of vigorous debate. Critics have questioned the motives and intentions of the missionary establishment, categorizing all missionaries as agents of colonization, conquest, and capitalism, as well as destroyers of autochthonous culture. Others, like the husband-and-wife team of John and Jean Comaroff, while examining the influences of culture, symbolism, and ideology, have nonetheless drawn sweeping generalizations from too small a base of specific empirical evidence, regarding missionaries as "the human vehicles of a hegemonic worldview."[40] Still others have examined the impact of the missionaries primarily through studies of African converts (the *kholwa*) and the linkages between mission stations and the rise of South African Black Nationalism. Norman Etherington has contributed an impressive personal canon of publications on southern African missions over the last thirty or more years. His scholarly significance runs deeply within the genre and leaves a substantial imprint on broader southern African issues.[41]

Individual missionaries approached their spiritual and temporal tasks in the Eastern Cape in different ways. The humanitarian Dr. John Philip presented an illuminating counterposition to the Comaroff motif. Philip committed his missionary and personal life to relentless and outspoken opposition to the injustices perpetrated by the colonial government in the dispossession and dehumanization of the amaXhosa. His battle for justice and human rights brought him into conflict not only with the colonial powers but also with the white settlers of the Eastern Cape and with the majority of his fellow missionaries.[42]

The Reverend Tiyo Soga, on the other hand, conveyed a more ambivalent picture of the missionaries' role. On the one hand, suspicion and resentment bred hostility against the intruding Christianizing force in the midst of the amaXhosa. This was matched, on the other hand, by a desire for education and the material benefits enjoyed by the invading strangers.[43]

Lovedale Mission, begun in 1823 through the efforts of the Glasgow Missionary Society, spawned the leading missionary institution in the Eastern Cape—arguably in the country—which opened its doors nearly twenty years later in 1841. The primary focus of the Scottish missionaries on the Eastern Cape frontier was education. They imparted their belief in equality and Christian brotherhood along with some useful secular teaching. However, working within the context of colonial influence and controls meant that they could not always match their ideals with their actions. They raised African hopes and expectations that could not be met in the context of the Cape political environment. Nonetheless, they offered Africans at their institutions the opportunity for a new, common identity that could transcend both clan rivalries and national divides.[44]

Countering this interpretation is the postmodernist view of missionary discourse and African response, which suggests, inter alia, that Victorian Christians (like James Stewart at Lovedale) spearheaded "a narrative in which Africans are metaphorically characterised as an 'infant' race in the more general march of 'civilisation' worldwide."[45]

Gender issues in the mission context have prompted considerable discussion on subjects including missionary education that reinforced the stereotypes of women's roles in home, classroom, and workplace. Nineteenth-century missionaries and educators never quite lost sight of the gendered, domestic, and largely inferior role of young African women.[46] A feminist subset of critics suggest that the missionaries wanted to turn young African girls into Victorian women, with their place firmly rooted in the home. However, placing women in the home released them from agricultural labor. In defense of the missionaries' more complex motives, they wished to emancipate women from the fields and to render the males into Christian yeomen. This movement began with the Watson Institute at Farmerfield in the Eastern Cape in 1838 and spread throughout South Africa.[47]

Support for this notion comes in an essay (included in this book; see appendix D) written by one of the Oromo boys, Gutama Tarafo, while at Lovedale. Drawing a direct comparison between the Oromo and the Xhosa people, Gutama insisted that Oromo men would never allow their wives to work in the fields. Instead, the Oromo women had dominion over the family home. As a male Oromo teenager, Gutama tellingly championed the right of women to be relieved of heavy manual field labor and to regard their position in their homes as one of domain rather than servitude.

Ethiopia and the Oromo People

Ethiopia, of all African countries, has a sui generis historiography.[48] However, the preponderance of Ethiopian studies have largely bypassed the history of the Oromo people, focusing on the agencies of power rather than on those who have been, and remain, powerless. Even those critical of the successive monarchies remained state-centered, focused on the rulers rather than the ruled, giving little attention to the powerless and the ordinary people in the southern regions below the geographical boundaries of old Abyssinia.[49]

The middle years of the twentieth century saw a surge in both Ethiopian and Oromo scholarship. However, the tendency remained to valorize the elite and powerful with barely a nod to the conquered peoples—including the Oromo. Identity politics wielded in Ethiopian halls of power played a powerful role in suppressing the history, the culture, and even the language of the Oromo people. Given that the Oromo were (and are) the largest population group in Ethiopia, the leading Tigrayan elite feared that to permit recognition and widespread knowledge would promote a sense of Oromo identity. Given their superior numbers, this would, in their view, place Ethiopian identity at risk. However, at the height of the period of the Derg—the administration put in place following the socialist military revolution that overthrew the Ethiopian monarchy in 1974—Oromo scholars, many of whom had already fled the country and were living in the diaspora, took the reins into their own hands. In the vanguard of these were Mekuria Bulcha, Mohammed Hassen, and Asafa Jalata, who began writing about their own and others' experiences, exposing the historical, political, and social causes of forced migrations of Oromo from Ethiopia. These studies initiated a burgeoning of nationalist—particularly Oromo—scholarship.[50]

Interestingly, in the early twenty-first century and echoing evolving changes in historiographical approach, non-Oromo scholars like Bahru Zewde, who had hitherto focused on the history of the ruling elite, began exploring Ethiopian democracy from the bottom up, partly redressing the criticisms of their earlier work.[51] In recent years, Oromo scholarship has responded to the intransigency of the ruling party and the growing oppression of the Oromo by becoming increasingly militant regarding the tensions between the Oromo and southern nations on the one hand, and the Ethiopian state on the other, from the era of Emperor Menelik II to date.[52] Issues of Oromo identity, slavery, dispossession, land tenure, and political contestation underpin the history and nature of escalating Oromo nationalism today.[53]

When the Oromo children arrived at Lovedale in 1890, they were no longer slaves, but theirs was, nonetheless, a form of forced migration. In recent years we have witnessed the forced migration of Oromo individuals and groups fleeing widespread repression, arbitrary arrests, detention without charge, enforced disappearance, torture, and possible death. While Oromo migrants and refugees have been seeking protection in other African countries—including South Africa—for decades, an "Addis Ababa Master Plan," proposed by the authorities in Ethiopia for the expansion of the capital city, triggered major Oromo protest and heavy government response. For the Oromo, the majority of whom are agriculturalists and nomadic pastoralists, the plan meant expropriation of their land. In response the government declared a state of emergency in October 2016, shut down communications (including Internet connectivity), and closed Ethiopia's doors to foreign journalists, observers, and human rights organizations. Hundreds were killed, and many more were injured, arrested, or detained.

Since then, the Master Plan has been shelved and an apology issued for the deaths, while in April 2018 an Oromo member who had served in the Ethiopian Parliament since 2010, Dr. Abiy Ahmed, was elected the twelfth prime minister of Ethiopia. This was doubtless a strategic move designed, at least in part, to placate the Oromo people. Though his vision is believed to be at odds with the Oromo people's demands for self-determination within their Oromia region without federal interference, toward the end of 2017 he issued a statement that may signal hope: "[Ethiopian citizens] expect a different rhetoric from us . . . we have to debate the issues openly and respectfully. It's easier to win people over to democracy than push them towards democracy. This can only succeed peacefully and through political participation."[54]

When the Oromo runner Feyisa Lilesa crossed the finish line on 21 August 2016 to win the silver medal for the marathon at the Olympics in Rio de Janeiro, he raised his arms above his head and crossed his wrists. In that silent sign of protest, he signaled his support for the hundreds of thousands of protesters back home in his Oromia state in Ethiopia. With that simple gesture Feyisa Lilesa was more effective in delivering a startling wake-up call to the world that all is not well in today's Ethiopia than any number of mainline media articles or NGO reports.[55] As one South African online newspaper headlined his story: "Ethiopia's Feyisa Lilesa Gets a Silver for Running—and a Gold for Bravery."[56]

What many among the world's reading and viewing public discovered in the backwash of Feyisa Lilesa's graphic message was that the ongoing protests and the injustices meted out to the Oromo in Ethiopia were not new. The Oromo people have been marginalized and oppressed as a political, economic, and social minority in modern Ethiopia since Emperor Menelik II ascended the imperial throne in old Abyssinia in 1889—the year the final group of Oromo children of the following story were liberated.

Roots: Memories of Home

CHAPTER 1

Ethiopia: The Lie of the Land

Modern, landlocked Ethiopia occupies the largest portion of the territory known as the Horn of Africa. Bordered on the south by Kenya and on the west by Sudan and South Sudan, Ethiopia's access to the Red Sea in the north is blocked by Eritrea and in the northeast by Djibouti. The eastern tip of Ethiopia is wrapped by large, number-7-shaped Somalia, whose long coastline takes in both the Red Sea and the Indian Ocean. The topography of Ethiopia is complex, but the center of the country is dominated by a high plateau with an altitude ranging from 1,290 meters to a peak of more than 4,500 meters. The central plateau is intersected diagonally by the Great Rift Valley. From this plateau, the land drops away—in places sharply—to the lowlands of the north, west, south, and east. Lake Assal, in the Afar or Danakil Depression, one of the hottest and driest places on earth, constitutes Ethiopia's lowest point at 155 meters below sea level. The country is watered by the many rivers that rise in the mountainous regions of the plateau and wash down toward the Nile on the west, with others, like the Awash, flowing into Djibouti and Somalia; and the Omo, feeding into Lake Turkana.

Drawing an arc from the western border of Ethiopia with Sudan to the Kenyan border in the southwest is Oromia, the region occupied by the Oromo people (see map 1.1). Oromia, constituting one of nine ethnically defined administrative regions (or *kililoch*), occupies the largest land allocation of all the regions (353,007 square kilometers), which accommodates the largest single population group (approximately 40 percent of a total estimated Ethiopian population in 2016 of 102,374,044).[1]

The topography of the Oromia region is varied and is generally divided into three principal topographical categories, ranging from the mountainous areas of the Ethiopian central plateau in the north to the grassy lowlands in the east, west, and south. Despite several substantial rivers and other water sources in Oromia, the region, like the rest of Ethiopia, is vulnerable to periodic and often devastating climate-driven droughts and famine.

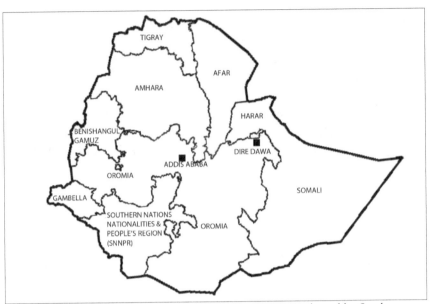

MAP I.I. Modern Ethiopian administrative regions (source: adapted by Sandra Rowoldt Shell).

More specifically, the three major topographical localities of the Oromia region can be divided into (a) the western highlands and lowlands; (b) the eastern highlands and lowlands; and (c) the areas falling within the East African Rift Valley region.

In the context of the Oromo slave children, the most significant of these localities are the western highlands and lowlands. Under the present political dispensation, this area of Oromia takes in the modern administrative zones of North Shewa, West Shewa, Jimma, Illubabor, East Wellega, and West Wellega. In general, the region features a rugged plateau with a slightly lower altitude than the land farther north. The highest peak is Mount Badda, rising to 3,350 meters above sea level. The western lowlands cover a smaller area of this region.

The eastern highlands and lowlands, incorporating the Arsi, Bale, Borena, East, and West Hararge zones, have an altitude ranging from 500 meters above sea level in the undulating lowlands to Batu Mountain, which peaks at 4,307 meters above sea level. The plateau here features inhospitable rocky desert land supporting a sparse population.

Some forty million years ago, one of Africa's most spectacular geological phenomena resulted in the splitting of the African tectonic plate, forming a continuous rift stretching 6,000 kilometers from northern Syria to Mozambique. The entire geological phenomenon, still often described loosely as the Great Rift Valley, is actually a series of separate rifts. Where the valley intersects Ethiopia from the Red Sea in the north through to the Kenyan border in the south, it is more accurately described as the Great East African Rift. Splitting Oromia from north to south, the East African Rift Valley region takes in part of the Arsi and East Shewa zones. Volcanic hills, lakes, and depressions fill the valley, while high mountains frame the ridge of the rift.

FIGURE 1.1. Mountainous terrain between Axum and Lalibela in Ethiopia (photograph by Johann Wassermann, 1994).

Terrain and topography impact patterns of human settlement and mobility. Clearly, the particular ruggedness of Ethiopia's terrain has had, over time, a distinct bearing not only on human settlement and mobility but also on security and the economy. The more rugged the terrain, the greater the challenges for transportation and trade. Over the centuries, humans have used ruggedness and altitude to defend their homes and their livelihoods. Fortresses and fastnesses built at higher altitudes allowed for visual and strategic advantage in times of hostility. Accordingly, the Oromo commonly used the terrain to secure their settlements and strongholds in the mountainous regions of Oromoland against marauders and slave raiders. The mountains and the rocky terrain served as a natural fortress.

In Ethiopia, the rugged topography not only provided a modicum of protection against the predations of slave raiders but also presented traders with the problem of postcapture transportation. The external Ethiopian slave trade, which supplied the markets of Arabia and India, was predicated on the successful transportation of slaves from inland regions to established entrepôts on the Red Sea coast. Negotiation of the towering mountains, craggy outcrops, and steep escarpments of the Ethiopian centroid was only possible via treacherous, rocky pathways.

Ethiopian Population and Demographics

Polyethnic present-day Ethiopia comprises as many as eighty different population groups, speaking some eighty-four languages and divided across its nine ethnic regions in a system of ethnic federalism. That Ethiopia's nine regions are ethnically defined has enabled critics of the system to draw comparisons with the racially driven Bantustans and the general spatial engineering of South Africa's pre-1994 apartheid regime. The Ethiopian system of ethnic federalism has, in practice, proved one of ethnic dominance, and, as in apartheid South Africa, the ruling group makes up a tiny minority. In 2016, the ruling Tigrayans constituted a mere 6 percent of the total population of 102,374,000. By contrast, the Oromo people amounted to approximately 40 percent and the Amhara roughly 27 percent of the total population.[2] Historically, the Oromo have consistently constituted the numerically dominant proportion of the population since incorporation into Abyssinia (old Ethiopia) by Emperor Menelik II in the late nineteenth century. However, as in previous centuries, the Oromo today remain a political minority occupying the administrative region of Oromia.

In earlier writings about the peoples of Ethiopia and in earlier accounts of the Oromo—including in the narratives of the freed Oromo slave children at Lovedale Institution— writers commonly used the term "Galla" to describe the Oromo people. However, in Amharic, the language of the politically and economically dominant Amhara people of Ethiopia, the word *Galla* means "uncultured" or "immigrants." The term has long been considered pejorative by the Oromo people, and the use of the old ethnonym, now considered both obsolete and offensive, was declared illegal in 1974.[3]

In this work, the term "Oromo" is used to describe the largest Cushitic-speaking people of Ethiopia. Although they occupied, in the late nineteenth century, a plurality of principalities, the Oromo people were, as now, united in language, religion, and political culture, most notably the democratic administrative system of *gadaa* and a collective Oromo identity. While occupying different principalities, each under the leadership of a local king or chief, the Oromo shared what Mekuria Bulcha refers to as the "myth of common descent."[4] In the late nineteenth century, although they shared a common language, they did not, at that time, share a formally defined and named Oromo territory. Despite this, the Oromo principalities hung together across contiguous territory to the south and southwest of Abyssinia in what was then referred to collectively by cartographers like John Bartholomew as "Galla Land" and more recently as "Oromoland." It was these territories that Sahlé Mariam, king of Shewa (later Menelik II),[5] expropriated—and effectively colonized—in the late nineteenth century, absorbing them into his vision for a new, united Ethiopia.[6] The unity of Oromo ethnonationalism would finally be recognized in 1991 with the establishment of their own "state-space" in the modern administrative region of Oromia.[7] But of course the granting of a state-space within a supposedly unified country neither ensures nor implies self-determination.

Writing in 1885, Rawson W. Rawson, a renowned British nineteenth-century public figure, geographer, and statistician, cites figures given by the celebrated French geographer Jacques Élisée Reclus in an article on European interests in the Red Sea hinterland.[8]

Map 1.2 uses proportional circles to represent Reclus's relative land and population figures for the different groups in the region roughly covering the area of modern Ethiopia.[9]

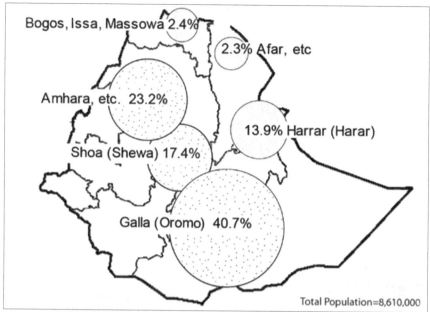

MAP 1.2. Reclus's population figures overlaid on a modern outline map of Ethiopia (source: generated from Reclus's data by Sandra Rowoldt Shell).

According to Reclus's figures, the Oromo represented 41 percent of the total population. The map demonstrates this numerical dominance. Rawson adds a caveat regarding the accuracy of these figures, saying, "They can, of course, only be approximate."[10] Reclus's figures nonetheless provide an acceptable estimated base of core population data for the region and era in which to embed the Oromo children's narratives.

Language

Ethiopia's rulers—and many non-Oromo scholars—often insist that the Oromo people are united only by the Oromo language (Afaan Oromoo). Oromo is an East Cushitic tongue of the Afro-Asiatic language family written in either the ancient Geez script or a modified Latin alphabet named Qubee. While more people (33.8 percent) speak Oromo than any other single language in Ethiopia, the language is also spoken in both northern and eastern Kenya, in Somalia, and in Sudan. It has also been carried farther across Africa by thousands of Oromo people who have fled oppression in Ethiopia in the twenty-first century, seeking asylum or refuge in other countries from Egypt and Libya to South Africa. Across the continent, as the fourth-largest language after the Arabic languages Swahili, and Hausa, Afaan Oromoo is spoken by an estimated fifty million people.[11] However, use of the language was significantly repressed from the late nineteenth century until the revolution of 1974. There were few publications by or about the Oromo in their language, and those that did exist were written in the Geez alphabet. In 1956, an Oromo scholar and poet named Sheikh Bakri Sapalo developed a script specifically for Afaan Oromoo, probably designed to conceal the existence of Oromo publications from the Ethiopian authorities. After 1991, the Qubee alphabet was formally adopted. Despite all these politically inspired linguistic hurdles, language is a bonding factor for the Oromo people. However, those who challenge the unity of the Oromo would aver that in every way other than language, they have been—and remain—a disparate people, divided by religion, by interclan squabbling, and by their ready acculturation into the groups among whom they settle.

Religion

While a student at Lovedale, Gutama Tarafo, one of the freed Oromo slave children, wrote a descriptive essay titled "My Essay Is upon Gallaland" (see appendix D in this book), which details an array of features including topography, diet, culture, climate, and religion. Gutama wrote: "The Gallas are heathens in religion. They worship a big tree, and in the mountains. They obey just as the king tells them, and the rule is if a person breaks the king's commandment, he is taken to the market and punished, by being beaten, or sold as a slave."

This is the only comment in Gutama's essay on the religious practices of the Oromo people. Oromo traditional religion is essentially monotheistic, centering on Waaqa, acknowledged as a "Sky God," a Supreme Being responsible for the creation of the universe. Attached to Waaqa is what Ioan Lewis referred to as a "vague hierarchy of

FIGURE 1.2. Holy tree festooned with cloth and votive offerings for Oromo worship (source: Guglielmo Massaia IV, 49, in Richard Pankhurst and Leila Ingrams, *Ethiopia Engraved: An Illustrated Catalogue of Engravings by Foreign Travellers from 1681 to 1900* [London: Kegan Paul, 1988], 134).

refractions" embracing the natural phenomena—"the sun, moon and stars, the winds, rainbow, rains . . . the hills, trees and water"—the full environmental experience of the Oromo people, hence their reverence for trees and mountains.[12]

These traditional beliefs, embracing the profound interconnectedness among "human, non-human and the supernatural," have shaped the Oromo ecological cosmology, which underpins their *Weltanschauung*—an enduring conservation ethic and culture in their relationship to their land, flora, and fauna.[13]

Although there were zealous but rarely successful attempts at proselytization by foreign Christian missionaries among the Oromo, particularly during the nineteenth century, there was scant influence exerted on the Oromo belief system by the monophysite Abyssinian Orthodox Church or, till the mid-nineteenth century, by Islam. Carl Isenberg, a German missionary and linguist, hints at reasons for this in his disheartened summary of spiritual interactions between the Oromo and their neighbors:

> The relation of the Gallas to their neighbours is hostile. The Abyssinian
> Christians only visit them for the sake of plunder; and the Mahomedans come
> among them in order to carry their sons and daughters away, by stealth or
> force, into slavery. The Gallas are, therefore, a nation hating all, and hated
> by all. They glory not in the promotion of the glory of their Creator, nor of
> the happiness of their fellow-creatures, neither in the enjoyment of happiness
> or the possession of wealth; but they glory in the murder of men that are not
> of their nation. The Abyssinians, indeed, have attempted, by force and by
> persuasion, to bring them over to a profession of Christianity; but, except in a
> few instances, quite in vain.[14]

Oromo scholar Mekuria Bulcha points to the analyses of Amharic intellectual and historian Asma Giyorgis (or Giyorghis), who converted to Catholicism and pursued a career in the administration of Menelik II. Asma Giyorgis believed that the dearth of conversions to the Abyssinian Orthodox Church, particularly during the Menelik era, could be attributed in the main to a general reluctance on the part of the Orthodox clergy. He suggested that the clergy preferred to leave the Oromo as a "pagan" and subjugated people, making it easier for them to maintain a certain dominance over them, ruling "the Galla like slaves."[15]

Asma Giyorgis wrote emphatically of the mutual antipathy simmering between the Oromo and the Amhara during the era of Menelik's reign: "Even now, the rest of the Galla prefer to be Muslim rather than Christian, because they hate the Amhara; the Amhara priests, the bishop and the clergy do not like the Galla. They believe that Christianity cannot be understood by those whose ancestors were not Christians. Therefore, they do not teach them."[16]

Bulcha argues that the Abyssinian Orthodox Church not only lacked a sense of mission but was also elitist and espoused a "chosen people" ideology that informed their reluctance to proselytize among the "Gallas," whom they regarded as uncultured foreigners, interlopers, and strangers—decidedly "the other." Bulcha also suggests that because of the indivisibility of Abyssinian church and state, "the clergy made attempts to convert non-Abyssinians only when it served the interest of their patron the king."[17] In respect of the interests of Sahle Mariam (Menelik), the king of Shewa, there was greater political and financial advantage in enslaving the Oromo than in converting them. Conversion to Christianity would have placed them outside the potential slave trade pool that was such a fundamental source for feeding Menelik's economic and political interests. As Bulcha explains, "While recommending the capture and enslavement of the 'pagans,' the *Fetha Nagast* prohibited the sale of Christians to non-believers. Therefore, it may not be surprising that Abyssinian rulers, whose external trade was dependent on the exportation of slaves, were reluctant to spread their faith to the neighbours they constantly raided for slaves."[18]

The Fetha Nagast, the Abyssinian "Law of Kings," which had its origins in a thirteenth-century Arabic document compiled by a Coptic scholar and jurist named Ibn Al'-Assal, included highly wrought regulations and instructions regarding slavery that were underpinned by numerous religious justifications. Slavery, slave raiding, and the trading of slaves were all clearly condoned—and indeed supported—by ecclesiastical and secular powers alike. Since the inception of the original document, those practices had been codified as legitimate Abyssinian economic dealings. Though the ban on the sale of Christians by Christians to non-Christians was often violated, the embargo would nonetheless have held as a deterrent to the proselytization and conversion of "the neighbours they constantly raided for slaves," including the Oromo who were located in territories surrounding the kingdom of Shewa on the west, south, and east.

This is not to say there were no conversions to Christianity, whether to Abyssinian Orthodoxy or to Western—Roman Catholic and Protestant—denominations. However, Western missionaries were regarded with suspicion and hostility, with Amharic and Tigrayan adherents proudly defending the independence of their own long-established Abyssinian Orthodox Church that was so intertwined with the state apparatus. As a result, Western missionaries experienced significant difficulties accessing Ethiopia as well as the territories occupied by the Oromo. There were those who were successful in getting approval for their applications to operate within Ethiopian borders and beyond. However, they were invariably expelled within a few years as suspicion and hostility mounted concerning their activities. The Oromo themselves were generally wary of both Abyssinian Orthodoxy and Western Christianity. Asma Giyorgis suggested that the Oromo's antipathy toward the Amhara and Tigrayan elites in Ethiopia extended to include an antipathy toward their faith and attempts to convert them. Certainly, there is evidence that while the Oromo had been exposed to both major monotheistic faiths over many centuries, Islam would exert the greater influence.

Abbas Haji Gnamo, an Oromo anthropologist, contrasts the "official/establishment" nature of Christianity with the perception of Islam as an "anti-establishment" faith—"the religion of oppressed peoples"—a faith that would have appeared as abhorrent to the ruling elites who regarded Ethiopia as an "Island of Christianity in an Ocean of Muslims and pagans." Abbas Gnamo believes that Asma Giyorgis was being simplistic and even anachronistic in his explanation that the Oromo would prefer Islam over Christianity because of their hatred of the Amhara elite, on the grounds that Islam's influence had begun to take hold prior to the imperial conquest of the Oromo.

However, it would seem that even divorced from religious influence, the antipathies between the two nations had a long historical reach.[19]

Certainly, there is a persuasive logic in why the Oromo, a populous but oppressed people, would be drawn to a religion of the masses. Steven Kaplan, a religious and social historian, differentiates between Orthodox Christianity, which he maintains took initial hold among the elite core, filtering outward and downward toward the periphery; and Islam, which traditionally grew from the periphery inward toward the core. Kaplan notes that for most of its history in Ethiopia, Islam existed on the periphery of a strong Christian state. It was the religion of traders, craftsmen, and pastoralists, rather than that of rulers and officials.[20] Mohammed Hassen, who limits his study of the Oromo mainly to those in the Gibe states, maintains that while there were pockets of sedentary Oromo who espoused Islam in earlier centuries, the more itinerant pastoral Oromo groups tended to adhere to their traditional animist belief system.[21] Explaining that the spread of Islam was gradual and multifaceted, Hassen presents a rather more nuanced view of the spread of Islam than that of either Abbas Gnamo or Kaplan. Hassen observes that as the spread of Islam was largely through the contact and influence of Muslim traders, there was a practical necessity for seller and buyer to be able to communicate with each other. This meant the adoption of the Oromo language as the lingua franca of trade, and it rapidly became the primary medium for the transmission of Islamic tenets and principles.[22]

Hassen suggests a complex dynamic in the spread of Islam among the Gibe Oromo through a "series of gradations in the conversion of the Oromo to Islam which acted as an insulator absorbing Islamic radiation without violently uprooting their traditional values."[23] First, traders were largely responsible for the geographic distribution of Islam to the marketplaces along the caravan routes. These traders were able to set up strong relations with the Oromo nobility based on mutual commercial benefits. Many of these traders also gradually took over responsibility for the teaching of the children of Oromo nobility and were therefore, in part, responsible for the preparation of future generations of Oromo leaders, at least in the Gibe states of Limmu-Ennarya and Gomma. By the middle of the nineteenth century, Islam had taken hold among the elite throughout all the Gibe states with the exception of Gomma. The kings, in turn, believed they had the responsibility of spreading Islam among their subjects and encouraged Muslim preachers and teachers to establish Muslim schools.[24]

Hassen indicates that consistent with his "series of gradations," a duality persisted between Islam and the traditional religion of the Oromo during this spread and growth of Islam throughout the Gibe states. Both change and acceptance were largely syncretic, particularly among the grassroots Oromo population. According to Hassen: "In the end Islam replaced the old religion mainly because it had the full support of the state, while the old religion lacked a literate class, organized preachers, and the ideological strength of Islam. The Oromo believed in Waaqa (sky god), the creator of the universe. To pass from believing in Waaqa to accepting Allah as the creator of the universe was not a formidable transition."[25]

Old traditions and rituals were often modified syncretically to embrace the new Islam.

Myths of Origin

There is a widely held view among many historians that the Oromo were latecomers to the highland plateau territory of Ethiopia, entering and settling there only during the sixteenth century. However, Oromo historian Mohammed Hassen challenges this view, claiming that the Oromo, as the largest group of Cushitic-speaking peoples who are known to have populated the Ethiopian region for millennia, are one of the indigenous groups of Ethiopia.[26] In support of this claim, he alludes to the assertion by British army officer, colonial administrator, and journalist Sir Darrell Bates that "the Galla were a very ancient race, the indigenous stock, perhaps, on which most other peoples in this part of eastern Africa had been grafted."[27]

Bates claims that the Oromo had earlier been driven out of the same lands that were most in contention during the first part of the sixteenth century by the Abyssinian Christians and the followers of Islam. According to Bates, the Oromo, who were then in the lands to the south and west of these territories whence they had been driven, observed the tussles between the two factions with interest, "waiting in the wings for opportunities to exact revenge and to recover lands which had been taken from them." Regrettably, Bates fails to source these statements, which Hassen later picked up and used as evidence in support of his argument.[28] Hassen points to evidence that the Oromo were largely agropastoralists and originally practiced mixed farming.[29]

In the 1880s, when the Oromo children's narratives begin, the Oromo were entrenched in the territories to the south and southwest of Abyssinia and Menelik's kingdom of Shewa. These were the final years of the reign of Abyssinia's "King of Kings," Emperor Yohannes IV, who claimed descent from King Solomon through two female lines and had come to power in 1872. By the mid-1880s, Sahle Maryam, king of Shewa (who could claim uninterrupted direct male descent from King Solomon and the queen of Sheba), was determined to place himself first in line to replace Yohannes when the time came.[30] This was the era of ascendancy for the man who would become Emperor Menelik II.

In his active pursuit of the imperial crown, Menelik knew that he needed to augment his material wealth and firepower. In that era, firearms had become "a precondition for satisfying wider political ambitions."[31] He also needed to expand his territorial domain, which he had achieved through an ongoing program of incursions, particularly to the south and southwest.

Menelik steadily augmented the territorial dominion and power of his realm, principally by expanding into the Oromo lands to the south and west through successive battles, including that fought at Embabo near the Abbay-Gibe watershed. He was also careful to extend his Shewan hegemony northward by incorporating the Wollo (or Wello) region to the northeast.

To cement his ascendancy, he recognized above all the strategic importance of securing the old trade routes to the southeast, thus opening up access to the sea and foreign trading opportunities. This would mean taking the ancient walled city of Harar (see fig. 1.3). The city had fallen temporarily under Egyptian control in 1875 when,

FIGURE 1.3. Ancient walled city of Harar (source: Richard F. Burton, *First Footsteps in East Africa; or, An Exploration of Harar* [London: Longman, Brown, Green, and Longmans, 1856], frontispiece).

by establishing this foothold, they hoped to take control of the whole of Ethiopia. This proved to be an abortive exploit, and they eventually abandoned Harar in 1885. Seizing the moment, Menelik attacked and conquered Harar at the battle of Chelenko in January 1887, thus adding considerable heft to his growing imperial ambitions.[32] When Emperor Yohannes died from a wound sustained in battle against the Sudanese Mahdists in March 1889, there was little doubt that Menelik would be his successor.[33]

Menelik's ambitions were not limited to his successful territorial and hegemonic advantages. He was equally bent on raiding these—and other territories he had no intention of colonizing—for whatever spoils and levies they might yield. The spoils included livestock and slaves. Menelik, as king of Shewa, had long benefited substantially from the slave trade. Despite his public lip service to the abolition of the slave trade, he actively promoted its expansion during these latter decades of the nineteenth century. Simply put, there was too much potential for profit in the trade in slaves and he was, arguably, the trade's greatest beneficiary in Ethiopia.[34] Harold Marcus maintains that Menelik was Ethiopia's "greatest slave entrepreneur."[35] He demanded that taxes be levied on slaves passing through Shewa, as well as a tax of one Maria Theresa (MT) dollar (or thaler) on every slave sold within his kingdom. Prisoners captured in the course of his predatory battles, or *zamacha*, were sold in slave markets, and he built up his own court's slave allocation through tributes paid in slaves.[36]

With the monies accrued from the profits of the slave trade, Menelik was able to satisfy not only his tactical need but also his personal passion for weapons. According to Marcus, Giovanni Chiarini—an Italian explorer who spent two years in the kingdom of Shewa (1876 to 1878)—described Menelik as "fatalistic and a good soldier, [who] loves weapons above all else."[37] To acquire his weaponry, he courted the European powers, notably the French, with whom he had established his first European contact and of whom he is reported to have said, "The French are my friends; it is upon them that I shall base the hope of my reign. I give you all my confidence and my friendship; my country is yours, and you are amidst a people who also love you."[38] Among his principal French gunrunners was, rather surprisingly, the celebrated French poet Arthur Rimbaud.[39]

The Oromo largely resisted Menelik's predatory attacks until 1886. Thereafter, despite their larger numbers, the insufficiency of their firepower was no match for Menelik's superior and growing ordnance strength. Enslaving the Oromo offered him an open opportunity to continue to augment his mounting military superiority. According to the historian Jon R. Edwards, by the late nineteenth century, slaves had become one of the most significant Ethiopian export commodities, and "in addition to the fillip to the trade generated by his disruptive wars of expansion, [Menelik]'s generals brought thousands of slaves home to Shewa after their expeditions."[40]

Menelik's efforts bore fruit. When the wounded Emperor Yohannes died on 10 March 1889, Menelik finally claimed the imperial throne thanks to his determination, his ruthless political ambitions, and his augmented purse and military power. He was crowned Emperor Menelik II in the Entotto Maryam Church on 3 November 1889.

The Famine Days

In the same period, coupled with the danger posed by Menelik's territorial predations and the incursions of his slave raiders, the southern regions were on the cusp of what came to be called *bara beelaa* (or *bâraa balliyyaa*) by the Oromo—the "famine days," "cruel days," or "time of suffering." This period materialized into the worst drought and famine in Ethiopian history, extending from 1887 to 1892, peaking in 1890–1891. The onset was signaled by the failure of the summer rains in 1887, resulting in drought and excessive heat that shriveled the crops.[41] Researchers working in the field of climate, water, and weather information have attributed the incidence of various droughts across the continent of Africa, but particularly in southern Africa and in the Horn, to climate phenomena linked with El Niño–Southern Oscillation (ENSO), "a coupled air and ocean phenomenon with global weather implications."[42] The effects of ENSO may manifest themselves thousands of kilometers away from the epicenters of these phenomena. Researcher Tsegay Wolde-Georgis, in a study examining the Ethiopian climate over time, posits that the El Niño phenomenon may be regarded as an early warning indicator of drought in Ethiopia. In his chronology of El Niño and drought and famine in Ethiopia covering more than four centuries, from 1539 to 1993, Tsegay Wolde-Georgis tables 1887 through 1889 as El Niño years in Ethiopia.[43]

In the first week of April 1888, it was reported that men were "starving and suffering from dysentery."[44] Crops had failed. Food was at a premium. In November 1888, one of the Roman Catholic mission journals published a letter from Monsignor Nicolas Bettembourg, the *procureur* of the Roman Catholic Congregation of the Mission, reporting on worsening environmental conditions in Ethiopia in the preceding months:

> Almost all Abyssinians are under arms, and this state of hostility is causing great misery to our poor Catholics. To the continual arson and looting that had almost ruined them, is added an epidemic [rinderpest] which deprives them of much of their herds. To make matters worse, crops have been lost through lack of rain and famine has begun to reign in the districts of our Christians. Even at Massawa commodity prices have doubled and it is very difficult to get food, so the dearth of supplies has been even more marked.[45]

Plagues of locusts, caterpillars, armyworms, and rats swarmed across the country, destroying crops and carrying disease.[46] On 8 November 1887, by which time Ethiopian cattle were beginning to feel the impact of the onset of drought conditions and were increasingly vulnerable to disease, an Italian expedition, under the leadership of General San Marzano, arrived at the port of Massawa and was stationed in the Hamasien province, the ancient political and economic center of Eritrea. Lamberto Andreolis, an Italian "contractor, purveyor, and ship-owner," is believed to have imported a shipment of cattle for these troops from India through the Red Sea port of Massawa.[47] Unbeknownst to the Italians, these imported cattle proved to be riddled with rinderpest. As early as 2 April 1888, there were reports that "transport animals [were] dying of rinderpest."[48] The disease ripped through the Ethiopian bovine population like a bushfire fanned by savage winds and then swept down the continent of Africa, reaching the southernmost tip in 1896, when southern Africa's cattle herds began to succumb to the disease.[49]

The human population of Ethiopia was similarly crushed. Many starved to death and many fell ill. Famine, cholera, bubonic plague, and associated diseases took hold and thousands died. Swarms of locusts and caterpillars invaded the lands and decimated what was left of the crops. Conditions during this period, as recounted across the literature, attained biblical proportions in terms of the multiple climatic and ecological calamities enveloping the land. When the drought eventually broke in 1892, observers reported that between one-third and one-half of the human population of Ethiopia had died.[50]

It was in this climate of political vulnerability and ecological disaster that the families of the Oromo children central to this study found themselves in the late 1880s.

The complex topography of Ethiopia—with its highland plateaus, grassy lowlands, and also hot desert lowlands ending in the Afar Depression—provided a dramatic topographical backdrop for the ordeals of the Oromo children. Distributed across these landscapes, the population of Ethiopia was (and remains) complex and ideologically divided, with the Oromo people the numerically dominant group. Three religious systems predominated among the Oromo: traditional religion, Islam, and Christianity. All three coexist in modern Oromia, the home of the majority of Oromo in Ethiopia and one of the nine regional states of Ethiopia designed around ethnic identity. The unique Oromo *gadaa* system provided a democratic framework until its influence waned in the face of conquest. Nonetheless, it retains a strong symbolic significance and could serve as the basis of a mechanism of regional governance for Oromia under the existing federal system. Nationally speaking, however, the plurality of ethnicities, cultures, languages, and religions suggests that Ethiopia is destined to remain a divided country. This division has been glaringly evident in view of the protests in Oromia and farther afield in recent years against the then Tigrayan-led minority regime. Dr. Abiy Ahmed, the new Prime Minister since April 2018, is an Oromo. Hopes run high that much-needed reforms in the system of governance in federal Ethiopia may take place under his leadership.

CHAPTER 2

The Family Structure of the Oromo Captives

There is a general lacuna in the slave trade literature of the Horn of Africa and elsewhere in Africa relating to the family structure of those who were captured and enslaved. Fred Morton's examination of a small body of narratives by East African child slaves offers some insights.[1] The sixty-four personal first-passage narratives of the Oromo children in *Children of Hope* illuminate slavery and family structure as few sources have done to date. Each of the narratives opens with the child's name, age, parents' names, orphanhood, number of siblings, total family composition, and kinship structures.

Inevitably, all the Oromo children would experience the impact of what the economic historian Mike Davis has described as "a truly biblical conjugation of natural and man-made plagues"[2] at some stage of their enslavement and to one degree or another.

For example, Bisho Jarsa, who had two brothers, was fourteen years of age when first sold into slavery. Both her parents were dead by the time she was first taken away from her own country. Her explanation of their deaths goes some way toward explaining the high rate of orphanhood among the Oromo children and their enslavement. According to Bisho's narrative, her mother and father "both died at the same time, during the prevalence of a sickness which carried away a great many people. The cattle also died in large numbers. . . . A famine was all over the land at the time" (appendix B; narrative 48).

Bisho was captured in the middle of May 1889, when the "cruel days" (referred to by the Oromo as the *bara beelaa* or *bâraa balliyyaa*) of famine and the onset of human diseases had begun to creep in on the coattails of drought and failing crops. As early as 1888, starvation, bubonic plague, cholera, typhoid, smallpox, dysentery, and a host of other diseases had begun to make inroads. Bisho's parents succumbed to one of these.[3]

As indicated in the excerpt from her narrative cited above, Bisho also alluded to the rinderpest, introduced into Ethiopia in November 1887. Some reports posit that by the time the disease had run its course, as many as 90–95 percent of the Ethiopian

29

cattle population had succumbed to the disease (see discussion on page 27). Cattle were central to the lives and livelihood of the Oromo farmers. They were their primary source of meat and milk, oxen were essential for pulling their plows, and the size of their herds constituted an important indicator of wealth and status. Bulls in particular represented wealth and feature prominently in Oromo memorial grave art depicting the principal accomplishments of the deceased.[4]

Bisho was sent with a man to buy food in a neighboring county called Gobu, today the administrative center of the Goba administrative region renowned for its thriving marketplace. No sooner had they arrived than she was told that she was to be sold for corn. Given the severity of the drought, the value of all food, including corn, was hugely inflated. People were starving throughout the land. Bartering children for food became a desperate means of survival.

Family, Kinship, and Slavery

Suzanne Miers, a historian, and Igor Kopytoff, an anthropologist, suggest that Western notions of slavery—that the slave was "first and foremost a commodity, to be bought and sold and inherited"—were, at best, questionable in the context of traditional African societies. They contend that in the common "Western" image, the slave was simply chattel possessed totally by another, with no control over his own life or destiny. This chattel status allowed the slave to be inherited, transferred, or sold at will. Ill-treatment, even to the point of death, was legal. Slave status was intergenerational; slaves occupied the lowest rung of the social ladder and stayed there.[5] Miers and Kopytoff emphasize the need to consider the influence of "rights-in-persons" within African social and kinship relationships. These rights, which Miers and Kopytoff aver are "usually mutual but seldom equal," are present in virtually every social relationship. In terms of these rights, children can expect to be cared for and protected by their parents, husbands have certain rights over their wives, and parents have rights over their children.[6] Transactions in terms of these rights-in-persons, say Miers and Kopytoff, are fundamental to African kinship and marriage systems and distinguish African from other slave systems.

The analyses of the data documenting the composition of the children's families and the conditions of their enslavement suggest a reexamination of the concepts of kinship and slavery in the context of this study. Paul Bohannan, an anthropologist, suggests that in precolonial Africa, slave owners exchanged slaves for other slaves, never for money. In his article on the Tiv people of Nigeria, Bohannan emphasizes the unique exchangeable values of rights in human beings, particularly of dependent women and children, expressed in terms of kinship and marriage.[7] This notion is consistent with the Africanist suggestion that owners did not buy slaves in precolonial Africa for money, but rather incorporated them into their families. On the other hand, Ned Alpers, a historian focusing on the political economy of the Indian Ocean slave trade, alludes to Yao male relatives selling their children "for what was very likely the simple acquisition of trading goods."[8] According to Richard Allen, a historian of the slave trade of the Indian Ocean, the sale of children by their parents or relatives was a "common mechanism" in southern Asia. The catalyst for such sales was often indigence or want in the wake of droughts, floods, and other natural calamities. "Human life," Allen writes, "became exceedingly cheap during these periods of severe economic hardship."[9] Families selling their children is neither a new nor an uncommon phenomenon.

Within kin groups, where "rights-in-persons" prevail across a range of relationships, the acquisition or absorption of kin could be used to increase the size of a kin group and thereby to augment a kin group's influence, wealth, and power.[10] Miers and Kopytoff describe the concept of the "slavery-to-kinship" continuum wherein the status of slave and kin member merge and where neat definitions become blurred and slavery itself becomes ambiguous. Kin, in Africa, whether adopted, dependent, client, or slave, stood side by side and could meld and merge in the way that tenants, serfs, and slaves did in feudal Europe.[11] The most marginalized in African societies could occupy a form of chattel status, but the chattel nonetheless remained along a "continuum of marginality whose progressive reduction led in the direction of quasi kinship and, finally, kinship." The overlap and blending of slavery and kinship, in the view of Miers and Kopytoff, occurs in the latter portion of the continuum, "and it is here that the redefinitions of relationships we have described took place."[12] They believe that the singular stamp of African "slavery" is the existence of this slavery-to-kinship continuum.

Much of what Miers and Kopytoff address applies to the Oromo family structure. For example, the Oromo have a long-established tradition of adoption, or *guddifachaa*. Mekuria Bulcha, in dealing with the centrality of the Oromo kinship system to Oromo history and sociology, confirms what Miers and Kopytoff claim, explaining the *guddifachaa* as a system through which the Oromo could adopt individuals who would thereafter be regarded as members of the household's putative descent group, or *gosa*. Further, through *gosa* membership, they were integrated into the larger collective of the community and, ultimately, of the nation.[13] *Guddifachaa* not only accords with Miers and Kopytoff's concept, but the practice goes further, penetrating the realm of the wider Oromo society.

Ayalew Duressa, a social anthropologist, observes that most scholars have ascribed the practice of *guddifachaa* among the Oromo to their love of children, maintenance of the family line, and as a means of acquiring labor power and access to an economic resource at both household and community levels. He notes further that some historians consider it a mechanism used by the Oromo people to incorporate (or assimilate) non-Oromo ethnic groups in the vicinity or as a means of alliance creation. However, few such studies have taken into account the influences of kinship, the economy of the people, family size, and household structure on its practice—nor, conversely, the impact that *guddifachaa* might have had on these issues.[14] One such study is that of Dessalegn Negeri, an Oromo social work scholar, who has also explored the societal impact of the *guddifachaa* system among the Oromo, noting, inter alia, its role in the creation of social bonds and building up resources where additional children were regarded as potential material assets.[15] The Oromo sociocultural system of *guddifachaa* has its roots in the Oromo *gadaa* system of democratic governance and, as such, both endorses and transcends the individual Oromo family structure, impacting and shaping Oromo society at community and national levels.

Evidence emerging from the narratives of the Oromo children suggests substantive deviations from the kinship continuum model as well as from either the Bohannan or the Africanist notion of internal African slavery as outlined above. Nor can the *guddifachaa* system incorporate the diverse experiences of many if not most of the children in the group.

These considerations of family incorporation are key as we explore the age and family structure of the Oromo children.

Age Structure

As with the differential in the sex ratio between the Atlantic and the Horn of Africa slave trade,[16] age is particularly significant in any study of the local slave trade (see the full discussion of the sex ratio of the Oromo children on page 209–210). Unlike the Atlantic trade from West Africa to the North American, Brazilian, or Caribbean territories, the most sought-after slaves were not young men intended directly for the plantation. Mekuria Bulcha, alluding to the reports of nineteenth-century travelers, maintains that the majority of captives exported across the Red Sea were young girls between the ages of seven and fourteen years, with a general ratio of two females to one male. There were virtually no slaves over thirty years old.[17] Bulcha underscores this point further, using data derived from observations made at the ports of Massawa and Tadjoura, by stating that "a large proportion of captives exported from the Red Sea ports during the nineteenth-century were children and adolescents. Young girls between the ages of seven and 14 years represented the largest group." He goes on to cite figures given by Belgian diplomat Edouard Blondeel van Cuelebroeck in the report of his sojourn in Ethiopia between 1840 and 1842. According to Bulcha, Blondeel quoted official figures that excluded numbers gained through smuggling, reflecting that about "600 captives, mainly Oromo, including 300 girls (most 12 or 13 years old), 200 boys and 100 eunuchs were exported from Massawa in 1839."[18] In the Horn of Africa, the trade was manifestly a trade in children.

When the missionaries and their Afaan Oromoo–speaking colleagues interviewed the Oromo children at Sheikh Othman, not all of the children were able to tell the missionaries their date of birth. Instead, the missionaries had to rely on visual observation, physical attributes (including height and developmental level), and the knowledge and assumptions of the children and their peers. The missionaries accordingly assigned each child an approximate age at the time of their interviews in 1890.

The following box and whisker plots (graph 2.1) show the different age ranges of the boys and girls. The chart demonstrates that the boys were generally younger than the girls with an age range of 10 to 18 years, a mean age of 14.33 years, and a median of 14 years. Ten-year-old Katshi Wolamo was the youngest in the group. Six boys were age 18 when interviewed.

The girls, on the other hand, were overall about a year older than the boys. Their ages ranged from 11 to 19 years, with a slightly higher average age of 14.73 years and a median age of 15 years.

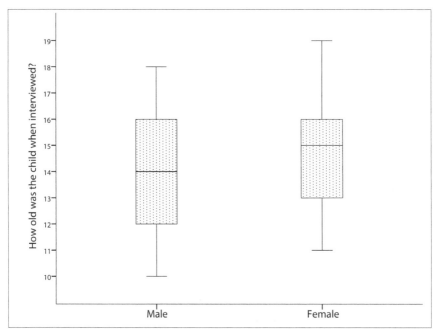

GRAPH 2.1. Ages of boys and girls when interviewed (source: Sandra Rowoldt Shell).

The children's narratives both confirm the general consensus on the youthfulness of the slave trade in the Horn of Africa and provide the sort of specific age detail not found elsewhere. To know what the children experienced in respect to the family-slavery continuum, we must first know more about the family structure.

The Oromo children were well documented in photographs. From this view of the children at the mission house in Sheikh Othman (see fig. 2.1), there can be no doubt as to their young ages. Half the girls (pictured on the upper floor) can barely peek over a standard balcony railing. Below them, the majority of the boys range from waist to shoulder height of the adult accompanying them—a portrait of mass vulnerability.

Family Composition

The travelers' accounts of this area and era indicate that youth characterizes the export slave trade of the Red Sea region. This was primarily a trade in children—and of Oromo children in particular. This meant that the tender years of this group of Oromo children undoubtedly contributed to their vulnerability. But there were other factors impinging on their personal security as well. For example, Fred Morton, in his exploration of the narratives of thirty-nine East African slave children, found that most had been separated from their parents by the time they were taken captive.[19] How does this compare with the Oromo families in the present study? Did the Oromo child have the protection of a secure family environment?

Figure 2.1. Oromo children shortly after their arrival at the Keith-Falconer Mission (source: Acc. 10023/417 [packet 3], Foreign Mission Records of the Church of Scotland, World Mission, National Library of Scotland).

A solid 15.1 percent of the Oromo children were sold into slavery by members of their families or by neighbors. Of these, slightly more than half (53.8 percent) were paternal, maternal, or full orphans. As has been evident from the experiences recounted above, the children's narratives reflect that when one or both parents of a child or children died, it was not uncommon for an uncle or other relative to step in to take over the late parent's (or parents') children and property as part of the *guddifachaa* system. Despite this initial gesture of kinship solidarity and sense of familial responsibility, these relatives often sold the child to a slave trader. Timothy Fernyhough, an economic historian, suggests some mitigating factors. Extreme poverty and crime, suggests Fernyhough, could result in a drop in social status to servitude, while natural disasters like drought and famine led to tougher times for those who lived off the land (see graph 2.2). This in turn led to an increase in enslavement as families found they could no longer survive independently. In these circumstances, wrote Fernyhough, "the famished offered their offspring to merchants who would feed them."[20]

It would be natural to assume from this that the pressures on parents, relatives, and neighbors to sell the children entrusted to their care for gain would have increased incrementally as the effects of what is known as Ethiopia's great drought and famine began to take hold in the southwestern regions after the summer rains failed in 1887.[21]

Fernyhough confirms the peak period of the famine as being 1890–1891, a year or two after the liberation of the Oromo children. Further, a cross-tabulation of the instances where a relative or neighbor sold a child indicates that more than two-thirds (69.2 percent) of the children who were sold were among those rescued off the *Osprey* in September 1888 when the drought and famine had begun to take their toll but had not yet peaked.

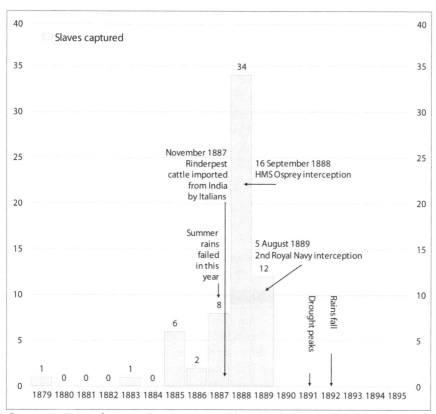

GRAPH 2.2. Years of capture showing onset of drought, famine, and rinderpest (source: Sandra Rowoldt Shell).

Only 30.8 percent of the children were from the later dhows. This second tranche of children were rescued and liberated in the summer of 1889, by which time the drought and famine had the territories to the south and southwest of Ethiopia firmly in its grip. The chart above (see graph 2.2) depicts the years in which the children were enslaved, the dates of their liberation, and the relative concurrence of external factors such as the drought, famine, and rinderpest. The bulk of the kinship sales, then, were in the early days of the drought and famine and cannot have been a precipitating cause for any reversal of the Oromo adoption system.

For example, Hawe Sukute was one of the children who had been rescued and liberated aboard the HMS *Osprey*. When her parents both died, she and her two brothers went to stay with their maternal uncle. However, another uncle, this time on her father's side, "claimed them as his property and took them to his house where they worked for him" (appendix B; narrative 56). As Miers and Kopytoff point out, it was not simply a matter of a relative taking initial responsibility for the children—effectively adopting them—when they were orphaned or when the family had fallen on hard times. What happened thereafter was significant, shifting the focus away from the mode of kin acquisition to mundane and pecuniary outcomes.[22] Hawe reported that her paternal uncle was in debt to the Garjeja king, so he sold her to pay the debt. Here, familial solidarity did not hold sway.

Other *Osprey* children experienced the profound trauma of being "disposed of" by relatives, sometimes by their own fathers. Liban Bultum's (see appendix B; narrative 27) father was clearly wealthy, owning a large piece of land, a number of oxen, sheep, and goats, and two horses. So Liban was perplexed and distressed to discover that when a group of Sidama came to collect their tribute money, his father inexplicably refused to pay what he owed. Instead, his father, Bultum, stood by while the Sidama seized his son in lieu of the tribute debt, carrying him off to a nearby slave market and selling him to the "Nagadi," a group of established slave traders and merchants.

While "Sidama" could refer to the neighboring people in the area south of old Abyssinia, the term is more likely to refer to the Abyssinians. In later life, Liban Bultum returned to the newly constituted and expanded Ethiopia and assisted missionary and lexicologist Edwin C. Foot in the compilation of the second Afaan Oromoo–English/English–Afaan Oromoo dictionary ever published. Given Liban's own identification of the Sidama as "Abyssinian" in his dictionary (indicating he was only too aware of their identity), it would seem inappropriate to assume that the people who seized him in lieu of taxes were the neighboring southern Sidama people—who were as vulnerable as the Oromo: "They [the Sidama] share many similarities in terms of language, culture, values, and psychological make-up with their Cushitic neighbors. They also share the common history of conquest by the army of Menelik of Shawa in the late nineteenth-century which is by far the most critical and perverse event in Sidama history."[23]

Not only family members took advantage of the more vulnerable of the children. Fayissa Murki (see appendix B; narrative 14), another child rescued off the later dhows, started off in a normal and secure family environment, living with his parents and two sisters. His father owned a small piece of land, about twenty head of cattle, and some goats in the village of Alle in the country of Danno. However, this familial stability was nonetheless fragile. While playing near his home one afternoon, a neighbor approached and asked Fayissa to accompany him to his home nearby. Fayissa complied, but once there, he must have been terrified when the neighbor detained him in his house. That night, the neighbor took Fayissa to a nearby slave market and sold him to a group of Atari merchants, who, in turn, took him to a place called Dalotti in Tigre country, where he became entrapped in the remorseless slave traffic destined for the Red Sea ports. We can presume the neighbor knew that the newly enslaved person would never be seen again.

Establishing household size, including the average family size among the general Oromo population in 1888 or 1889, is a challenging task, and estimates of the average number of children per family in sub-Saharan Africa during precolonial times have a broad range. Economic historian Gwyn Campbell, in his article on the precolonial historical demography of Madagascar, cites an average of "between 4.9 and 5.25 children per household estimated for sub-Saharan Africa in general during pre-colonial and recent times."[24] While scholars like Elisée Reclus have provided approximate

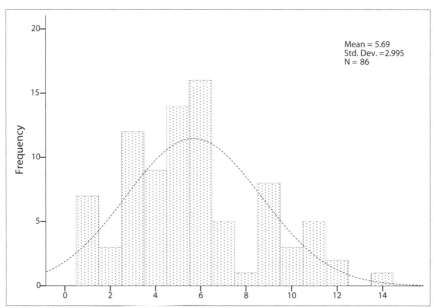

Mean = 5.69
Std. Dev. = 2.995
N = 86

GRAPH 2.3. Family sizes of boys and girls (source: Sandra Rowoldt Shell).

population totals for the region in general and for the Oromo population in particular for 1885 (see map 1.2 and discussion on page 19),[25] detailed demographic data for the Oromo in the late nineteenth century are elusive. Geographer R. T. Jackson, in his research on the influence of population size on market size and density in southern Ethiopia, estimated an average family size of five among the inhabitants of this region bordering present-day Oromia.[26] This figure at least gives a rough yardstick by which to suggest a regional estimate of trends relating to family size. The average number of children per Oromo family in this study is snugly commensurate with this figure.

The histogram above shows the family sizes of all the Oromo children (see graph 2.3). Gender differences in family size patterns were minor.[27] Most of the boys and girls (80.2 percent) lived in families of between three and nine family members. A small proportion of children (3.5 percent) either had no memory of any other family members (Gilo Kashe, Faraja Jimma, and Galgalli Shangalla; see appendix B; narratives 19, 12, and 54, respectively) or were full orphans with no siblings (Meshinge Salban and Isho Karabe; see appendix B; narratives 59 and 23, respectively). These are included as single-member families.

At the upper end of the scale, 15.1 percent of the children had families of between ten and fourteen family members. However, even the Oromo families with larger than the average number of siblings in the home did not provide the sort of protection to an individual child that might have been imagined. Safety in numbers carried little weight against the forces that were driving the internal and export slave trade.

Orphanhood

UNICEF defines an orphan as "a child who has lost one or both parents," so those Oromo children who lost either their father or their mother were ranked as orphans.[28] Nearly one-fifth (19.77 percent) of the children (11.63 percent girls and 8.14 percent boys) either could not remember one or both of their parents or did not mention them in giving details of their family composition. These figures tell their own story. Of the majority 81.2 percent who could supply these details, as many as 12.8 percent of the children were full or double orphans when they were captured—with boys accounting for 3.5 percent of that total and girls nearly three times that proportion at 9.3 percent.[29]

These figures compare negatively when ranked against comparable statistics from twenty-first-century Ethiopia, Oromia, or even South Africa, where the death toll of men and women between the ages of nineteen and forty-four—many of them victims of the massive HIV/AIDS pandemic—is distressingly high. Graph 2.4 shows the clear discrepancy between the percentage of orphans among our group of Oromo children and the prevalence of orphanhood in any of the regions selected for comparative purposes.

A total of 12.8 percent of the Oromo slave children were full orphans, 17.4 percent were paternal orphans, and 1.2 percent were maternal orphans. In aggregate, 31.4 percent of the children had lost either one or both parents. This figure falls just short of three times the aggregated national Ethiopian orphan prevalence percentage of 11.9 percent in 2005, more than three times the aggregated national Ethiopian orphanhood total in 2007, and 3.27 times the aggregated orphanhood total in Oromia in the same year. The prevalence of orphanhood among the sixty-four Oromo children is therefore significantly higher than might be anticipated.[30]

Fred Morton believes that the deaths or absence of the parents of the East African slave children of his study certainly rendered them unprotected and at greater risk.[31] Raiders probably regarded orphaned Oromo children as easier quarry without the usual protection of a full family-unit complement. They may also have regarded orphans as generally more acquiescent and less likely to run away, given that they had no families to which they could return.

Orphanhood in Ethiopia is an old and still-growing phenomenon. Laura Camfield, a social anthropologist, has written recently that parental mortality, more specifically maternal mortality, is increasing in Ethiopia. She ascribes this not only to the growth in the incidence of HIV/AIDS, but also to high maternal mortality, acute illness, and the effects of drought, famine, displacement, migration, and conflict.[32] The conditions experienced by the Oromo children in the late 1880s were not dissimilar—acute illness, drought, famine, displacement, migration, and conflict.

Of the fifty children rescued aboard the *Osprey* in September 1888, 28.4 percent were orphans. This figure contrasts starkly with the 47.4 percent of orphans aboard the dhows who were rescued and liberated eleven months later on 5 August 1889. While it is not possible to draw a straight line of causality, the considerably

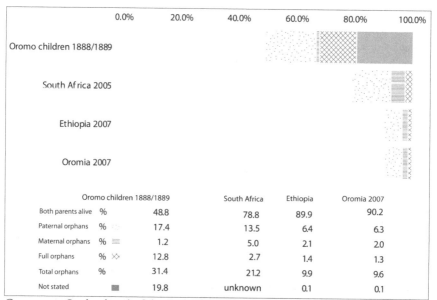

		Oromo children 1888/1889	South Africa	Ethiopia	Oromia 2007
Both parents alive	%	48.8	78.8	89.9	90.2
Paternal orphans	%	17.4	13.5	6.4	6.3
Maternal orphans	%	1.2	5.0	2.1	2.0
Full orphans	%	12.8	2.7	1.4	1.3
Total orphans	%	31.4	21.2	9.9	9.6
Not stated		19.8	unknown	0.1	0.1

GRAPH 2.4. Orphanhood of the Oromo children vs. children in South Africa, Ethiopia, and Oromia (source: Sandra Rowoldt Shell).

higher prevalence of parental mortality in the later, non-*Osprey* group could be considered consistent with the increased impact of the drought and famine by the end of 1888.

Were children also at risk if they lived with their mother but there was no father in the household? According to Abbi Kedir and Lul Admasachew, "There is a great degree of stigma attached to children who are raised without a father figure" in Ethiopia.[33] Without the paterfamilias, the children were clearly vulnerable. There was only one example of maternal orphanhood. That all other Oromo orphans were paternal or full suggests the significance of the presence of the father for the protection of the family. Nearly one-fifth (17.4 percent) of all the Oromo children were paternal orphans, a total that was distributed more or less evenly between the boys (8.1 percent) and the girls (9.3 percent). Male relatives (uncles and elder brothers) were again quick to intervene following the deaths of the fathers of six of these paternal orphans, five boys (Badassa Nonno, Bayan Liliso, Fayissa Umbe, Rufo Gangila, and Wakinne Nagesso) and one girl (Galani Warabu). (See appendix B; narratives 5, 9, 15, 32, 39, and 53, respectively.) The intentions of these appear to have been relatively benign, in most cases assuming the care of the family and working the properties. Galani Warabu's uncle laid claim to all the family's assets, that is, all his brother's cattle and property, and took care of the family until the Sidama (i.e., Abyssinians) raided the country, killing the two eldest of Galani's five brothers. Galani and her sisters successfully evaded capture by hiding from the Sidama and, after the raiders left, the siblings returned home. Their restored sense of security was short-lived.

Soon after their return, a "cousin" came to visit and took Galani back to his home. However, one day she told him she wanted to go home, prompting him to take her to the market in Macharro, situated in West Hararge in the modern Oromia region, where he sold her to a group of slave traders.

Fayissi Gemo (see appendix B; narrative 52), who was a young girl approximately twelve years of age when captured, was the daughter of Gemo and Yarachi. Gemo, her father, had been a secure landowner in a village called Upa in the Kaffa country. He owned several oxen, sheep, and goats, but he had died before Fayissi was abducted. After her father's death, Yarachi supported the family, employing laborers to plow the land. However, the family was no longer secure. While Yarachi was away visiting her homeland, the chief of their village of Upa took the opportunity to abduct Fayissi—and promptly sold her to some passing merchants, leaving her mother and sisters behind.

Jifari Roba (see appendix B; narrative 57) was a little Oromo girl of about eleven when she was sold into slavery. Her father, Roba, her mother, Dongoshe, and her three brothers and four sisters lived in Galani, a village in the Sayo country. When Roba died, Dongoshe sought work reaping for others in the fields. In what seemed to be a compassionate gesture, a neighbor offered to look after Jifari. Immediately after taking Jifari into her home, the woman sold her to a passing group of "Nagadi" (slave traders) for ten pieces of salt (amole).

The only maternal orphan, a young boy named Galgal Dikko, was very young when he left home but was nonetheless able to remember that his mother (Hudo) was dead and that he had five brothers and one sister. He recalled:

> A party of men on horseback, with guns, coming down upon his village, and, after a fierce fight, carrying himself and one of his brothers away. He became very ill as they were taking him away, and he was left by them on the wayside, near a place called Gobbu. Here he was found by a man who took him to his house. The chief of the country hearing the circumstances of this man's finding Galgal, claimed him as his property, and promised to allow him to return to his own country when he grew up. (appendix B; narrative 17)

However, during another battle the Sidama (Abyssinians) raided the village and seized all the guns they could find. Galgal thought he was safe, but the Sidama soon returned, this time seeking slaves rather than guns, and they carried him off to a place called Tibbe, in modern Oromia.

One family member selling another is widely regarded as repugnant. One of the most familiar instances is the biblical story of Joseph.[34] This practice has a long history and universality. That it was practiced in Ethiopia should therefore come as no surprise.

Given the exceptionally high prevalence of orphanhood, the incidence of parental mortality seems to have played a role in leaving the children more vulnerable than if both parents had been alive and present at the time of enslavement. From the evidence of the children's narratives, there is a sense that the loss of a parent was likely to trigger the intervention of relatives or neighbors. In terms of the assumption of family incorporation held by African historian Suzanne Miers and anthropologist Igor Kopytoff, this intervention should have led to a continuance of familial protection as a manifestation of the kinship continuum.[35] The reality, regrettably, was that these children found themselves caught in the slave trade sweep to the Red Sea coast, often directly through the actions of their kin. Whatever it meant to some, familial incorporation did not protect all the children.

Only the broadest brushstrokes have depicted what is known about the slaves and their family backgrounds in the Red Sea slave trade. Contemporary accounts and later scholarly studies of the trade concur that this was a trade in children. The Oromo children's narratives ipso facto support this interpretation but also provide much more intimate detail. Details of Oromo family structure and kinship patterns emerge that both partially align with and significantly depart from the concept of the slavery-to-kinship continuum espoused by Miers and Kopytoff. On the one hand, there were well-established Oromo traditions of familial solidarity, namely the Oromo adoption (or *guddifachaa*) system. In the Miers and Kopytoff model, kin would be expected to assume responsibility for a deceased relative's children. One cannot know about the "good" relatives, who may have looked after their wards and kept them from the slave trade. However, on the other hand, we know from the children that relatives sold many of the Oromo children to slave traders. Such sales for monetary gain or barter diverged from that kinship model. Some of these sales may be regarded as distressed sales, resulting from the drought and famine of 1887–1892. But such sales also occurred before the "cruel days" had fully caught hold. Notable among the new information emanating from the narratives was the high proportion of orphans among children traded as slaves. Orphans were potentially easier targets than those embedded in secure, full family units. Paternal orphans were perhaps the most vulnerable. Orphans could be expected to be more docile and acquiescent slaves as they had a lower motivation for escape without a family to return to. One may also speculate that orphans made perfect candidates for what psychologists have termed the Stockholm syndrome. These new considerations suggest new avenues for exploration in this underresearched area of the African slave trade.

CHAPTER 3

Wealth and Status of the Oromo Captives' Families

Scholars exploring the background and social status of the families of slave children in Ethiopia (and more broadly in Africa) have had to formulate their sometimes hazardous interpretations based on travelers' and other third-person accounts. Records of captives, such as they are, document the experiences of slaves after capture or after manumission. This applies especially in Islamic societies, where there was no clearly defined slave class, and integration into general society was possible and even planned.[1] In the case of the Oromo captivity narratives, there is direct information on their families' wealth and social status. Their accounts, as well as the memoir of an Oromo child written at Lovedale (see appendix D) and letters by some of the Oromo repatriates after their return home,[2] go some way toward answering the question and help define the range of social strata from which the Oromo children were drawn.

There are, of course, studies of the social structure of societies in which slave raiding occurred and where there was a culture of local enslavement. In his study of Senegambian society, for example, historian Philip Curtin positions slaves or *captifs* among the social strata, with the caveat that Senegambian slaves could not be considered as a social stratum in the Western sense. Instead, he distinguishes the social group of slaves as foreigners who were purchased or captured as spoils of war and integrated into Senegambian society.[3] Curtin also examines two different types of enslavement. One, a "political" model, would constitute not an economic process but one where slaves were acquired as the spoils of a war waged for prestige and power rather than profit. Another, which he terms an "economic" model, would involve the enslaver in calculating the costs of his raiding and slaving against the potential income he could expect from a slave dealer. In this scenario, the captor would organize a raid or simply kidnap a child from a neighboring village.[4] However, none of these studies engage with the social status of the people targeted for enslavement. The question, then, remains: What was the social status of the people who were enslaved in Ethiopia? The key to answering this lies in the first-person accounts of the slaves themselves.

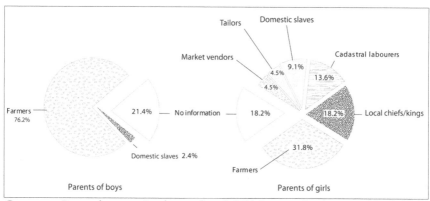

GRAPH 3.1. Parental occupation by gender of child (source: Sandra Rowoldt Shell).

Parental Occupation

According to the children's firsthand accounts, all but one of the parents were engaged in farming (see the assertion in Wakinni Ugga's account in appendix B; narrative 63). The present analysis is rather more detailed than that broad stroke would suggest. The reason for this has been in recognition of issues of status underwriting some of the occupations—for example, where a father was a village chief, or a mother was engaged in domestic work as a slave in a household environment, or where widows were forced to find employment following the deaths of their husbands.

Just under one-fifth of the children (19.8 percent)—mostly very young or, in a few cases, mentally compromised—did not give the missionaries any details regarding their parents' occupations. Of the rest, marginally more than two-thirds of the group (66.7 percent) indicated that their parents made their living off the land. The most striking finding is the difference between the proportion of farmers among the boys' families (76.2 percent) and the girls' (31.8 percent). The following double pie diagram (graph 3.1) clearly shows the predominance of agricultural endeavor, particularly in the families of the boys. Only 2.4 percent of the boys' parents were in domestic servitude. This agricultural concentration was the natural result of the higher level of freehold tenure among the boys' families.

The diagram shows that 18.2 percent of the girls were the daughters of village chiefs. The parents of 13.6 percent of the girls hired themselves out as cadastral laborers (plowmen, tillers, sowers, or reapers), including those widowed mothers who were engaged in manual labor in the fields after the deaths of their husbands: Damara, mother of Damuli Diso (see appendix B; narrative 49), cut wood to sell to local men who made earthenware; Dongoshe, Jifari Roba's (narrative 57) mother, went to reap in the fields; and Dabeche, mother of Turungo Gudda (narrative 61), went into the fields to sow or reap or do any other labor required by Turungo's uncle. One widow, Damuli Dunge's (narrative 50) mother, became a market vendor. A total of 9.1 percent of the girls' parents were engaged as domestic slaves. Wakinni Ugga's (narrative 63) father, the only artisan and Matthew Lochhead's single occupational exception, was a village tailor.

Measures of Land

In addition to occupation, the extent of a family's immovable property is also a strong indicator of relative wealth. In their interviews with the missionaries, 69.7 percent of the children gave rough details of property size through either precise or approximate acreage. These approximations have been aggregated as follows: land the children described as "small" measured up to two acres; land the children described in approximate terms such as "some" or "a few" acres was classified as medium; and land the children described as "large" measured six acres and up. Of the 30.3 percent of the children who did not give any indication of property size, some were in nonownership circumstances, while others either did not know or could not remember.

Graph 3.2 shows the proportional sizes of property occupied by the families of the Oromo children by gender of child. All but one of the children giving the size of the family's land were raised on freehold farms. The exception was Amaye Tiksa, whose father was a small crofter working "about two acres of land" (appendix B; narrative 4).

Most of the boys (36.8 percent) also indicated that their families owned large pieces of land. Liban Bultum, for example, reported that his father "was the owner of a large piece of land in the Ilu country" (appendix B; narrative 27). One boy, who stated that his father owned a "small piece of land" (appendix D), told an unusual story. Gutama Tarafo (see appendix D), who would have been about thirteen years old when he was captured, lived near the village of Gamoje in the Gera country. The word *gamoje* in general use means "the cool country." In this case, Gamoje is the name of a small village that presumably had a climate cool enough to keep bees for the production of honey.

While fewer girls were raised on freehold farms than boys, a higher proportion (57.1 percent) were from families owning what they described as a "large" piece of land (i.e., land of six acres or more). Among these girls were four daughters of local chiefs, whose fathers appear to have had wealth to match their stations. Berille Boko, for example, gave a graphic description of her family's socioeconomic status, saying that her father was "the chief of the village and possessed land which it would take a whole day to go round" (appendix B; narrative 46). Dinkitu Boensa's home was in a village called Garjeda in the Gindo country. She told the missionaries that her father was the chief of Garjeda and that "he had large lands" (narrative 51). Similarly, Galani Warabu's father was "the chief of a village" and died before she left home. Galani's information about her homestead is skimpy, but there is a suggestion of considerable holdings, as she reported that when her father died, her uncle claimed "all his cattle and property" (narrative 53). Kanatu Danke also gave a response that implied rather than detailed her family's circumstances. She reported that her father, who was the chief of the village of Lalo in the Sayo country, "possessed a piece of land on which he employed many labourers" (narrative 58).

In an anonymous essay—which may be classed as a small memoir, written later at Lovedale Institution—one of the Oromo children wrote about the prevalence of beekeeping and honey cultivation among the Oromo. The author of the memoir is almost certainly Gutama Tarafo, as he provided the only reference to honey and beekeeping in the narratives: "There is plenty of honey. The people don't keep bees as

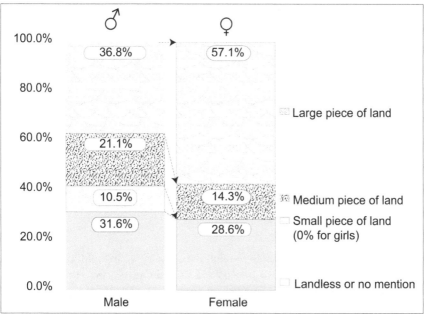

GRAPH 3.2. Relative sizes of land occupied by Oromo families (source: Sandra Rowoldt Shell).

in this country. They hang a kind of basket made of reeds high on a tree. When the honey is ready, the people climb the tree, and get the honey. They sell it in the markets, of which there are many" (appendix B; narrative 20). Beekeeping in Ethiopia has a long history. According to Kassaye Ayalew, cited in a study by two biologists, Gidey Yirga and Kibrom Ftwi, Ethiopians are believed to have been raising bees since 3500–3000 BC. In the same study, Yirga and Ftwi indicate that the success of box hive beekeeping is largely due to the country's moderate climate.[5] In recent years, Ethiopia has been responsible for almost a quarter of Africa's total honey production.

Gutama's father, Tarafo, was apprehended while selling honey to a neighboring clan. Gutama does not explain why this should have been an illegal act, given the proliferation of honey production in the country, but Gutama told the missionaries that it was deemed to "have been an offence against the King of the country." The village chief who found out about Tarafo's honey-selling reported him to the king of Gera. The king's response was to send his men to seize Tarafo's land and possessions. The entire family was also seized and given as slaves to the village chief—one may assume as a reward for blowing the whistle on Tarafo's honey-selling (see appendix B; narrative 20).

In "My Essay," Gutama also wrote about the houses and properties occupied by the Oromo in his region:

> The houses are not the same as those here. The Galla huts are [always] four or
> five times bigger than these Kaffir huts. I may say the Galla house has got two

storeys. In the upper storey they keep corn and other things; but in the lower one the people sleep. There are two rooms in the lower storey, one is where the mother of the house does her work and the other one is for sleeping and eating. There are many kinds of grain, as wheat, barley, maize, and bishinga, that is Kaffir-corn, also pumpkins, potatoes, and other things like potatoes, beans, coffee, peas, bananas, also cabbages and tobacco and many other things which I can't name in English. . . . The Galla people are rich in cattle and corn. Some of them have farms for cattle, and some for corn. (appendix D)

Gutama wrote about his home and homeland as he remembered them prior to his capture in September 1886. His premature departure from home predated the onset of the great drought and famine that was to blight the land after the rains failed in the summer of 1887. In Gutama's description, the crops of the Oromo were still abundant and the cattle plentiful.

Livestock

Although as many as 61.6 percent of the children did not give any information regarding whether their families owned livestock, the remaining 38.4 percent not only reported that their families owned livestock, but followed up by identifying which types of animals they held and even, in some cases, how many head of each species. More than three times as many boys' families owned livestock (69.7 percent) against only 30.3 percent of the girls. The double pie diagram below (graph 3.3) shows the combination of livestock species mentioned by the children tabulated by gender of child.

As the diagram indicates, cattle clearly predominate, featuring alone and in every combination of livestock mentioned by the children. As might be expected, there is a high correlation between freehold tenure and livestock ownership, so on those grounds alone there would have been an expectation of higher livestock holdings for the boys' families than for the girls'. The boys' families held the full range of livestock species except for the combination of cattle and donkeys: cattle only (30.3 percent); cattle and sheep (12.1 percent); cattle, goats, and sheep (9.1 percent); oxen, sheep, goats, and horses (9.1 percent); cattle and goats (6.1 percent); and cattle, horses, and sheep (3 percent). The girls' families held either only cattle on their own (12.1 percent); cattle and sheep (6.1 percent); cattle, goats, and sheep (6.1 percent); or cattle and donkeys (also 6.1 percent).

Tolassa Wayessa's father, for example, had "about twenty oxen, fifteen sheep, also a horse" (appendix B; narrative 38). What Tolassa does not mention is that along with the landed property and livestock, his father also owned several slaves. Many years later, Liban Bultum wrote to Lovedale from Addis Ababa to say that

> Tolassa Wayessa, who returned some years ago, has a good position in the German Legation. Wayessa's father and mother were dead before he reached Abyssinia; but he found an old woman who used to live with his parents when he was child. Through her help he has been able to recover all his father's property with the exception of four slaves belonging to his father, which another man claims.[6]

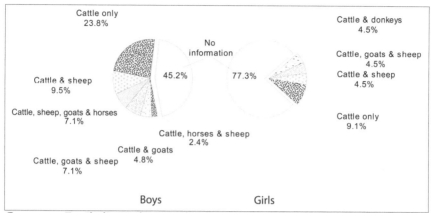

GRAPH 3.3. Family livestock ownership by gender of child (source: Sandra Rowoldt Shell).

Slave ownership was obviously a further mark of relative wealth. Only the families of Tolassa and Bisho Jarsa (appendix B; narrative 48) are recorded as owning slaves. This was a sensitive area, however; and the fact that Tolassa did not mention his family owning slaves in his narrative may suggest that there might have been further—unspoken of—instances among the wealthier Oromo families.

Gutama continued his essay by giving details of the livestock commonly kept by the Oromo, beginning with cattle, and he also included information on the use of the plow on Oromo farms (see fig. 3.1). The Oromo were long-term users of the plow, so cattle held a special value for them both as plow oxen and as beef or dairy stock:

> The bullocks in Gallaland are very big, much bigger than those in South Africa, as high as a horse. The yokes are nearly like those used in this country. It is a custom to train one of the oxen to guard the Kraal and they sharpen its horns to fight. It does no work but just keeps the kraal. The kraals in Gallaland are bigger than those here, but are made of bushes too. Many people's cattle go into one kraal. Nearly every cow or ox has a name, and they like very much to eat salt. There are blacksmiths who make the ploughs, long narrow ploughs, and only two oxen draw them. (appendix D)

While Gutama's nostalgia and innate pride in his country might be considered to be at work in enhancing his memory of the bullocks' size, Oromo cattle are indeed larger than average.

James McCann, a historian, emphasizes the pivotal role played by oxen in the highland areas, describing them as the preeminent mode of capital and often the economic resource that was hardest to come by.[7] The highland ox, larger and heavier than the norm, continues as the draft animal of choice in the highland areas because of its superior pulling power.[8]

More girls than boys responded with information about their families' cattle—39.5 percent of girls as opposed to 23.3 percent of boys. Most families (26.7 percent)

FIGURE 3.1. Oromo oxen (source: *Tourist* 1, no. 35 [8 April 1833]: 281).

held what the children described as "a few" or "some" cattle. The rest of the girls were able to give the number of cattle their families held, ranging between one and nineteen head.

A small number (3.5 percent) of boys reported that their families held between twenty and fifty-nine head of cattle. Among these were Fayissa Murki, who said his father owned a small piece of land and "about twenty head of cattle" (appendix B; narrative 14); Tolassa Wayessa, whose father "possessed a large piece of land and about twenty oxen" (narrative 38); and Tola Lual, whose father had a large piece of land and "about twenty ploughing oxen" (narrative 36). Tola Urgessa, who said his father "had a large piece of land of his own, with about sixty oxen" (narrative 37), was one of the 2.3 percent of the families who held between 60 and 99 head of cattle. In the same proportion, the families of 2.3 percent of the girls and 1.2 percent of the boys had more than one hundred head of cattle. Balcha Billo reported that his father held "a great many cattle" (narrative 8); and among the girls, Dinkitu Boensa said that her father, the chief Boensa, had "some hundred of cattle" (narrative 51). Both of these children fell into the final class, coded "100 plus."

Gutama Tarafo bragged in his memoir that "the Galla horses are just the same as the Arab horses; they all look like race horses" (appendix D). The Oromo, who bred one of the world's oldest recorded breed of horses,[9] were a cavalry people, using horses to traverse their inhospitable territory. This lent them a natural defense against foreign, noncavalry marauders but afforded little protection against slave raiders who were fellow Oromo on horseback (see fig. 3.2). Economists Nathan Nunn and Diego Puga have argued that raids and kidnapping were the principal methods of enslavement in Africa, either by members of one ethnicity against another or within the same ethnicity. Rugged terrain provided a natural defense against slave raiders as well as providing caves in which to hide. High altitudes meant the ability to monitor incoming routes for invaders.[10]

Bred for its strength and agility as a mountain packhorse or workhorse, the Oromo horse's bloodlines originated in Ethiopia and spread along the Red Sea coastline. Today, these bloodlines have been diluted to such a degree with centuries of interbreeding that the strain has almost disappeared.

Only four children reported owning one or more horses, all of them boys. Tolassa Wayessa's (see appendix B; narrative 38) father owned one horse; and the fathers of Liban Bultum (narrative 27) and Wayessa Tikse (narrative 41) owned two apiece; while Tola Urgessa's (narrative 37) father owned four horses. Although Tola's was a home of considerable wealth in the context of the other families, each of these boys came from advantaged circumstances when compared with the rest of the children. One anomaly emerges: If horses were a mark of wealth, why did none of the chiefly daughters mention horses in their narratives?

Only 17.5 percent of the children mentioned owning any sheep: 14 percent owned "several," while 3.5 percent owned "many."[11] Gutama, the putative young essayist on "Gallaland," does not mention sheep among the animals commonly farmed by the Oromo. However, his perspective could have been compromised by his youth and was likely to have been limited to his own experience, particularly if his father farmed the honey-producing bees that led to his arrest. Although Gutama's family appear not to have owned any livestock, he explains in his memoir that Oromo women were responsible only for the domestic work within the house and had no outdoor, agricultural role: "The Gallas are not lazy people. The men never allow their wives to go and build the house for them, and they won't allow them to go and labour in the fields all day for food, while they sit down in their huts and smoke their long pipes. The women there do not work like that but they only work in the house while their husbands till the ground" (appendix D).

The kingdom of Gera, where Gutama lived, is now one of the *woredas* (or administrative zones) in the Oromia region and occupies much the same territory as the old kingdom. With an altitude ranging between 1,390 and 2,980 meters above sea level, much of the land in Gera is not arable. Coffee, grain, and spices are the primary crops, but the terrain remains largely inhospitable to livestock. Gutama's personal experience of husbandry might therefore have been scant and his knowledge of gender roles in other regions could have been skimpy. Certainly, among the Oromo children's families in this study, some widowed mothers were forced by straitened circumstances to venture into the fields to engage in reaping or other agricultural manual labor (see mentions of widows' field labor on pages 43, 190).

Even fewer children mentioned goats. Only 15.1 percent said their families held any goats, and of these, 10.5 percent of the boys and 2.3 percent of the girls said their

FIGURE 3.2. Cavalry on the Wadela plateau in Ethiopia (source: Trevenen J. Holland and Henry Hozier, *Record of the Expedition to Abyssinia* [London: Her Majesty's Stationery Office, 1870]).

families owned "several goats." The same proportion of girls (2.3 percent) and none of the boys claimed that their families owned "many goats."

Mixed livestock holdings would have been common, as meat and milk formed core components of the Oromo diet. However, according to Gutama's memoir, they eschewed game, pork, and wild fowl, while most avoided poultry and eggs as well: "Gallas never eat wild animals. They don't eat pigs in northern Gallaland; and they don't eat any kind of birds; and few people eat fowls or eggs. But there are some tribes that live among the Gallas, that eat nearly everything" (appendix D).

When the Oromo children reached Lovedale Institution in the Eastern Cape in South Africa, the children did not take long to acclimatize to local ways. A happy discovery was that the *amasi* (sour milk) and *mealies/mielies* (corn or maize) on which they had been raised at home were part of their daily food regimen at the institution.[12]

From the details provided by the children, the relative levels of wealth and status of the Oromo families emerge as crossing all social strata, from the humblest level of servitude to the elevated thresholds of the local royal houses. Any a priori assumptions that slaves were garnered from only the poorest and humblest of Ethiopian society have to be abandoned. The trends suggested by the children's evidence suggest that captives were acquired from a broader spectrum of social strata than hitherto suspected. The existence of slaves drawn from the more affluent strata is not unknown. Published personal accounts of slaves coming from wealthy, high-status families do exist, but these have numbered few to date.[13] Without further first-person, eyewitness accounts, the social origins of African slaves will probably remain one of the many conundra of the first passage, but historians should not be able to assume any uniformity of wealth or status.

A convincing majority of the boys emanated from agricultural origins rooted firmly in the peasant class. They were differentiated by type of land tenure, which determined gradations of status and material wealth. The girls' families, equally freehold and feudal (35.3 percent each), and with almost as many born into slavery (29.4 percent) at the lower end of the social ladder, ironically included four daughters of chiefs at the upper extreme. The boys had a far stronger freehold tenure representation (64.5 percent) against 25.8 percent brought up in a feudal environment and only 9.7 percent already living under servitude, with neither royalty at one extreme nor large numbers born or already absorbed into domestic slavery at the other. The majority of families with freehold tenure should, in theory, have been able to enjoy the stability of a higher standard of living and greater family security. In reality, the individualistic nature of freehold tenure—without the potential for protection by landlord or overlord—actually increased their vulnerability to enslavement. Even the demonstrated wealth of some of the boys and the chiefly status of four of the girls did not insulate them from being captured.

In sum, the families of the Oromo children were drawn from every social stratum—from the lowliest slave environment to local royalty. Captors and raiders did not seek out the lowliest as the most vulnerable. Instead, they targeted families from all strata, driven in part by the exigencies of Menelik's invading forces to feed Oromo slaves in large numbers into the train of the external slave trade. The insights into wealth and status of the targeted families made possible by the children's narratives may open the way to further examination in future studies. No class or group was safe from the slave raiders in Oromoland.

CHAPTER 4

Topography, Domicile, and Ethnicity of the Oromo Captives

Scholarly research on Oromo slavery suggests that slaves were drawn from a broad area to the south and southwest of Ethiopia, roughly the area of today's Oromia. Mekuria Bulcha, Timothy Fernyhough, and the authors of localized studies of slavery among the Oromo in the late nineteenth century have drawn their information largely from the accounts of travelers and other commentators.[1] The eyewitness narratives of the Oromo children provide the names not only of their countries of origin but of their regions, towns, and villages. Using data drawn from the narratives, the use of geographical information systems (GIS) methodologies made it possible to generate data-specific maps. In addition, variables derived from the narratives have made it possible to pinpoint and analyze their places of domicile and ethnicity against the topography of the country.[2]

The Topography

Elevated plateaus, escarpments, tablelands, and mountains dominate the dramatic topography of central Ethiopia that frames the journeys of the Oromo captives. The country of Ethiopia boasts as many as half of the highest peaks in Africa—including Badda, a volcanic peak in the Bale mountain range soaring to 4,200 meters (13,650 feet). The country also lays claim to some of the lowest-lying land on earth, including the below–sea level desert on the edge of the Afar or Danakil Depression, through which all the children passed on their way to the entrepôts. The Bale Mountains are separated from the former Abyssinian highlands by the Great Rift Valley. The land of the central plateau, intersected diagonally by the Great Rift Valley, falls away—in places sharply—to the lowlands of the north, west, south, and east.

The lateral escarpments of the rift drop down and diverge to the northeast and northwest, where they transect the Afar or Danakil Depression toward the Red Sea coastal regions, including the children's destination entrepôts of Araito (Rahayta) and Tajurrah (Tadjoura).[3] The Danakil Depression constitutes one of the hottest and driest places on earth and is Ethiopia's lowest point at 120 meters (393.70 feet) *below* sea level. Archaeologists consider the entire rift area one of the cradles of humankind.

Mapping the captives' places of origin against the topography of Ethiopia shows that an overwhelming majority came from highland regions, with their homes dotted along the ridges of the mountain ranges (see map 4.1).

Symbols have been attached to the girls' homes to highlight gender differences in the children's geographic and orographic distribution. Note that with only two exceptions, the girls' homes lie to the west of the escarpment, whereas the boys' homes for the most part follow the mountain ridges on either side of the main Ethiopian rift. These mountain ridges, with their rugged terrain, provided a degree of natural protection from all comers, but they were not sufficient to deter the invading cavalry from the north. Only the homes of Isho Karabe (see appendix B; narrative 23), who lived in the village of Imo in the southeast; Hawe Sukute (narrative 56), from the village of Gani in Garjeja country in the west; and Turungo Tinno (narrative 62), from Saate, a village in the Kaffa country in the south, lay at altitudes of less than 1,000 meters (3,281 feet). Two boys (Amaye Tiksa [narrative 4] and Badassa Wulli [narrative 6]), came from the village of Badda, standing at 3,820 meters (12,415 feet) on the slopes of Mount Badda, a volcanic mountain peaking at 4,200 meters (13,650 feet).

An unanticipated finding was the pronounced gender difference that emerged in respect to altitude. While the average altitude of the boys' homes was 2,156.52 meters (7,008.69 feet), the girls' average was almost 400 meters (1,290 feet) lower, at 1,759.33 meters (5,717.82 feet). The boys had a wider altitude range, from a low of 441.36 meters (1,434.42 feet) to a high of 3,819.97 meters (12,414.90 feet). The girls, on the other hand, ranged from 653.83 meters (2,145 feet) to 2,745.22 meters (9,006 feet). The full explanation of this gender difference related to altitude remains obscure.

There may be virtue in remembering that young Oromo girls realized the highest prices in the external slave markets, so traders might have sought out girl children in places that were easier to access than those living in the higher mountainous regions of the highlands. Ease of access meant a quicker journey to the Red Sea. The children's evidence shows that fewer girls than boys were sold into local servitude initially. Nearly three-quarters (73.8 percent) of the boys were enslaved locally, compared with only half of the girls (50 percent). Some boys spent years—one as long as nine years—in local servitude before being sold into the external network headed for the coast (see pages 84–94 for further discussion).

Graphs 4.1 and 4.2 are based on two different measures of central tendency. The first, a bar graph, is based on the mean, or average, altitude; while the second, a box and whisker plot, is based on the median, or midpoint. The bar graph shows the descending altitude at which each child was captured. This view, not possible with the otherwise effective box plot, provides a statistical cross section of the topography of capture in which the statistically significant gender differentiation is clear.

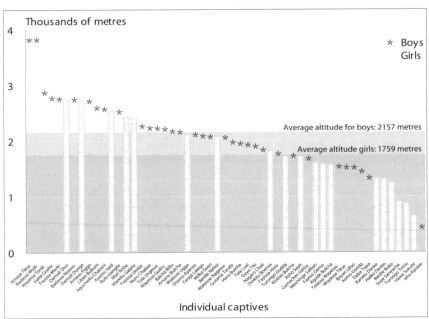

GRAPH 4.1. Altitude at which each child was captured (source: Sandra Rowoldt Shell).

The complementary box and whisker plots (graph 4.2) give a better idea of the gender differences in altitude range. Here, the median, as the midpoint, is unaffected by the outliers at either end of the boys' range.

Note that 50 percent of the girls fall within a discernibly lower second and third quartile range than the boys, with no extreme measures at either high or low altitudes. Using both graphs allows us to visualize the altitude range in two different ways and to appreciate the gender discrepancies more clearly.

The Homelands of the Oromo Children

Most of the children (84.88 percent) remembered some details of where they had been living at the time of their capture. The remaining 15.12 percent could not give the name of their village, town, region, or even their country of origin. The linked pic diagram (graph 4.3) represents the home countries of the Oromo children.

As the diagram illustrates, the children originated in twenty-six different principalities. The majority of the children were concentrated in six of these "countries" (as they termed them). The rest of the children were sparsely distributed at a rate of one or two per principality. For clarity, these have been aggregated in the pie within the category of "Other" principalities, which compose a significant geographic spread, as the map showing the children's places of origin and domicile demonstrates (see map 4.1). This multiplicity of principalities is indicative of the extent of subinfeudation in the region. Some of the monarchies were more prominent and powerful than others; the kingdoms of Jimma, Enarya, Goma, and Guma coexisted, often uncomfortably, in what some might regard as a retrospective federation of principalities.

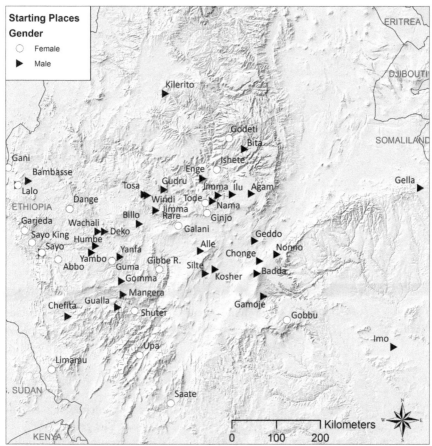

MAP 4.1. Places of domicile of the Oromo captives (source: Sandra Rowoldt Shell and GIS Laboratory, University of Cape Town).

Further, while there was a limited amount of country-level congruence, with small numbers of children coming from each of six countries, the same congruence was not reflected at the more localized level. With only two exceptions, the children all came from different towns and villages. However, in one case, Amaye Tiksa (see appendix B; narrative 4) was carried off by marauding raiders after a battle with his people in November 1887; while Badassa Wulli (narrative 6) was kidnapped from his home in Badda three years earlier, in May 1884. Similarly, two girls and one boy came from Sayo. Kintiso Bulcha (narrative 25) was snatched from his home after Sidama raiders emerged victorious after having invaded his country and engaged in battle against his chief in October 1888. The two girls, Asho Sayo (narrative 44) and Soye Sanyacha (narrative 60), were both taken as spoils of war by invading Sidama raiders in November 1887. This is possibly the same raid, but each child had a different captor and followed a different route thereafter. The Oromo children had no group experience as captives until they neared the coast.

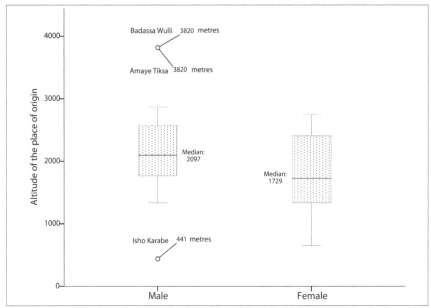

GRAPH 4.2. Altitudes of places of origin by gender of child (source: Sandra Rowoldt Shell).

Ethnicity

The multiplicity of locales might suggest a multiplicity of ethnicities. This is not the case, as a detailed examination by experts has revealed.[4] The graph (4.4) gives a breakdown of ethnicity by gender of child, showing that the overwhelming majority of the boys (81 percent), and an even greater majority of the girls (86.4 percent), were Oromo, giving an overall Oromo majority among the entire group of 83.7 percent, an astonishing homogeneity considering the chaotic process of slave raiding.

This convincing ethnic homogeneity among the children is borne out further in examining the handful of children whose ethnicity could not be attributed as directly Oromo. Of those who were not classified as Oromo, 7 percent were Kafficho (4.8 percent of the boys and 9.1 percent of the girls); and 2.4 percent of the boys were Shangalla, Gurage, and Yambo. The ethnicity of 7.1 percent of the boys and 4.5 percent of the girls could not be determined. These few who could be classified other than Oromo were all from groups cognate with the Oromo or with strong genealogical or political links to the Oromo. The graph shows the Oromo positioned within modern Oromia with the cognate ethnicities placed in the adjacent regions. The girls had a simpler ethnic profile than the boys, with only a single exception (Kafficho) to their high Oromo majority.

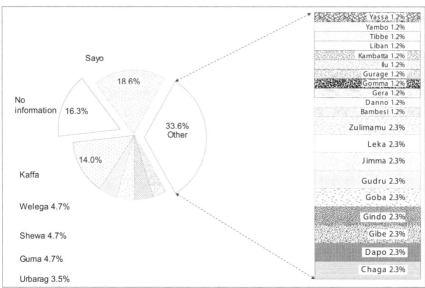

GRAPH 4.3. Home countries of the Oromo children (source: Sandra Rowoldt Shell).

Why Were These Regions Targeted?

Having delineated the areas in which slave raiding was focused, the question arises, Why were these particular areas targeted for enslavement? One possible approach to answering this question is through the prism of Immanuel Wallerstein's model of modernization, specifically his concept of the core and the periphery of empires or political systems.[5] Wallerstein, who began his scholarship as an African sociologist, proposed that the modernization of any state required a core area with a powerful central government, developed bureaucratic structure, and extensive military capability. Surrounding the core were the peripheral areas, which lacked strong government as well as well-trained and well-equipped armies. Though conceived initially to explain the history of Western Europe, Wallerstein's model may be used on the micro as well as the macro level and is applicable to any society.

In the history of Ethiopia, we can locate Wallerstein's core area as that defined as Abyssinia, comprising Menelik's core kingdom. The heavily subinfeudated Oromo regions lay south of Menelik's core area, straddling the main Ethiopian rift. While demographically speaking this area had a high population density, the interfeuding and subinfeudation within the region made it a perfect periphery in Wallerstein's terms.

In his discussion of state machinery, Wallerstein pointed to the juxtaposition of two tipping mechanisms—one where strength created still more strength; and, conversely, one where weakness could lead to further weakness. Expanding on this, Wallerstein explained that in states where the state machinery was weak, those in charge did not control the whole but simply became one set of landlords among others without any

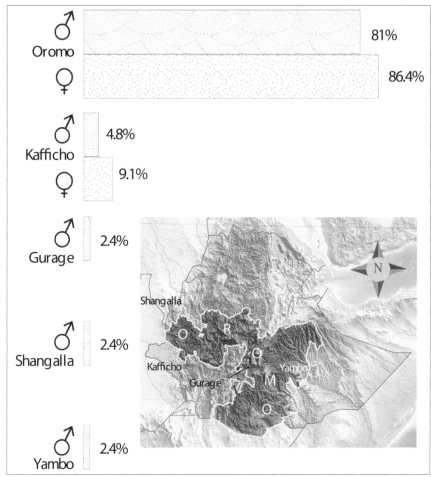

GRAPH 4.4. Ethnicities of the children (source: Sandra Rowoldt Shell).

real claim to legitimate authority over the whole.[6] The views of Jack Goody, noted social anthropologist, would support Wallerstein's tipping mechanisms, pointing out that Ethiopia, which had early on adopted the plow, was the only country in Africa where there was a system of landlordism. Where there were landlords, he notes, there would also be tenants and serfs. Goody adds that where there was shifting cultivation, slavery (in which slaves were acquired mostly as war captives or through purchase) rather than serfdom would be likely to emerge.[7] There were, in addition, what Goody referred to as "lords of the land," local chiefs who had power over people rather than land and lived largely off the labor of their people.[8]

Using status and the promise of wealth, Menelik succeeded in enlisting the services of the Shewa-born Gobana Dacche, who was both Oromo and Christian. Menelik promoted Gobana to commander of the armed forces with the rank of *Dajazmach* and later awarded him the title of *Ras* (head) with the hint of future promotion to the title of *Negus*, or king. In return, Gobana worked tirelessly toward the conquest of the Oromo territories and succeeded in bringing the Oromo territories of Illubabor, Wallaga, and the Gibe region under Menelik's control. As these three regions constituted the wealthiest of all the Oromo territories, they considerably strengthened and consolidated Menelik's power and economic superiority. It was Gobana, for example, who won the critical battle of Embabo for Menelik in 1882, thus creating one of the most important watershed moments in Oromo history, and marking the beginning of the collapse of Oromo power and sovereignty. Among the Oromo, of course, Gobana would have been regarded as a traitor. At lesser levels than the powerful Gobana (whom Menelik regarded—for as long as he still needed him—as his most powerful and competent general), local and regional chiefs in the conquered Oromo territories and in the neighboring regions also gradually fell under Menelik's authority. With that co-option came the obligation to collect additional tithes and taxes from local peasant farmers and villagers. Again, in these terms the Oromo regions sit firmly in Wallerstein's periphery.

Sociologist Solomon Gashaw endorses Wallerstein's core-periphery dichotomy in Ethiopia in his work on nationalism and ethnic conflict. In his words:

> The survival of Ethiopia has required that all—the Amhara core culture and groups at the periphery—consider themselves as belonging to one Ethiopian nation. The basic resources of nationalism, however, will erode away if a nation is engaged in a continual political conflict. The ongoing political impasse of recent years has created a crisis of hegemony for Ethiopian nationalism.[9]

The area of the Oromo at this time comprised a proliferation of small principalities, each vying for power. One of the Oromo teenagers, Gutama Tarafo, in his Lovedale schoolboy essay on his homeland, wrote wryly of the constant regional squabbling:

> Each part of the country has got a king or a chief of its own. For instance, let us take the Jimma country. That country has got a king or a chief of its own. These Kings are always wanting to fight each other, and everyone wants to be the greatest of all the kings. If he conquers one of these kings, first of all he asks for a tax; and if that king won't pay it, he just comes and destroys him. Sometime that king wants about 200 oxen or he wants some horses, and the other king has to give, because if he won't he knows that his life will be taken from him, and what he has too. (appendix D)

Gutama's firsthand evidence graphically describes the proliferation of subinfeudation that threaded through the region and provides the best evidence for Immanuel Wallerstein's subinfeudation concept in the context of this study.

What we see in this period as Menelik rose to power is that the Oromo people increasingly became en prise. They lacked the strength of Menelik's wealth and firearms. They had few guns and weak defenses.[10] According to Mekuria Bulcha, the Oromo were prevented from purchasing guns through a system of strategic blockades and because rulers did not have the necessary arms dealer contacts in the north.[11] Menelik's biographer, Harold Marcus, cites a letter by Pietro Antonelli written in 1882, in which Antonelli alludes to the superior numbers of Menelik's invading Amhara forces, who were armed with thousands of rifles and pistols and even the occasional cannon. The vulnerability of the Oromo was exacerbated by not having any weapons except "a lance, a knife and a shield."[12] Their potential for an effective rebuttal of the raiding forces from the north using firepower was minimal. Instead, the Oromo used the natural fastnesses of their country's topography as their first line of defense against all comers. However, even nature's fortification of their high-altitude homesteads did not protect the male captives from the determination of slave-raiding invaders.

No people can be enslaved without there arising a reciprocal attitude of defiance— what Wallerstein refers to as the "counter-assertiveness of the oppressed"[13]—which may lead to a growth in proto-nationalist thinking. Thus, as Menelik's power grew, the Oromo became more unified. The ethnic homogeneity of the group resulted in a reciprocal proto-nationalism over time. This gradually coalesced in the names of the administrative regions of the emergent country of Ethiopia, more specifically the delineation and naming of the modern administrative region of Oromia and even the emergence of the Oromo Liberation Front and calls for independence.

The ethnicity of the children was overwhelmingly Oromo, with only a handful of other ethnicities with strong genetic and political ties with the Oromo. Homogeneity characterized the captivity. The children came from towns and villages dispersed across a wide stretch of Oromo territory, primarily following the lines of the mountainous regions along the rim of the escarpment. A statistically significant gender difference emerged, with the boys coming mostly from homes in the highland regions, while the girls came from areas as much as 400 meters lower in altitude on average. The full significance of this disparity is unclear. Perhaps the girls, highly sought after for the external slave trade, were easier to capture in the lower altitude regions, making for a speedier passage to the coastal entrepôts. The children's evidence, opening up the geographic and topographic range of slave raiding among the Oromo in the late nineteenth century, allowed for a full and precise placement.

If we can consider the Oromo captives of this study as a snapshot of the process of enslavement of vulnerable people in that territory, we see that the captives were remarkably homogeneous in terms of their ethnicity, and this is reflected in the profile of modern Ethiopia. The secular effect of this core and periphery was to establish a reciprocal nationalism in the south, which we can recognize in the contemporary demand for Oromo liberation and independence. This was an ancient reaction evident in the Greek and Roman Empires and in such a familiar biblical example as the Jews—the original peripheral people—fleeing their Egyptian slavers. In considering the Jews and their potent ideas of nationhood, who could deny that this was a response to their enslavement? The model of the core and the periphery helps explain the particular case of Abyssinia and the emergent Oromo nation.

PART II

Routes: From Capture to the Coast

CHAPTER 5

The Moment of Capture

Scholars of the Oromo slave trade, informed by the accounts of travelers and other observers, have recorded that slave raiders generally either kidnapped, purchased, or seized their Oromo captives as spoils of war.[1] Timothy Fernyhough goes further, mentioning a broad spectrum of ways in which the trade in slaves was augmented. These included state-sponsored expeditions, the thefts of those already enslaved (confirmed by Henry Darley, a traveler), the seizure of children as they tended livestock, housebreaking at night, ambushes, natural disasters such as famine and drought, debt redemption, and retributive procedures for real or fabricated crimes.[2] Mordechai Abir and Timothy Fernyhough both refer to instances whereby Oromo parents even used trickery and deception to sell their children or other kin into slavery.[3] These are broad allusions drawn from travelers such as Antonio Cecchi, Henry Darley, William Cornwallis Harris, Charles William Isenberg, and Johann Ludwig Krapf, as well as from other sources. The Oromo captives' firsthand accounts informing this study provide a rare opportunity to go further and to explore in detail the moment of capture in the life of a slave child.

Fred Morton, in his study of thirty-nine East African child slave narratives, posits that for the children, "life's memory was anchored in that place and moment."[4] This chapter will focus on that moment, examining the identity of those who captured the children, as well as their ethnicity, gender (both men and women were involved in the slave trade), occupation, and slaving group. The children also indicated whether or not they recognized their captors, whether they had any existing kinship bond or other relationship with the captors, and whether the captors acted alone or in a group. In addition, they told of how they were captured, whether their captors used violence during the captures, whether their captors were mounted or on foot, and whether they were sold for money or bartered for food or goods.

Who Captured the Children?

The external Red Sea and Horn of Africa slave trade is regarded in the older, secondary sources as having been instigated and driven largely by "Arabs."[5] At point of capture, however, the agencies were different. All but two gangs of slave raiders were drawn from local groups. Even at trading level on the way to the coast, Arab intervention emerged only at, or close to, the termination points of the journeys. Though the Red Sea maritime slave trade was ultimately Arab-controlled, it was not, in this study, Arab-initiated in the interior, or at point of capture.

The majority of the children (70.9 percent) did not recognize their captors, while 9.3 percent recognized kin, 3.5 percent recognized neighbors, and a further 16.3 percent recognized persons known to them. There were two noticeable gender differences: more girls did not know their captors, and no girls recognized any of their captors as neighbors. That the children recognized almost one-third of those who initially enslaved them is not altogether surprising, given that the majority of their captors were local. However, that more girls than boys did not recognize their captors and were not enslaved by their neighbors would support the notion that the majority of slave raiders targeting the girls came from farther afield, possibly as direct agents of the external trade. (This subject is developed further in chapter 6, "On the Road.")

The following graph (5.1) illustrates the range of ethnicities and places of origin of the captors. Just under a quarter of the children (23.3 percent) identified the Sidama as the raiders who enslaved them. There is a degree of ambiguity surrounding the term "Sidama." The word means "Abyssinian" in Afaan Oromoo (see the discussion on page 36).[6] There is also a small ethnic group situated farther south named the Sidama, who, like the Oromo, were victims of Menelik's expansionism from the late 1880s.

Today, the Sidama occupy their own administrative zone within Ethiopia's Southern Nations, Nationalities, and People's Region (SNNPR). With their own language and traditions, and a long administrative history dating back to the ninth century, they currently make up 4.1 percent of the Ethiopian population. The pressures on the Sidama people at the time the children were captured were similar to those experienced by the Oromo themselves.[7]

Almost one-tenth of the captors (9.3 percent) were from Sayo, an Oromo kingdom; a further 8.1 percent of the captors came from Kaffa (a territory with whom the Oromo shared strong historical links and a border); 4.7 percent were from Leka (now a part of modern Oromia); and 3.5 percent of the captors originated in Jimma, also now a part of modern Oromia. The rest of the captors came—mostly singly—from some thirteen other local territories, almost all within the borders of modern Oromia.

Three of the boys referred to their captors' identity not by geographical allusion but by ethnicity, religion, or hue. For example, Aguchello Chabani referred to "black Arabs" (see appendix B; narrative 1); Bayan Liliso referred to "Mahommedan raiders" (narrative 9); and Amanu Bulcha referred to his captors as "three black men" who came out of the forest, pounced on him, gagged him with a piece of cloth, and carried him off (narrative 2). With nineteenth-century Christian missionaries recording the

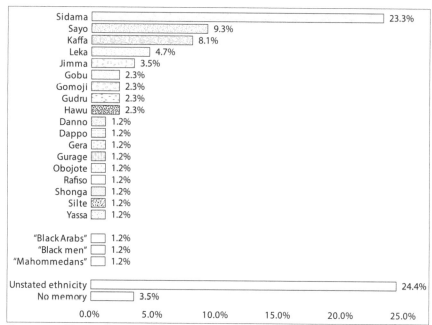

GRAPH 5.1. Places of origin of the children's captors (source: Sandra Rowoldt Shell).

children's narratives, the researcher needs to be alert to possible missionary bias against Islam in their accounts. However, there is no firm evidence of this.

The diversity in location of the children's homes is echoed in the range of territories from which their captors were drawn. Almost half (48.8 percent) of the captors hailed from five principal regions, and nearly a third (31.3 percent) came from thirteen additional territories. The evidence in this study is of a widespread practice of slave raiding within the southern and southwestern regions below Abyssinia. This evidence indicates that slave raiding in the south and southwestern regions, while feeding into the Red Sea slave trade, was also part of a widespread domestic slaving system. The raiders came from a wide range of local groupings, including raiders from within Oromo subgroups.

Who Captured Whom?

Linking the places of origin of the raiders with those of their captives produced some consistent patterns. The following graph (5.2) shows the relative proportions of both raider and child origins in a cross-tabulation.

The graph includes a map of modern Ethiopia with the administrative region of Oromia shaded. The places of domicile of the five dominant raider identities or ethnicities are indicated by arrows. All of them lived either within what is now Oromia or in adjacent territories. Only the three outsider groups—the "black Arabs," the "black men," and the "Mahommedans"—constituted foreign agencies. Note that the Sidama

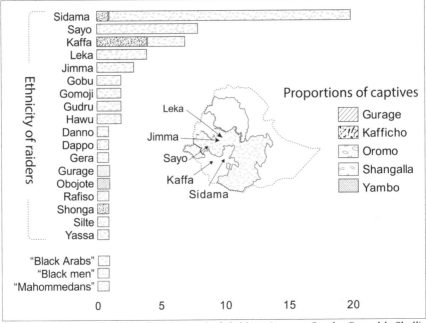

GRAPH 5.2. Places of origin of raiders and of children (source: Sandra Rowoldt Shell).

(Abyssinians), the dominant raiders, targeted mostly the children identified as Oromo plus a far smaller proportion of Kafficho. The raiders from Sayo and Leka, both places in what is now Oromia, were interested in seizing only Oromo children, while raiders from Kaffa, like those from Sayo and Leka, also targeted their own. Slightly more than half of the children they captured were Kafficho, with the remainder being Oromo. A Gurage raider captured the single Gurage child in the group, "Black men" captured the one Shangalla child, and a raider from Obojote seized the only Yambo child.

Gender of the Captors

Slave raiding in the Horn of Africa was decisively a male preserve: 93 percent of the Oromo children's captors were men. The women enslavers, who made up the remaining 7 percent, lured the children away from their homes rather than seizing them by force, possible examples of the "trickery" to which Fernyhough and Abir allude.[8]

Modes of Capture

The following polar pie diagram (graph 5.3) illustrates the gender differences in the capture experience. The inner, middle, and outer rings show the experiences of the girls, boys, and all the children, respectively.

The aggregated majority of the children (55.8 percent) were subjected to some form of violence at the moment of capture. They were seized either with a show of force (29.1 percent) or through other forms of violence (26.7 percent). A total of 17.4 per-

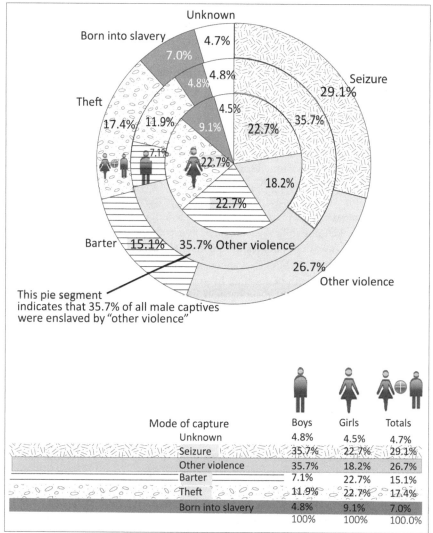

GRAPH 5.3. Modes of capture by gender of child (source: Sandra Rowoldt Shell).

cent of the children were taken by nonviolent means, namely, kidnapping; while 15.1 percent were bartered. A small percentage (7 percent) were born into slavery. However, there were clear differences between the experiences of the girls and the boys.

Many more boys than girls were captured after a show of force: 35.7 percent of the boys were captured through "seizure," compared with 22.7 percent of the girls. A further 35.7 percent of the boys were captured through a form of violence other than "seizure" (i.e., "other violence"), as were 18.2 percent of the girls. Adding the two variables of "seizure" and "other violence" for each group allows for a more comprehensive view of the difference between the genders. The aggregated totals show that 71.4 percent of the boys were enslaved using some sort of violence, as opposed to 40.9 percent of the girls. On the other hand, adding all the nonviolent modes (barter, theft, and enslavement from birth) shows that 23.8 percent of the boys were enslaved without violence, compared to 54.5 percent of the girls—more than double.

Not all the enslavers were armed and not all of them used violence to acquire their slaves. Here the major gender differences emerge. For example, as graph 5.3 illustrates, many more girls than boys were captured following the nonviolent process of barter and negotiation. Traders and raiders entered into negotiations to acquire 15.1 percent of the children. Of these, 11.64 percent were girls and 3.5 percent were boys. Nonviolent theft accounted for another 17.4 percent of the children, 11.6 percent being girls and 5.8 percent being boys. A gender breakdown of the aggregation of these two nonviolent modes of capture (38.9 percent) shows that just under a quarter of these were girls (23.2 percent); while less than a tenth, or 9.3 percent, of those children taken nonviolently were boys. Twice as many girls (4.7 percent) were born into slavery (i.e., their families were already enslaved when these children were taken from their homes) as boys (2.3 percent).[9] Far more boys than girls experienced violent capture of one form or another. In treating the girls more gently, the raiders were likely to have been influenced by their higher export demand and buyers' insistence on intact girls.

A majority (57 percent) of those who enslaved the children acted alone, particularly in the process of enslaving the girls compared with the boys. Only a handful of the enslavers acted in groups of two (4.7 percent, split evenly between girls and boys); groups of three (4.7 percent, all boys); and groups of four (2.3 percent, all boys). The rest of the children (31.4 percent) did not comment on the number of their captors. Two boys reported that gangs of four men had abducted them. One of them, Nuro Chabse (see appendix B; narrative 31), was seized by four men while looking after his father's oxen and sheep. The other boy, Gamaches Garba (narrative 18), told of a group of four men who seized him and carried him off while he was herding his father's cattle. Three men abducted Tolassa Wayessa (narrative 38) while he was playing not far from his house. One may conclude that kidnapping teams were involved in the capture of boys, but did not dominate the slave capture.

As graph 5.4 indicates, almost four times as many boys (38.4 percent) were captured to service the domestic slave system as were sold directly into the external slave trade network (10.5 percent). This is in clear contrast to the girls, of whom half (50 percent) were sold into the export network; the other half entered domestic servitude.

Oromo girls and eunuchs were the highest valued of all slaves in the Horn of Africa external trade.[10] This might account for the higher percentage of girls than boys being captured specifically for the export network.

The enslavement of the children was not, at least at point of capture, a mass or overtly syndicated operation, though it is possible that single captors acted alone in the field but were part of a larger slave trade network controlled from elsewhere. However, the high proportion of children who were seized in the first instance to service the internal slave system (64 percent) rather than the external slave trade chain

78.6%	Domestic trade	50.0%	
21.7%	Export trade	50.0%	
Boys			Girls

GRAPH 5.4. Domestic and external slave trade networks (source: Sandra Rowoldt Shell).

indicates that domestic slavery was endemic and was initiated for the most part on an individual basis.

Prices

While the children had more vivid memories of what happened at the moment they moved from freedom to slavery than of subsequent transactions, none of the children gave a monetary price for this first exchange. As shown in the earlier discussion on the mode of capture, there was a variety of transactions at the moment of capture. Most children were simply the spoils of raids; only a few captures involved any form of exchange, in monetary or commodity terms. For example, one boy (Liban Bultum; see appendix B; narrative 27) and two girls (Hawe Sukute [narrative 56] and Turungo Gudda [narrative 61]) were taken in lieu of debts.

Hawe Sukute was about sixteen years old when interviewed but was considerably younger when she first encountered slavery. Her father, Sukute, died when she was very young. Her mother, Ibse, was left vulnerable and was taken as a slave (with Sukute and two brothers and a sister) by the Sayo people, who were feuding with those in her own country, Garjeja. When her mother died, she and her brothers were taken by their uncle into his home. But her father's brother intervened, claiming the children as his own property. This uncle put the children to work, but, as he was also indebted to the Garjeja king, he sold Hawe to a Leka merchant to pay off his debt.

There were two Oromo girls called Turungo in the group: Turungo Tinno (meaning "little Turungo"; narrative 62) and Turungo Gudda (meaning "big Turungo"; narrative 61). Both girls were paternal orphans and did not carry their fathers' names, hence the descriptors to distinguish them from each other. Turungo Gudda was about fourteen when interviewed. Her mother, Dabeche, worked for one of their uncles sowing and reaping in the fields. However, before her father died, he had borrowed various items from his brother, and the family was not able to reimburse the loan. To compensate for the unpaid debt, the uncle sold Turungo to Jimma merchants in a market nearby.

Berille Nehor (narrative 47), who was approximately thirteen years old at the time of her interview, was the daughter of Nehor and Bushaseche and had several brothers and sisters. Her father, Nehor, was a slave in a place called Ishete in the Kaffa country. He held a piece of land that he cultivated for his master, while the mistress of the household employed Berille as a nursemaid to her child. Berille's master lost his *goga*, or kaross, in an altercation with a neighboring ethnic group and saw Berille as an asset he could sell to pay for a new one. He told Berille to go to a neighboring hut to fetch his sword, but when she reached the hut, a stranger was waiting for her. The stranger gagged her and carried her off to Jimma, where he sold her on the slave owner's behalf.

Other girls were bartered, like the orphaned Bisho Jarsa (see page 30 and narrative 48), who was sold for a little corn. Jifari Roba (narrative 57), the daughter of Roba and Dongoshe, was around age thirteen when she was interviewed. The family, comprising Jifari and three brothers and four sisters, lived in a village called Galani in the Sayo country. When her father died (about a year before she was enslaved), her mother went out to work, sowing and reaping in the fields. A woman in a neighboring village offered to look after Jifari but betrayed the trust placed in her by selling Jifari almost immediately to a group of Nagadi people for ten pieces of salt (called *amole*).

Fayissi Gemo (narrative 52) was also approximately thirteen years old when the missionaries interviewed her at Shaikh Othman. She lived with her father, Gemo, and her mother, Yarachi, in a village called Upa in the Kaffa country. After her father died, her mother had to support the family, employing laborers to plow the land. However, when her mother returned to her home village for a short period, Upa, the chief, seized the opportunity to abduct Fayissi and exchanged her for a horse in a deal with passing merchants.

Aguchello Chabani (narrative 1), son of Chabani and Gurdenfi, was a young boy of about twelve at the time of his interview. He was born in a village called Enge in the district of Barsinge in the Shangalla country, where his father co-owned six acres of land. Aguchello, at that time only ten or eleven years old, was playing near his family home one afternoon when a group of people he described as "black Arabs" came to the house and entered into a heated discussion with his father. Angry and frustrated, the strangers seized Aguchello and, using considerable force, began to carry him off. Both Chabani and Gurdenfi pleaded with the strangers not to take their child. The "black Arabs" said they would return Aguchello if his parents would bring all their cattle in his place. However, when the cattle were handed over to them, the "black Arabs" double-crossed the parents and took not only the cattle but Aguchello as well.

The children identified nearly two-thirds of their captors as professional slave raiders (59.3 percent). However, their captors also emanated from local and regional royal circles as agents of their king or chief (12.8 percent). Almost the same number (11.6 percent) were seizing children for purposes of cadastral or agricultural slavery, and a smaller proportion (2.3 percent) were merchants or traders (see graph 5.5).

Military captors formed the smallest category identified by the children. Few of the children were enslaved directly by foreign agencies. The 1880s were a decade of considerable upheaval for the Oromo as Menelik, king of Shewa, looked to the south and southwest of his kingdom to augment his territorial dominance. He concentrated on the co-option of as many Oromo and other southern leaders as could be persuaded to submit to his power and act as his agents.

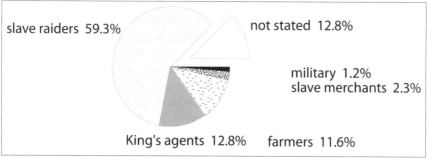

slave raiders 59.3%

not stated 12.8%

military 1.2%
slave merchants 2.3%

King's agents 12.8%   farmers 11.6%

GRAPH 5.5. Occupations of captors (source: Sandra Rowoldt Shell).

Timothy Fernyhough has pointed to an elaborate slave trade system in the southern regions that supported the interregional and international commodity trade in the north—including the trade in slaves—to supply the export trade off the Red Sea coast. Fernyhough highlights the interdependency of the system whereby the local, southern small traders (known in the Gibe kingdoms as *afcala* or *abshala*—literally, "clever") acted as agents for southern rulers as well as supplying human merchandise for the external trade of the north.[11] The afcala played an important commercial role in the trade nexus between north and south. With this in mind, there is the possibility that some of the local and regional raiders may have become co-opted agents, but the children could not have been aware of such details.

As previously stated, the successful abduction of children in the highlands of Oromo territory required a rapid escape. The terrain in much of Oromoland was mountainous and rugged, and many captors used nimble, fleet-footed Oromo horses to carry off their prey.

In addition to those children who specified the use of horses by their captors, there seems to have been a deliberate distinction in the children's narratives between those who described their capture experience as being "carried away" and those who simply said they were captured and taken to a given destination. The consistent use of the phrase "carried away" seems to imply the use of horses, but there is no way to be certain of this. There is certainly a sense that the phraseology suggests something other than that the children were simply being led away from their homes. To assume both descriptors apply to mounted raiders, an aggregation would amount to more than a third (35 percent) using horses to seize their captives (7.09 percent specifying "horseback" and 27.9 percent indicating "carried away").

The issue of terrain suggested a cross-tabulation of the use of horses and the incompletely defined "carried away" against the children's places of domicile. Sayo, Kaffa, Shewa, Guma, Urbarag, and Welega are all mountainous areas. Captors used horses when seizing slave children in Sayo, Shewa, and Guma (each 2.7 percent); while captors "carried away" children from Kaffa (5.5 percent); from Shewa and Guma (2.7 percent each); and from Sayo, Urbarag, and Welega (1.4 percent each).

The majority of the children identified their captors as Sidama as well as raiders from neighboring territories, primarily the neighboring Kaffa, or from among

Oromo regions such as Sayo, Leka, and Jimma. Included among the local captors were people the children knew; some were neighbors or even kin. These raiders acted on their own initiative or as agents of their king as local chief. Whether or not any of them had been co-opted locally to boost Menelik's slaving forays did not emerge from the children's narratives. Again, the children would not have known such details. The raiders certainly did not feed all their captives directly into the external slave trade network. Instead, they sold or absorbed more than three quarters of the boys (78.6 percent) and half (50 percent) of the girls into domestic servitude. Perhaps they sold more of the young Oromo girls directly into the external network because they fetched higher prices on the external market, and they therefore had the certainty of quick and profitable sales. Gender differences were marked at several other points of the capture experience. The boys experienced considerably more violence than the girls at point of capture, while more of the girls were bartered or kidnapped without overt brutality.

CHAPTER 6

On the Road

In the general absence of eyewitness accounts of the slave route experience in the Horn of Africa, scholars have necessarily had to pin their interpretations on a modest number of travelers' accounts. Most have accepted the injunction of historian David Henige, who enjoins scholars of precolonial Africa to resign themselves to the assumption that there will always be an "absence of data" regarding the first passages in Africa generally. In warning of the dangers of arguing from silence, Henige has assumed not only that historians do not have access to eyewitness first-passage accounts but that such sources will never be located.[1] The Oromo children's narratives at the core of this study—together with a small number of other known slave narratives from the Horn and East Africa[2]—stand in modest but visible refutation of this.

The Oromo children's recall of their journeys from capture to arrival at the Red Sea ports provides a level of detail that goes far beyond the assumptions and estimates of the secondary literature. The children detailed each segment of their journeys, giving the names of every place they visited, how long each segment took, how long they paused or stayed in servitude in each place, how they were treated en route, whether or not they tried to escape, how they were punished for their attempts, how many times they changed hands, the identities of the slave traders and their owners, and how much the traders demanded in cash or kind for their human merchandise. The children's personal narratives also revealed whether or not they were sold into the local slave trade system, what their duties were, and the length of time they spent enslaved domestically. In short, this detailed eyewitness evidence of the slave trade provides ample scope for a preliminary examination of Henige's elusive first passage.

Mapping the places of origin of the Oromo children against the complex topography of Ethiopia (see chapter 4) shows that a clear majority of the boys came from highland regions, with their homes dotted along the ridges of the mountain ranges (see map 4.1 on page 55). The average altitude of the children's homes was 2,019 meters (see the descending altitude range shown in graph 4.1 on page 54). From these heights,

the children were marched down to the Red Sea coast along disparate and compli-
cated routes. As the captives descended one steep gradient, that of topography, they
ascended another—temperature. Gutama Tarafo, writing from Lovedale, began his
reminiscences with comments on the climate of his highland home:

> First of all, I want to speak about the climate of the country. Perhaps many
> of you won't believe about the climate, because none of you have been there,
> except those that came from there. But you read in the books of Geography,
> and those books say the climate is very hot. I can tell you the climate is
> not all very hot. But it is quite true that the southern part of the country is
> exceedingly hot, because there are no mountains there. The upper country is
> much cooler than Cape Colony, although it is near the Equator, because there
> are many high mountains near Abyssinia. (appendix D)

The children not only had to deal with negotiating the rocky passages down the
mountains to regions lying at or below sea level in the desert area around Aussa, but
they were also exposed to increasing extremes of temperature, from the cool heights
of their mountain homes where the average annual temperature was about 16°C to
the Danakil desert, where temperatures hovered around 48° to 50°C. Theirs can only
have been a hellish descent that must have exacted an even higher than average first-
passage mortality toll. Trauma, tiredness, and temperature extremes were their constant companions.

A rare contemporary aquatint of the first-passage experience has survived among
a series of six drawings of "Billy King," a liberated slave in Mahé, Seychelles. These
sketches, with Billy's own captions, recorded his capture and first-passage experience in East Africa until his liberation by a British naval gunship. He began with a
drawing of his capture (along with a number of other children) by Arab slavers,[3] and
then sketched the descent of the slaves in a coffle from mountains to the coast (see
fig. 6.1),[4] illustrating an experience similar to that of many of the Oromo children
from the highland areas. Billy also depicted his time as a captive settling down for
the night under guard in his third drawing.[5] The fourth sketch portrayed a dhow
awaiting its cargo of slaves.[6] The penultimate sketch illustrated a dramatic and violent encounter between the dhow and a British warship during interception and the
liberation of the slaves aboard.[7] The final drawing recorded the firing and sinking of
the dhow by the British Royal Navy.[8] This little collection stands as a unique record
of the first passage sketched by the only known slave to have recorded the sequence
of his experiences graphically and, according to Billy's employer, with a good idea
of color and perspective.

Back and Forth

Fred Morton emphasizes the lengths of the journeys covered by the small group of
East African slave children whose narratives are lodged in the correspondence of the
Church Missionary Society. Nonetheless, despite changing hands multiple times, the
children appeared to head for the coast—albeit slowly—from the time of capture.
These East African narratives, and most scholars of the East African slave trade, chal-

FIGURE 6.1. Billy King's descent from highlands to coast (source: *Graphic*, 25 November 1893, 656).

lenge the validity of author James Mbotela's popular account of simple, Arab-initiated captures in the interior followed by direct treks to the sea.[9] The East African narratives also bear comparison with those of the Oromo in the present study.[10]

Scholars such as Mekuria Bulcha and Timothy Fernyhough have emphasized that the journeys could be long and intricate, but, beyond their valuable studies of the Oromo slave trade, little has been learned about the extent of backtracking routes feeding the domestic slave needs.[11] Few of the itineraries progressed directly from the children's homes to the Red Sea entrepôts. Most reflected lengthy and complex cross-country treks, often backtracking, sometimes even randomly and cruelly returning to the child's hometown (see, e.g., the story of Balcha Billo [appendix B; narrative 8] for an example of this).

As many as 12.8 percent of the children are estimated to have been ten years old or younger at the time of capture, the youngest being only seven. So it is not surprising that some of the children could not remember the names of all the towns or villages to which they were taken or that the details they gave were too vague to be mapped. For example, Amaye Tiksa reported being carried off by an unnamed neighboring tribe on a two-day journey to "their own country" (narrative 4); and Fayissa Murki told how he was taken to "a slave market near[by]" (narrative 14). Two children said only that they had been taken to "another place." In these cases, the segments of their journeys were included in the segment count, but, as their precise location could not be identified nor the segment distance calculated, these places could not always be reflected on the base route map. Such elisions were rare, however. Slave traders and slave merchants shunted the young captives back and forth and back again across the vast complex of sidings, dead ends, detours, slave entrepôts, and termini that formed the Oromo and Abyssinian slave trade networks. Their itineraries had a shockingly high number of segments, ranging from three to twenty-two places, with a median of eight.

Wakinni Ugga (narrative 63) and Gilo Kashe (narrative 19) were the only two children whose itineraries appear as proceeding directly from hearth to dhow. However, youth or reduced intellectual capacity hampered their recall. Wakinni, the youngest of the girls when taken captive at only ten years old, could not remember details of all the places she was taken. Her journey, featuring only her home, one stop en route, and her destination port, is therefore similarly truncated on her route map (see map B.63).

While the trauma of the first passage impacted each of the Oromo children to some degree physically or mentally, Gilo Kashe suffered the most visible evidence of profound trauma of all the group. It is highly unlikely that Gilo presented as intellectually or physically compromised prior to his initial enslavement. Slave traders worldwide were anxious that the slaves they were buying be in good health and worth the price, and that those they were offering for sale be sound of mind and body to earn them a good price in the marketplace. Milko Guyo, another one of the boys, recalled that while he was in the hands of a Sodo merchant in 1888, he was taken through Tigre before being taken on to Dawe. In Tigre he recalled seeing Gilo working for a man named Butta, "going round from house to house gathering up cow dung which when dried was used as fuel" (narrative 28). The following year (1889), Butta sold him to a passing trader who took him to the port of Tadjoura. There is a sense that even at that stage, Gilo was limited in what he was capable of doing, presumably a consequence of his brain damage. Logically, then, the trauma that robbed him of his wits and ease of mobility occurred between his home and Tigre. Whatever that trauma was, it left Gilo with no memory of his mother, not even her name. Matthew Lochhead, the missionary who interviewed Gilo and the other children at Sheikh Othman, an oasis north of Aden, wrote that it was impossible to get any accurate information from Gilo at all (with the exception of his father's name—Kashe). (See Gilo Kashe's narrative, number 19, and map B.19 in appendix B.)

The Lovedale authorities believed Gilo Kashe suffered a head injury during his capture or captivity, leaving him brain-damaged.[12] One medical doctor has suggested that a mild case of the bubonic plague that was sweeping the country at the time on the back of the worst Ethiopian drought and famine in history could have precipitated Gilo's intellectual impairment and his oft-described "crouching gait."[13]

Coincidentally, in the first group of Oromo children liberated through the interventions of the Royal Navy on 16 September 1888, there was another boy named "Gilo" or "Geelo." On reaching Aden, this boy was taken to hospital where he was diagnosed with "general dropsy."[14] Dropsy, or edema, is a major indication of severe malnutrition and kwashiorkor. This level of malnutrition can also lead to permanent cognitive impairment as well as general developmental delay, loss of knee and ankle reflexes, and impaired memory.[15] Gilo Kashe was liberated nearly a year later, at the height of the worst drought and famine in Ethiopian history. Starvation and malnutrition were rampant across the

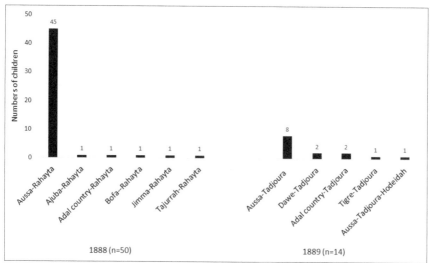

GRAPH 6.I. Final legs to entrepôts (source: Sandra Rowoldt Shell).

country. The experience of the earlier "Gilo" might also have been the experience of Gilo Kashe a year later and is worth considering as a possible cause for his cerebral damage.[16]

The rest of the children, however, had clear memories of their journeys. For example, Guyo Tiki was marched back and forth across the country, stopping at as many as twenty-two places (see narrative 21). His itinerary, featured in map B.21, vividly illustrates his bewildering crisscross journey. Guyo's route traversed the country from east to west and back again repeatedly until a group of Adal traders bought him at Dawe. Only from this point on did his route even face the coast. The Adal merchants took him the last two legs to Aussa and, finally, to the trading port of Araito (hereafter Rahayta, the modern spelling of Araito). The captives' journeys were not uninterrupted lines from home to the coast—the near universal but unexamined assumption in the secondary literature on the first passage.

The Oromo children were captured one at a time.[17] No two were captured together, and there is no evidence that any of the children knew one another prior to their capture. Altogether, fifty-five of the sixty-four Oromo children traveled through Aussa: forty-six in the 1888 group and nine in the group of 1889. However, despite this majority traveling through the same penultimate point, there were no shared itineraries.

Not only were there no shared itineraries, but the traders did not travel to the same terminal entrepôts in successive years. Traders delivered the first large tranche of Oromo (fifty children) to the coastal village of Rahayta in 1888. Eleven months later, in 1889, another group of traders took a smaller group of fourteen children to Tajurrah (hereafter Tadjoura, the modern spelling of Tajurrah), some 107 kilometers to the southwest of Rahayta. Regardless of the destination entrepôt, most routes passing through Menelik's kingdom of Shewa converged (mostly at different times) in Aussa,[18]

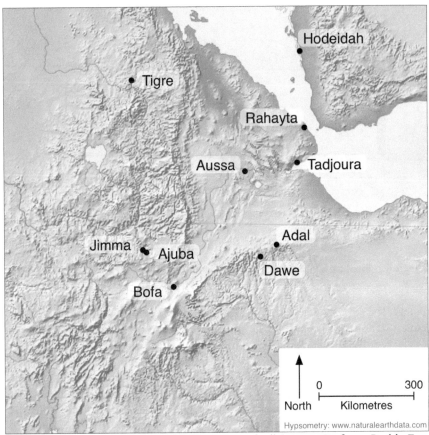

MAP 6.1. Two entrepôts and penultimate points of call (source: Professor Roddy Fox, Department of Geography, Rhodes University).

the major slave market governing external trade and the seat of the powerful and wealthy Sultanate of Aussa. Aussa was laid out expressly for the slave trade, one part being occupied by buyers and the other by sellers.[19] The sultan of Aussa was effectively instrumental, in conjunction with the sultan of Tadjoura,[20] in controlling almost all of the external, maritime trade emanating from Shewa.

According to Charles Gissing, commander of the Royal Navy's HMS *Osprey*, the sultan of Aussa, to whom Gissing referred as "one of the greatest slave catchers and dealers in these parts," owned 111 out of the total cargo of 204 slaves liberated by his crew in September 1888.[21] Tadjoura and its "smaller sister village," Rahayta, were the destination entrepôts of choice for those trading out of Aussa.[22] Despite the disparate nature of the children's itineraries, these hubs were where the bulk of the power, wealth, and control of the commercial external trade from Shewa resided.

GIS technology allows for an overlay of all sixty-four routes, revealing a complex network of itineraries, often crisscrossing, some backtracking, and only slowly inch-

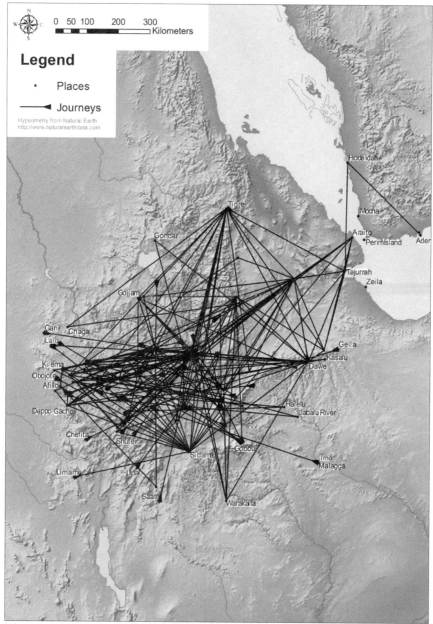

MAP 6.2. Crisscrossed journeys of the sixty-four Oromo children (source: Sandra Rowoldt Shell and GIS Laboratory, University of Cape Town).

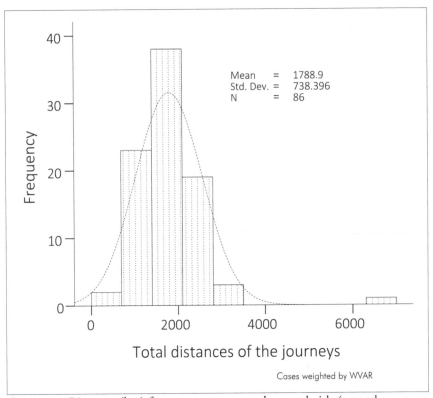

Mean   =   1788.9
Std. Dev. =   738.396
N   =   86

Cases weighted by WVAR

GRAPH 6.2. Distances (km) from capture to coast: boys and girls (2,000 km = 1,243 miles; 4,000 km = 2,485 miles; 6,000 km = 3,728 miles; source: Sandra Rowoldt Shell).

ing coastward. However, there was no consonance of time or route until the children reached their last three or four destinations. Map 6.2 shows the intricate, intersecting network of all sixty-four journeys. Clearly visible are the many common places the children visited as they traversed the country, but, importantly, there were no common itineraries.

Mapping the sixty-four individual itineraries graphically reveals the Oromo children's ordeals in ways travelers' accounts and other sources cannot. The sixty-four individual itineraries and route maps are shown in appendix B, "The Oromo Narratives." The routes as plotted here in map 6.2, with their neat, intersecting crow's-flight straight lines, belie a more complex reality. They represent the minimal distance between two points. In reality, the individual journeys were considerably longer. The map traces the routes against the topography of the region, hinting at some of the rigors of the children's itineraries. Their paths wound up and down mountains, crossed streams and rivers, circumnavigated expedient detours (to avoid tax collectors and brigands) and dangers, and ended with the brutal heat of the desert lowlands as they neared Aussa and the coast. Mekuria Bulcha has pointed out that detours were also frequently necessary in the highlands of Abyssinia to dodge the many customs posts along the way, or to steer clear of armed conflicts between warlords and highwaymen who frequently attacked the caravans.[23] Thus nature and man combined to ensure their journeys were not only tortuous but hazardous as well.

More realistic routes, factoring in circumnavigation of mountains, streams and rivers, and detours, would require cost-surface modeling, an extensive procedure falling outside the scope of the present study.[24] We have to make do with summary measures. For example, the histogram (graph 6.2) is a proportional distribution of minimal distances for the entire group of boys and girls.

Adding the segments of each of the children's itineraries reveals distances greater than indicated in any secondary accounts. The mean was 1,789 kilometers—only a little farther than the distance from Addis Ababa to Dar es Salaam (1,752 kilometers). We can compare the 1,668-kilometer median of the children's journeys roughly with the distance from Dar es Salaam to Harare (1,511 kilometers). Half the journeys fell above and half below this distance. Gilo Kashe's (narrative 19) truncated journey of 417 kilometers lies at the lowest point on the scale. On the other hand, Guyo Tiki (narrative 21) trudged twenty-two segments back and forth across the country and eventually from south to north. His journey totaled 6,350 kilometers—the longest recorded walk into slavery. This total measured only the minimal distance he could have walked, and is easily comparable with walking from Cape Town to Cairo—7,189 kilometers as the crow flies. While some scholars have acknowledged that first passages were lengthy and could take months, the children's journeys, whether interpreted textually, cartographically, or in statistical charts, were not only complex and convoluted but also indisputably longer than earlier thought.[25]

Every aspect of the first passage demonstrated significant gender differences. The distances covered were not exceptions. There were distinct gender differences relating to these distances, as the following two histograms demonstrate. The boys covered greater distances (see graph 6.3). The average distance covered by the boys was 1,942 kilometers, longer than for the whole group. The median was 1,728 kilometers. The range of the boys' journeys was considerable—from 417 kilometers to 6,350 kilometers.

On the other hand, the girls—marginally older than the boys on average (see section titled "Age Structure" in chapter 2)—covered an average distance of 1,644 kilometers, almost 300 kilometers shorter than the boys' average. That their median distance was a close 1,623 kilometers indicates the relatively compact distribution of the distances they covered—half the girls fell above this mark and half below (see graph 6.4).

The range of the girls' journeys was also considerably shorter than those of the boys—from 889 kilometers to 2,677 kilometers. This may indicate a need to get the girls to the coast by the shortest routes possible. "Shortest" usually meant speediest. "Speediest" meant the early realization of good prices on the most valuable of their human merchandise—young, intact Oromo girl captives. This may have been sufficient motivation for the traders of girl captives to hurry them along to the coastal routes.

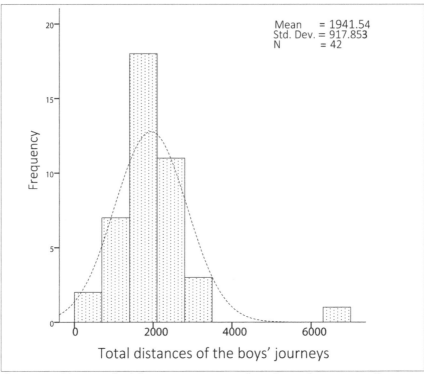

GRAPH 6.3. Distances (km) from capture to coast: boys (2,000 km = 1,243 miles; 4,000 km = 2,485 miles; 6,000 km = 3,728 miles; source: Sandra Rowoldt Shell).

Time on the Road

Estimations of the time slaves spent on the road are few. Historian Philip Curtin, in his study of the Senegambian slave trade, estimated that a coffle or caravan of slaves, spending seven to seven and a half hours on the road each day, could travel a maximum of thirty kilometers a day. Curtin assessed the pace as the average speed a donkey could achieve, namely, between four and four and a half kilometers per hour.[26] This assumes comfortable climatic conditions and a good road with no detours, deviations, or diversions. Nor does the rate allow for sale transaction times, mealtimes, or rest periods during the working (i.e., walking) day. Curtin assumed the economics of delivery of human merchandise to the coast. Clearly, the sooner slaves reached the coast, the lower the cost of supporting them en route. "Idle people do not increase in value," wrote Curtin, "and idle slaves were simply unemployed workers, whose maintenance was a dead loss to the master."[27] So, in Curtin's view, it was in the trader's best interest to get his merchandise to the destination as quickly as possible. However, routes were not always simple, nor conditions ideal. As Fernyhough pointed out, the merchants in the north relied on the small traders to locate and extract slaves and other export commodities for them

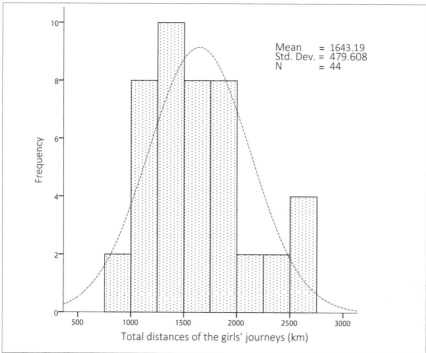

Mean = 1643.19
Std. Dev. = 479.608
N = 44

GRAPH 6.4. Distances (km) from capture to coast: girls (2,000 km = 1,243 miles; 4,000 km = 2,485 miles; 6,000 km = 3,728 miles; source: Sandra Rowoldt Shell).

from otherwise inaccessible areas in the interior. Fernyhough also observed that the use of small traders sped up the journeys, reducing the time on the road from months to days. In other words, he shared a set of assumptions similar to Curtin's.[28]

Those who bought, sold, and transported the Oromo children were likely to have been part of this small trader network. However, the children's eyewitness evidence of the length of time they spent on the road challenges both Curtin's and Fernyhough's assumptions that the use of small traders would reduce their journey time to a matter of days.[29] Citing Richard Pankhurst, Mekuria Bulcha acknowledged that the journeys from the slaves' homes to the coastal entrepôts were long.[30] He also recognized that captives often changed hands several times over the course of the journeys. He was sensitive to the hardships they endured along the way and that the death rate on the road to the slave markets in the north was high, citing Pankhurst's figure of up to 60 percent of a caravan dying on the way to the coast. However, the captives' accounts of their journeys include figures that stretch even beyond Bulcha's informed estimates.[31]

Curtin's formula for calculating time on the road made it possible to assess a minimum time each Oromo child spent on each segment of their journey, with a total for each child's entire itinerary. Their recorded time on the road is therefore the minimum

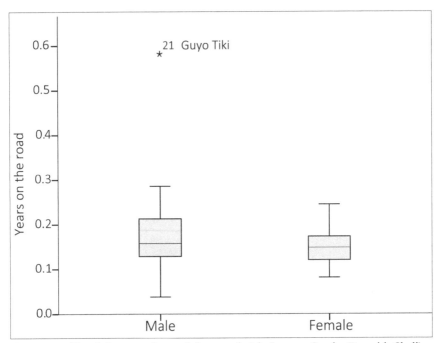

GRAPH 6.5. Travel times on the road: boys and girls (source: Sandra Rowoldt Shell).

they could have spent traveling. Despite being minimal, the figures challenge both West and East African estimates of the first passage.

Graph 6.5 shows the duration of the children's journeys and highlights the distinct gender differences. As the separate plots indicate, the boys' range was visibly greater than that of the girls. They spent a minimum of a fortnight and a maximum of seven months on the road, representing Guyo Tiki's (narrative 21) marathon trudge back and forth across Oromoland and Abyssinia. The average for the group, however, was fifty-eight days, while the median was a close fifty-five days.

The girls, on the other hand, spent a minimum of just short of a month and a maximum of three months on the road. Looking at the midrange for both boys and girls on the plots, however, the differences narrowed. The boys' average time on the road was sixty-five days, compared with the girls' average time of fifty-five days. The median demonstrates that half the boys' times on the road fell above and half below fifty-eight days. The same measure for the girls was a comparable fifty-four days.

Servitude within the Country

Gender differences become still more marked when adding the time spent in servitude within the country to time on the road to give the full first-passage period. Summation of the total time from home to harbor underscores what is already manifest: that traders were keen to get their highly valued female slaves to the coast quicker than the males. The boys often languished in the established and extensive system of domestic slavery.[32]

Historian John Grace, in his 1975 study of Sierra Leone, established a clear dichotomy between "domestic slaves" and "trade slaves." He conceded that the one could become the other under certain circumstances, particularly if the domestic slave was not sufficiently acquiescent or, worse, tried to run away. In such circumstances, the domestic slave would in all probability be sold.[33] In Grace's terms, many of the Oromo children were "domestic slaves," but *all* would eventually be reclassified as "trade slaves." More specifically, and moving beyond the confines of Grace's definitions, the Oromo children transitioned seamlessly from one mode to the other. Grace's dichotomy between his two posited streams of servitude falls away in the face of the children's evidence that they were, de facto, both. Almost two-thirds (62 percent) of the captive children reported that they were retained as slaves during their first passage. The remaining third did not mention any period of enslavement during their journeys.

In his remarks on the domestic slave trade, Mekuria Bulcha has pinpointed the importance of the influence of the social and religious ethos intrinsic to the Oromo *gadaa* (administrative) system in discouraging the practice of local enslavement. He has pointed out that until the nineteenth century, slave owning rarely occurred among the Oromo people, with the exception of those occupying the western regions of Oromoland, specifically among the Oromo of the Gibe region. He saw this development of domestic slavery as the result of the weakening of the *gadaa* system, the growth of local monarchies, and the gradual Islamization of the region.[34] The children's narratives demonstrate unequivocally that while some went directly into the external trade network, there was also an entrenched domestic slavery system in the areas where they were captured.

The following box and whisker plot (graph 6.6) shows at a glance the marked gender differences in the Oromo children's experiences.

Almost three-quarters (73.8 percent) of the boys, compared with only half the girls (50 percent), were enslaved locally.[35] Tola Lual (see appendix B; narrative 36) was an extreme outlier, being enslaved for a total of nine years. The experiences of Faraja Jimma (narrative 12); Nagaro Chali (narrative 30); Badassa Wulli (narrative 5); Bayan Liliso (narrative 9); and Komo Gonda (narrative 26) all lay outside the box and whisker quartile delineation, each being enslaved locally for periods between three and four and a half years. At the lower end of the scale, just short of a quarter of the boys (24.2 percent) were held captive locally for thirty-five days or less.

The plots also show that the girls experienced a shorter range of domestic enslavement, from a minimum of two days to a maximum of three years. Like the boys, there were several outliers. Dinkitu Boensa (narrative 51); Kanatu Danke (narrative 58); Damuli Diso (narrative 49); Halko Danko (narrative 55); and Jifari Roba (narrative 57) were enslaved for periods ranging from one to three years. However, three-quarters (75 percent) of the girls were enslaved locally for less than a year, markedly less than for the same proportion of boys.

The gender difference in the children's domestic enslavement experiences is significant. The boys were enslaved in greater numbers and for longer periods, probably because of their increased suitability for working in the fields and with livestock, both

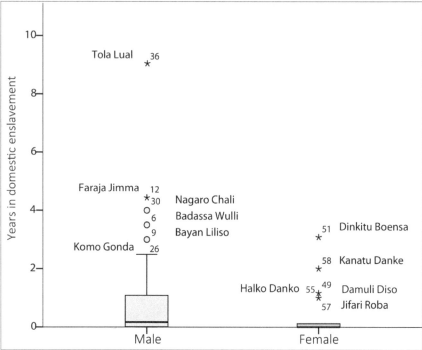

GRAPH 6.6. Years in domestic enslavement by gender of child (source: Sandra Rowoldt Shell).

by virtue of their superior strength and because culturally, manual and agricultural labor were masculine preserves. All except two of the boys who listed their local slave duties said they were forced to herd cattle. Girls were not used for such work. Their work and their value were confined to within the home.

The slave raiders and traders were anxious to get their female merchandise to the coast as soon as possible in view of their enhanced price. Young Oromo girls were reputedly beautiful and were eagerly sought after in the coastal slave markets for the external trade.[36] This flies in the face of the notion promulgated by Claude Meillassoux that females were more likely to be enslaved for their labor potential than for their beauty or fecundity. He posited that raising a slave from birth was more expensive than purchasing a strong young slave in the marketplace.[37] But in the Horn of Africa trade, the beautiful young girls were valued most highly of all slaves—with the possible exception of eunuchs. As Fernyhough points out, determinants of value in the Horn of Africa slave trade included ethnicity, gender, physique, health, and age, pointing out that the price of a female captive in the Red Sea ports was ten to fifteen times more than at the place of capture in the interior.[38] Traders selected young girls and women in the *fondaks*, or slave markets, for indoor domestic work and, in some cases, for harems.

Commander Charles Edward Gissing, skipper of the HMS *Osprey*, wrote after his successful intervention of the dhows carrying fifty of the Oromo children in 1888 about the enhanced prices for beautiful young Oromo girls: "The profits are very great, prices for slaves in Tajourra being: girls, 60 to 70 dollars; boys, 50 dollars; at Hodeida and Jeddah: girls, 120 to 130 dollars; boys, 70 to 80 dollars; if the girls are good-looking, as very many of them are, fancy prices are paid for them up to 600 dollars."[39] Gissing commented again on the beauty of the young Oromo girls his crew had rescued and brought aboard the *Osprey*:

> But once out of the filthy boats that brought them from Africa, the demonstrative greetings they bestowed upon their relatives as they recognized one another on the deck of the *Osprey* were peculiarly affecting; hugging, kissing, and crying with delight was the order of the hour. Two young girls particularly attracted notice. They seemed to be about fifteen and sixteen years of age, were very good-looking, and evidently sisters. The elder was brought on board first, where she watched with the most intense eagerness until she saw her sister handed through the port, when, with a shriek of joy, she bounded to meet her, clasped her neck, and covered her with caresses.[40]

Matthew Lochhead and, later, David A. Hunter took photographs that confirm the Oromo girls' attractiveness.[41] There is also no hint anywhere in their narratives that traders purchased the girls for their capacity to do manual labor. Indeed, Berille Nehor (narrative 46) was the only girl who listed her local slave duties (nursemaid). We may need, therefore, to approach Meillassoux's hypothesis, in the context of the Red Sea slave trade, with some caution. Be that as it may, traders moved the Oromo girls to the entrepôts faster than the boys.

Aggregating the time spent traveling the roads to the coast and the time retained in domestic servitude after capture results in the total duration of the children's first passage. The range was dramatic, from a fortnight to fractionally over nine years. Particularly startling was the difference, clearly illustrated in graph 6.7, in gender experience.

The flattened box reflecting the total first-passage time spent by the girls—with the exception of only five outliers—supports the earlier finding that most traders hurried the girls to the coast as expeditiously as possible. Even the upper-end outlier girls experienced markedly shorter periods of enslavement—from Jifari Roba's (narrative 57) fourteen months to Dinkitu Boensa's (narrative 51) thirty-nine months (just under three and a quarter years)—than the boys. This is further confirmation that fewer girls than boys were enslaved locally en route and that they spent shorter periods of time on the road.

By contrast, the boys had a longer, more variegated experience. In the midregions, the boys' average first-passage time length (fourteen months) was slightly more than twice that of the girls (just over six months). Similarly, the median for the boys was four months, compared with fractionally over two months for the girls.

As illustrated in the box plots, the ranges confirm the contrast: two weeks to just over nine years for the boys, compared with the much smaller range of the girls: thirty-three days to a little less than three and a quarter years. Boys on average traveled longer and endured longer interludes within the domestic slave network than the girls.

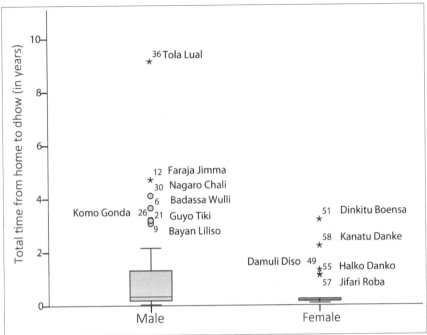

GRAPH 6.7. Total first-passage time in years from home to dhow (source: Sandra Rowoldt Shell).

Changing Hands

Moving the focus from the children to their captors reveals more of the intricacies of the first passage. The following bar graph (6.8) uses a simple tally of all raiders and captors, traders, merchants, and owners to illustrate the uneven distribution.

The northern Adal merchants dominate the list, followed by the Sidama, the Gudru, the Atari, the Leka, and the Jimma.[42] With the exception of a handful identifiably from the north, including the Sidama, the Adal, the Atari, and the Tigrayan, the groups were all local or regional—some even kin. However, this tally tells only a small part of the story.

The children changed hands up to ten times. An important factor to keep in mind is that these exchanges happened over a decade: the first enslavement was in 1879, the last in 1889. The 100 percent surface chart (graph 6.9) lays bare the mechanism of the domestic and export wings of the Ethiopian slave trade over time. At one end of the slave catching process, the chart reveals a host of opportunistic raiders and adventitious traders who were acquiring captives seemingly indiscriminately. At the other end are the broad swaths of activity of the networks and major groupings. The Sidama and the syndicated trading networks of the Adal, Atari, and their ilk dominate the lower portion of the chart. The chart shows how they commanded much of the process from the first (or capture) exchange to the third change of hands, persisting in decreasing measure to the seventh sale.

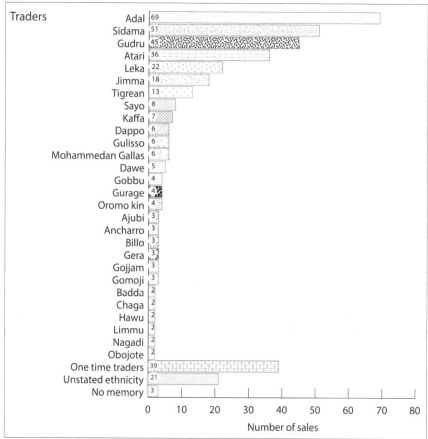

GRAPH 6.8. Ethnic identities of slave traders and owners (source: Sandra Rowoldt Shell).

Note the persistence in particular of the Adal and Atari merchants, who feature from the second sale right through to the coast and the final, tenth sale. By the time of the fifth sale, the Adal and Atari networks alone dominate more than half of all transactions. Few raiding groups (i.e., the slave catchers) were also trading groups. However, note the dominance of local groupings such as the Gudru and Leka, who were active in the first through sixth sales, then tailed off dramatically. The rest, the opportunistic raiders and traders who appear in angled slivers in the upper-left-hand corner of the chart, have a brief and slender showing. There was a rapid reduction in their role from point of capture through the early sales as they scribbled their way across the landscape. These proximate traders, who included kin and neighbors, represented the true terror of the slave trade.[43] As an Oromo child, you could trust no one. Even in adulthood, Liban Bultum (see narrative 27) still could not understand why his father, a wealthy man, refused to pay the tribute the Sidama demanded, electing to sacrifice his own son in lieu of tribute. These unanticipated results paint a clear picture

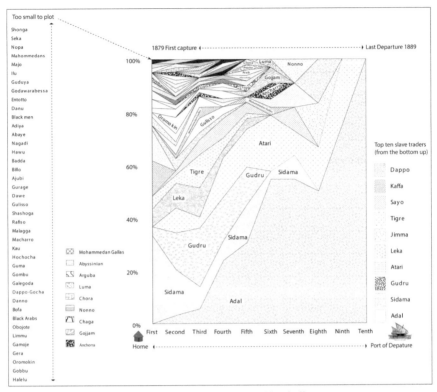

GRAPH 6.9. Changing hands (source: Sandra Rowoldt Shell).

of the dynamic patterns of both the internal and the external slaving mechanisms in the region as well as the severity of drought, famine, and disease throughout northeast Africa during this period.

Scholars of the economics of the external Horn of Africa slave trade have used the observations of travelers to focus on prices and commodity exchanges at the various slave markets in the trading regions of West, East, and North Africa. Timothy Fernyhough cites values observed by travelers including Henry Salt, William Cornwallis Harris, John Ludwig Krapf, George Annesley Mountnorris, and Samuel White Baker.[44] These usually comprised ranges of observed sales of slaves by gender and age in specific slave markets along the trade routes.

All the Oromo children experienced being sold or bartered at some stage after their initial enslavement. The bulk of the sales they reported occurred when they changed hands for the second time (i.e., the first ownership exchange after their capture). More than three-quarters (81.4 percent) said they had been sold but could give no further information. The rest (18.6 percent) reported a cash sale or commodity exchange (in Maria Theresa dollars [or thalers], salt; or livestock/farm produce) in equal proportions. Traders and merchants purchased four of the children for between MT$5 and

MT$16. Baki Malakka (narrative 7) reported that a trader in Gojjam bought him for ten pieces of silver—plus a handful of peppers. Humiliating exchanges, such as Baki's handful of peppers; Bisho Jarsa's corn (on first exchange; narrative 48); and Berille Nehor's father's new kaross (narrative 47), evidently were burned indelibly into the memories of these children. A Gulisso merchant paid five cows for Tola Lual (narrative 36). Traders paid a horse for each of two children, Guyo Tiki (narrative 21) and Amanu Bulcha—but the party of traders who bought Amanu in Leka added MT$1 to their horse (narrative 2). A stranger who had deceived Shamo Ayanso into following him sold the boy for the price of a donkey (narrative 34), as did the group of Sidama merchants who bought Wayessa Tonki (narrative 41). Traders paid between four and one hundred *amole*, or salt bars (the alternative currency), for each of five boys. The Gudru merchant who bought Kintiso Bulcha at Kau paid four *amole*, plus an additional MT$3. These second sales and exchanges reflected the replacement of the raiders and captors of the first exchange—the capture—with the traders and merchants of the domestic and external slave trading networks.

The children's memories, as might be expected, diminished as they were taken deeper into these trading networks, changing hands time and again. By the time of the third and later sales, they all knew they were being sold as slaves, but only three boys remembered details of these sales. Milko Guyo remembered being exchanged for 2 amole plus MT$9 (narrative 28); Tola Lual fetched 12 amole at the Nakante slave market (narrative 36); and a trader bought Shamo Ayanso for 106 amole (narrative 34). Only one girl remembered any sale: Dinkitu Boensa was held for several years by the Sidama man who had captured her until she was "ransomed" by a passing stranger for MT$8 (narrative 51). This stranger tricked both the Sidama man and Dinkitu into believing he wanted to take her home. However, he reneged on this promise and, probably with an eye on a good profit, took her instead to Tadjoura—her export entrepôt—where he sold her for an undisclosed amount. The highest exchange was not for a sale but for a manumission. William Grant paid MT$175 to manumit Berille Boko at the slave market in Hodeidah in 1889 (narrative 46).[45] These details reveal not only the relative worth redeemed for these captive children—influenced by gender, place, and agencys—but also something of the chicanery and expediency that preceded some of the sales.

Ill-Health and Ill-Treatment

While the foregoing themes have analyzed the parameters of duration, distance, agency, and economics of the first passage, the following analyze instances of ill-treatment, which the children also vividly remembered. Anecdotes abound in the secondary literature regarding the treatment of slaves in their coffles, ranging from the benign to the cruel.[46] The Oromo children add a new dimension to our understanding of the first-passage ordeal with their accounts of sickness, ill-treatment, torture, and torment. With regard to sickness, and despite instances of ill-treatment, only a handful of children reported suffering any illness during their journeys. Two of the boys endured unidentified but severe illnesses that lasted for protracted periods. A third boy told how he had contracted *finno*—the Afaan

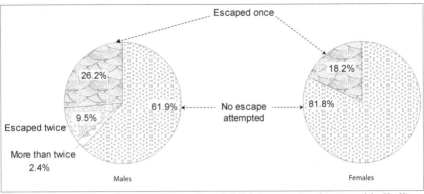

GRAPH 6.10. Attempted escapes by gender of child (source: Sandra Rowoldt Shell).

Oromoo word for "smallpox." Perhaps the children did not bother to report any of their minor ailments along the road.

The children reported fully on the incidences of cruelty, abuse, and other ill-treatment they experienced during the first passage. Nine children (all but one being boys) told of specific acts of cruelty. Tolassa Wayessa (narrative 38) and Gamaches Garba (narrative 18) said their captors chained their feet, while Damuli Diso told how her captor chained her hands together (narrative 49). Faraja Lalego reported that he was included in a group of unknown slave children who remained chained together for a week (narrative 11). Isho Karabe said his captor tied rather than chained his hands (narrative 23); while Nuro Chabse described how he was both tied up and locked up (narrative 31). Wayessa Tikse went with his cousin's cousin, whom he was visiting, to their friend's house. The next morning, his kin and their friend stuffed a piece of leather into his mouth, tied and chained him, and then forced him beneath a bed, where they kept him for a week. They then sold him in the Gudru market (narrative 41). In the only instance of branding, Aguchello Chabani related how the Arab merchants who captured him scarred three marks into each cheek as punishment for his attempt to run away (narrative 1). Gaite Goshe described how the Sidama raiders who carried him off took him into a forest where, for no particular reason it seems, they put his feet into stocks for two days (narrative 16). When they released him from the stocks, he tried to escape but was foiled in the attempt and promptly sold to a "Mohammedan Galla" and onward into the external trade.

Some of these punishments were consequences of attempted escapes (we know nothing, of course, of any successful attempts). Again, there were distinct gender differences, as the diagram (graph 6.10) demonstrates. Unlike Fred Morton's examination of the East African slave children's narratives, during which he found that running away was "strikingly rare,"[47] more than one quarter (27.9 percent) of the children attempted escape at some point along their journeys. Of these, a majority two-thirds (66.7 percent) were boys.

Commander Charles Edward Gissing, master of the ship responsible for the children's liberation in September 1888, gave an eyewitness endorsement of the difference in treatment between the genders. He remarked on the "pitiable condition, particularly that of the little boys," when the children were carried aboard the *Osprey*.[48]

Less than one-fifth (18.2 percent) of the girls attempted to run away, compared with 38.1 percent—more than twice the proportion—of the boys. Two actually succeeded in initially evading their Sidama and Gojjam captors, but both were eventually captured when the raiders made a surprise return and successfully claimed their human booty. One girl, Galani Warabu (narrative 53), told of the Sidama raiding her village and killing her two brothers. She and her sisters managed to escape, hiding in the forest until the Sidama had left their village in peace. When they returned to their home, Galani's cousin arrived and took her home with him. When she asked to go back to her mother, her cousin promptly sold her into the trade.

The boys were more of a flight risk, with more than a quarter of them (26.2 percent) trying to escape once. Only four boys (9.5 percent) tried to run away a second time, and only Gamaches Garba (2.4 percent; narrative 18) was resolute enough to try many more times. The trader who owned him at that time chained his feet every night as a punishment and deterrent. Fewer than half of the instances of harsh treatment were meted out as a punitive measure for attempting to escape, and the degree of harshness of the treatment was not determined by whether a child had attempted to escape or not. Nor was cruelty the province of one particular group of traders—the abusers ranged from kin to black Arabs, Atari, Sidama, and traders from Entotto and Gombu.

Much has been written about the ordeals of the lengthy Atlantic middle passage. However, we cannot—and must not—discount slavery's primary ordeal, the first passage. The Oromo captives' slave routes were far more complex than current assumptions suggest. They were also a great deal longer. The children's reports of extended periods of domestic servitude during their journeys point to an entrenched domestic slavery system within the region. Gender differences were marked throughout the children's first-passage experiences, suggesting that we might consider a "boys' experience" and a "girls' experience." The boys' journeys were longer and more convoluted, as was the duration of their entire first passage. Boys were also treated more harshly en route, which led to more escape attempts, and boys suffered more serious illnesses.

That the girls spent less time both on the road and in domestic servitude suggests a need to get them to the coast expeditiously. Traders were likely to have been driven by the opportunity to realize an early return on their higher-valued young Oromo female captives, spurring them on to their destinations. The young Oromo girls were valued more highly in the most part because of their legendary beauty. This would have made them more precious as cargo, and traders may also have feared that keeping them too close to home for too long would risk attempted rescue by parents or kin.

Analyses of the identities of the slave captors and raiders, as well as of the traders, merchants, and owners, yielded unexpected but clear results. Raiding and capture were largely opportunistic and brief. The syndicated slave trading networks—of the Adal, Atari, and Sidama in particular—revealed their dominance throughout the trading experience from the first or second exchange to the final sale prior to loading the dhows. The evidence analyzed in this chapter has thrown up many new aspects of the first-passage experiences that require further examination.

PART III

Revival: From *Osprey* to *Lovedale*

CHAPTER 7

Interception to Aden

The middle passage looms large in the minds of historians of slavery, thanks to generations of nineteenth-century abolitionists who earnestly sought an end to the oceanic slave trade. In the Red Sea, the situation was quite different from that elsewhere. The middle-passage experiences of the Oromo slaves aboard the dhows lasted only a few hours. Captain Charles Edward Gissing, the commander of the first intercepting ship, the *Osprey*, was able to provide a detailed description of the dramatic—and traumatic—rescue and liberation of the Oromo children. His description complements those of the slave children themselves. In particular, Gissing's striking commentary on the physical state of the children as they were brought aboard the *Osprey* points not to the effects of their brief middle passage but to the trauma of their lengthy first-passage ordeal.

Though the children's first-passage narratives end when they reached their embarkation ports, two members of the *Osprey* crew compiled detailed records of their encounters with the slave children. Seaman A. T. V. Wright, the youngest of the *Osprey* crew, wrote his memoir of the event many years later. Chief among these observer accounts, however, were those of Commander Gissing, whose reports form part of the extensive official documentation on the Red Sea slave trade in general and on his ship's interception of the three dhows carrying the children in particular.

During the late 1880s, the British Parliament charged the Royal Navy with intensifying its efforts to intercept vessels suspected of carrying cargoes of slaves.[1] Britain mandated the Royal Navy, by a succession of bilateral treaties dating back to 1807 with a range of cooperating slave trading states, to act against vessels engaged in slave trading in both the Atlantic Ocean and the Indian Ocean, with the mutual right to search suspect vessels belonging to cosignatory nations.

At the Berlin Conference of 1885, the European powers agreed, broadly, to "help in suppressing slavery"; and Germany, Britain, and Italy blockaded the coast of Zanzibar, ostensibly to suppress the slave trade, in 1888.[2] A system of Vice Admiralty and other courts had been established in ports along the Indian Ocean and Atlantic Ocean coasts to try slave traders and liberate slaves.[3]

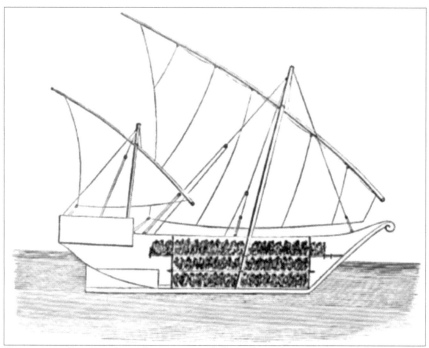

FIGURE 7.1. Cross section of a two-masted slave dhow (source: G. L. Sulivan, *Dhow Chasing in Zanzibar Waters and on the Eastern Coast of Africa* [London: Sampson Low, 1873], 114).

The Osprey *Dhows, September* 1888

Agents in the slave trading entrepôts loaded the Oromo children aboard their respective slave dhows in two groups almost a year apart—the first on 15 September 1888, the second on 5 August 1889. Both groups were bound for the Arabian slave markets. In the first group, agents at Rahayta boarded a total cargo of 204 slaves, comprising 183 Oromo children (91 boys and 92 girls, including the children of this study) and 21 adult slaves (5 men and 16 women). Table 7.1 gives details of the children's dhows, including the names of the dhow owners and masters, and the numbers of slaves aboard.

Dhows had intrinsic design advantages that helped them resist the steam- and sail-powered gunships of the British Royal Navy. Speed, maneuverability, and local knowledge were their key advantages. Usually single-masted, with a large triangular sail and shallow draft, the dhow could skate over the surface of the water like a gerrid water strider.[4] Whatever speed the average steam-driven naval sloops could achieve, none were maneuverable. The skilled dhow master would counter naval speed with rapid tacks and could dart off for a quick getaway.

For years these tactics confounded the British fleet patroling the eastern coastlines, leading one ship's captain to write despairingly to the Admiralty that the dhow "could sail like a witch."[5] Vice Admiral Philip Howard Colomb, who directed many dhow chases and interceptions during his antislavery patrols of the Indian Ocean, describes dhows as "enormously swift" and with which the speediest naval vessel under steam and sail would battle to keep pace. In his experience, a dhow would outstrip a naval gunship doing ten and a half miles an hour (seventeen kilometers per hour, or nine knots).[6]

Table 7.1. Details of three dhows intercepted by HMS *Osprey*

Details				Totals
Ship making capture	*Osprey*	*Osprey*	*Osprey*	
Place	Mokha	Mokha	Mokha	
Date	16 Sept 1888	16 Sept 1888	16 Sept 1888	
Name of vessel	*Al Heshima*	*Bakheita*	*Alkathora*	
Name of master	Ibrahim Ali	Saladin Ibrahim	Ali Kira Mahomed	
Name of owner	unknown	unknown	unknown	
How rigged	Dhow	Dhow	Dhow	
Number of men	8	17	8	
Number of guns	Small arms	Small arms	Small arms	
Tons	13	21.9	14.9	
From	Rahayta	Rahayta	Rahayta	
Bound	Jeddah	Jeddah	Jeddah	
Date of sailing from last port	15 Sept 1888	15 Sept 1888	15 Sept 1888	
Nature of cargo	Slaves	Slaves	Slaves	
If slaves aboard, no. of men	0	4	1	5
If slaves aboard, no. of women	5	7	4	16
If slaves aboard, no. of boys	32	31	28	91
If slaves aboard, no. of girls	24	39	29	92
Where shipped	Rahayta	Rahayta	Rahayta	
Port sent for adjudication?	Aden	Aden	Aden	
If condemned: Yes or No	Yes	Yes	Yes	
Condition of slaves	Very good	Very good	Very good	
Condition of vessel	Very good	Very good	Very good	
Deaths before adjudication	0	0	5	
Number emancipated	61	81	62	204

Source: Compiled from "List of Dhows Captured, 21 Apr–31 Dec 1888," BPP, C.5821, 1889, 34–35.

The Royal Navy's only successful means of countering the maneuvers of the dhows was firepower. On the *Osprey*, newly developed and lethal Gardner guns were mounted on the mainmast (see fig. 7.2).[7]

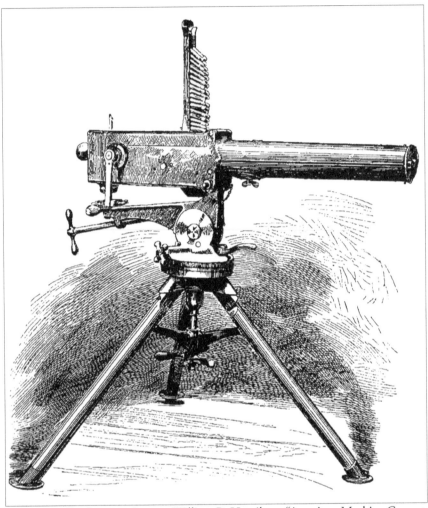

FIGURE 7.2. Gardner gun (source: William R. Hamilton, "American Machine Cannon and Dynamite Guns," *Century Illustrated* 36, no. 6 [October 1888]: 885–93).

The Royal Navy, for their part, positioned several vessels in the Red Sea to intercept dhows and other vessels suspected of carrying cargoes of slaves.

In October 1883, Commander Charles Edward Gissing was appointed British vice-consul in the dominions of the sultan of Zanzibar. His duties were clear. He was to suppress the slave trade by every legitimate means, and do all in his power "to develop the civilization and commerce of East Africa."[8] In 1888, he took command of the British sloop HMS *Osprey*,[9] and on 5 July that year he began his surveillance of the Red Sea coastline.

Prize money motivated enlistment for service aboard the antislavery patrols. Vice Admiralty courts awarded this prize money for each slave dhow. Successful British ships earned the reward en bloc. Each crew member—not just those in the boarding parties—received a proportion according to rank. Overall, the prize money for each freed slave was £5.10s. The British ships had to tow the offending dhows safely to port so they could be weighed. Prize money awarded was also dependent on tonnage at a rate of £1.10s per ton. If no slaves were found aboard the condemned dhow, the prize money was £4 per ton, but of course, with no slaves aboard, there was no reward for the crew. There was even an award price tag of £2.10s for any slave who died aboard a prize dhow.[10] Critics of this system charge that the lure of substantial reward—with half-price for dead slaves—meant, for some naval crews, the cheapening of life itself.[11]

In July 1888, the British Foreign Office authorized Gissing to investigate a rumored Russian occupation of the African coast south of Zeila (also known as Zaila or Zayla), a port city on the coast of the Gulf of Aden. Following a coastal reconnoiter in the vicinity of Tadjoura, he submitted a report to Colonel Edward Vincent Stace, who occupied the chief civil officer post of first resident at Aden.

Gissing was, however, alarmed, not by the presence of Russians in and around Tadjoura, but by the large numbers of slaves he observed in the town and neighborhood:

> All information points to the fact of there being a considerable trade in
> slaves about the Gulf of Tadjoura. When I visited the town of Tadjoura there
> were a large number of Abyssinian slaves, boys and girls, in the town and
> neighbourhood. Reports vary as to numbers, but seem to agree to over 100
> waiting to be taken overland to Rahayta, south of Assab Bay, from whence they
> are shipped in dhows for Hodeida, Jeddah, &c.[12]

On 6 September 1888, Gissing submitted an official report to the Admiralty for tabling in the House of Commons, in which he recorded his own observations of slave trading activities in the Red Sea region:

> The slave trade in the southern part of the Red Sea during the past six months
> has been very active. The season of its greatest activity is during the time of
> the Hadj, or pilgrimage to Mecca. . . . To meet this demand the slave-caravans
> start from Shoa and march to the coast by two routes, either by Harrar on the
> road to Zeyla, . . . [or] they pass a little north of Shoa, marching to Aussa, the
> chief town of Danakil-land, where Mahommed Kumfereh, the Danakil King,
> lives, who is one of the greatest slave catchers and dealers in these parts. Out
> of the 204 captured by Her Majesty's ship *Osprey* in September 1888, no less
> than 111 were his personal property. At Aussa there is abundance of water and
> food. From there they proceed to the east, either to Tajurrah, or branching off
> to Rahayta[13] or to Beilul. At Rahayta and Beilul the slaves are not embarked
> actually at the towns, but from the beach in their neighbourhood.[14]

Gissing remarked on a lack of French commitment to the bilateral agreements signed in 1885 in several of his official reports.[15] In a report to the assistant political resident in Aden, Gissing wrote that "all information points to the fact of there being

FIGURE 7.3. Tadjoura in the mid-nineteenth century (source: Guglielmo Massaia, 128, in Richard Pankhurst and Leila Ingrams, *Ethiopia Engraved: An Illustrated Catalogue of Engravings by Foreign Travellers from 1681 to 1900* [London: Kegan Paul, 1988], 74).

a considerable trade in slaves about the Gulf of Tadjoura."[16] On 6 September 1888, he reported that he believed the Dankali or Adal merchants (see graph 6.9 on page 90), who largely controlled the export of human cargoes across the Red Sea, brought the slaves from villages through Shewa to Tadjoura.[17] Writing further on the Adal slave traders, Gissing had few kind words:

> These Danakil are a semi-Somali tribe, very cowardly, cruel, and deceitful
> to a degree, but much more intelligent than the other Somalis; they are
> Mahommedans in religion, fanatical as all Mahommedans are; their name
> is a by-word among other Somalis for treachery; they always cut the private
> parts off any prisoner that falls into their hands, and leave him to die; they are
> inveterate slave-traders, and have so long carried it on with impunity that they
> are very indignant at the capture made by *Osprey*, and have turned all the other
> Somalis and the Arab traders out of Tadjoura, as they believe it was there I
> obtained the information which led to the capture.[18]

Gissing pointed out that the challenges facing the "Aden ship" in trying to deal with the Red Sea slave trade were exacerbated because major slave dealers in Aden, led by members of the Abu Bakr family, constantly monitored their movements.[19] These deal-ers maintained a close watch on ship movements and would telegraph details to their contacts in Perim, a small island off the Yemen coast in the Strait of Mandeb at the southern entrance of the Red Sea, where a dhow carrying the news would set sail for Rahayta.[20] Aboard the *Osprey* in September 1888, Gissing decided to dock at Perim for several days to allow the Arab crews sufficient time to begin loading their slave cargoes

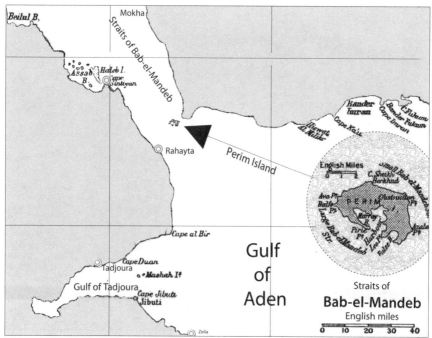

MAP 7.1. Perim Island in the Strait of Mandeb (source: adapted from Map of Straits of Bab-El-Mandeb 1932, New Society for the Diffusion of Knowledge, Internet Map Archive, http://www.probertencyclopaedia.com/photolib/maps/).

aboard the three dhows. From Perim, he positioned the *Osprey* strategically off the coast so that he would be in a good position to intercept these dhows at sea. The crossings from the entrepôts to the Arabian ports were fraught with danger for slave dhow masters, so they generally chose to launch their dhows after dark. Map 7.1 shows the lower reaches of the Red Sea as it opens into the Gulf of Aden and marks Perim, where Gissing waited aboard the *Osprey*, as well as the relative positions of Tadjoura and Rahayta.

Given these risks, dhow captains were able to charge inflated fees for carrying their contraband cargo. For example, charges at Rahayta averaged MT$5 per slave, plus an additional surcharge to cover the loss of any dhow captured and confiscated by the British fleet.[21]

On 15 September, as Gissing had predicted, three dhows loaded with slaves set off from Rahayta heading for Jeddah: the *Bakheita* (21.9 tons), commanded by Saladin Ibrahim, with seventeen crew and eighty-one slaves (four men, seven women, thirty-one boys, and thirty-nine girls); the *Alkathora* (14.9 tons), commanded by Ali Kira Mahomed, with eight crew and sixty-two slaves (one man, four women, twenty-eight boys, and twenty-nine girls); and the *Al Heshima* (13 tons), commanded by Ibrahim Ali, with eight crew and sixty-one slaves (five women, thirty-two boys, and twenty-four girls). There were 204 slaves (five men, sixteen women, ninety-one boys, and ninety-two girls) aboard the three dhows. All three dhows carried small arms.[22]

FIGURE 7.4. Modern Rahayta/Raheita/Araito (source: Panoramio, http://static.panoramio
.com/photos/large/69876460.jpg).

The *Osprey* set sail to intercept the three suspect vessels. Seaman A. T. V. Wright,
the youngest member of the crew at eighteen years of age, was acting as lookout that
September morning:

> On 16th September 1888 [*sic*] we left Aden in execution of orders received to
> the effect that a slave caravan was on the way to Tadjoura, on the Somaliland
> coast. Tajura is west of "Obokh" (now called Djibouti). We arrived at Tadjoura
> on Saturday the 17th September [*sic*].[23] After obtaining information that the
> slaves had been embarked in three dhows and had left the night before for
> a destination on the Red Sea, we left Tadjoura, in an attempt to capture the
> dhows, which proved successful. I had been ordered to be at the foretop mast
> head by dawn . . . and when dawn broke, I reported to the "deck" "Three
> dhows right ahead," this would be at about 5.45 a.m.[24]

Gissing reported:

> On the morning of Sunday, the 16th, at daylight, being about seven miles from
> Mokha Point, I sighted three dhows standing to the northward, the wind being
> southwesterly. I took up a position about half a-mile to leeward of them, and
> between them and the shore, when I fired several blank charges to bring them to.
> They immediately altered course in various directions, making for the shore.[25]

When Gissing again signaled them to stop and the masters of the dhows ignored his signals, he ordered his crew to fire several blank charges across their bows, hoping to halt their progress. In response, the dhows sped off in different directions. Gissing then fired live shells across their bows. He called on them to lower their sails. However, all three dhows continued toward the shore.[26] The dhow masters' plan was to put all the slaves ashore. The dhows would then be empty by the time the naval vessel caught up with them. They were well aware that they ran the risk of having their dhows confiscated and destroyed should they be taken in tow by the British navy.[27]

Gissing then ordered his men to fire his seven-pounder and sixty-four-pounder guns directly at the masts of the dhows. Instead, the shots pierced the sails. There is no indication of any return fire. The dhows barely slowed their pace. Gissing then decided to use the Gardner guns mounted on the fore and main top masts of the *Osprey*.[28] At 07h00, the first dhow, the *Alkathora*, lowered her sails.[29] Gissing lowered a fully armed boat from the *Osprey* and sent gunner John W. H. Budge to board the *Alkathora*.[30] On boarding, Budge discovered that they had killed Ali Kira Mahomed, the master of the *Alkathora*, and four of the slaves held captive aboard his dhow. Four additional slaves were wounded.[31]

Five minutes later, the second dhow, the *Al Heshima*, followed suit by lowering her sails and surrendering to the British sloop. The third dhow, the *Bakheita*, however, was already some three miles distant. Gissing gave chase, firing shots through her sails until, when he had again ordered the deployment of the Gardner guns, they, too, finally surrendered. Meanwhile, the second dhow had rehoisted her sails and was trying to make a quick getaway while the *Osprey* was focusing on the other two dhows. Mr. Budge, the gunner, still on the *Alkathora* some five hundred yards away, opened fire on the fleeing dhow until the crew capitulated and again lowered their sails.[32] At 07h30, the *Bakheita* finally came into the wind and luffed her sail.[33]

Eventually, all three dhows were brought alongside the *Osprey*, and the dhows' crews were placed under guard in the starboard wing passage.[34] Gissing continued his account: "I then took all the crews, agents, and owners of the slaves on board, making them prisoners, thirty-three in number, consisting of Arabs from Turkish ports of Red Sea, and Dankali [Adal] merchants. I then removed all the slaves on board the *Osprey*, 204 in number, took the three dhows in tow, and proceeded to Aden."[35] Wright recorded that they found the slave children bundled into the holds of the dhows, stacked atop sacks of rice, unable to move.[36] Conditions belowdecks were cramped. The hours that the children were squeezed into the cargo holds had made them lame. Members of the *Osprey* crew had to carry most of them aboard their ship.[37]

Tightly packed out of sight aboard the dhows, the children were terror-stricken, not only in consequence of their first-passage experiences and the violence of the events unfolding around them aboard the dhows, but also by the scare tactics that had been used by their captors. The crews of the dhows and the children's earlier slave masters had told them that if they fell into the hands of white men, "they would be eaten."[38] Tolassa Wayessa had tried to run away from the Atari merchants after they threatened to sell him to the Bulgu (men eaters), who populated various myths and legends among the Somali, the Oromo, and other East African peoples.[39] The Atari

Slave-Ship captured by H.M.S "Osprey"

FIGURE 7.5. Slave ship captured by HMS *Osprey*, ca. 1885 (source: watercolor by one of the Osprey crew, ZBA2714, Michael Graham-Stewart Slavery Collection, University Christian Missions Archive, National Maritime Museum, London).

and other slave traders frequently used such stories to scare the children and discourage them from trying to escape. According to historian Lindsay Doulton, captives aboard slave dhows found the moment of seizure physically and mentally distressing, adding to their litany of traumas.[40] Their physical traumas were mostly acute, and the extent of their psychological scarring can only be imagined.

Matthew Lochhead, in his introduction to the published children's narratives, reported that the Arab dhow masters and crew covered the children with tarpaulins, telling them to remain totally still, "as the man-eaters were after them."[41] This ruse was intended to dupe any English gunboat coming alongside their dhow for a visual inspection of the dhow's cargo. Hiding their canvas-covered human cargo would, they hoped, convince the crews aboard the gunboats that they were innocently carrying a general cargo.

Gissing commented on the way in which slaves were typically treated aboard the Arab dhows in the Red Sea and, notably, described the effects of their first passage:

> The great loss of life takes place at their capture in their own country, and
> during the voyage down. Europeans have travelled with these caravans, and
> have told me that to their certain knowledge 50 per cent died coming down,
> and many more after reaching; this can easily be seen to be the case where so
> many are children and quite young girls, utterly unable to stand so long and so
> rough a journey.[42]

His observations on first-passage mortality in this report are compelling. On seeing the Oromo children for the first time as he watched them being carried aboard the *Osprey*, Gissing noticed their woeful condition:

Except four men, all the rest were women and children, and their pitiable condition, particularly that of the little boys, was heartrending to witness. The latter looked like small ebony skeletons, many of their wee miserable bodies exhibiting the traces of recent ill-treatment. . . . All of them nearly had to be lifted on board their limbs being so cramped by confinement.[43]

This description corroborates what the children were later to tell of their ordeals. That they, particularly the boys, were all emaciated was obviously a consequence not of their brief middle-passage experience aboard the dhows but of their long and punitive first-passage ordeal. This eyewitness description and that of Seaman Wright are at odds with the official manifest describing their condition as "very good"—a phrase applied to only one other cargo of slaves aboard any of the forty-seven slave-carrying dhows captured between 1 July 1887 and 31 December 1888.[44] Gissing augmented his account with a later synopsis of what he believed had been the children's experiences of the slave trade: "Of the two hundred and thirteen [*sic*] slaves rescued by *HMS Osprey* eighteen months ago, most of them had been kidnapped by Mohammedan Gallas, taken to the slave markets and sold, many of them passing through the hands of ten merchants before reaching the coast."[45] In this passage, Gissing confirms the multiple sales the children later reported to the missionaries. While "Mohammedan Gallas" played a minimal role in the captures and sales of the Oromo children of this study, Gissing is here referring to the entire group of 204 (not 213) liberated Oromo slaves aboard his ship. As he remarked in a later report, approximately half of that total number were Muslim: "The majority of the 204 slaves were girls or very young boys; of the boys three were eunuchs; they were all well cared for, especially the girls, who sell from 200 to 300 dollars in Jeddah; out of the whole party quite half were Christians, the remainder Mussulmans."[46]

Seaman Wright, the other commentator aboard the *Osprey*, was also clearly moved by the sight of the 204 Oromo slaves as they were helped aboard the *Osprey*: "All were crying. But what a change came over them, for within a half hour they learnt that they were free. Embracing each other (some were brothers and sisters)."[47] The siblings and other family members to whom Gissing and Wright refer were among the larger group of Oromo slaves aboard the *Osprey*, not the children of this study.

According to Wright, two government interpreters aboard the *Osprey*—Mahomet Ali and Mahomet Sayed—were able to converse with and comfort the children and to communicate what the children told them about their experiences. One young girl, who attracted the special notice of the interpreters and crew, "turned out to be of Royal descent."[48] Though there were four royal daughters among the sixty-four Oromo children who eventually arrived at Lovedale, only one, Dinkitu Boensa (narrative 51), was aboard the *Osprey*.

Wright continued in his reminiscence:

The two Government Interpreters, Mahomet Ali and Mahomet Sayed, who accompanied us on this operation, told me a lot, after these children had had a refreshing bath, & a nice meal, they both complimented me, and whilst they were talking to these children, they all looked towards me, and the white

ensign which was flying at the "Peak," and smiled. . . . The Interpreters told me
. . . how the Sultan of Tadjoura professed to know nothing about the slaves,—
that the information which the Interpreters gained was from Somalis on the
beach to the effect that the slaves had embarked on these dhows, and had left
during the night of the 16th Sept. I have wondered, if the Sultan of Tadjoura
ever missed his three dhows, and their crews.[49]

Wright's account both supports Gissing's interpretation and goes a little further,
based on the interpreters' information, about events back on the mainland, pointing
clearly to the dominant role of the sultan of Tadjoura in the export slave trade in the
area. Musing on the children's future, Wright added that "it would be impossible to
return these children to their homes in the Galla District of Abyssinia, as they would
probably have been captured again by Slave Dealers."[50] Technically, the middle passage of the surviving children ended when they were carried aboard the *Osprey*, for
that signified the beginning of their automatic liberation in terms of the 1807 statute
and the subsequent multilateral treaties.[51]

The *Osprey* docked at Aden on the evening of 17 September 1888. The next morning, Gissing handed his prisoners, the surviving dhow masters and crews, over to the
police. In his official report, written aboard the *Osprey* on 18 September 1888 in dock
at Aden, Gissing reported that he had landed the slaves at Aden that morning and that
they were in the care of government authorities there.[52] The *Osprey* incident became a
matter for the Vice Admiralty Court at Aden, to which the thirty-three captive masters and crews of the dhows were referred. The three dhows that the *Osprey* had towed
to Aden were quartered and burned on the beach.[53]

Skirmishes and battles of most military hostilities invariably result in "collateral
damage." The armed interventions used by the British navy in their efforts to intercept suspect vessels all too often resulted in slave mortalities. Historian Lindsay
Doulton confirms this, writing that "both the official and unofficial records of naval
suppression are littered with frequent accounts of bungled rescue attempts."[54] She
goes beyond this by suggesting that for some naval crews, slave lives were cheap and
the prize money, even for dead slaves at half the price of the living, was considerable.
Questions hung over Gissing's decision to order the firing of the Gardner guns, but
the permanent secretary to the Admiralty was able to report to the Foreign Office on
2 November 1888 that the commissioners of the Admiralty considered the firing of the
Gardner gun justifiable under the circumstances.[55]

The Tadjoura Dhows, August 1889

Eleven months later, on 5 August 1889, agents assembled a second group of Oromo
children at Tadjoura (now in modern Djibouti). This group was put aboard a cluster of
slave dhows bound for Arabia's slave markets. Interspersed among them was a smaller
group of fourteen children—nine boys and five girls. Beyond knowing the names of
these children, little is known of their experiences aboard their respective dhows.[56]

Daba Tobo (narrative 10) told of being initially put aboard a dhow in a group of
seven dhows that had embarked from Tadjoura two months previously. Bisho Jarsa's

(narrative 48) memory of their experience differed slightly from the story Daba told. She remembered being aboard one of six dhows setting out from Tadjoura. The masters of two of the dhows, having spotted a British naval patrol, set course to return to Tadjoura. After the crew had kept their cargoes of slaves captive in Tadjoura for six weeks, the two dhows set sail again. However, the trade winds betrayed them and they found themselves becalmed. A Royal Navy ship pursued both dhows, successfully intercepting the first dhow and securing all the slaves carried aboard. The Oromo children known to have been aboard this first dhow were five girls: Bisho Jarsa (narrative 48); Damuli Dunge (narrative 50); Fayissi Gemo (narrative 52); Galani Warabu (narrative 53); and Kanatu Danke (narrative 58); and eight boys: Daba Tobo (narrative 10); Fayissa Hora (narrative 13); Galgal Dikko (narrative 17); Gilo Kashe (narrative 19); Mulatta Billi (narrative 29); Nagaro Chali (narrative 30); Shamo Ayanso (narrative 34); and Wayessa Tonki (narrative 42).

When the captain of the second dhow in this group realized capture was inevitable, he ordered all forty-one slaves on board his dhow to be thrown overboard before he and his crew leaped into the sea themselves.[57] What they did not know was that one Oromo child, Isho Karabe (narrative 23), had hidden below some planks in the dhow and remained there for the whole day, not daring to move or make a sound. In the evening, one of the English officers from the British gunship boarded the dhow to inspect her and discovered Isho cowering beneath the planks.

The middle passage of this group of children was even briefer than that of the *Osprey* children in 1888. With the exception of Isho Karabe, their middle passage endured no more than a handful of hours, and there is no record of violence or slave mortalities during the engagement between the dhows and the British gunship.

Berille Boko, 1890

There would be one final addition to the Oromo children. In April 1890, a Gudru merchant took a young Oromo girl named Berille Boko (narrative 46) to Tadjoura and sold her to a group of Adal merchants who put her aboard a dhow with twenty-two other girls and twenty-eight boys. This dhow set sail from Tadjoura alongside another fully laden with a cargo of slaves heading toward the Turkish Arabian port of Hodeidah.[58] As they neared the Arabian coast, a Royal Navy gunship spotted and pursued them. To avoid capture, the two dhows put ashore, and, with their captured slave cargoes, the crew escaped into the forest where they remained hidden for two days. The slave children were then put onto camels and led into the nearby port town of Hodeidah, where they were displayed for sale in a *fondak* (described by Matthew Lochhead as a "native caravanserai" in Berille Boko's story; see appendix B, narrative 46). Arabian *fondaks* or *fondouks* and caravanserais were, typically, enclosed rectangular courtyards designed to shelter humans, animals, and goods. They were situated along ancient caravan routes where traders and travelers could rest and refresh themselves and their transport animals. They could also display and sell their wares, including their captured slaves.[59]

A young Scotsman named William Grant spotted Berille among the slave children displayed for sale in this fondak and paid MT$175 to secure her manumission and freedom.[60] Grant took her with him to Aden, where he put her into the care of the missionaries at the Keith-Falconer Mission, "to be educated at his expense." He is believed to have continued to support Berille for many years.[61] She was the last of the Oromo slave children to be captured and liberated.

In many respects, the Red Sea slave trade was different from that of the West African/Atlantic trade. Most marked of the differences, perhaps, was the far shorter middle-passage experience of Red Sea slaves, whose voyages ranged between six and thirty-six hours. The absence of a lengthy middle passage had a compensatory, evidentiary advantage. Obviously the children's conditions on being carried aboard the dhows in September 1888 could not be ascribed to their middle passage. The cumulated effects of the children's first passage took a hefty toll in the short and the long term. Gissing's account supported what the children later told the missionaries about their ordeals. Emaciation, to the point of Gissing's description of "small ebony skeletons," does not occur in consequence of an hours-long middle passage. Their pitiful conditions and the evidence of physical abuse that Gissing reported were the direct result of their lengthy and merciless first-passage experiences, not of their middle passages.

CHAPTER 8

Sojourn in the Desert
and the Onward Voyage

After the protracted trauma of the children's first passage and their brief but violent rescue, a period of recuperation followed. Decisions about their future now lay in the hands of the assistant political resident in Aden, the Aden administration, and a group of Scottish missionaries at Sheikh Othman, an oasis just north of Aden.[1] The missionaries documented this sojourn of the Oromo children in letters, photographs, telegrams, reports, and missionary newsletters. This was also where the children recounted their life stories, which were transcribed and translated by Matthew Lochhead, assisted by interpreters. While there is no firm evidence of when the missionaries interviewed the children, they would have taken advantage of having three fluent Oromo speakers at the mission to assist them in interviewing the children regarding their first-passage experience. The interviews must have taken place after the arrival of Berille Boko, the last of the Oromo children to reach the mission sometime between May and June 1890, and before the children departed for South Africa in July 1890. This was also where the first tangible evidence of the impact of their first-passage ordeals manifested itself, for one-fifth of the children died within three months. The legacy of the ordeal of their first passage would dog the rest of the survivors' lives even as they acquired their freedom and education.

On their arrival at Aden, the 204 newly liberated Oromo were placed under the care of Colonel Edward Vincent Stace, the chief civil officer in Aden, who was charged with finding an appropriate sanctuary for them. Stace contacted Dr. Alexander Paterson, a Free Church of Scotland medical missionary stationed at the Keith-Falconer Mission. Paterson wrote after the *Osprey* had docked at Aden:

> The three cargoes of slaves which were captured off Perim [Island] by Her Majesty's gunboat Osprey—217 or thereabouts in all—are quartered under strict Government surveillance. None, not even Government officials, except

FIGURE 8.1. Aden in 1882 (source: sketch by Jose Rizal, Aden College, http://adencollege .nethtmlbody_aden_ history.html.jpg).

the one or two in charge, are allowed to see them without a pass from Colonel Stace, interim First Political Resident; and those who obtain a pass are enjoined to see it destroyed on being delivered up.[2]

Though Gissing had estimated that about half of the 183 children aboard the *Osprey* were Christian and the other half Muslim,[3] those he considered "Christian" were almost certainly followers of the traditional Oromo religion or animists (see chapter 1).

Identifying which children were Muslim and which were not was not easy because, according to Paterson:

> Intriguing Mohammedans . . . , at the very first, forbade, in common with
> all comers, free access. These were anxious to secure as many of the girls and
> young women for their licentious purposes as they could, and tried to persuade
> them to profess themselves Muslim, rather than Christian. Under such pretexts
> as prayer and fasting, they sought to identify them as Muslim—as if, as
> Colonel Stace sharply reminded them, only Mohammedans prayed and fasted.[4]

Stace classified the children according to their names and other indications. He recorded their names "with his own hand," his task the more difficult as he could not, initially, find anyone fluent in Oromo to help him. The practice was for Arab families in Aden to apply to adopt liberated Muslim children and to look after and educate them until they were able to provide for themselves. Paterson wrote in the same article: "The few Mohammedan women and girls will probably be given to those of their own religion for service or, where they are too old or otherwise unfitted for service, given in marriage."[5] Both Stace and the Keith-Falconer missionaries respected the Islamic faith by ensuring that the liberated Muslim slave children were placed with established Muslim families.

In the case of those he determined to be non-Muslim, Stace asked the authorities at the Keith-Falconer Mission if they could take at least some of the children. Paterson wrote of his encounter with Stace:

> He was exceedingly anxious that we should take . . . some of them. . . . We stipulated for a selection, so as to secure the healthiest and, if possible, those who seemed the most intelligent. . . . A difficulty that has presented itself is the want of a lady to take charge, but as we should choose the youngest among the girls, our present task should be less formidable.[6]

Paterson, in response to Stace's urging, exchanged telegrams with the Free Church of Scotland Foreign Missions Committee in Edinburgh about the fate of the recently liberated Oromo children. This exchange would change their demographic composition. On 28 September 1888, the committee wired Paterson, saying: "Take fifty youngest boys—doubts about girls great." Despite Edinburgh's doubts, Paterson selected twenty-five girls (finally whittled down to twenty-three) and thirty-nine boys. He anticipated that the rest of the Christian children among the original *Osprey* group would be taken in by other missions in Zanzibar or Mumbai, India.[7] A few days later, this group of sixty-two children, about one-third of the original group of 183 *Osprey* children, arrived at the mission.[8] The sex ratio of the Oromo children who were selected for the mission at Sheikh Othman was now 170 males to 100 females. This was clearly not the result of the sex ratio of the dhow cargoes, but rather a direct result of the missionaries' selections based on the male potential for agricultural work—and a coincidental imposition of Atlantic slave trade ratios.

Paterson clearly wanted to take only the healthiest and most intelligent males. He added a cynical rider to his account, one that reveals how, even though the children had been liberated, Paterson still regarded them as sources of labor: "Even now, the boys at least may be an indirect source of profit; in building and gardening we will be able to dispense with much outside labour."[9] While such shocking considerations appear to conflict with the purely evangelical purpose of all missions, hints of financial strain are evident throughout the missionaries' discussions around the long-term care of the Oromo children, and Paterson here sounds a pragmatic note to put the best gloss on his selection of male Oromo children.

Lochhead took detailed photographs of the children from the time of their arrival at the mission until he left Lovedale in 1892.

The first known photograph taken of them (see fig. 8.2) shows the children shortly after they were transferred on foot from Aden, their last march. Their small stature, thin limbs, and ragged clothes reflect their recent ordeal.

At the mission their health continued to deteriorate. When Lochhead and Paterson tried to start a school at the mission for the children, they had to abandon the idea initially when the children succumbed to malaria, whooping cough, bronchitis, and

FIGURE 8.2. Oromo children on arrival at Sheikh Othman, September 1888 (source: PIC/A 1320, Cory Library for Humanities Research, Rhodes University).

lingering scurvy. The children in the photograph (fig. 8.2) were truly Gissing's "small ebony skeletons" (see Gissing's full description of the children on pages 105–108).

These emaciated children had little resistance to the new opportunistic infections they now encountered. By the end of 1888, "fully one-fifth" of this group had died, dwindling their number to fifty-one—thirty-three boys and eighteen girls—changing the sex ratio to 183 boys to 100 girls.[10] These children's deaths constituted the earliest postliberation manifestation of the impact of their first-passage experiences.

The missionaries were determined to restart the school for those who survived. When the children first arrived, the school relied not only on the involvement of the missionaries attached to the station but also on the services of an unnamed Muslim teacher, "whose influence over the children," the missionaries felt, "was very questionable."[11] In early 1889, Dr. Gulian Lansing, a missionary in Cairo, sent two Ethiopian female teachers to help with the care and education of the Oromo children.[12] They were both fluent in Afaan Oromoo, and one spoke English "with ease and readiness."[13] In addition, William Gardner (see the following photograph, fig. 8.3), the youthful, dapper, and brilliant successor to Ion Keith-Falconer, devoted all his time to learning Afaan Oromoo.[14]

Lochhead was already fluent in Afaan Oromoo. Later, he taught the Oromo children at Lovedale in their mother tongue. Within a few months, however, the mission relieved the Muslim teacher of his duties.

In the meantime, news of the Oromo children's rescue had reached Gebru Desta, a highly educated missionary at the Basel Mission in East Africa, who is recognized as the first evangelist to the Oromo people. While in Dar es Salaam toward the end

FIGURE 8.3. Reverend William Gardner at Sheikh Othman (source: Acc.10023/417 [packet 3], Capture One [03168], National Library of Scotland).

of 1888, Gebru—who was fluent in Afaan Oromoo, Amharic, German, French, and English—read a report about the children at the Keith-Falconer Mission.[15]

The Reverend John Fairley Daly, Free Church of Scotland minister and honorary secretary of the Livingstonia Committee in Scotland from 1901 to 1932, wrote about Gebru's reaction to this report:

> He at once said to himself, "I may be of some use there," and packing up his things, took steamer to Aden. Shortly afterward, to the astonishment of the missionaries he appeared at the door of the mission-house with all his luggage, asking if they would take him in. He was the very man that was wanted, and, pending inquiry, it was agreed he should stay. The best of testimonials were received, and the result is that a valuable and trustworthy Christian teacher has been found for the boys, thereby relieving Mr. Gardner of a serious burden, and setting free his time for other important work.[16]

Daly, who must have been close to Lochhead and Gardner, provides the first physical description of the Oromo children at the Mission.

On 13 March 1889, Lochhead and Gardner set off for Aden. They headed for the harbor, where Daly was a passenger aboard a steamer just in from Bombay. At one o'clock in the morning, the two missionaries knocked at Daly's cabin door, offering to take him to visit Sheikh Othman. They promised to have him back on the steamer in time for its departure.

Daly responded with spontaneous enthusiasm. They passed through what Daly regarded as the "dreary and uninviting" Aden while Lochhead and Gardner updated the visitor with news of the mission and the children. They told Daly that the bungalow the late Keith-Falconer had occupied had been converted into the schoolhouse for the Oromo, enclosed by a brick wall on land of more than four acres. Daly wrote of their visit to the sleeping children inside this schoolhouse:

> Going first to the school, we entered the large central room on the ground flat, and found twenty-one sleeping figures wrapped in their mats and lying on the floor. Some wakened as we walked between the rows, and starting up, rubbed their eyes and asked, "Father, is it morning?" It was only 4 a.m. A kindly hand laid on the shoulder, and a pat on the cheek, quieted the disturbed sleepers, who could not understand the unreasonable intrusion. Passing into the next room, we found the remaining twelve deep in peaceful slumber. In the large upper room the eighteen girls lay sound asleep. This room, with its broad, cool veranda round and round, it is intended to use as a place for public worship. It was impossible not to be impressed with the interesting character of the charge intrusted to the mission, and of the responsibility attaching to it. It will entail much anxiety and labour.[17]

The photograph below (fig. 8.4) shows the schoolhouse, with the girls ranked along the first-floor veranda and the boys below.

Part of the schoolhouse was also used by the doctor as his dispensary and medical store. For the first time since their arrival, the children were well. In his account of this

FIGURE 8.4. Keith-Falconer School: boys on ground floor; girls on upper floor, 1889 (source: Acc.10023/417 [packet 3], No. 3 [97131493], National Library of Scotland).

visit, Daly confirmed that of the sixty-two originally received, eleven had died, leaving fifty-one—eighteen girls and thirty-three boys—in the mission's care.[18]

Lochhead and Gardner continued their explanations as they led Daly through the rest of the mission premises. Work was proceeding on two buildings that would serve as dormitories for the boys and girls. Totally separate from the school, these two dormitories were separated by a small house for the female teachers. Gardner and Lochhead occupied the upper flat of what they described as "a comfortable home."[19]

The missionaries told Daly that medical work at the mission was at a standstill because of Paterson's continuing ill-health, but they hoped the work would soon be resumed. On a more encouraging note, Lochhead was able to assure Daly that the school was now in full working order. He was busy with brickmaking, buying building materials, housebuilding, and generally managing the details of the project; while the Oromo boys enjoyed working in the garden and caring for the grounds in their spare time. Daly returned to his ship that morning without further commentary on the schoolhouse (pictured again in figure 8.5 with the children in more relaxed array).

In August 1889, a further contingent of Oromo children, also liberated at sea by the Royal Navy, arrived at Aden. Gardner, then in charge of the mission, consulted with Thomas Martin Lindsay, convener of the Foreign Missions Committee and in India at the time. He decided to take fourteen more Oromo children—nine boys and five girls.[20] The last of the Oromo children, Berille Boko (the only manumitted slave; narrative 46), arrived sometime between May and July 1890. The photograph (see fig. 8.6) shows Berille toward the end of her time at Lovedale, circa 1899.

FIGURE 8.5. Keith-Falconer Mission: Oromo children and missionaries (source: Acc.10023/417 [packet 3], No. 3 [97131490], National Library of Scotland: Matthew Lochhead reclining left foreground, William Gardner and Gebru Desta, seated far right).

Two Oromo girls must have died sometime between August 1889 and July 1890. The Reverend George Smith, in a letter from Edinburgh written on 4 July 1890 to accompany a photograph of the children he was preparing for publication, confirms the heavy mortality:

> Most of the children in this print are of the party captured by *HMS Osprey*. Dr Paterson, our medical missionary, selected upwards of these, and the rest were taken by the Roman Catholic Mission at Aden. Owing to rough usage by their captors, and the malaria of Shaikh Othman subsequently, the mortality among seventy-five, to which the number was raised by additions from a later capture, was fifteen. The mortality among the Roman Catholic lot was greater.[21]

Compromised resistance as a result of the trauma of the first passage made the children vulnerable to all infections, including the malaria that seems to have stalked Sheikh Othman. With Berille's arrival, the group had a final tally of sixty-four: forty-two boys and twenty-two girls, a sex ratio of 191 males to 100 females.

An African Alternative

The missionaries were now faced with the dilemma of the children's future. One thing was certain: the missionaries had to find an alternative, malaria-free destination for the children. Any thought of sending them home was dismissed. The missionaries concluded that if they were to do so, the children would be at a triple

FIGURE 8.6. Berille Boko at Lovedale, ca. 1899 (source: CL PIC/A 1319, Lovedale Collection).

FIGURE 8.7. Oromo children at Sheikh Othman, 1890 (source: CL PIC/A 1320, Lovedale Collection; shown: Gebru Desta, center back; Alexander Paterson, reclining left front; Matthew Lochhead, reclining right front; William Gardner cross-legged in center).

disadvantage: they were children, Oromo, and former captives. Reenslavement, abuse, sickness, and an early death would have been the probable outcome for most of them. As Christopher Saunders, a South African historian writing in the context of liberated Africans in the Cape Colony, pointed out: "To return them to where they came from, it was argued, would make possible their re-enslavement."[22] The Foreign Mission Committee considered suggestions of Poona in India or Mombasa, while the Keith-Falconer missionaries favored Egypt.[23] Formerly, the authorities in Aden had sent Ethiopian "prize slaves" to Lower Egypt for sale, but because of lingering hostility between Egypt and Ethiopia, the British intervened to ensure this was no longer an option.[24]

There was a sense that it would be best for the children to be cared for in a mission environment somewhere on the African continent. T. M. Lindsay wrote to James Stewart,[25] the principal of the Lovedale Institution in South Africa:

> Poona has been suggested but there are great difficulties in the way there. Mr Stephen and Mrs Stewart have both suggested Lovedale. Others have thought of Mombase. The more I think of it the more I like your wife's suggestion, but I have not indicated any preference to the Committee. Can you take them in at

Lovedale and, and this is an important question, at what cost annually? Aden is an expensive place, but so is Lovedale in comparison with India.[26]

After much debate, the committee decided the best destination for the sixty-four children would be Lovedale. In 1824, Glasgow Missionary Society missionaries John Bennie and John Ross had founded a station on the Ncerha River about twenty kilometers southeast of Tyhume in the Eastern Cape. Initially named "Incerha," they renamed the station "Lovedale" in honor of Dr. John Love after his death in 1825. Love had been the first secretary of the London Missionary Society and was later a leading figure in the Glasgow Missionary Society. The site of the old Lovedale was abandoned in 1836 in favor of one on the east bank of the Tyhume River some seven kilometers distant. Within two decades, the missionaries extended the mission to include an educational facility. This new Lovedale Institution opened in 1841, with the Reverend William Govan as its first principal.[27] The Reverend Dr. James Stewart took over from Govan and was principal at the time of the children's arrival in 1890.[28]

The group photograph (figure 8.7) shows all sixty-four children with the missionaries Lochhead, Paterson, and Gardner in the foreground and Gebru Desta (see earlier discussion regarding Gebru Desta on pages 114, 116) standing in the middle of the second row from the back. This picture must have been taken shortly before they sailed for Lovedale Institution in South Africa in July 1890, as it includes Berille Boko, the last arrival, in a white dress, standing second from the right in the middle row.

The liberation of the Oromo children signaled the beginning of the next major phase in their lives. But liberation from the bonds of slavery did not mean an escape from the deleterious impact of their first passage. The emaciated, frail, and susceptible children were defenseless against the adverse conditions of climate and infection. The first manifestation of early mortality in consequence of their harsh first-passage experiences came all too soon after their arrival at the Keith-Falconer Mission. Nearly one-fifth died within three months, six of the eleven mortalities being the vulnerable boys who had endured the worst first-passage experiences. The search for a new, healthier environment for them led to Lovedale Institution in the Eastern Cape, South Africa.

CHAPTER 9

By Sea and Land to Lovedale

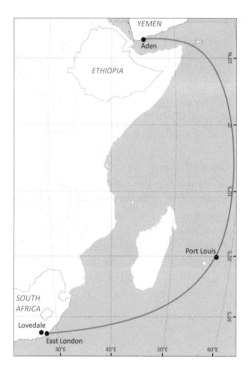

MAP 9.1. Sea voyage from Aden, Yemen, to East London, South Africa (source: Sandra Rowoldt Shell and GIS Laboratory, University of Cape Town).

To reach Lovedale meant a pair of sea voyages and a final, land-based leg to the institution itself. Letters, photographs, reminiscences, and reports from the Lovedale staff, as well as shipping news and newspaper articles, underpin this final journey. The contrast between this and the Oromo children's initial first-passage journeys is marked. Whereas the first-passage trek was a harsh, grim, and fear-filled ordeal, the stretch to Lovedale promised to be gentler, characterized by expectation rather than fear.

FIGURE 9.1. *Conway Castle*, 1880 (source: South African Genealogy, http://www.sagenealogy.co.za/Conway_Info&Pic.htm).

Embarkation for Mauritius and South Africa

On the night of 24 July 1890, the children, along with Alexander Paterson and Matthew Lochhead, embarked on the mailship *Rio Grande* of the French shipping line Messageries Maritimes. They put to sea from Aden, stopping at Zanzibar and Madagascar before reaching Mauritius. The *Rio Grande* sailed into the harbor at Port Louis, Mauritius, on 12 August 1890.

To reach the east coast of South Africa meant transshipping from a Messageries liner to a steamer of the Castle Line, held by the Castle Mail Packets Company. The Oromo children boarded the *Conway Castle* for the new service's maiden voyage to Durban and East London.[1] However, once the commander, Captain Warden, had learned of their dramatic story, he decided that the children were in need of a treat before their departure.[2] That treat was a performance of the Fillis Circus in Port Louis.[3] Warden had just shipped the entire entourage of this circus from East London in South Africa to Mauritius on the *Conway Castle*'s outward voyage. A poster survives advertising the circus (see fig. 9.2).

Accordingly, his crew—"the kindly British tars no doubt enjoying the children's pleasure as much as their worthy captain"—took the children ashore and returned them safely on board thereafter.[4]

The circus program, which included burlesque, variously skilled artists, and four performing lions, was predominantly equestrian, despite what the poster promised.[5] One can only imagine the reaction of the former captives to this exhibition. This was the first documented, lighthearted moment in the children's lives since their capture. The circus visit may be considered a turning point. The children were changing more than ships; they were turning their backs on their former harrowing lives. Freedom and a new life lay beyond their circus outing.

FIGURE 9.2. Fillis Circus poster for World's Fair, Chicago, 1893 (source: Vintage Circus Collectibles [beginning of Fillis Circus history to 1975]).

Arrival in South Africa

Within days, Captain Warden set sail for East London.

On Tuesday, 19 August 1890, the Reverend William J. B. Moir, a Lovedale mathematics teacher and one-time editor of the *Christian Express*, received a telegram from Durban announcing their imminent arrival:

> [The telegram] was handed to me about ten minutes to one in my class, &
> I fear the boys thought I had suddenly forgot all my geometry, for it was so
> unexpected that it quite confused me. Our arrangements had been made for
> the end of the week at the earliest. The Tuesday afternoon was spent in securing
> that the waggons should start next day, & in getting ready to go myself. I got
> away about 6 a.m. and the waggons got underway an hour later.[6]

Moir reached East London before 16h30 on Wednesday, 20 August 1890. He was surprised to find that the *Conway Castle* had docked more than an hour earlier. Lochhead was still on the quayside finalizing arrangements for their luggage. The Oromo children, however, had already disembarked. Large crowds of East London's citizenry had greeted them with enthusiasm.[7] James Coutts, a leading wool trader and shipping agent, described by R. H. W. Shepherd as a "sympathetic merchant," had generously made one of his large woolsheds available for the occasion, and the organizers had taken the children there.[8]

Moir found the Oromo children making themselves at home in the immense, dimly lit woolshed, enjoying the coffee and cakes members of the East London Presbyterian Church Sunday School had provided. The children were chatting with some of the people who had come to welcome them. However, Moir noted sourly:

> Conversation tended chiefly in two directions—the intelligent look of the
> young people and the possibility of getting any of them for servants. This last
> idea took a strong hold. It applied specially to the girls, of course, who it was
> thought were not so likely to be sent back to the north. It was suggested that
> if more slaves were captured & government had a difficulty in disposing of
> them, they should be sent south to the Colony and apprenticed out to suitable
> applicants for them.[9]

Moir did not record his response.

The Lovedale authorities had arranged for them all to travel by train from East London to King William's Town, an inland town some fifty kilometers away. The Oromo children had never seen a train, let alone traveled on one.[10] Lovedale had arranged for three ox-wagons to be in readiness in King William's Town to carry the children to Lovedale. Moir continued his account: "Now for the first time I really saw the children, and Dr Paterson, who had been with Mr Ferguson overnight. The Railway people took us all up for £3.6.6, a really nominal sum. Of course the railway journey was a great wonder and delight to all. They recognized many things as being like their country—herd boys in skin karosses, huts, the general look of the land, etc."[11]

At King William's Town, James W. Weir (son of one of Lovedale's early missionaries and also a businessman) and his wife provided a meal as well as a place to rest awhile once the children arrived. Moir recorded an awkward moment:

> They sat down in the courtyard of his [Weir's] place & here the only morsel of unpleasantness in the whole journey occurred. A crowd of rude natives—men—gathered round the girls, & discussed them, not too delicately. The moment this was seen, & it was seen at once, we cleared the yard; but the sun was rather strong, and we moved the whole to Xiniwe's former place, now unoccupied, up in the same street as Mr Weir's house. All got under roofs here and were much more sheltered. They got food twice in town, having soup for dinner with their bread.[12]

According to Moir, Paul Xiniwe, a former Lovedale pupil who, in 1890, was the owner of the Temperance Hotel in King William's Town, catered for them:[13] "He led the whole troop two & two down the street & over the Market Square, marching two & two behind him in his crimson jacket, the observed of all observers."[14]

The wagons had reached King William's Town about the same time as the train. As the September evening threatened to be chilly, Moir bought a blanket for each of the sixty-four children from James Weir's store. The missionaries divided the children across the three wagons. Of the first two, one wagon belonged to a Mr. Odendaal (who drove the wagon personally, taking with him twenty of the smaller boys); and the other was owned by a Mr. Mzimba (a large tent wagon, driven by a man named Hani, carrying all the girls). These first two wagons left King William's Town at 15h00. The third wagon, leaving an hour later at 16h00, was an open wagon carrying the remaining twenty-two boys and the missionaries Paterson, Lochhead, and Moir.

Map 9.2 shows the route from East London via King William's Town and Middle-drift (crossing the Keiskamma River) to Lovedale.

The late-winter evening turned out to be more than chilly. When a cold wind sprang up, the blankets were put to good use. At about 18h30, the wagons arrived at Green River, their rendezvous for the night. The wagons were drawn close together on a grassy patch next to the river. The missionaries prepared their evening meal. Moir noted that before eating, "the children all stood up & asked a blessing & after returned thanks. Both at East London & here, they also sang one or two simple English hymns very sweetly, & repeated the Lord's Prayer before going to sleep." The marks of Christian influence are evident in the children's spontaneous appeal for a blessing before their meal and in giving thanks thereafter. They also had by then a sufficient command of English to enable them to sing the hymns and to recite the Lord's Prayer.[15]

After supper, they settled for the night. Some chose to sleep inside the wagons, while other preferred to sleep under the wagons, protected by canvas. The wind dropped and the night was mild although overcast. Moir, Paterson, and Lochhead agreed that one of them should act as guard throughout the night. As Lochhead had had little sleep the previous night in East London, Paterson volunteered.

Moir slept a few hours, but at about 02h00, he joined Paterson on the watch: "We talked over most things connected with the party. . . . They have done the work

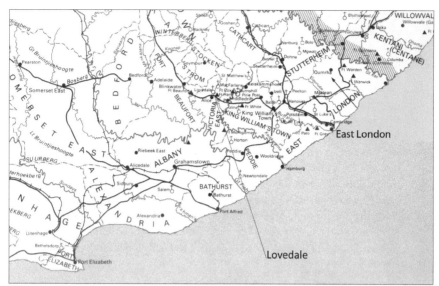

MAP 9.2. Route from East London to Lovedale (source: adapted from J. S. Bergh and J. C. Visagie, *The Eastern Cape Frontier Zone, 1660–1980: A Cartographic Guide for Historical Research* [Durban: Butterworths, 1985], map 23, p. 65).

very well, & with great care & attention to detail. The children were well provided & everything was as tidy & neat as could be, with both boys & girls."[16]

With the first hint of dawn, the missionaries roused the children for a six o'clock start. The plan was to give the children time to wash and have breakfast on the banks of the Keiskamma River, some forty kilometers farther on.

> By 11:30 we were all at the place, and our fires were lit and the tea getting ready. . . . A good many visitors came to see us. Some women helped & one brought a dish of Kaffir corn, for which she got as a return present, our surplus sugar, two or three pounds. All were pleasant & interested. The Kaffir corn [*mielies*] brought many smiles of recognition to the children's faces—"it also grows in our country," they said.[17]

By 13h00 the wagons began the last stage of their journey to Lovedale. Two hours later the two leading wagons reached the institution, with Odendaal's wagon arriving soon after 17h00. A Lovedale student—identified only as "K"—remembered: "I saw [the Oromo children] squatted on the bed planks of the three wagons crossing the [Tyhume] River at Fort Hare as I stood on the Victoria Suspension Bridge one Spring evening so many years ago, on their way to Lovedale."[18] Their journey was done.

Arrival at Lovedale

The question of the Oromo children and preparations for their arrival became "the most absorbing interest of the present time" when word of the rescued children first reached the Lovedale authorities late in the year of 1888.[19] The construction of two buildings—one for the boys and one for the girls—each to bear the name "Galla House"—was well underway by the beginning of 1890. On 5 July 1890, the Reverend William J. B. Moir wrote:

> All the departments are busy working for them, and we shall have temporary
> quarters ready by the time they arrive. The building specially intended for the
> boys is on the way. It will be a plain brick building with stone foundation,
> measuring 50 feet by 32 feet inside. It will be divided into two rooms of equal
> size by a single cross wall carrying fireplaces. The cost will, we hope, not
> exceed, or not much exceed, £400. The temporary accommodation proposed
> for the girls will be of wood, lined in part with sun-dried brick. It will be 36
> feet by 24 feet, also with a simple cross-wall of brick-carrying fireplaces. The
> cost will be about £150. Afterwards, when the extension of the girls' school
> is completed, the Galla girls will be moved into the other buildings, and this
> wooden house will become the outside store and bath-room for the whole
> school.[20]

Moir reported in the same letter that the lady superintendent of the Girls' School, Margaret Muirhead,[21] and her daughter, May,[22] spent their holidays in East London, fostering interest among the local population in the impending arrival of the Oromo children. Within Lovedale itself there was considerable interest, curiosity, anticipation, and excitement among the pupils. Several of them had been selected to assist in receiving and welcoming the children when they arrived.[23]

Margaret Muirhead gave her own account of the arrival of the children at the institution:

> About four in the afternoon Mrs Geddes drove me out some distance to
> meet the party, and we had just crossed the Chumie when we caught sight
> of the waggons. The first waggon brought all the small boys—bright, merry,
> bewitching little fellows.[24] Then Mr Mzimba's, containing all the girls—timid,
> spiritless-looking creatures; then the farm-waggon with the big boys—fine and
> manly-looking. All Alice turned out to have a look at the quaint procession,
> and as we drove Lovedale-ward we met all the European boys and many
> others. Then on crossing the Gaga everybody, native and European, seemed to
> appear—all sorts and conditions of men, women, and children.[25]

Mrs. Muirhead described how, having met up with the wagons, they left the boys at the old wagonmakers' shops while they accompanied the girls to their new premises: "Their waggon drove by the new avenue and halted in front of the sewing-room, where all our girls were assembled. They cheered the new arrivals and rang the bell of welcome. Then they all went into the sewing-room where we had a nice, bright fire, and everything looked so cozy. Baths of hot water were in the room, and each girl was presented with a towel, with which she seemed delighted."[26] Two of the older girls were left to look after the Oromo girls until suppertime. The Oromo girls filed into the hall alongside the other Lovedale girls and took their seats among them for a meal of tea and bread. This was considered a treat as the other girls had to eat their regular "crushed maize."[27]

> Then after supper the red flannel petticoats were produced, and caused us great amusement. It was a bitterly cold night, and the poor things were clad in cotton skirts, rather tight, and loose jackets, with the inevitable handkerchief folded so as to let a corner hang down behind—rather picturesque-looking. Well, the girls who had made the petticoats out of school hours, had written their own names on the tapes, so each possessed herself of her own handiwork, and had the pleasure of presenting the gift to the girl the petticoat fitted. They were delighted. Next a set of dolls was produced (they came in Mrs Hanson's box), and the little ones got a doll each: still more mirth. Then we thought they should go to bed, and we once more adjourned to the sewing-room; but they were very modest, and would not undress till we retired. The baths and hot water were again produced, and they got clean and comfortable to bed; and when we went to see them they all had on flannel night-dresses, which must have come from some kind person in Scotland. They all looked so clean and nice; each had a bag made of canvas, with her own number marked on it, and it contained their requisites, even to a small looking-glass.[28]

Moir, too, documented his impressions of the children on arrival at Lovedale:

> There was much excitement. Everybody was out. The newcomers were almost frightened at their welcome, but the boys very quickly fraternized and finding everybody more than friendly were at ease in an extremely short time. The emotion at the Girls' School was more irrepressible, but we got as many employed as possible in carrying the things from the waggon inside, & gradually they calmed down. The amount of handshaking was worthy of an induction service! The boys were very comfortably housed in the old waggon shop. The girls were put in the sewing room, their own rooms being too wet in the floors, but they took possession of them a few days after.[29]

Several of the Lovedale staff, including Mrs. Muirhead, remarked on the girls being more subdued and unhappy than the boys. Some of them were still less than happy on their first morning at Lovedale:

> This morning they were all up to breakfast and looking less down-trodden than yesterday; but the boys are far happier and brighter and more interesting in appearance than the girls. After breakfast one or two began to cry—they wanted "father"; so it was quite a relief to me when Dr Paterson came down. I sent to Alice for shawls, and each girl got one . . . and they looked happier. Mr Lochhead presented them. I asked Dr Paterson to bring all the boys down in the afternoon (it is not evening), as I thought the girls would feel more at home if they saw them; so the rollicking little chaps all appeared after dinner.

They jumped on the tables, and made such a noise I can't say I was sorry when they took their departure. They look so nice in their jackets and trousers, with bright brass buttons, and very neat round-about caps.[30]

Moir included some further details about the boys, his remarks again underlining the gender differences in their responses: "Next day the Galla boys were as much at home as if they had always been here. They taught our boys their games & their language & played from morning till night. The Girls were shyer but only for a day or two, & have been most kindly treated by the others in every way."[31]

Lovedale personnel consistently remarked on the gender differences in emotion and attitude. The girls were quiet, obedient, shy, and unhappy. The boys, on the other hand, were ebullient, noisy, talkative, merry, and "naughty." The relative ease with which the boys relaxed and engaged with the other Lovedale boys was a mark of their resilience.

The trauma of the first passage left not only an indelible physical impact on the lives of the young Oromo, but also a legacy of psychological trauma that manifested itself differently in the boy's and the girls' behavior. The boys had, by and large, experienced more severe treatment at capture and en route to the coast, endured longer journeys, with a greater number of stopovers, and changed hands more frequently than the girls. Yet their behavior on arrival at Lovedale seemed to belie the severity of the trauma. The boys seemed instead to have sprung back to normality with their spirited and rambunctious behavior.

The girls, on the other hand, demonstrated more evident trauma in their restrained and unhappy demeanor. This could suggest that added to their known first-passage vicissitudes, the silence surrounding any reports of the inevitable sexual abuse they would almost certainly have experienced could have concealed some massive instances of personal trauma. The validity of these opposing behavioral observations is hard to assess. Dominick LaCapra, a historian focusing on trauma studies in the context of historiography, favors a "middle voice" approach to writing about this sort of historical trauma. He advocates the marrying of the "documentary or self-sufficient research model" (as evidenced in this study) with more performative, figurative, and ideological factors to arrive at a heightened sensitivity to the nature, signification, and impact of past trauma—the relationship between empathy and critical analysis.[32]

The children had experienced another kind of journey. This time they had known where they were going and had kindly guardians along the way. Not only had there been ample food, but their wheeled transport had made forced marches a thing of their past. There were no deaths. Instead of a trek into terror, they had journeyed into hope and a new life at Lovedale. The arrival of the Oromo children at Lovedale also signaled a rare, unexpected link between South Africa and Ethiopia during the nineteenth century.

CHAPTER 10

Education at Lovedale

When the Oromo arrived at Lovedale, they constituted a body of sixty-four foreign students who had to fit into a much larger body of scholars in a huge educational establishment.[1] They had to adjust to a new environment, a new language, new customs, and a new curriculum. The Lovedale missionaries were assiduous in documenting the children's time at Lovedale from 1890 to 1900 in school reports, letters, photographs, submissions to missionary newsletters, and, most frequently, in contributions to the regular "Lovedale News" column.

This chapter is in three main parts, consisting of what the children were taught, drawn from existing published syllabi; who taught them, drawn from annual reports; and, finally, their academic progress, drawn from class marks.[2] Together these data enable a satisfactory overview of the Oromo children's scholastic careers within the mission environment.

South African missionary historiography has often been critical of the missionaries, particularly following Dora Taylor's 1952 polemic.[3] Such criticism usually fails to marshal evidence in support of what is argued. The weight of such criticism is in inverse proportion to the evidence presented in support of the argumentation (see page 9 for a discussion of some of these critiques). The following descriptive analysis will examine missionary life as experienced by the Oromo boys and girls.

What Were the Oromo Children Taught at Lovedale?

In 1890, the Oromo, with little cultural preparedness, entered a strange new South African curriculum. However, they had received sound and intensive basic grounding at Sheikh Othman, where they had the advantage of three teachers who were fluent in Oromo to interpret and supplement the teaching of the three Scottish missionaries, Matthew Lochhead, William Gardner, and Alexander Paterson.

Within three months, Lovedale determined that the Oromo children's potential should be independently estimated by the Cape school inspector. The results would

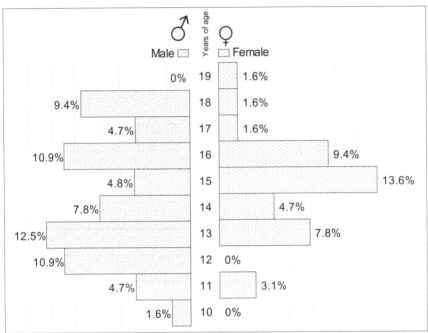

GRAPH 10.1. Ages of Oromo children on arrival at Lovedale, 1890   (source: Sandra Rowoldt Shell).

provide a benchmark by which to place the Oromo children. Paterson modestly hoped most of the Oromo children would pass the first and the second standards, which would allow the Oromo children to be appropriately placed in the mainstream of Lovedale courses and curricula.[4]

Lochhead commented on the early progress of the Oromo boys in his first report to the institution. He maintained that the 1890 inspection was the first time the missionary teachers had a "fair opportunity" to test the children's abilities. In addition, testing them at Lovedale alongside the other pupils in their respective classes would allow the missionaries to evaluate the children's relative performance against their non-Oromo peers: "Having a standard at which to aim was an incentive to diligence and perseverance. The boys and girls being at present mixed in the classes we had also a fair opportunity of testing the relative progress of both," Lochhead said.[5]

One of the first considerations in placing the Oromo children was their age (see graph 10.1). When the children arrived, they ranged from ten to nineteen years. The slightly younger age range of the males (ten to eighteen years) and the heavy clustering of females in the midteen levels was the consequence of slave raiders' preferences at point of capture, with raiders and traders seeking the more highly valued pubescent Oromo girls (see chapter 5, "The Moment of Capture").

Lovedale offered a full range of classes divided into broad schools. Scholars who were not familiar with isiXhosa began in the entry-level Lower Classes (Standards I, II, and III); and the Oromo and children from Lake Nyasa, Bechuanaland, Basutoland, and other African countries fitted into these classes.[6]

The School Department, covering Standards IV through VI, taught scholars in the Teachers' Class (Scripture, English, mathematics, geography, and drawing),[7] as well as the matriculation and School Higher classes.[8] The Intermediate Class in the Normal Department moved scholars forward into the Teachers' Examination. Though the Girls' School offered nothing beyond this point, a few young women studied higher subjects alongside the men. Tolassa Wayessa (narrative 38) and Warkitu Galatu (narrative 64) would both study in the Normal Department on the way to their teaching qualifications.[9]

The Literary Course, spread over three years, aimed at matriculation in the University of the Cape of Good Hope, which was responsible for setting the annual matriculation examinations for all component colleges in the Cape of Good Hope education system to ensure a consistent national standard. The course embraced all the subjects prescribed for the matriculation examination and for the School Higher Certificate, plus logic and the basics of mental and moral science. Tolassa Wayessa, one of the Oromo boys, would matriculate from this class in 1897.[10]

From time to time, Lovedale published the syllabi for each of these schools and classes, with the exception of the lower classes. The entry-level Standard I was where the Oromo children learned the fundamentals of the three R's. In Standard II, the children were taught reading and recitation. Lovedale required that by the end of that year the children be able to read intelligently from their Standard II reader. They should also be able to read twenty lines of poetry with an understanding of the meaning. They learned writing and spelling and were required to be able to write three lines on a slate dictated word by word from the reading book. They were expected to show a completed copybook by year's end, in large and medium hand, including one page of figures. They studied written and mental arithmetic, through which they needed to be able to read and write numbers of not more than seven figures, add six numbers of not more than six figures, subtract one number from another (fewer than seven figures), and divide numbers by any number under thirteen. For mental arithmetic they underwent exercises in addition, subtraction, multiplication, and division, with no figures exceeding 100. Lovedale included basic geography in the Standard II syllabus, by which they were expected to know the main natural features of the country in the locality around the school and the cardinal points. They were to possess the knowledge to draw a plan of their schoolroom and to understand a map of their immediate neighborhood. Their drawing classes taught them to draw lines, angles, and simple boxes with or without the aid of a ruler.[11] This was a secular toolbox of life skills.

Standard III offered the same basics but at a higher standard. Here, the children had to be able to read intelligently from their readers. More challenging, they were required to memorize thirty-two lines of poetry and understand their meaning as well. Lovedale introduced spelling at this level. The children also had to be able to write six lines of dictation from their reading books onto their slates. In addition, the institution introduced simple English grammar and prosody. In arithmetic, the calculations became progressively more demanding. In Standard III, the children must add, subtract, multiply, and divide whole numbers and sums of money using the British denominations of £.s.d. In their geography classes, the children became familiar with a map of the Victoria East Division in which the school was situated, and were required to position this division correctly on a map of the Cape Colony.[12]

By the time the children completed Standard IV, they were expected to read fluently and intelligently from their reading books,[13] one of their histories,[14] and an ordinary narrative from any other source. Classes in English grammar demanded the ability to analyze a simple sentence and to recognize and correct grammatical errors. The number of lines of poetry to recite increased to forty. In arithmetic, new additions to the syllabus included the use of weights and measures and elementary operations using fractions. The first elements of comprehension entered their syllabus at this level under "Composition." They had to reproduce a simple story read to them twice, in ten lines or fewer, testing their summarizing and comprehension skills. Geography gradually extended to embrace the entire Cape Colony and the position of South Africa on the globe. The children learned fundamental facts such as the form of the earth, the planetary reasons for day and night, and understanding the principles of latitude and longitude. Freehand drawing became more complex and included their first exposure to drawing to scale.[15] These skills were by no means narrow and mission-oriented, but rather general knowledge. This is not mentioned by mission critics.

The Standard V curriculum included studies of the Bible (i.e., the four Gospels). Levels of difficulty in their reading and writing requirements advanced progressively, helping the students to learn parsing and analysis.[16] They extended their comprehension and composition skills by doing exercises that included reproducing a short historical narrative after having heard it read twice. At this level, their arithmetic classes introduced the concept of proportion in addition to the growing complexity of both their numerical problem solving and mental arithmetic. In geography the children were taught about the seasons and the fundamentals of map drawing. They also studied the continents of Africa and Europe.[17] Lovedale introduced English history covering the time of the Norman Conquest in 1066 to the battle of Bosworth and the ushering in of the Tudor dynasty in 1485.[18] The scholars also studied "the early period" of the Cape, covering the time up to the arrival of the British settlers in 1820.[19]

Scholars in the Standard VI class had to be able to read fluently and intelligently from their reading books, to recite eighty lines of poetry, and to understand the poems' meanings and allusions. In arithmetic, the scholars learned about decimal fractions, the calculation of percentages (including interest), and the mensuration of rectangular surfaces and solids. Their English grammar classes trained them to analyze a complex prose sentence containing at least two subordinate clauses. They were required to learn parsing, error detection, and the meanings of prefixes and suffixes. In their composition classes, the students wrote a business letter on a given topic. Geography at this level included climate, winds, and rainfall. Scholars learned about the remaining continents and had to draw maps from memory. They studied English history from 1485 to 1688 and Cape history from the 1820 settlement to date. Their drawing classes taught them how to create freehand and geometrical drawings and to draw from models. In addition, in trade classes the boys trained as artisans in fields as diverse as woodworking and carpentry, printing and bookbinding, shoemaking, wagon-building, and agriculture.

Girls prepared for domestic service by learning to sew, clean, and cook.[20] Feminist critics may find fault with the missionary focus on the training of young women for domestic work. However, a more complex analysis of missionary motive may indicate that in so doing, the missionaries were intentionally emancipating young women from agricultural labor.[21]

Lovedale positioned the Oromo children (following their placement exam) in this complex, multilevel class structure and the various streams to accommodate different levels of preparedness and talent.

Integration

Natasha Erlank, a historian writing of missions in the Eastern Cape, maintains that missionaries were influenced by anti-African propaganda generated from the tussle between settler and amaXhosa for land and labor, as well as the legacy of animosity in the wake of the frontier wars. By the end of the century, she believes, the missionaries had absorbed these views, alongside social Darwinian perceptions of racial inferiority, "which meant that a perception of racial equality was less a possibility for [missionaries] at the end of the century."[22] A former Lovedale student, on the other hand, a contemporary of the Oromo children who signed himself only as "K," emphasized the radical racial integration he experienced at Lovedale: "Here I found sixty other students in the same classroom, both Europeans and Natives. There was no discrimination, we were pupils to be taught Education and that was the first consideration of our Teacher."[23]

André Germond, who was in charge of the Lower Classes catering largely to scholars from beyond South Africa's borders, remarked on the level of integration in his own classes: "As regards class work, I have perhaps more than any other teacher, a variety of nations amongst my pupils. There are English, Gallas, Kaffirs, Dutch, Bechuana and Lake Nyassa lads."[24] This personal evidence of the lack of discrimination on the basis of skin color at Lovedale gainsays Erlank's assertion of growing racial divides in mission environments in the late nineteenth century. The Oromo were deeply integrated into Lovedale's education system and were distributed among nearly all the classes. Initially, there were one or two classes tagged specifically for the Oromo, for example, the Galla trade class.[25] As the Oromo children's English skills and general acclimatization developed, the need for such special provisions fell away.

Who Taught the Oromo Children?

Matthew Lochhead and Alexander Paterson accompanied the Oromo children to Lovedale and shared the teaching—two classes each—during their initial year. Lochhead had charge of the boys, Paterson of the girls. William J. B. Moir tried to encourage Paterson to take some of the higher work, "but he would not do so."[26] Moir did not elaborate on Paterson's reasons for this reluctance, seemingly so out of step with missionary commitment. As the Foreign Missions Committee of the Free Church of Scotland no longer had funding to sustain both Lochhead and Paterson at Lovedale, both positions were

FIGURE 10.1. Oromo boys at Lovedale shortly after their arrival, ca. 1890 (source: Library of Parliament, 41866 [iv] 13).

due to be terminated for reasons of finance and redeployment. Thomas M. Lindsay, convenor of the Foreign Missions Committee of the Free Church of Scotland, wrote to Paterson on 24 January 1891 regarding Paterson's intention to relocate to the mission in Cairo, Egypt.[27] After Margaret Muirhead, the lady superintendent of the Girls' School, who had been closely involved with the Oromo girls from their arrival, died, her daughter, May, married Paterson and the couple left the institution the same day, leaving Lochhead to carry the primary responsibility for the Oromo children.[28]

Lindsay later wrote to Lochhead, in June 1892, explaining that there was no more money to retain his services at Lovedale and that the committee would, reluctantly, have to let him go.[29] Lochhead's time at Lovedale also came to a sudden and dramatic end a few months later, for on 1 October 1892, the *Christian Express* ran a front-page article with the headline "A Sad Admission," announcing that the Lovedale authorities had declared Lochhead guilty of "a serious charge of immorality." The nature of his misdemeanor is disclosed neither in the article nor elsewhere in the Lovedale archives:

> Against an assistant teacher—who was temporarily employed, and not on the permanent staff,—there was brought lately a serious charge of immorality. . . . It is but right to state that he has all along solemnly protested his innocence. But in the face of evidence on the other side, this protestation cannot be received. It is now intimated, that his connection with the mission has formally ceased, as it did practically when the charge was made; he having left the place at the same date. No comment is needed to express our sense of this disaster, for such we cannot help regarding it.[30]

Lochhead's name and deeds were expunged from Lovedale annals after 1892 except for an oblique, anonymized allusion to the incident in R. H. W. Shepherd's centenary history of the institution: "Very unfortunately, in connection with the Gallas, there was a happening that plunged Lovedale into shame. To the grief of Dr Paterson, his teacher colleague, who came with them from Aden, betrayed his trust and was guilty of gross immorality among the Gallas."[31] What is curious is that none of the Oromo children who mentioned Lochhead in their letters written on 20 October 1892 to Mrs. Mina Stewart (James Stewart's wife) displayed any animosity toward him or knowledge of the scandal. Gamaches Garba wrote about staff comings and goings: "Now Dr Stewart was going away from us. We are very sorry because Mr Geddes was going always from us only Mr Moir was left with us another which we was last they are left us Dr Paterson and Mr Lochhead and Mr Geddes and Mrs Geddes all these are left us in Lovedale."[32]

On the same day, Fayissa Hora wrote: "Mr Lochhead is not with us, and all his things had been take away and were in Alice and I think he is Pietermaritzburg Now. Your loving friend, Fayissa Hora."[33] Bayan Liliso, writing to Mina Stewart two years later in September 1894, alluded in passing to Lochhead: "I think most of the people have read our Biography [sic] which was written by Mr Lochhead when he was still with us here. If not perhaps Mr Moir has got the copy of it perhaps he will give it to you."[34] Far from censuring Lochhead, Bayan implicitly applauds his efforts in documenting and publishing their experiences, to the point of recommending that Mina Stewart try to acquire a copy through William J. B. Moir.

Several other boys wrote letters, undoubtedly as part of a classroom exercise, but none mentioned their former teacher.[35] Can this silence be construed as censure? Or could it simply demonstrate the reticence of commissioned classroom letters written to the wife of the institution's principal? Or maybe the children simply did not know that Lochhead had been dismissed, let alone the reason for his dismissal. Or does this newly discovered, uncaptioned photograph from the Library of Parliament in Cape Town hold a clue (see fig. 10.1)?

This is the first photograph of the Oromo boys after their arrival at Lovedale in 1890, with Lochhead seated in the middle. Victorian missionary sensitivities might have recoiled at the affectionate familiarity of the young boy's hands on Lochhead's shoulders. However innocent, this was a rare public display of intimacy in that closeted era. So keen was Lovedale on erasure that they skillfully doctored this photograph for use by Robert Young in his book *African Wastes Reclaimed* ten years later (see fig. 10.2).[36]

Only careful scrutiny revealed the telltale shadow around Geddes's head indicating the careful excision and cutout replacement of the image.

With the departure in quick succession of the two Sheikh Othman missionaries who had charge of the Oromo children, responsibility for the Oromo children now fell directly on the Lovedale staff. Chief among the staff, and much trusted, respected, and loved by the Oromo children, was Alexander Geddes, the boarding master at Lovedale. The children called him Abba, meaning "Father."[37] William J. B. Moir, reputedly a kindly man, taught the Oromo children English literature, including poetry. He de-

FIGURE 10.2. Oromo boys at Lovedale shortly after their arrival, ca. 1890 (same photo as 10.1, with Lochhead replaced by Alexander Geddes; source: Library of Parliament, 41866 [iv] 13; and Robert Young, *African Wastes Reclaimed: Illustrated in the Story of the Lovedale Mission* [London: Dent, 1902], facing page 198).

termined that by the end of 1890, some of the Oromo children would be able to join the regular Standard III classes. Moir reported in a letter written in early September 1890 that he regarded them all as diligent and that some of them had already made considerable progress in English.[38] André Germond (son of the Paris Evangelical Society missionary Paul Germond, in what was then Basutoland) was in charge of and taught the Oromo in the Lower Classes. He had a high regard for the ability and diligence of the Oromo scholars. Alexander Paterson believed the Oromo girls' women teachers contributed in considerable part to their rapid progress from 1891 onward. Miss M. J. Dodds, head of the Girls' School; Miss F. J. Barnley, the principal teacher in the Girls' School; and Mrs. J. A. Bennie, head of the Industrial Department in the Girls' School, taught and cared for the Oromo girls in those early years at Lovedale, with good results.

First Inspection

Gender differences marked every aspect of the Oromo children's experiences, and their education and academic progress were no exception. The results of the inspection examination, which took place only three months after the Oromo children arrived, are presented in the following graph (10.2). The pass marks, which were aggregated figures for the whole class, reveal a low average for the general population of the institution. The Oromo children, however, performed much better, especially given their recent arrival and the ordeal of their enslavement. The graph shows clearly that the average for the non-Oromo children over the ten-year period was only 37.3 percent. The Oromo scored 77.4 percent—the boys achieving a spectacular 86.0 percent, while the girls were behind with 54.5 percent. The girls' relatively poor showing could have been influenced by the emotional trauma of the first passage and all the subsequent changes in their lives. Clearly by the time they arrived at Lovedale they were severely

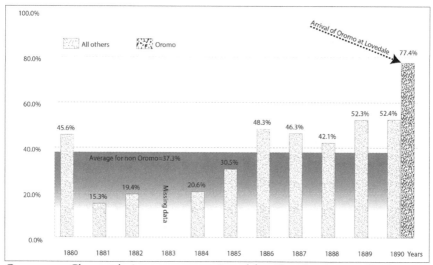

GRAPH 10.2. Class marks in percentages at Lovedale, 1880–1890 (source: Sandra Rowoldt Shell).

traumatized, with little will or strength to apply themselves fully to their schooling. Reinforcing perceptions of their lack of will, Paterson remarked on how listless they had been on their arrival at Lovedale in August 1890.[39]

Margaret Muirhead, who had been closely involved with the preparations for the children's arrival and took care of them at Lovedale in their first few months, described the girls as "timid, spiritless-looking creatures" on their first evening.[40] The next morning they were still tearful, and the girls remained quiet and withdrawn for several weeks. During those first few months, Paterson remarked that they were passive and unresponsive— almost "taciturn"—in class.[41] They took longer to acclimatize than the Oromo boys, and their distress partly explains their poor performance.

Academic Progress

Individual class scores inform the sets of graphs that follow. Using the 1,053 class marks over their core years at Lovedale, clear patterns of progress and gendered differences emerge more precisely. The paneled histograms below (graph 10.3) demonstrate the different patterns for the Oromo males and females compared with the other males and female scholars at Lovedale. Despite the false start of the Oromo girls, they made rapid progress in the following years.

Lochhead noted the Oromo boys' prowess and promise in the industrial and other class departments as early as his first report to the institution in January 1891: "In the Industrial Department they have not been behind, and although many of them prefer play to work,—what boy would not?—they have shown intelligence and smartness which are promising features in young artisans. This is the opinion of the managers of the various departments."[42]

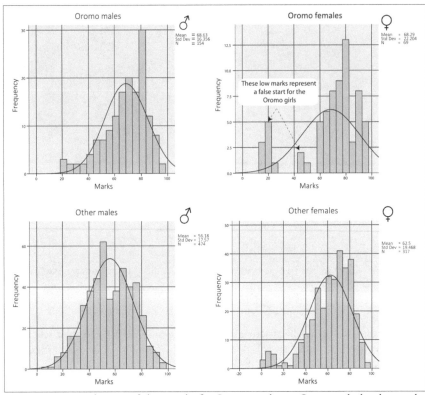

GRAPH 10.3. Distribution of class marks for Oromo and non-Oromo scholars by gender (source: Sandra Rowoldt Shell).

The same data are rendered differently in the following group of box plots (graph 10.4), which give the results sorted by gender and by Oromo and non-Oromo scholars. The box plots are oriented around the quartiles and the median rather than the mean. Note the higher median of the Oromo girls' scores and the higher second and third quartile range. Conversely, the non-Oromo boys came off a low base in their first quartile, with one quarter of them achieving class scores between 10 percent and 45 percent. Non-Oromo girls had a handful of low-scoring outliers in the 20 percent to 30 percent range, but generally ranked above their male counterparts.

In short, the Oromo children, males and females, were quickly establishing themselves and, moreover, taking the lead at Lovedale.

Nowhere is their excellent progress more noticeable than in the number of top class positions they achieved over the three to four core years for which we have data. The following bar chart (graph 10.5) shows how the Oromo children dominated the top ten class positions. They achieved higher class positions than could have been anticipated, as can be seen by the juxtaposition of the statistically generated expected

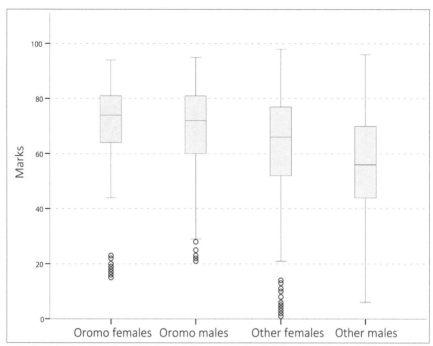

GRAPH 10.4. Marks of Oromo and other Lovedale scholars by gender of child (source: Sandra Rowoldt Shell).

counts. The liberated children were ahead of all expected values until reaching the eighth class position.

Lochhead, in his 1891 report on the children, appreciated the Oromos' diligence and commitment to hard work, commenting on the reluctance of the children to take time off for the Christmas break. He also recalled the children's surprise at being told at the Keith-Falconer Mission that they would be able to enjoy an end-of-year holiday from school in 1889: "They have not yet got the length of appreciating holidays and have asked for their books for next session so as to study while the classes are closed. Last Christmas also, in Aden when we intimated a few days' holidays, they asked their teachers what they wanted holidays for!"[43] The Oromo had been given a second chance, and they made the most of their time at Lovedale.

Paterson, in his own January 1891 report, commented on the progress of the twenty-two Oromo girls, whom he considered to have improved even more noticeably than the boys in the few months they had been at Lovedale. He attributed this improvement in part to the influence of Lovedale's female teachers, including Dodds, Barnley, and Bennie, who both taught and cared for them. The newfound contact with other girls, the routine of domestic duty, and the impact of overall superintendence had provided, Paterson believed, the essential structure and impetus that had

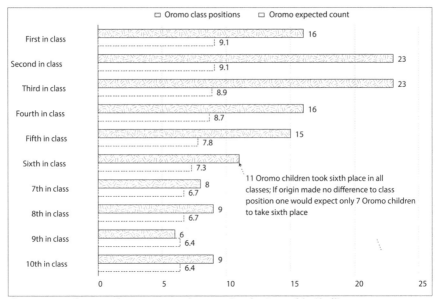

GRAPH 10.5. Oromo class positions (source: Sandra Rowoldt Shell).

been lacking from their young lives: "No doubt their docility and frank and easy manner—except perhaps occasionally in school—and their naturally tidy habits have lent themselves to training and thus afforded early marks of improvement." By the end of the year, he was able to report a further favorable transformation from their former "ill-favoured condition" into "fat and healthy-looking" children whose bearing was steadily becoming "sprightly and vigorous." Physical exercise and care-free romping and playing, he believed, were also largely responsible for this progress. However, he pointed to a further factor, which was the role of their South African peers who had been "attracted into displaying a genuine interest in initiating their exiled companions into their new life and ways," further evidence of the level of integration at Lovedale.[44]

Paterson also remarked that the girls' earlier taciturnity was "giving way to a franker and freer manner but is probably responsible in some measure for the apparent mental superiority of the cleverer boys. With some exceptions they are diligent in the prepara-tion of home-lessons and almost at any hour may be seen poring over book or slate." Paterson included in his report a vivid description of the girls in their Sunday best: "On Sundays they present a very attractive appearance, in white flannel dresses with red sashes and white straw hats trimmed to match. The kerchiefs and print frocks which most are familiar with in the photographs, have been relegated to every day wear."[45]

The following photograph (fig. 10.3), the first of the girls after their arrival at Love-dale, shows them in their Sunday best—but still barefoot. Note that the girl at the back has her hands on the shoulders of the Oromo girl seated in the row in front of

FIGURE 10.3. Oromo girls in their Sunday best at Lovedale, ca. 1892 (source: Library of Parliament, 41866 [iv] 17).

her (one of her female peers), a stance reminiscent of the photograph of the boys with the later-excised Matthew Lochhead. However, those who excised Lochhead from the picture did not make any attempt to replace the boy's hands on Geddes's shoulders (this would have been technically possible by slotting the cutout of Geddes behind that of the boy's hands). The missionaries did not do this, which could confirm their censure of the public display of intimacy between the Oromo boy and a male teacher. In Lochhead's case, the serious same-sex factor was compounded by the difference in status (teacher/pupil and possibly race).

Reporting on the progress of all the Oromo scholars in their report for 1892, Lovedale commented on their "steady and in every way encouraging progress. . . . In book work, they are almost without exception, attentive and intelligent."[46] André Germond, heading the Lower Classes, was acutely aware of Oromo scholastic ascendancy. In 1892 he wrote, "During the course of the session, it was easy enough to notice that the most satisfactory boys were those from distant countries, such as Gallas, Bechuanas, and Nyassa boys."[47] All of these were boarders, which might also explain their growing competence. According to the same 1892 annual report, the Lovedale boarders included seven boys from Nyasaland (Malawi); five boys from Bechuanaland (one being Sekhoma/Sekgoma II, son of Khama III, who would become king of the Bamangwato people of Botswana); and one boy from Matabeleland (in today's Zimbabwe).[48]

Natasha Erlank has written that "most converts were socially peripheral to Xhosa society, but maintained links with their chiefs while treating mission stations as spaces that were part of their annual cattle-grazing circuits."[49] This was hardly the case at Lovedale during the last decade of the nineteenth century. The Oromo children took

FIGURE 10.4. Samuel Edward Krune Mqhayi (source: adapted from S. E. K. Mqhayi, Wikimedia Commons).

their places in class alongside several South African children whose names would become well known in households across the nation, a cross section of twentieth-century African political leaders and intelligentsia. Lovedale was in that era the leading missionary educational institution in the country, with the reputation of nurturing and training many of the country's future leaders across a wide array of fields.

Celebrated Xhosa poet, novelist, and historian Samuel Edward Krune Mqhayi (see fig. 10.4), was in the Standard VI class in 1894. He ranked eighteenth in the class with 59 percent, behind five Oromo boys: Shamo Ayanso, who was first with 88 percent; Liban Bultum, second with 79 percent; Gutama Tarafo, ninth with 73 percent; Bayan Liliso, eleventh with 69 percent; and Nuro Chabse, sixteenth with 62 percent.[50]

The familiar family names of Balfour, Bokwe, Mabandla, Matshikiza, Mqhayi, Mzimba, Sekgoma II, Tywakadi, Tyamzashe, Wauchope, and many others dot the pages of Lovedale's academic records during the Oromo period.[51]

Morbidity and Mortality at Lovedale

While Lochhead could report with discernible relief that the Oromo children experienced vastly improved health after they had settled down at Lovedale in comparison with their time at the Keith-Falconer Mission, the group remained susceptible to changes in climate, diet, infections, and endemic diseases after his departure. His remarks were too sanguine.

The best summary of the Oromo mortality experience can be found in the following two Gantt graphs, which chart all phases of their lives (the Oromo males are represented in graph 10.6; the Oromo females are represented in graph 10.7). The graphs, of course, cannot convey the pathos of their individual deaths, but the missionaries wrote movingly about each loss.

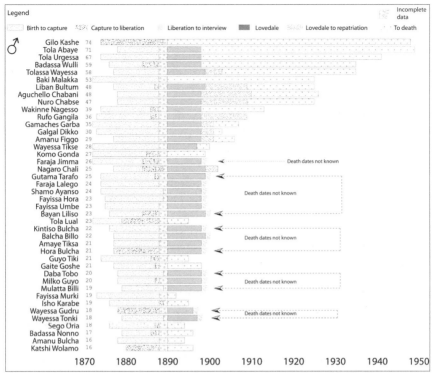

GRAPH 10.6. Mortality of the Oromo boys (source: Sandra Rowoldt Shell).

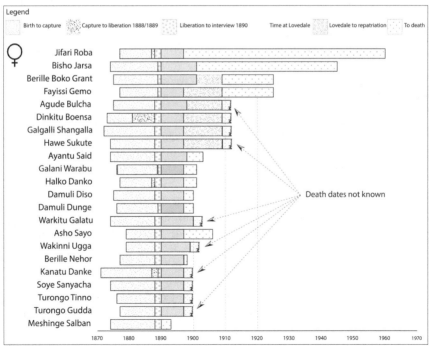

GRAPH 10.7. Mortality of the Oromo girls (source: Sandra Rowoldt Shell).

On 30 September 1892, death claimed its first Oromo victim when one of the girls, Meshinge Salban, died of an acute chest infection at an estimated age of seventeen years.[52] Meshinge was an orphan, her mother having died when she was young and her father when she was about fourteen years old. She was reared by her father's principal wife until she was seized by slave raiders from Gojjam. From her account it would seem that although the time from her capture to the Red Sea was relatively short, she nonetheless had to endure being sold five times en route. She did not report falling ill along the way, being beaten, or being otherwise badly treated.

Three months later, an Oromo boy, Fayissa Yadatta Murki, died after "a long and painful illness" at an estimated eighteen years of age, casting a shadow on Christmas Day, 1892. Fayissa had been ill for several months prior to his death. Gamaches Garba wrote about Meshinge's death and Fayissa's illness in his letter to Mina Stewart: "Now we are very sorry boy this time our sister was which we came with him left us in this world she was dead now two weeks ago at this time. Dr Stewart was here in Lovedale another one Galla boy was very sick by this time. Now Goodbye my dear mother, I am, Your truely [*sic*], Gamaches Garba."[53]

A second Oromo boy, Amanu Bulcha, died on 20 November 1894. According to his class record for the second session of 1894, his natural ability had been fair, he was a "nice, quiet boy, earnest and painstaking in his work," he had displayed good diligence and attention, and he had been a volunteer in Lovedale's Student Volunteer Missionary movement. However, "he was but little in the classroom this session being absent through illness. He died Nov. 20th [1894]."[54] Amanu was about seventeen years old when he died.

Three Oromo boys—Sego Oria, Tola Lual, and Isho Karabe—died during 1895. The date and the cause of Sego Oria's death are not known, but he would have been approximately sixteen years old when he died. In the summer of 1895, several Oromo children fell ill and, to facilitate their recuperation, the Lovedale authorities decided— in desperation—to send them to East London, where they hoped the sea air would restore them to health. On 14 March 1895, Wayessa Tikse wrote to James Stewart from the Kennaway Hotel, Union Street, in East London:

> My Dear Father: I am very glad to write you a few lines this morning & tell about the boys. All the boys are feeling well. Their faces are pretty good-looking very good. I daresay they do not like to go back to Lovedale at present. Tola Lual also a little better, but he use to get a little fever at the 11th hour. . . .
> We did enjoyed our-selves with a picnic whole day, except Tola was not. Mr Ferguson was wondering about us because he was waiting for all of the Galla children to come down he did not thought of us that we are come for a present. So he want us very much to come down during the holiday time. . . . The Rev. W.B. Rubusana asked us to go to Location on Tuesday evening there was a especially meeting & we went down to Location & spoke to the natives there two of us Faraja Jimma & myself & many confessing, or repentances was made amongst them. Tola Lual said that he is feeling tired of

that waggon's shaking so he told me to tell you If please kindly keep him for another week. I think as he said he is improofing if he can get another week to keep him more. Of course Dear Father I can stay with him as far as you want him stay. I am quite willing to do so. Please dearest Father answer him with telegraphy or letter please. Goodbye dear Father. God may comfort with all your friends.[55]

Tola never returned to Lovedale. In June, a brief news item in the *Christian Express* recorded his death on Friday, 17 May 1895, after suffering "much from a long and trying illness which he bore with great patience." Tola was about twenty years old at the time of his death and had proved to be, according to the writer of the report, "a quiet industrious Galla boy, and an influence for good among his companions."[56] Evidence of this surfaced early in his time at Lovedale when he and Shamo Ayanso were appointed as the institution's "postmen" during 1891.[57]

Lovedale reported on the death of sixteen-year-old Isho Karabe, who died at two o'clock in the morning on 31 October 1895 after an illness lasting many months. The report states that he was "a boy of good character and manifested great interest in his work."[58] The story of his early life was one of the more distressing accounts. An orphan reared by his uncle, Isho was abducted by a stranger who tied his hands behind his back in an effort to restrain him. The king of the region happened to be passing by and heard Isho's cries for help. The king stopped, demanded Isho's release, and sent the unsuccessful kidnapper to prison. He then gave Isho away to one of his chiefs. Desperate to escape, Isho took a spear one evening and tried to run away. He was unsuccessful in his escape bid and was taken captive again. Some time later he was purchased by a group of merchants from Nopa, whereafter he was sold five or more times before Adal merchants took him to Rahayta. When the Royal Navy boarded an abandoned slave dhow in the Red Sea in August 1889, the only person they found on board was Isho, lying terrified beneath sacks of rice. The crew took him to Aden and then to the Keith-Falconer Mission.

Guyo Tiki also died during 1895, at about eighteen years of age. Only three years earlier he had penned a letter, at the urging of his teacher André Germond, to Mina Stewart, which focused on the death of Meshinge Salban and makes poignant reading: "My dear Mrs Stewart, . . . are all well boys all well (one) Except one of Galla girls she is gone way from us on Septeber [sic] 20 she is died and God keep us Jesus Chist [sic] didd [died] for all the people for me. . . . [Tiki]."[59]

Badassa Nonno and Katshi Wolamo both died during 1896. Little is known about Badassa after he arrived at Lovedale, beyond his letter to Mina Stewart in October 1892: "Lovedale, 20th October 1892. Now Mrs Bergh is sick and one of the Galla boy Fayisa Morke Gadatta.[60] There are 6 Nyessa [Nyasa] boys now. Dr Love bring 4 of them and now there are two of them came already. Now I must say thank-you for all your kindness to me. Your loving boy, Badassa Nonno."[61]

The Lovedale annual report for 1896 recorded that seventeen-year-old Badassa died "after a long time of weakness and suffering," but the nature of his affliction is not divulged. While Badassa's death was almost inevitable, that of another boy, Katshi

Wolamo, came with little warning. According to the same report, "Katshi's death was at the end, very unexpected."[62] Katshi was a year younger than Badassa, dying at the estimated age of sixteen. Four years earlier he, too, had responded to André Germond's instruction to write to Mina Stewart:

> Lovedale, 20th October [1892], My Dr Mrs Stewart: I was very glad you sent me close [clothes] for all Galla boys and Galls Grils [sic]. I am very sorrow you gone away from Lovedale to see Mrs Geddes and Misses Geddes and Willie Geddes. I can['t] right a very long letter because I dont I know English. If you know Galla I write to you in Galla. I am your loving boy, Kache Wolamo.[63]

There is a curious report in one of Lovedale's sporadic updates on the activities of the Oromo that Gaite Goshe was living and working in King William's Town in 1898.[64] If this was indeed so, he must have left Lovedale to take up a carpentry or other position in King William's Town late in 1897 or very early in 1898. One can only speculate that he fell ill very soon after making this move and, with no one to take care of him, he returned to Lovedale. Gaite, who had earlier been apprenticed in the Lovedale carpentry department, died in March 1898, reportedly "after a severe illness."[65]

Komo Gonda was described as one of two invalids remaining at Lovedale at the beginning of 1898, Gilo Kashe being the other. At the time of this report, Komo was still able to do a little work in Lovedale's shoemaking department, having begun his training in the trade in 1897.[66] Lovedale recorded that he had "long been in poor health" by the time he eventually died on 15 March 1899. His post office savings bank account registered a nineteen-shilling credit in the record of his liquidation and distribution account. In the absence of any family or any other beneficiaries, this amount was paid from his estate to Alexander Geddes of Lovedale—a poignant footnote to Komo's lonely life and death.

In the same year, Asho Sayo finally gave up her fight for life. She was lame when she arrived at Lovedale, and, over the years, her condition—probably multiple sclerosis—deteriorated steadily, robbing her of one faculty after another. Within a few years, she became almost totally paralyzed. She then progressively lost her hearing and, finally, a year or two prior to her death, her sight. In the closing years of her debilitating disease, she could communicate only through manual sign language. She eventually died on 17 April 1899.[67] By all accounts, Asho had a special place in everyone's heart and several wrote affectionately about her, including David Hunter,[68] and the anonymous author of the account of her funeral service, conducted by the Reverend John Lennox and attended by the Lovedale staff and students of the whole institution. According to this account, Asho was "wonderfully patient, and cheerful. She seldom complained even when suffering great pain and discomfort. Indeed none could see her without being rebuked by the patience of the blind, deaf girl. Asho was also very unselfish. She was always thinking of others, and remembering all who had ever been kind to her."[69] She was buried, along with the other Oromo who had died, in the Lovedale graveyard.

This raises the questions: How did this high percentage compare with the rest of the students at Lovedale during the same period? What were the comparative

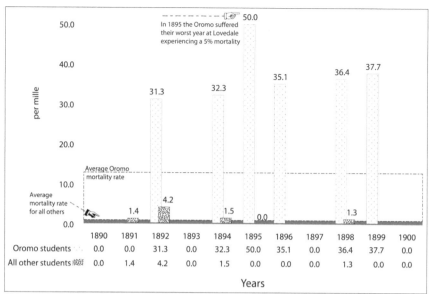

GRAPH 10.8. Mortality rates of Oromo and non-Oromo students, 1891–1899 (source: Sandra Rowoldt Shell).

mortality rates? Table 10.1 (see page 150) illustrates the comparative mortality rate between the Oromo and their non-Oromo peers at Lovedale. The year-on-year death tallies varied from zero for both groups to a dramatic contrast in 1895, when the mortality rate for the Oromo students was 50 per thousand. This stark difference demonstrates the long-term deleterious impact of the Oromos' enslavement and first-passage experiences as evidenced in the early deaths of these young people.

In all, thirteen (or 20.31 percent) of the original sixty-four Oromo children died during the ten years they spent at Lovedale.[70] Graph 10.8 illustrates the comparative mortality rate between the Oromo and their non-Oromo peers at Lovedale.

Reliable scientific demographic data for the Cape of Good Hope were scarce prior to the census of 1891. The data presented in the two earlier censuses of 1865 and 1875 were rudimentary, and no state machinery was put in place to collect, record, and analyze the nation's vital statistics until the 1890s. The census published in 1891 registered the arrival of the sixty-four Oromo children, who at that time constituted the entire "Abyssinian" segment of the Cape population. The next census was scheduled for 1901, but publication was delayed due to the exigencies of the Anglo-Boer War. When this census finally appeared in 1904, the attrition experienced by the Oromo was recorded in the diminished Abyssinian total of fifty-one for the colony. Charles Simkins, an economist, and Elizabeth van Heyningen, a historian, computed and analyzed these census data and presented crude death rates for the component years against which the Lovedale and Oromo data for 1891–1901 may be ranked.[71]

TABLE 10.1. Comparative crude death rates, 1891–1901

Date	Simkins: Cape of Good Hope: crude death rate	Lovedale: Oromo mortality rate	Lovedale: non-Oromo mortality rate
1891 – 1896	15.6	24.8	1.2
1896 –1901	14.7	18.4	0.4
Average	15.2	21.6	0.8

Sources: Charles Simkins and Elizabeth van Heyningen, "Fertility, Mortality, and Migration in the Cape Colony, 1891–1904," International Journal of African Historical Studies 22, no. 1 (1989); Oromo database; and Lovedale annual reports.

While the non-Oromo component of the Lovedale student population registers a notably low mortality rate, the mortality rate of the Oromo children demonstrates the heavy toll of their first-passage experiences on their young lives.

After Lovedale

Between 1891 and 1895, fifty-one (79.6 percent) of the Oromo students were baptized into the Free Church of Scotland. Over half (54.0 percent) of the thirteen who died before 1900 had been baptized. From 1895 to 1898, thirteen of the Oromo were admitted to full membership of the church.[72] After spending six years at the institution, the young adult Oromo began leaving Lovedale to fend for themselves. During 1896–1897, ten boys left in search of employment and new, independent lives.[73] Despite the option of Lovedale's Theological Course for aspirant African ministers of religion, none of the Oromo opted for a career in the church, unlike Fred Morton's "Bombay Africans," who supplied the Church Missionary Society with nearly all of their African teachers and evangelists in East Africa.[74] Only two are known to have retained strong links to the church post-Lovedale; both were women and both trained as teachers: Warkitu Galatu, who took up a teaching position at the Free Church Mission School at Macfarlan, near Lovedale;[75] and Bisho Jarsa, who became a teacher in Cradock, some 160 kilometers northwest of Lovedale.[76]

At Lovedale, Bisho Jarsa trained initially in the girls' work department, where she learned to sew, wash, and iron. However, she had no intention of being confined to domestic service. Instead, she had set her sights on training as a teacher.[77] By May 1899, three young women remained at Lovedale: Bisho, Berille Boko, and the only other female trainee teacher, Warkitu Galatu.[78]

In August 1903, Lovedale polled the former captives by distributing questionnaires nationwide asking them if they would wish to return home if offered a subsidized passage. Bisho completed and returned her questionnaire on 15 September 1903, giving her address as c/o Mr. S. Walstroom in Cradock, and saying, "I am on duty at present,

FIGURE 10.5. Berille Boko at Lovedale, ca. 1898 (source: detail from BC 106, C.254.19, James Stewart Papers, University of Cape Town Manuscripts and Archives).

[I would] rather remain [a] few years longer." She included a letter to the principal with her response:

> I have received the copy of the information and I found myself in great difficulty, as to what to decide, being quite ignorant of the news before this time. I came to Cradock at the end of last year and I am teacher, as an assistant teacher. When I left Lovedale I was not full certificated, therefore since I began teaching I see the necessity of having full certificate, so I have engaged myself to work up for it while teaching or else I could not see any other way of getting it, so I am on duty at present. I am not able to give my wish of returning to Abyssinia at present year. Moreover, I like to know the detail of the conditions of returning. I rather wait few years and have more experience. So if it will be God's will to have me do something, to show my gratitude to Him. I am willing when the way is clear. Please be kind enough to let me know a little of the news if possible. I am quite interested to hear. I shall fill [in] my address and occupation.[79]

In 1911, Bisho married fellow Lovedalian Reverend Frederick Scheepers, a minister in the Congregational Union of South Africa (CUSA) in Port Elizabeth.[80] One of their children was a daughter named Dimbiti Bisho Scheepers. Dimbiti, following in her mother's footsteps, became a teacher and later married a carpenter from Cradock named David James Alexander. Their first son, born in Cradock on 22 October 1936, was Neville Edward Alexander. After his schooling at Holy Rosary Convent in Cradock, Neville entered the University of Cape Town, where he earned a BA in 1955, his honor's degree in 1956, and a master's degree in German. He won an Alexander von

FIGURE 10.6. Bisho Jarsa at Lovedale, ca. 1898 (source: detail from BC 106, C.254.19, James Stewart Papers, University of Cape Town Manuscripts and Archives).

Humboldt Foundation fellowship, Germany's premier scholarship; and a place in the University of Tübingen, where he gained his PhD in German literature in 1961. From 1964 to 1974, Neville was imprisoned on Robben Island (concurrently with Nelson Mandela)[81] for his antiapartheid activities. After Neville's release, he emerged as one of South Africa's leading intellectuals, recognized as a scholar of linguistic theory and a noted educationalist. He believed passionately in education, linguistic diversity, justice, and equality. He publicly denounced both racism and xenophobia vehemently and specifically rejected "race" as a biological concept. Instead, he dealt with notions of color, caste, class, and identities in developing "an indigenous theory of knowledge about humanity's genealogy and evolving consciousness."[82]

Neville Alexander directed the Project for the Study of Alternative Education in South Africa (PRAESA) in the University of Cape Town's education department, focusing on the fundamental need for mother-tongue education in a multilingual South African society, until he died of cancer on 27 August 2012. Despite his impressive stature as an intellectual and activist, he was noted for his compassion and humility.[83]

For the Oromo children entering adulthood, the bulk of their young lives had been dominated by captivity and institutionalization. As they reached maturity, the urge to strike out on their own would have been compelling. For these children, their education constituted a springboard for redemption and independence. Given their troubled pasts, several foreign environments, daunting syllabi, and a new language, the Oromo children performed extraordinarily well. Through the education Lovedale

FIGURE 10.7. Dr. Neville Alexander in 2008 (photo courtesy of Dr. Neville Alexander).

gave her, Bisho was able to realize her personal freedom and potential, and to achieve her ambitions as a teacher. In an interview with the BBC in 2011, Neville declared that Bisho's "real liberation was not the British warship but the education she later received in South Africa."[84] His insight could apply not only to Bisho but to all the Oromo who were able to leave Lovedale as resourceful and courageous young adults. That was the redemption Lovedale bestowed upon Bisho and her Oromo peers.

PART IV

Return: Forging a Future

CHAPTER 11

Going Home

Introduction

In the era between the outbreak of the Anglo-Boer War in October 1899 and the guns of August heralding the start of the First World War in 1914, imperial rivalries multiplied. During this complex era, the Oromo left Lovedale as literate adults, free to determine their own futures. Their first choice was to decide whether to return to their troubled homelands or stay in South Africa. Their departures from Lovedale were as dramatic as their arrivals, for different reasons. Whereas they arrived as newly liberated slave children—in the care of the missionaries—their departures signaled a new self-determination. To the personal narratives that shaped their first passage as slaves, the literate Oromo now added their considerable personal correspondence. These letters documented their own interpretation of the events of the day and plans for the future.

The reluctance of the missionaries and the British authorities to facilitate their return resulted in the Oromo turning to a most unlikely philanthropic agency, the German government. German diplomats were active in Menelik's court, pressing ahead for the dream of a Mittelafrika. Some German diplomats now suggested that Menelik's subjects—the Lovedale Oromo—were being prevented from returning to Ethiopia by the British. A questionnaire presented to the former slave children, one of the earliest such questionnaires in South Africa, is one of the various sources that document the stages of their decision to quit South Africa. Now adult Oromo, they left behind all vestiges of their chattel condition and took control of their own lives as actors on a crowded global stage.

The Independent Repatriates

By early 1900, the Lovedale authorities learned of the first Oromo who had made the decision to return. Galgal Dikko, who had worked as a railway porter in Kimberley, set off for Aden on his own.[1] From Aden, Galgal headed for the medieval walled city of Harar in eastern Abyssinia. But less than a year after he left South Africa, the *Christian Express* reported his death.[2]

Figure 11.1. Wreck of the *König*, East Africa, 1914 (source: Wreck Site, http://www.wrecksite.eu /wreck.aspx?122060).

Gamaches Garba left Lovedale in 1899 around the time of the outbreak of the Anglo-Boer War and enlisted for service as a mule driver with the Royal Artillery in Pietermaritzburg at £3.12.0 a month. He saw action in northern Natal and was one of the "beleaguered garrison" serving under Sir George White during the siege of Ladysmith between 30 October 1899 and 28 February 1900.[3] He saw out the siege, but the horrors had taken their toll. He no longer had the stomach for war—nor for horse or mule meat. As a result, by the time the siege was raised, he was in an emaciated and weakened state. He did not wait to recover his strength. Instead, he set off immediately for Aden.[4] Milko Guyo suggests in a letter to Lovedale on 27 April 1900 that Gamaches's move was not entirely unexpected: "You won't be surprised to hear that Gamaches went to Aden to proceed to Abyssinia. He left on the 11th of this month [April] on the big German steamer *Koenig* (or *König*). He has not written me since he left. I would not go; I am wanting to see the end of this war."[5] See the illustration in figure 11.1 of the *König*, wrecked on the East African coast fourteen years later.

Gamaches seemed to have recovered a sufficient level of his health to take charge of the mission briefly during the absence of the resident missionaries. However, he soon had a serious relapse. Dr. John Young, one of the missionaries at the Keith-Falconer Mission, wrote less than a year later:

> Poor Gamaches [Garba], the Galla lad who had made his way back to Aden, and has been living with us, has not had a single day's freedom from fever [malaria?] since my return. He is, however, better than he was, although I greatly fear that his life here will be short. Of his genuine Christian spirit and love, his patience in suffering, his earnestness and faithfulness, his zeal and hopefulness, no one could say too much. That such a boy has been trained in one of our own mission schools makes us thank God for Lovedale, and take courage for our own work in this place.[6]

Within a month, the *Christian Express* carried a report of his death, at age thirty-five, on 4 February 1901:

> You will be sorry to hear that Gamaches Garba died on Monday last. He had had a very hard time just previously, and it was a relief to us all when he entered into rest. He told me some days before that he trusted altogether in

Christ. We buried the remains the same night. The white-covered coffin was carried along the high road on the shoulders of four Arabs. We reached the deep, narrow grave in the Sheikh-Othman burying-ground in the part set aside for Christians. We stood there in sight of the white mission bungalow in the bright moonlight. Beside us were the graves of the Galla children who died at Sheikh-Othman. The coffin was lowered, Dr Young prayed, and soon our little ceremony was over.[7]

Amanu Figgo was the next independent returnee. On leaving Lovedale, he traveled to the diamond fields and Kimberley, where he was employed as a store messenger.[8] Toward the end of September 1900, Amanu, with Oromo friend Shamo Ayanso, traveled to East London intent on sailing for Aden and then going on to Oromoland. However, Shamo became seriously ill, coughing and spitting blood.[9] Despite his illness, the two men were determined to continue, believing that skilled Arab doctors near Aden would be able to cure Shamo.[10] In the end, however, it seems Amanu had to board ship without his friend. There is no report of Shamo ever sailing, nor has any official death record been located.

Amanu carried letters, given to him by the other Oromo living in Kimberley, that contained the names of all the Oromo still in South Africa. These letters, intended for Menelik II, included the names of their parents, their family members, and their king—and told how they longed to return home. They hoped that the emperor would recognize the advantage of introducing some educated Oromo into their own communities and this would persuade him to underwrite their return passage. The record does not indicate if Menelik ever received these letters.[11] Amanu made his way to Addis Ababa. Writing from that city in 1907, George Clerk told Liban Bultum that "Amanu Figgo died here [Addis Ababa] about three years ago [circa 1904]," but he gave no further details.[12]

Nagaro Chali completed the three-year Normal Course at Lovedale and was awarded his Third Year Teacher's Certificate in December 1897.[13] Leaving Lovedale, he set out for Bulawayo (in the southwest of today's Zimbabwe), where he was employed as a railway carriage attendant. However, by January 1901 Lovedale learned that Nagaro had arrived in Aden.[14]

There he became a colporteur,[15] peddling religious and devotional literature for the British and Foreign Bible Society under the supervision of Dr. John Young at the Keith-Falconer Mission. Based in the key sea-road nexus of Aden, and commuting between Aden and Harar, Nagaro was ideally positioned for contact with other shipboard travelers.

Undoubtedly the most significant of these contacts was the interview he had with a group of Ethiopian envoys when they docked at Aden on their way home from the coronation of Britain's King Edward VII on 9 August 1902 (see fig. 11.2):

Yesterday I met his Highness Ras Makonnen and suite, who are very glad to see me, especially his Excellency Kentiba Ghebroa [Gebru Desta], the Governor of Gondar, who, seeing me, at once jumped up from his seat and shook hands with me. He took me round to his Highness Ras Makonnen, and

FIGURE 11.2. Ethiopian delegation at the coronation of Edward VII, 1902; the Ethiopian envoys in the photograph are, from left to right: the chief priest of Harar; unidentified; Abba Tabor; Haile Sellassie Abayneh; Kentiba Gebru Desta; and Ras Makonnen, seated (source: Lafayette Studio Collection, Victoria and Albert Museum London, [L] 3453B).

introduced me to him. As for his officers, they are also glad to see me, being known to them during my stay in Harar last year. Yet I stayed together with his Excellency Kentiba Ghebroa from 8. a.m. to 2 p.m.—being an old teacher of mine in Sheikh-Othman in 1889—and we conversed about things passed [*sic*] during these many years we stayed away from one another, especially about Galla boys and girls, that are in South Africa. Yet he promised that he will try all his best to persuade King Menelik to bring them back to Abyssinia. His idea is this, as he have told me, that he shall ask King Menelik for a piece of ground, and then put on an industrious department and a school, if only these young men and girls are willing to come. . . . When I left the steamer they all bade me a hearty good-bye.[16]

By 1907, George Clerk, the British chargé d'affaires in Addis Ababa, noted that Nagaro was in the service of "a German gentleman" in Dire-Dawa.[17] Milko Guyo included Nagaro in his list of those Oromo who were still alive in 1925 when he reported to Lovedale on the fate of all the returnee Oromos.[18]

Figure 11.3. Tolassa Wayessa at Lovedale (source: detail from CL PIC/M 1093).

Map 11.1. Arena of Buller's forces in Natal, January–July 1900 (direction of Acton Homes arrowed; source: adaptation from New Map, Briton or Boer [Cape Town: Wood and Ortlepp, 1900], UCT Digital Collections: BMX 684.b.1 [110], inset: Ladysmith).

Of all the repatriates, Tolassa Wayessa is by far the best documented (see fig. 11.3, a portrait identified from a group photograph by his relatives). He left Lovedale in 1898 having been awarded his Teacher's Elementary Certificate. By May 1899, he was employed in East London as a photographer's assistant and later as a restaurant waiter in the same city.[19] In the meantime, the Anglo-Boer War had broken out, and in 1900 Tolassa enlisted, serving in the British Army as a transport driver under General Sir Redvers Buller in Natal.[20]

He wrote several letters to Lovedale recording his horrific wartime experiences, which convinced him to return home.[21] Stationed at a place called Acton Homes in Natal, Tolassa wrote on 22 January 1900:

> We left Maritzburg on New Year's Day and . . . came on to Springfield. In all these marchings, man after man dropped out on the way. Some were worn out by the long marching and others through want of water. . . . Yesterday and the day before yesterday 12 cannon were in action. To-day there are more of them in action. It is said that 322 men are killed and wounded today. Of course, we do not know exactly how many are killed on the side of the Boers. It is said that their trenches are full of dead. In every engagement the Boers are being driven back farther and farther. Before yesterday they shelled the position where we were and killed one man, wounded about half-a-dozen others and killed a number of transport horses and mules.

The Oromo people live in harmony with nature, regarding humans as part of a symbiotic relationship with the earth, its plants, and its animals. So the killing of the horses and the mules, in addition to the deaths of hundreds of men, had a profound impact on Tolassa. He continued:

> It is easy to speak about war, but it is very hard to look on dead and wounded men. I did not like to look at the man who was shot by the shell of the Boers. The shell knocked through his breast and came out at the back. . . . General Buller was here yesterday and today. Our transport is in the fighting line, while the transport belonging to other regiments keeps about half a mile from the regiments. Being under cover of the guns a number of our mules were shot. I cannot tell you all that is going on just now, but I will tell you some time, if I return safely.[22]

Six months later, in July 1900, he wrote again, this time from their position at Glencoe:

> At Hussar Hill and Colenso I was very nearly blown to pieces by shells. The one at Hussar Hill was a 40 pound shell, and at Colenso a shell from a 15 pounder long range gun. At the relief of Ladysmith my regiment was the second to enter the town, and I tell you the town was in a very bad condition. The soldiers were just like moving skeletons. How these men, who were scarcely able to handle a rifle or carbine, kept out the Boers is really wonderful. . . . After the relief of Ladysmith I was transferred to the Special Ammunition

Column of the Royal Artillery. We were stationed at Ladysmith about one month; at Elandslaagte over a month; and now my column is here at Glencoe. Dundee, Glencoe and Hadding Spruit were taken with scarcely any fighting. We are leaving for Newcastle perhaps to-day or to-morrow. . . . At another place a lot of Cape Boys and Kaffirs came round the unfortunate prisoners and began asking for "Pass!" "Pass!" which no doubt must have cut them to the heart.[23]

In January 1902 he wrote to the Lovedale missionaries saying that he intended to leave South Africa that month. Tolassa had returned to East London from his military service and, at the time of writing, had "been for some time in business in East London." He told them that he intended to travel via Bombay to Broach (now known as Bharuch), a town in southern Gujarat, about two hundred miles north of Bombay.[24] From there, he expected to continue his voyage to Aden.[25] He sailed aboard the SS *Kaiser* from East London on 9 January 1902, a voyage that took him home via India to Aden.[26] Eventually, in July 1903, Tolassa reached Aden and returned to the Keith-Falconer Mission at Sheikh Othman where he visited the Reverend Dr. John Cameron Young, then medical missionary of the Keith-Falconer Mission. On 16 July 1903 he arrived back in Ethiopia.[27]

After recovering his late father's farm and other property, Tolassa found employment in Addis Ababa, working as an interpreter for Captain R. Brian England, appointed by the London-based International Railway Trust and Construction Company to take charge of its agency in Abyssinia. He left England's service to take up "a good position" in the German legation. While he retained ownership of his family farm, he settled in Kebena near the German embassy.[28] Here Tolassa married a woman by the name of Getenesh Woldeyes and raised a family of two boys and one girl.[29] Tolassa's own descendants (today living in Addis Ababa, Canada, and England) believe he died in Addis Ababa in the mid-1930s.[30]

In 1903, a sixth Oromo, Fayissa Umbe, who had gone to Bulawayo where he was employed as a railway carriage attendant and who had later settled in Kimberley, told Lovedale of his plans to return home with his Oromo wife, Ayantu Said.[31] There is even an erroneous report indicating that they and their seven-month-old baby, Foyate, had sailed for Mombasa on 9 October 1903. This report was retracted a month later when the *Christian Express* informed its readers of Ayantu Said's death in Kimberley on 1 November 1903.[32] In due course, Fayissa resumed his plans to return home and by 1907 was reported to be living with a group of Oromo in Wallaga, an area to the southwest of Abyssinia, today known as the Mirab Welega administrative zone in western Oromia.[33]

The remaining two Oromo who chose to return home unaided were Daba Tobo and Fayissa Hora. Immediately after leaving Lovedale, Daba took a position in a store in Cape Town, earning eighteen shillings per week. In 1900, he shifted to employment in an aerated water factory in the same city.[34] By 1903, he was living at 152 Caledon Street and was working as a hall porter in central Cape Town. David Hunter annotated his questionnaire with "gone to Gallaland Aug[ust] 1906."[35]

Fayissa Hora also moved to Cape Town, where he was initially employed as a wag-onmaker. By 1900 he was known to be working as a waiter in a Cape Town restau-rant.[36] In 1903 he was living in the Union Hotel in Plein Street, Cape Town, where he was employed as a bottle washer; he was listed by Lovedale in November 1903 as married.[37] In his response to Hunter's questionnaire, Fayissa wrote that he was "willing to go home."[38] He followed up with an appeal on the same day: "I am willing to go home but I have a request to ask: is my wife entitled to a free passage with me as I am a married man with one Child and [I am a] Gentlemen."[39] Hunter added a later, undated handwritten annotation to Fayissa's response to the questionnaire reading "Returned to Gallaland."[40] The record is silent thereafter, so all that can be construed is that he and his family sailed for home sometime between 1903 and 1909. He was the only married independent returnee.

These eight voluntary, self-funded repatriations symbolize the first of the redemp-tive, restorative actions of the adult Oromo group. Free will, determination, and as-tonishing courage lay behind these homeward migrations. There were enormous risks attendant on their return, and their future was by no means certain, but they went. The decision to return—and to return unaided—signified the successful routing of the last vestiges of any passivity imposed on them by their slavery.

The 1903 Poll

In 1892, two years after the children's arrival, the Lovedale missionaries had mused in their annual report on the length of time the children would remain in their care. "This cannot be fixed," ran the report. "They came in a body, but they will probably leave in groups."[41] The missionaries stood by as, one by one, the Oromo left to seek work in different urban centers throughout South Africa and farther afield. Nagaro Chali and Fayissa Umbe headed for Bulawayo and took on positions in the Rhodesian railways. Mulatta Billi became a sailor and settled in the United States. By 1912, he was listed in the *San Diego City and County Directory* as a laborer in the city sewer depart-ment. Eighteen years later, the compilers of the *St. Louis, Missouri City Directory, 1930*, listed M. Billi as a clerk in that city.[42]

By 1903, the Oromo were seriously on the move. Eight had already financed their own voyages home, boarding their respective ships alone. The Lovedale authorities an-ticipated that still more would also venture out on their own but voiced misgivings about the wisdom of their repatriation, whether solo or in a group, "unless accompanied by some Europeans."[43] In keeping with the paternalism of the era, they believed that without "the supervision of a European missionary who might act as their friend, coun-cillor and guide,"[44] the returning Oromo would flounder materially as they struggled to find the means to survive without their missionary mentors. But there were also profound health concerns. Gebru Desta, their former teacher and later mayor (*Kentiba*) of Gondar, seems to have endorsed Hunter's fears in a letter from Addis Ababa in 1903:

> How delighted I was to have received your unexpected kind letter and
> "*Christians* [sic] *Express*" (Newspaper) including concerning my dear Christian
> old Galla friends. It was always my hearty desire after the education & maturity

of those homeless friends to be useful in their own country without losing their Christian freedom. Your careful proposal if the Gallas to Abyssinia return it would be wiser to be accompanied by some Europeans is quite right; otherwise they might be orphaned and lose soon their moral worth.[45]

In May 1903, Sir John Harrington, British diplomatic agent and consul general in Addis Ababa, responded to an exploratory letter from Lovedale regarding the possibility of Emperor Menelik II funding the repatriation of the Oromo:

H.M. the Emperor Menelik has desired me to inform you that he is prepared to pay the passages of those Gallas who have been educated at Lovedale Mission and who are desirous of returning to this country. His Majesty states that he is willing to pay the passages of those who have not the means of doing so themselves. If you will kindly inform me of the number who are desirous of returning and the amount necessary for their passages to Aden the amount will be remitted to you. If it is considered desirable to arrange their immediate departure, arrangements might possibly be made for their passages, and the amount remitted by me when the amount is known. A list of these returning and their occupation should be sent.[46]

Harrington wrote a confidential covering letter to this formal letter, evincing his own misgivings regarding any repatriation plan. He reportedly feared that "unless the Gallas were possessed of some trade, their future in Abyssinia was likely to be a miserable one, the Gallas being a conquered subject race, whose lot is hard."[47] By this time, he was aware of the full impact of Menelik's depredations in the south and southwest of Abyssinia, depredations that led to the eventual conquest of the Oromo people. As Oromo scholar Guluma Gemeda has indicated, the disastrous consequences of disunity—caused by internal strife and rivalry among western Oromo leaders—were principally responsible for undermining any effective opposition to Menelik's forces.[48] Repression, dispossession, and enslavement of the Oromo followed.[49]

On 26 August 1903, Hunter polled all the surviving Oromo he could trace using a simple questionnaire, asking them if they would favor returning to Ethiopia on the condition that they be offered an assisted passage.[50] By the time of the 1903 questionnaire, 31.4 percent of the Oromo had already died and 3.5 percent had repatriated independently. Lovedale sent forms to all the other known surviving Oromo. There were no forms returned nor any added information for almost one-third (or 29.1 percent) of the group; 17.4 percent responded in the affirmative, saying that they would be interested in returning with an assisted passage; and 5.8 percent replied saying they were planning to repatriate independently. A further 5.8 percent of the forms were blank when returned. These blank returns indicated either that an Oromo had changed address, was not interested in participating in the poll at all, or had died without Lovedale's knowledge. A conditional response was given by 4.7 percent, who asked for more information before making a final decision, while 2.3 percent wanted to remain in South Africa and were not interested in repatriating, with or without an assisted passage (see graph 11.1).

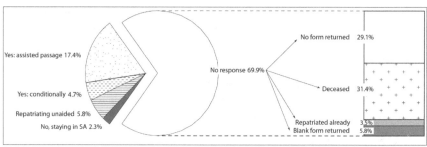

GRAPH 11.1. Results of Lovedale's 1903 repatriation poll (source: Sandra Rowoldt Shell).

Of all the Oromo, only Bisho Jarsa gave a negative response: "I am on duty at present, rather remain few years longer."[51] She followed up with a fuller explanation in a brief letter to Lovedale. As indicated in the previous chapter, she remained teaching a few more years, then married the Reverend Frederick Scheepers, a Lovedale classmate. Arguably her greatest gift to her adopted country came in the form of her eldest grandson, the late Dr. Neville Alexander, a renowned intellectual, educationalist, human rights activist, and struggle hero (see chapter 10, pages 151–153).

Of all the men who responded, slightly more than a quarter (21.4 percent) responded in the affirmative. The proportion for the women in this regard was considerably less at 13.6 percent. All but one of the men and women who responded in the affirmative were married to Oromo spouses. The marital status of the remaining "yes" voter—a woman—was not known.

One revealing—if a little fractious—response to the questionnaire came from Dinkitu Boensa. Writing from her Sans Pareil home in Three Anchor Bay, Cape Town, she retorted, "If I wish to return to my native land I will do so at my own expense and convenience." She enclosed the envelope in which the questionnaire had been enclosed addressed simply "Dinkitu Boensa," commenting: "I think at least you might place *Miss* to my name."[52] She and her husband, Gutama Tarafo, both repatriated with the subsidized group in 1909.

In 1904, David Hunter wrote to Dr. John Young, sounding him out on the advisability of he and Mrs. Hunter accompanying any Oromo who might wish to return. In response, John Young expressed practical fears, based on his personal observations of several of the independent returnees, the impact of the protracted plague and famine years, poor transport, living costs, lack of medical support, and the possibility of political insurrection in the event of the ailing emperor's death:

> I am against the Gallas returning to Abyssinia as nearly every one has died
> who has attempted to get there, and those who have not died have with the
> exception of Tolasso [Tolassa Wayessa] fallen quickly back into their pristine
> state. The journey to Addis Ababa is a long and trying one.[53] The mule being
> used as a means of conveyance from Dire Darwah where the railways stops.

The railway journey is one of twelve hours and the mule journey from a fortnight to three weeks according to rate of travel. Addis Ababa is itself a very healthy station but it is feared by many that there will be an insurrection there when the reigning monarch (Emperor Menelik) dies. I would think Addis Ababa would be an extremely cheap place to live in if you were content with the food of the country but otherwise a very expensive place as it is so far from the [Red] Sea Coast. . . . The journey to Addis Ababa and then being there without a medical man would tell hard upon Mrs Hunter if she has not very robust health and therefore I could not undertake to advise your taking the journey but if you did the best time for landing in Abyssinia would be the month of April or the end of March. We have been having a trying time owing to plague and famine in our midst.[54]

Expectations ran high among the Oromo that Lovedale would follow through rapidly on the results after the poll and that an early return home would be imminent. However, both parties—Menelik's court in Addis Ababa and Lovedale itself—were experiencing periods of administrative disarray, both for reasons of ill-health. In Addis Ababa, Emperor Menelik II was becoming increasingly debilitated by the tertiary syphilis he had contracted as a youth. Successive strokes, at least one epileptic episode, and the onset of senility lessened his control of the affairs of state and he became progressively dependent on his court advisers, many of them German.[55]

Lovedale's Administrative Torpor

At Lovedale, after an extended spell in Scotland, the characteristic energy of Principal James Stewart—called Somgxada, "the long strider, or the man who is everywhere"[56]—began to flag in 1904.[57] In November 1905, Liban Bultum—fast emerging as the leader of the returnee hopefuls—wrote to James Stewart, urging him to respond to the appeal from Menelik's court for further information:

I have not written you any letter since I left Lovedale and so be not surprised to receive this note. I was very sorry and so are many of my country folks to hear of your ill-health and hope ere this you are restored to your good health. We all wish you a hearty recovery. I received a letter yesterday from General Harrington, British Legation, Addis Ababa informing me about our returning home. He says Emperor Menelik is willing to contribute £500 towards our expenses in going home but they want first the informations asked for in the letter addressed to you dated the 19th February 1904 copy of which is also sent to me, also copy of your acknowledgement to the letter, promising to write on the matter. General Harrington says if I am in a position to supply you with the informations asked for in the letter, he will move in the matter. I would like to know if you have written him again, and if so kindly oblige me with a copy of your letter to him and if not I am quite willing to supply you with any informations you may require.[58]

In all likelihood Stewart never read that letter. He died on 21 December 1905. Within months he was replaced by the Reverend James Henderson.[59] Despite a rapid leadership transition, Lovedale neglected to move forward with the repatriation process. As Henderson explained later, in a letter dated 12 May 1909, the Lovedale authorities acknowledged receipt of Harrington's communication from Addis Ababa in 1903, but they did not follow up with the details requested. Henderson explained that "owing to the late Dr. Stewart being in Scotland the matter had to be referred to him, and it took a very considerable time to get into communication with the Gallas and collect the necessary information."[60]

In desperation, Liban took matters into his own hands, writing on his own initiative to George Clerk in the British legation in Addis Ababa on 21 November 1906. He asked specifically about the £500 fare subsidy Menelik was purported to be willing to subscribe toward their repatriation. George Clerk responded to Liban on 28 February 1907:

> With reference to your letter of November 21st last, relative to the Five
> Hundred Pounds (£500) which the Emperor Menelik was willing to subscribe
> towards the repatriation of those Gallas who wished to return to Abyssinia, I
> have to inform you that this Legation is still awaiting the necessary information
> from Lovedale Mission.[61]

An exasperated Liban wrote to Alexander Geddes, his former boarding master at Lovedale, on 11 April 1907, again appealing to Lovedale to respond to the communications sent to them from Addis Ababa:

> I have just received a letter from the British Legation in Abyssinia in reply to
> mine of the 21st November 1906. . . . In order for you to see the contents of
> this letter and also to kindly refer to the responsible party which I think is Mr
> Henderson as principal and ask him to kindly reply to the letter which the
> British Legation still awaits reply, I enclose herewith for your information and
> Mr Henderson as well the copy of the letter I received today from the British
> Legation.[62]

David Hunter, who seems to have initiated the poll, must also have been a frustrated man. He could initiate action (as in the idea to poll the Oromo in 1903) but, as a lay missionary, did not have the necessary authority to carry matters through to their conclusion. He was, however, the first from Lovedale to respond to the British representatives in Addis Ababa. On 29 May 1908 he wrote to the chargé d'affaires, enclosing a tentative list of those he believed, from the 1903 poll results and subsequent feedback, would be interested in the repatriation scheme, giving details of their Lovedale training and work experience:

> This list comprises 16 men, 9 wives (of whom 2 are Cape coloured women, and
> one is a Kaffir) 12 children, and one single Galla woman. It is probable that
> before a reply comes to this letter response may be received from other Gallas,
> whose addresses are at present unknown, who wish to return. It is therefore

impossible at this stage to submit an accurate budget of the cost of repatriation. If the Emperor is willing to entrust this Institution with the £500 he offered, it would be carefully administered, and such portion (if any) as remained over, after paying passages and other necessary expenditure, would be remitted either to Addis Ababa, Jibuti, or Aden as may be directed. We understand the 3rd class fare from Port Elizabeth to Aden is about £15. You will know what could be the cost of transport from there to Jibuti, thence to rail-head and on to Addis Ababa. I shall be glad to have some information as to the overland journey, especially the part after leaving the Railway; also regarding prospects of employment, rate of remuneration, housing, cost of living, and generally as to the state of the country, some of these young men are capable and steady-going, and should prove of value in their country. I feel, however, that it would be better if they could return under the leadership of a suitable European. Would the Negus be willing to meet the additional expense this would entail?[63]

He pointed out that the Oromo, for their part, were anxious to know if they would be required to refund the money advanced to take them home. "If this is to be insisted on," Hunter remarked, "it would deter some of them from starting." He was also concerned that "enquiries are being made through the German Consul in Port Elizabeth regarding these Gallas." This oblique reference touched a highly sensitive spot. Hunter believed that Menelik had been given the impression that the Oromo were not allowed to dispose of any property they owned, nor to leave the country—effectively prisoners in their adopted land.[64] Hunter and the other Lovedale missionaries were obviously anxious to dispel these perceptions: "Such, of course, is not the case; and it seems a pity that these young people, on whom much British money and effort has been spent, should go back under German auspices, and thereby acquire and spread the idea that they owe their repatriation to German influence and effort."[65] Hunter closed his letter on this dramatic note, hoping it would strengthen his appeal to the chargé d'affaires to send a timely and definite response so as to forestall "this threatened interposition" and any further delay in expediting their own arrangements for the Oromos' repatriation.[66]

German Ascendancy

There was growing British jitteriness at the growth of German power and influence in Africa. From the watershed moment of the Berlin Conference of 1884–1885, in terms of which various European colonial powers continued to divide up the African continent in the scramble for Africa, Bismarck's ambitions for German territorial supremacy burgeoned. Bismarck's ultimate dream was for a "Mittelafrika" (see map 11.2), a wide band of German-controlled African territory stretching from the Atlantic to the Indian Ocean.

Against this background, only two African territories retained their independence by the close of the nineteenth century—Liberia on the west coast and Ethiopia. Like the Germans, the Italians were relative latecomers to the cluster of European imperialists but, having successfully secured Eritrea on Ethiopia's borders, they planned to

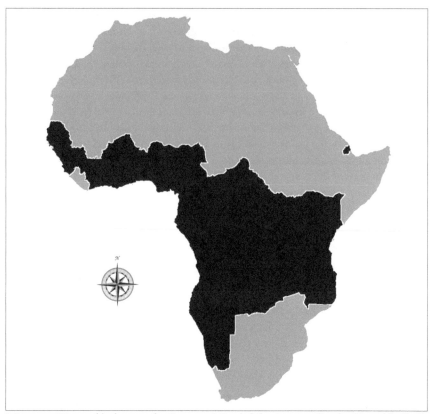

Map 11.2. Bismarck's dream of a German Mittelafrika (source: Sandra Rowoldt Shell, adaptation of base map).

extend their territorial ambitions in the Horn of Africa to include Ethiopia itself. In 1889, Menelik II agreed to sign the Treaty of Wuchale with the Italians, in terms of which, in the Amharic version, the emperor of Ethiopia had the option of making use of the goodwill of the Italian kingdom in his diplomatic interactions with other foreign powers. The Italian interpretation of the treaty, however, considered that the emperor consented to channeling all interactions with other foreign powers through Italy, thus effectively making Ethiopia a protectorate of the Italian kingdom.[67] The ensuing dispute led to the first Italo-Ethiopian War, culminating in the resounding defeat of the Italians at the battle of Adwa in 1896 and the signing of the Treaty of Addis Ababa, in which Italy recognized the sovereignty of Ethiopia.[68]

The British had not forgotten German involvement in and support of Paul Kruger during the Anglo-Boer War of 1899–1902. Immediately after the Peace of Vereeniging in 1902, ongoing concern developed concerning the prospect of Germany's diplomatic and naval expansion. Britain viewed German interventions in Ethiopia with suspicion. German-Ethiopian diplomacy began in earnest on 12 February 1905, when a special embassy, sent by Kaiser Wilhelm II and led by Friedrich Rosen,[69] arrived in Addis Ababa to negotiate a friendship and trade treaty with Menelik II.[70] Gebru Desta, who served as a volunteer tutor to the Oromo children at the Keith-Falconer Mission in Sheikh Othman during 1889–1890, acted as interpreter.[71]

On 12 February 1905, Rosen, leading a twenty-member delegation with a Prussian escort and one hundred servants liveried in the German national colors, rode into Addis Ababa.[72] On 7 March 1905, Menelik signed the Ethiopia-Germany Commercial Treaty with Rosen. The treaty was ratified in Berlin on 6 February 1906.[73] Sir John Harrington, British diplomatic agent and consul general in Addis Ababa, was alarmed by the sudden surge in German influence following the signing of this accord and would have been further disturbed by the Enno Littmann Expedition to Axum in January 1906, a joint archaeological undertaking between the German government and Princeton University, raised at Menelik's urging.[74]

In the meantime, the German campaign to quell the Maji-Maji rebellion in German East Africa resulted in scorched-earth tactics and a human massacre of vast proportions during 1905–1906. According to historians Robert Gellately and Ben Kiernan, between 200,000 and 300,000 Africans perished as a result—a number that eclipses the Herero Genocide of 1904–1907, in which approximately 24,000 to 100,000 Herero and 10,000 Nama were killed.[75] This evidence of German brutality "sparked outrage among leftist parties in Germany" and around the world.[76] In 1907, Wilhelm II appointed a new colonial secretary, Bernhard Dernburg, a liberal who was keen to ameliorate Germany's image on the African continent. Dernburg wanted to introduce reforms that would outlaw corporal punishment and strictly limit the exploitation of African labor in the German colonies.[77] He received limited support for these reforms. Dernburg therefore probably regarded the Oromo cri de coeur for assistance to help them find their way home after their harrowing slavery ordeal and two decades at the southern tip of Africa as an ideal opportunity, as William Patch surmises, "to promote the logic of the new public relations offensive emanating from [his] office."[78] Dernburg's liberal views were not popular, and he was never able to see all of his reformist ideas in the colonial arena come to fruition. He served a relatively short term as secretary for colonial affairs and head of the Imperial Colonial Office between May 1907 and June 1910. He later held the position of federal minister of finance and was vice-chancellor of Germany for an even briefer two-month period between April and June 1919.[79]

Britain's nervousness about German diplomatic and naval ascendancy reached a new level of intensity by early 1909:

> The uneasiness felt in Great Britain at the German Government's policy of naval expansion has been greatly intensified in the course of the past few weeks by information made public in the discussion on the Naval Estimates. It was stated that since the autumn of last year Germany's rate of construction of Dreadnoughts had been materially accelerated, that their shipbuilding yards had been working at full pressure night and day, and that contractors had been heavily subsidised in order to have work rapidly pushed through. The result was that the margin of Britain's naval preponderance and security has been dangerously reduced.[80]

Britain's fears would come to fruition two years later, when a German gunboat, the *Panther*, took the tensions to their apogee. In April 1911, a rebellion against Sultan Abdelhafid in Morocco resulted in France dispatching troops to support the incumbent regime. While the British opposed the French move, Spain took advantage of the general turmoil of events by occupying some of France's territory in Morocco. Germany, flexing its growing naval muscle, responded by deploying the gunboat *Panther* to Agadir in Morocco on 1 July 1911. The Germans believed, erroneously, that the British would support them against the French. The British chose instead to align themselves with the French in a formal alliance. The Germans insisted on being compensated by the French for protecting French interests in Morocco. Against British advice, the French eventually conceded, in small part, to Germany's demands. This incident, considered to be the most renowned case of "gunboat diplomacy," contributed significantly to the bridling tension among the imperial powers of Europe in the run-up to the First World War.[81]

At a diplomatic level, any hint of German ascendancy gave rise to a flurry of alarmed responses in British political circles. Lovedale gave vent to some of these fears in an article in the *Christian Express* in June 1909, the timing of the article possibly triggered by the ongoing repatriation issue:

> The present attitude of Germany seems in Europe to be almost universally
> recognized as one of preparation for war. Germans say that they are merely
> occupied in organizing a navy adequate to the defence of their now extensive
> commerce. Whichever view is accepted, the fact is undeniable that a forward
> policy is being pursued by Germany and that neighbouring nations are
> considering it necessary to add to their defences. If the present forces continue
> to act unchecked, it seems humanly certain that the end will be war. . . . We are
> glad to know that the South African colonies, so soon to be united, are shortly
> to meet in conference the other sections of the British Empire for the purpose
> of discussing measures for the common defence. But, after all, preparation for
> war is not a certain preventative, and in some circumstances preparation may
> even prove an actual incentive to war.[82]

The air was bristling with imperial rivalries, and the impact of those certainly touched the lives of the Oromo, starting with the Anglo-Boer War. As early as March 1905, Harrington had expressed his unhappiness at the upsurge of German leverage in Menelik's court.[83] The echoes of the scramble for Africa were still resounding across the continent, and Britain was wary of any hint of latent or blatant German imperial aggrandizement.

The tense political climate aggravated Lovedale's ultrasensitivity to the sudden appearance of the Germans in the negotiations for the Oromos' repatriation. The cat was very definitely among the pigeons. On 12 May 1909, Henderson wrote to the high commissioner in Pretoria, confirming that "the German interposition of which we heard rumours nearly a year ago, has become a *fait accompli*."[84] Henderson continued:

> I venture to think that Your Excellency may consider this a matter which
> should be brought before the Foreign Office for information and elucidation. It

would be dishonest to have these Gallas, on whom a great deal of British effort and money has been expended be repatriated under German auspices, and in such a way as to spread in Abyssinia, the idea that the German Government alone had been friendly and that His British Majesty's Government was unable or unwilling, to do for them what a foreign power could do and was willing to do. The haste with which the German Consul appears to wish to get these young people away gives colour to a suspicion that he fears some step may be taken on the part of the British authorities to interfere with his action.[85]

Henderson concluded his letter by warning that according to his information, the Oromo were due to sail within ten days of his letter, on 22 May 1909.[86] The British imperial secretary in Johannesburg responded by telegram, instructing Henderson to send all relevant documentation to the governor, Sir Walter Francis Hely-Hutchinson, in Cape Town. Henderson complied,[87] and a flurry of telegrams crisscrossed the country. Henderson cabled the governor on 29 May 1909, saying that the departure date had been changed to 2 June 1909.[88] On the same day (29 May 1909), Hely-Hutchinson forwarded all the documentation to his ministers for their observations.[89] He informed his ministers that he was in communication with the high commissioner, William Waldegrave Palmer, second Earl of Selborne, on the subject. He wrote further, stating the governor had stressed that "if any steps are to be taken to interfere with the repatriation of the Gallas under the auspices of the German authorities, they should originate with the High Commissioner, and [he] has informed Lord Selborne that, should he decide that such steps are to be taken, the Governor will be ready to render any assistance which Ministers may advise in the matter."[90]

The imperial secretary ("Gravido") cabled, informing the Government House ("Pendriver") that the papers relating to the Oromos' repatriation were by then lodged with the high commissioner, who was away at the time of cabling. The telegram referred to the tentative list of returnees, which, the writer noted, was "nearly a year old," continuing: "I telegraphed to [Henderson] asking reason Germans desired to repatriate them and number now requesting repatriation. He replied reason unknown."[91]

The telegram went on to say that Henderson had also revealed that the Oromos' departure had been postponed until July, that the number who would be boarding was still not known, and that the matter of repatriation had been referred to the German consul general in Cape Town. The telegram also indicated that Henderson had "omitted enclosures to his letter of 12th [May 1909]. Several days were lost thereby making interference with departure under German auspices on 22nd impossible even if such were contemplated. No steps have therefore been taken beyond instructing Henderson to refer to Governor Cape." According to this cable, no previous papers on the subject were traceable in their own offices.[92]

On 31 May 1909, the high commissioner told the governor that he would prefer the governor take any action that might be deemed necessary after consulting his ministers. If the governor believed such action should still originate from the high commissioner's office, he would be willing to telegraph the secretary of state for the colonies in London, for the information of the Foreign Office, giving the facts as James Henderson had reported them. The departure date had once again been rescheduled and was set for 3 July 1909.[93]

The governor responded in a draft dispatch saying that he was writing to James Henderson suggesting that he should not give any assistance to the German consul in the matter of "collecting the Gallas." He did not propose to take any further steps in the matter and was sending a copy of the dispatch to the secretary of state for the colonies.[94] In a postscript no. 96 to this dispatch, addressed to James Henderson, the private secretary expanded further on the contents of the despatch itself:

> The Governor desires to say that, after enquiring into the matter, he does not feel able to take any steps to prevent the Gallas from taking a passage in the German ship: and the Colonial Government does not feel disposed to take any steps, itself, for repatriating them. The Governor thinks it probable that the Gallas are much better off here than if they were to return to their native country, and suggests that you should not lend any assistance to the German Consul in the matter of collecting them. The Governor has laid the papers before the High Commissioner for South Africa and before the Secretary of State for the Colonies.[95]

Edward Dower, the secretary for native affairs, wrote in support of Henderson's opinion "as to the desirability of such of the Gallas as desire to return to the land of their birth being repatriated under British auspices. Some of them have turned out very well and would doubtless be very useful in their own country."[96]

However, Dower was puzzled by the intervention of the Germans and recommended that the prime minister's office ask James Henderson and the civil commissioner in Port Elizabeth to clarify the situation.[97]

On behalf of the ministers whom the governor had asked for observations, the prime minister, John X. Merriman, submitted a detailed minute dated 4 June 1909:

> It is a matter for speculation—looking to the condition of domestic slaves in Mohammedan countries—whether on the whole their lot would not have been happier if they had been left alone than it is likely to be if they are relegated to the care of that Christian, but ferocious, potentate, the so-called Emperor of Abyssinia. . . . Why they should be disturbed is not in any way shown—or why they should be sent back to a place where no doubt the servile condition from which they have been rescued would be renewed. Menelik's fitful intervention seems to have died out as soon as he became aware of the amount required to recapture [sic] his subjects.[98] What possible *locus standi* the German Consul can have in the matter is also not shown and most certainly Ministers would not advise that anything should be done to assist him in his efforts. On the other hand there is no law under which a free man can be prevented from taking a passage in a German ship. He may, in this case he probably will, have cause to regret it, but unless he is kidnapped he is free to go. As for the Colonial Government repatriating these people, that is quite out of the question. The most that can be done at present is to forward the correspondence to the High

FIGURE 11.4. *Kronprinz* (photograph by Witthöft, ca. 1910).

Commissioner, who will no doubt communicate with the Secretary of State. Mr Henderson might also be cautioned, in the interest of his protegés, not to give any assistance to the Germans in the matter of rounding them up. [signed] John X Merriman[99]

By this time, there were four powerful polities involved: Sir Walter Hely-Hutchinson, the governor of the Cape Colony, and John X. Merriman, the prime minister in Cape Town; the secretary of state for the colonies in London; the German authorities behind the scenes in Berlin; and Emperor Menelik II and his court advisers in Addis Ababa.

James Henderson responded to the postscript, echoing again his own misgivings, and agreeing that it was probable the Oromo would be better off in South Africa than they would be if they returned to their own country,

> but those who have been interested in them and concerned in their education and training have felt that repatriated under arrangements which would keep them together, they might become effective as a great civilising and educative force among their own people and bring benefit on a considerable scale to the land of their origin. The arrangement under which at present some of them are likely to be returned to their native land is not one that in any way commends itself to me, and I cannot countenance it.[100]

On 5 July 1909, E. Schnoster, the acting imperial German consul general, wrote to James Henderson:

> Referring to the letter addressed by you, on the 13th May last, to the Imperial German Consul at Port Elizabeth on the subject of certain Abyssinians in the Cape Colony I have the honour to inform you that it is at the request of their own Government that this Consulate General has taken in hand to arrange for the repatriation of certain Abyssinian subjects who are residing in this Colony and are in a destitute condition. Upon enquiries made several of the people concerned have declared that since a series of years they are no more in connection with the Lovedale Mission Station, that they have earned their

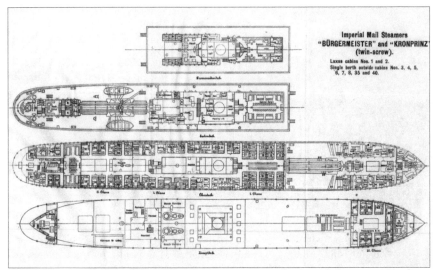

FIGURE 11.5. Deck plan of the *Kronprinz* (source: *Deutsche Ost-Afrika-Linie, Hamburg: Handbook* [Hamburg: DOAL, 1911], folded plan).

> living quite independently and not received any support from the Station. One part of the Abyssinians concerned had made all preparations for leaving this Colony, had sold their things, given up their abodes etc., so that, for this reason already it would have been impracticable to delay their departure. They have left Port Elizabeth on the 3rd inst. on board the S.S. *Kronprinz*.[101]

Liban Bultum had successfully completed his task, and he and his group of Oromo were finally sailing home.[102] There is no certainty as to precisely how many that group comprised on board, nor, of course, their identities. David Hunter's draft listing dated 1908 was clearly inaccurate by the time of sailing. For example, Wakinne Nagesso, who had indicated interest in the 1903 poll, was not on board. In the intervening period between the poll and embarkation, he had married a South African woman and settled in Cape Town. In addition, by 1909 one further Oromo had died—Amanu Figgo in 1904—bringing the total number of Oromo deaths since their arrival in 1890 to twenty-two, or 34.4 percent of their original number.

The *Kronprinz* was a liner in the service of the Deutsche Ost Africa Linie/Woermann Afrika Linie (see figure 11.4 and deck plan below, figure 11.5).[103] Attempts to locate a final boarding passenger list have been met with the same response from every quarter. All archives of the Deutsche Ost Afrika Linie/Woermann Linie were destroyed by fire when Allied forces bombed Hamburg during World War II.[104]

The different presses along the east coast of Africa tracked the journey of the *Kronprinz* on its northward journey to Aden. The *Beira Post* confirmed her arrival there on 16 July 1909, carrying seventeen passengers and a forty-ton cargo.[105] Without a passenger list, there is no way of knowing whether these seventeen passengers were the Oromo only or included other passengers.

Lovedale stubbornly ignored an obvious news item for their August 1909 issue of the *Christian Express*. They would indubitably have found the sequence of events from the poll in 1903 to the sailing of the SS *Kronprinz* in 1909 difficult to explain to their readers and supporters. In the political milieu, pique and embarrassment were masked by a bluster of indignation that German interference may have jeopardized the lives and futures of the Oromo repatriates. As John X. Merriman opined in his minute of 20 October 1909:

> Ministers cannot but observe, however, that it would seem quite likely that the fate of the Gallas in Abyssinia will be of a kind to serve as a warning to the well meant efforts of the foreign philanthropists responsible for the repatriation. In saying this, Ministers assume that the reasons for repatriation were purely altruistic and did not spring from political motives. A result such as Ministers fear would be most regrettable from the point of view of the hapless victims of the experiment, however useful the lesson conveyed in reproof of the interference. John X. Merriman.[106]

Merriman and other functionaries afforded no credit to the Oromo themselves, who, as young adults—mostly young married couples—in diaspora, had made considered, mature decisions to return home. The authorities probably had no idea that eight other young married Oromo couples had long since returned home using their own initiative and their hard-earned savings to do so. Certainly, three of these repatriates died shortly after arriving at Sheikh Othman or within a few years after reaching Abyssinia. However, observers need to consider the high mortality rate the group had experienced as a result within such a protected environment as that provided by the Lovedale Institution in the Eastern Cape, South Africa. The tentacles of the first-passage ordeal stretched deep within—and despite—that sanctuary for its young victims.

Justifications aside, the Lovedale authorities had raised hopes that they then failed to see through to fruition. With no follow-through, they could expect to incur only anger and frustration. That Liban Bultum approached other agencies for alternative options can have been no surprise to David Hunter nor to James Henderson.

Afterthought from Addis Ababa

On 18 August 1908, the British consul general in Addis Ababa, Herbert Hervey,[107] wrote to Sir Edward Grey in the Foreign Office in London summing up the repatriation saga from the viewpoint of the British legation in Addis Ababa. He reiterated Harrington's opposition to the repatriation of the Oromo in principle on the grounds that on return, "they would probably be considered as under an obligation to the Emperor, and where they might be made to work for nothing or next to nothing." James Henderson had suggested in an earlier missive that Harrington—a Roman Catholic—was not in sympathy with Protestant missions. Hervey was at pains to dispel this perception. He pointed instead to the gravity of Menelik's infirmity:

The grave illness of the Emperor for a long time prevented any steps being taken in the matter, but a few months ago when it became possible for non-controversial matters to be referred to him, I asked the Minister for Foreign Affairs whether His Majesty was prepared to fulfil his promise and advance the money for the repatriation of the Gallas. After much delay, during which full particulars of all those desiring to return was supplied to him, he declared that he had spoken to the Emperor, but His Majesty demurred at the large sum which would be required.[108]

Hervey explained that despite several subsequent inquiries, Menelik gave no definite response. It seemed to the legation that the idea had been mothballed in the imperial court. Then came the surprising news that the Oromo were on their way home. Hervey submitted his understanding of the level of German involvement in the repatriation process:

The explanation of this extraordinary procedure is that the Germans in the early months of this year were in high favour with the Abyssinians, who looked to them for advice and assistance in everything, and it is probable that at the very moment that I was taking representations on the subject of the Gallas, offers of assistance were coming from the German Legation, with the result that they preferred to accept the aid of those they considered at that time to be their best friends.[109]

Several of the parties involved in the repatriation plan doubted that Menelik had ever defrayed the cost of the Oromos' return voyage, based on the information passed on by the minister of foreign affairs in Addis Ababa. "Subsequent enquiries have elicited the fact that the Emperor himself defrayed the cost of the repatriation of the Gallas, which amounted to over Five thousand [Maria Theresa] dollars ([MT] $5,000). The Minister for Foreign Affairs makes no attempt to excuse his duplicity, which according to Abyssinian ideas is a synonym of diplomacy."[110]

Hervey concluded his letter with a commitment to keep himself informed after the arrival of the Oromo with regard to their treatment by the Abyssinian authorities, "with a view to rendering them any assistance that I properly can, but I do not think that those who have learnt useful trades and are industrious are likely to meet with trouble. From the British point of view their advent should be advantageous as after so many years under good government in a British Colony they will appreciate, and perhaps explain to their compatriots, the benefits to be derived from a civilised and orderly rule."[111]

After the reactions of Hervey's predecessor in Addis Ababa, the South African authorities, the Lovedale missionaries at Lovedale, and from within diplomatic circles, Hervey's own response showed a welcome pragmatism.

Within the year, Liban Bultum wrote once again to Lovedale. Writing from Addis Ababa on 15 March 1910, Liban reported that they were all comfortably settled, but that because of the emperor's illness, there had been a delay for some in finding work.[112] He reported that Milko Guyo's parents were also dead but that two of his brothers were still alive, and one was expected, at the time of writing, to come to see Milko.[113]

Table 11.1. Confirmed independent and *Kronprinz* repatriates

Independent repatriates		*Kronprinz* repatriates	
1	Amanu Figgo	1	Aguchello Chabani
2	Fayissa Hora	2	Agude Bulcha
3	Fayissa Umbe	3	Baki Malakka
4	Galgal Dikko	4	Berille Boko
5	Gamaches Garba	5	Daba Tobo
6	Nagaro Chali	6	Dinkitu Boensa
7	Nuro Chabse	7	Fayissi Gemo
8	Tolassa Wayessa	8	Galgalli Shangalla
		9	Gutama Tarafo
		10	Hawe Sukute
		11	Liban Bultum
		12	Milko Guyo
		13	Rufo Gangila
Total confirmed repatriates = 21			

(Source: Sandra Rowoldt Shell.)

Lovedale would continue to hear, from time to time, from the repatriated Oromo. These reports on the welfare of the repatriated Oromo provided important clues as to which of the Oromo had finally boarded the *Kronprinz* in 1909, allowing for a putative listing of all the Oromo who had returned home.

Most useful of all the communications was the letter from Milko Guyo, writing c/o the Bank of Abyssinia, Addis Ababa, in January 1925. Milko listed all those who were known to be have died and those whom he knew were still alive. Table 11.1 lists the eight independent returnees as well as those who returned on the *Kronprinz* in 1909. Several of the Oromo couples were accompanied by their children. For example, Aguchello Chabani had three children and Milko Guyo had one, as did Liban Bultum, Berille Boko, Rufo Gangila, and Hawe Sukute. The count of passengers aboard the *Kronprinz* when it docked at Beira may or may not have included these Oromo children. This is as accurate a passenger list as can be constructed.

By 1909, the Oromo fell into three categories: those who had died by the end of 1909; those who had repatriated; and those who had remained and made their lives either in South Africa or farther afield. The spread was remarkably similar for the three groups, resulting in roughly one-third for each.

Of the twenty-two Oromo who had died by the end of 1909, three were early independent repatriates, while nineteen died in South Africa, so these three could legitimately fall into either group. However, in the ensuing analyses, the three repatriate deaths have been grouped in the total of twenty-one confirmed repatriates, reducing the twenty-two deaths before the end of 1909 to nineteen. One Oromo male, Mulatta Billi, became a sailor and made his way to the United States. The remaining twenty-three felt sufficiently at home in their adopted country to settle in South Africa permanently.

The twenty-one Oromo who repatriated did not spell out their reasons for wanting to return home. Certainly, a sense of alienation in South Africa and nostalgia for home would have been significant factors to consider. Perhaps some of those who returned had reason to believe they were going home to their families and to the security of their families' immovable and movable property. As discussed in an earlier chapter, the extent of immovable property is one indicator of relative wealth (see pages 44–46). Well over two-thirds of the repatriates (69.2 percent) had given some indication of property size when interviewed as children at Sheikh Othman. Of these, 61.1 percent of those opting to return home came from families with large pieces of land. A further 27.8 percent came from families with medium-sized properties. A mere 11.1 percent came from families with small properties. Aggregating the repatriates from families with large or medium-sized properties indicates that as many as 88.9 percent of the repatriates were raised on fairly substantial pieces of land—certainly an incentive to consider.

The twenty-three Oromo who stayed in South Africa did so for several reasons, as cited in their responses to the repatriation questionnaire circulated by David A. Hunter in 1903. They usually wanted to stay because they had a secure job, or because they had a local relationship and/or a family. There is the unanswerable possibility as well, of course: some may not have wanted to return because memories of their trauma-filled early lives were too painful (see map 11.3, showing their distribution across the country).

Kimberley emerged as the destination of choice for almost one-third of these twenty-three Oromo. The country's economy in the late nineteenth century was dominated by the discovery and exploitation of its mineral deposits—diamonds in the Kimberley area, followed by gold on the Witwatersrand. One of the seven Oromo who settled in Kimberley was Wayessa Tonki, who opened his own photographic business in the "Malay" Camp.[114] Badassa Wulli, who had trained as a wagonmaker, was a storeman in Tarry & Company, a Kimberley engineering firm. He died in Kimberley in 1927. Faraja Lalego was employed in a grocery store; Tola Abaye, who had been partially trained as a cobbler at Lovedale, was working in a grocery store; and Tola Urgessa was employed as a railway porter. Jifari Roba, one of the two Oromo women who settled in Kimberley, married Tola Abaye; and the other woman, Turungo Gudda, married a local Kimberley man.

Six Oromo settled in Port Elizabeth. Of these, Amaye Tiksa was a storeman; Balcha Billo worked in a store; Bayan Liliso worked for some time in the bookshop at Lovedale before landing a position in a timber company's office in Port Elizabeth. Faraja Jimma worked as a carpenter and eventually opened his own carpentry business in Strangers' Location near Port Elizabeth.[115] Hora Bulcha had a position as a painter, and Wakinni Ugga was employed by a private household as a cook.

Three Oromo men and one woman settled in Cape Town. The lone woman was Turungo Tinno, who worked for J. Joseph on Commercial Street, Cape Town. Of

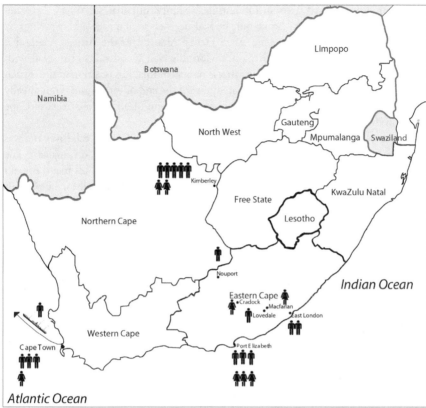

MAP 11.3. Domiciles of the Oromo in South Africa by 1909 (source: Sandra Rowoldt Shell).

the men, Faraja Jimma took up a post as a carpenter with the Table Bay Harbour Board, Wayessa Tikse was employed as a shop assistant in Hepworth Stores, and Wakinne Nagesso became an ostrich feather dresser.[116] In South Africa, the latter part of the nineteenth century and the first decade of the twentieth century saw a massive boom in the breeding of ostriches, as well as the plucking, packing, finishing, and provision of their feathers to eager international markets. The successful South African ostrich enterprise was run largely by a group of Jewish businessmen. Ostrich feathers had become the vogue for fashionable women in Europe and beyond, and it seemed the trade could not fail. But the unexpected happened. The outbreak of the First World War in 1914 sounded the sudden death knell for the commercial production of ostriches and their feathers. Wartime privation led rapidly to changes in fashion trends, primarily on grounds of affordability. From 1914, an estimated 80 percent of South African ostrich farmers suffered bankruptcy. They let their ostriches loose in the *veld* (open grasslands) or slaughtered them for their meat, primarily to make *biltong*.[117]

Wakinne was a man with an interesting life story, but that story had a sad denouement. By the time war broke out, he had been cheated out of all his savings by an American missionary, Reverend Allen Henry Attaway, of the African Methodist Episcopal Church. His South African bride (Sophie Nell Webster) had run away with a German sailor to Keetmanshoop in what is now Namibia. His position in the ostrich feather business may have been terminated toward the end of 1914—and if not already terminated, it was certainly at risk. He was found lying dead in the streets of Cape Town in the early hours of 2 January 1915.

Two chose East London as their home. One, Kintiso Bulcha, was a cabdriver and was in charge for a while of a conveyance owned by his Oromo friend Rufo Gangila.[118] The other, Shamo Ayanso, who had fallen ill in East London while he and his friend Amanu Figgo were preparing to board ship, headed for Aden. He did not sail for home with Amanu, and there is no known official death record, so one can only speculate on his fate.

Two resourceful Oromo women, Bisho Jarsa and Warkitu Galatu, took up teaching posts—Bisho in Cradock and Warkitu in the Free Church Mission School at Macfarlan, near Lovedale. Wayessa Gudru was last heard of during the Anglo-Boer War when he was a transport driver in Noupoort, a railway junction linking the Port Elizabeth–Bloemfontein and Cape Town–Johannesburg lines. Finally, the profoundly brain-damaged Gilo Kashe remained in the care of the staff at Lovedale until his death on 15 February 1948.

The Oromo have long held a reputation for easy assimilation into other ethnicities and cultures, so settling in South Africa may not have been too much of a challenge. Nonetheless, assimilation would probably have been easier for the five who married South African spouses than for the three who married fellow Oromo.

By 1909, the Oromo had already spent almost two decades in the southernmost country on the African continent, and they would have had a fair idea of both the hazards and the opportunities of deciding to stay. However, they might not have anticipated the increasing racial discrimination they would undoubtedly experience, culminating—for the few who survived that long—in the statutory apartheid that the incoming nationalist government imposed on the country in 1948.

The Oromo, despite their youth—and perhaps partly because of it—made their mark in South Africa from the day they disembarked from the *Conway Castle*. The attention of the public began in earnest with their arrival in East London in August 1890, which had the local populace agog with excitement and led to a large and curious dockside crowd and extensive press coverage. In the years they were to live and study at Lovedale, the institution would issue regular reports on their progress, published primarily but not exclusively in the institution's *Christian Express*. In addition, Lovedale would issue incidental reports throughout the year recording the more momentous of their life and death experiences until they dispersed on leaving Lovedale to fashion their lives on their own.

The departure of the group of seventeen in 1909 aboard the *Konprinz* was as dramatic as the children's arrival nearly two decades earlier. However, where their role in the drama of their arrival as recently liberated slave children in 1890 was essentially passive—even pathetic—the drama of their departure was generated by the Oromo themselves. In maneuvering their own way home, whether independently or in the 1909 group, they redefined themselves as free, fully fledged, self-determining adults.

The issue of the repatriation of a sizable group of Oromo in 1909 resulted in a diplomatic melee when the missionaries suddenly realized the determination of the returnee hopefuls to go home—no matter how or with whose help. That Liban Bultum, on behalf of the Oromo, approached the Germans to assist them was a particularly bitter pill, given the tension around maritime rights in which Germany and Britain vied for effective dominance of Africa's eastern coastline, together with Germany's sweeping territorial ambitions on the continent of Africa.

The involvement of the Germans led to international ramifications in which powerful political figures drawn from the Cape, Britain, Germany, and Ethiopia were involved. Animosity, mortification, guilt, and foreboding clouded the Oromos' embarkation.

An unrelentingly high mortality rate is a constant thread in the Oromo repatriation saga. By 1903, when David Hunter polled the surviving Oromo, twenty-one of the Oromo (33.7 percent) had already died. By 1909, when the group boarded the *Kronprinz* in Port Elizabeth, the death toll had risen slightly to twenty-two, or 34.4 percent. These Oromo had been cared for in a protected, nurturing environment from their arrival in 1890 until they dispersed on completion of their studies. The climate was mild, their nutrition was good, and their treatment benign. They had entered an alien disease environment but had adequate health facilities at their disposal to nurse them back to health. Despite their good treatment and diet, they died faster than their fellow students at Lovedale—a handy control group. What was common to the Oromo children, and differentiated them from their non-Oromo Lovedale peers, was their first-passage ordeal. The physical and psychological trauma of the first passage was unremitting in those formative years. Their continuing high mortality even after repatriation reflected how persistent that trauma turned out to be.

The first passage shaped their demographic destiny. Their triumph was their survival, coupled with their literacy, courage, initiative, and leadership in negotiating their own return home. Their repatriation came at the conjuncture of imperial rivalries: first, the overarching scramble for Africa; second, the Ethiopian triumph in defeating their would-be colonizers—the Italians, at Adwa in 1896; and third, the looming threat of world war. In the midst of this political ferment, the Oromo managed to slip between the interstices created by political rivalries to engineer their repatriation and their own—albeit uncertain—futures.

Reflections

The dearth of first-passage narratives in slave trade history has left significant historiographical gaps. Historians have assumed, as did David Henige, that first-passage sources did not exist. The absence of first-passage narratives in the history of the Horn of Africa slave trade has meant that scholars have been able to surmise little, beyond that it was predominantly a trade of Oromo children and that young Oromo girls, renowned for their beauty, attracted the highest monetary value. Consequently, scholars have had difficulty understanding who the enslaved children were, which regions they came from, what their ethnicity was, what types of homes they were raised in, what their parents' occupations were, their relative wealth and social status, and so on. Nor has it been possible to write anything substantive about the moment of capture, the identity of the captors, the prevalence and periods of domestic enslavement, or the length and nature of the journeys to the coast and the external, oceanic slave trade. The major contribution of this book is that the individual narratives provided by the sixty-four Oromo children taken to the Lovedale mission in South Africa provide answers to these questions.

Using prosopography, the preeminent tool for group analysis, this study has analyzed the common characteristics of this group of Oromo children from coded eyewitness accounts. That each account follows the same sequence of topics suggests that the missionaries who took down the children's statements used a common set of questions when interviewing each child.

Using the children's narratives, this study began with analyses of the Oromo group's family structure, land tenure, wealth and status, domicile, and ethnicity. The narratives then focus on details of the children's enslavement, their periods of domestic servitude, and their journeys to the Red Sea coast. The narratives cease at the point that the children board the slave dhows waiting to embark on the short middle passage to the Arabian slave markets on the opposite shores of the Red Sea. Their middle passage and rescue by the Royal Navy, their interim stationing at the Keith-Falconer Mission at Sheikh Othman north of Aden in Yemen, their final journey to Lovedale, their experiences at Lovedale and afterward, and their repatriation have been discussed using additional archival data, added to the core prosopography, in the remaining chapters. What conclusions emerge?

Family Structure

There is consensus in the secondary literature, based for the most part on travelers' accounts, that the slave trade of the Horn of Africa was primarily a trade of children. The narratives analyzed here broadly confirm this but go much further. Scholars of the Red Sea slave trade have, in the main, estimated that the majority of captured slaves were girls between seven and seventeen years, and that across the genders, the great majority were younger than twenty years. The ages of the Oromo children in the sample of this study are drawn from their own personal accounts—primary sources carrying more heft. Data provided in the children's narratives accord with the travelers' assessments but provide much more detail. Far beyond the secondary sources, they give us access, in the first place, to far more detailed aspects of age; for example, we know the youngest child was a boy aged eight and the oldest a girl aged seventeen at the time of capture, and that the average (median) age of the sample was 11.7 years, with half the children falling below this age and the other half above. Their tender years would have contributed to their vulnerability in the face of the agencies driving a thriving domestic and oceanic slave trade.

Second, the Oromo children disclose the degree of orphanhood, a facet of the first passage nowhere explored in the secondary sources. According to their own accounts, almost 13 percent of the Oromo children were double orphans, that is, children who had lost both parents; and, cumulatively, nearly one-third (31.4 percent) of the Oromo children in the sample were either paternal or maternal orphans or had lost both parents, that is, were orphans in terms of the standard UNICEF definition. However, we can go beyond the UNICEF definition for a more detailed breakdown of orphanhood. One child was a maternal orphan; fifteen had lost their fathers and were therefore paternal orphans (17.4 percent); and eleven (12.8 percent) were full or double orphans, that is, they had lost both parents. This factor, not even examined in earlier first-passage speculations, constitutes a hitherto unsuspected, but obviously important, psychological aspect of enslavement.

Though we cannot get into these children's minds, we can assume that those who were orphaned would have been acutely aware of having lost the security of home and hearth. We must, however, remember that all the children would have experienced loss through extraction from their family environments. Orphans made ideal slaves. They had less hope of survival on their own, had less motivation to flee, and were generally less rebellious than a child from a regular, fully populated nuclear family. When we consider what we know of the importance of the extended African family from the huge body of African anthropological literature, the lack of support experienced by these children would have made them especially vulnerable.

Slave Loyalty or the Stockholm Syndrome

Without their biological parents, some of these orphaned children could have been particularly susceptible to the Stockholm or "captor-bonding" syndrome, whereby they would have developed an irrational attachment to their captors—maybe even regarding their captors in *loco parentis*. Some historians have argued that this is a subject for "armchair psychologists." However, the phenomenon (also known as the "slave loyalty syndrome") has been studied in the context of slavery by scholars drawn from a range of disciplines. Ruth Scodel, a Greek and Latin scholar of the classical era, examined the behavior and motivation of Ajax's slave concubine Tecmessa, exploring her ability to reconcile her slave status with her genuinely deep feelings for her captor, Ajax. As Scodel explained: "This phenomenon of victims who adopt the world-view of those who have power over them is, of course, well known, as [the] Stockholm Syndrome."[1]

Claudia Card, a philosopher and feminist scholar, dealt extensively with the manifestation of Stockholm syndrome in slavery situations from Roman times, to the American Deep South, and through to the trafficking of sex slaves in the twenty-first century.[2] Two scholars in the social sciences, Barbara Huddleston-Mattai and P. Rudy Mattai, have explored the manifestation of the Stockholm syndrome and the long-term residual impact of slavery on the societal interrelationships of African Americans in twentieth-century America.[3]

Shortly after their arrival at Sheikh Othman, the children, the missionaries, and the people of Aden and Sheikh Othman all referred to the Oromo children as the "family."[4] There is evidence at Sheikh Othman of the children calling Matthew Lochhead "Father."

Later, at Lovedale, they accorded the title "Abba" to the master closest to them, their boarding master, Alexander Geddes. Gilo Kashe, the Oromo child who suffered the worst level of trauma of them all, could not leave Lovedale as he was intellectually and physically incapable of taking care of himself. In a recent study on Gilo's trauma, the author argues that Gilo

> represents a classic case of Stockholm syndrome. His lifetime accommodation within the Lovedale environment reveals the epitome of what the Stockholm syndrome means. His disfigured mind and body became a poignant living testament to the multiplicity of traumas which deprived him of the power of self-determination. Even the gentle care of the Lovedale missionaries exerted its own invisible subtle shackles. Gilo could not leave. He could not survive on his own. In a sense he was enslaved not by any external agency but by the legacy of his trauma. But Gilo readily adopted the world-view of those who cared for and had power over him.[5]

However, a strong and stable family structure was no guarantee of protection at point of capture. Numbers alone were no guarantee of protection. Most of the enslaved boys and girls (80.2 percent) lived in families of between three and nine family members. The mean (or average) family size across both genders was 5.69, with a median of 5.0. At the upper end of the scale, one boy (an orphan) had thirteen siblings. Even the presence of parents at the moment of capture was not always an effective shield against the determined slave raider. More than half of the children had at least one parent present when they were captured: 51.2 percent of the fathers and 58.1 percent of the mothers were at home when their children were captured. And almost one-third (32.6 percent) of the children had both parents present at the moment of capture.

Land Tenure

The dominant system among the Oromo was individual freehold tenure that could be passed on to a landholder's descendants in perpetuity. The proportion of individual freehold landowners among the families of the Oromo children in the sample is fairly consistent with the norm for the preconquest Oromo population as a whole. Nearly half (47.7 percent) of those children who responded to the missionaries' questions regarding landownership told them that their families owned their land. Not quite a third (32.3 percent) lived on leased land within a system comparable with feudal tenure. The remaining 20 percent were born into slavery or were cadastral slaves, that is, slaves who could be inherited or transferred along with the property on which they resided.

As Menelik conquered one Oromo territory after another, he replaced the entrenched system of freehold rights among the Oromo with his system of *naftanya-gabbar*, or "armed settler-serfs." This forced the Oromo to give up their landownership rights and resulted in a nation of *gabbars*, or serfs. However, at the time the children were enslaved, freehold tenure among the Oromo still predominated, indicating that Menelik's influence had not yet impacted their home regions. What emerged, however, was a distinct differentiation along gender lines. Many more boys (30.8 percent) came from freehold farms than girls (18.5 percent). Considerably more girls (18.5 percent) than boys (12.3 percent) came from families who were living under feudal conditions, leasing their lands from the local chiefs or kings. And many more girls (15.4 percent) than boys (4.6 percent) were already enslaved by the time they were impelled toward the Red Sea coast and the maritime slave trade.

Status and Wealth

While four of the Oromo girls were of royal descent, the majority of the remaining females lived in humbler circumstances than the males. The relative wealth and local power of the children's families—even this royal descent—did not protect them from servitude when raiders descended on their villages seizing children as slaves by force, or when creditors knocked on the doors of their homes demanding satisfaction on outstanding debts. Taking landholding size as one measure of wealth, there was an insignificant difference between the genders: 20.6 percent of the boys from freehold households, compared with 23.5 percent of the girls, were from what might be considered wealthy homes. For the rest, while fewer girls were raised on freehold farms than boys, a higher proportion of girls (57.1 percent) were from families owning what they described as a large piece of land (i.e., land of six acres and more). By comparison, 36.8 percent of the boys reported coming from such large freehold farms. The parents of an effective two-thirds of the group (66.7 percent) made their living off the land. The parents of 8.7 percent of the group hired themselves out as plowmen or tillers, while a further 8.7 percent (all widows) were engaged in manual labor in the fields. A total of 7.2 percent of the parents were engaged as domestic slaves. One widow became a market vendor; and one father, the only artisan, was a village tailor. The Oromo children, therefore, were not uniformly from any one social stratum and certainly not all from the lower strata. They grew up in homes that straddled a range of social strata, none of which proved more protected or more vulnerable than another. This resonates with the shock realization in Voltaire's satirical attack on eighteenth-century French society in his novel *Candide*, that enslavement could happen to anybody, even royalty.[6]

Domicile and Ethnicity

The question of the children's ethnicity is a critical one. They had an immediate, ascribed "Galla" identity aboard the *Osprey* and at Aden. At the Keith-Falconer Mission at Sheikh Othman, Matthew Lochhead and William Gardner reportedly wasted no time in learning the "Galla" or Oromo language (Afaan Oromoo). Shortly after their arrival at Lovedale, several of the children wrote letters in which they clearly identified themselves and their peers as "Galla," a term now considered pejorative ("Oromo" has been used universally since the middle of the twentieth century). Gutama Tarafo, one of the boys, penned a detailed commentary on his land and his people titled "My Essay Is upon Gallaland" (see appendix D). Despite their ready personal identification with a "Galla" ethnicity, none of the children volunteered a definition of their own ethnicity in their narratives.

This was assuredly more the result of not being asked the question than not giving an answer. Ethnicity was therefore derived from an analysis of family names and regions of domicile in terms of which a convincing majority—89.9 percent—could be identified as what we would now call Oromo. The four ethnic groupings from which the remaining 10.1 percent sprang all had strong historical links with—and most were ethnically cognate with—the Oromo. A further 7.4 percent were identified as Kaffa, now one of the nine administrative regions of Oromia. Only three other children could not be described as Oromo: one was Gurage, one Shangalla, and one Yambo. All three ethnicities occupied territories to the south and southwest of what was then known as Abyssinia.[7] While political geography is a human construct, it also signals the history and interethnic ties of the groupings. In 1888 and 1889, such groupings were as much a target for Menelik as the Oromo. Shared threats lead to shared bonds.

Although it was possible to group almost all the children by country of origin, there were a few cases where more than one child came from a particular town or village. Even in instances where two children came from the same village, they were enslaved at different times. No two children in the sample were enslaved in the same place at the same time. There was no collective capture of villages, no mass kidnapping to stock a caravan to the coast. Enslavement was an individuated, not a collective, process. The first time any of the children met one another happened when the routes of a small number of them converged in the littoral slave markets near the Red Sea coast entrepôts.

The Moment of Capture

Chapter 5 focused on a range of conditions at the moment of capture in an effort to understand the underlying motivations and practices in the acquisition of slaves for the local slave system and for the external slave trade. Establishing the identity of the captor is, I suggest, fundamental to understanding the operations of the trade. Secondary sources invariably implicate external Arab agencies. However, the children pointed emphatically to the roles of the Sidama (meaning "Abyssinian" in Afaan Oromoo) and the Sayo, Kaffa, Leka, and Jimma local agencies as their slave raiders. One boy named his captors as "a party of Mahommedan raiders"; another as "three men—

whom he calls black Arabs." So it was neighboring people in conflict with the Oromo, not outsiders, who were the principal slave raiders. The Christian missionaries recording the children's accounts would have been likely to exaggerate any Arab influence or involvement. That they faithfully recorded such limited Muslim involvement suggests that these sources are innocent of anti-Muslim bias.

That the slave raiders mostly (57 percent) acted singly indicates that the enslavement of the children was not, at least at point of capture, a mass or overtly syndicated operation. It is possible that each captor acted alone in the field but as part of a larger slave trade network. However, the high proportion of children who were seized in the first instance to service the internal slave network rather than the external slave trade chain (64 percent) indicates that domestic slavery was endemic. This was a thriving local system that undergirded the oceanic slave trade of the Horn of Africa.

The children confirmed that slave raiding was decisively a male preserve: 93 percent of their captors were men. Women enslavers, who made up the remaining 7 percent, lured the children away from their homes rather than seizing them by force. The children identified just under two-thirds of the captors as professional slave raiders (59.3 percent). A smaller number emanated from local and regional royal circles (12.8 percent), while 11.6 percent of the abductors seized children for purposes of cadastral or agricultural slavery, and a much smaller proportion (2.3 percent) of slave traders were merchants. Military captors formed the smallest category identified by the children, suggesting that the abductions were overwhelmingly initiated and enacted by local and regional civilian agencies. Unexpected findings were that 29.1 percent of the captors were people the children knew and 15.1 percent were kin. The children's evidence qualifies the Miers and Kopytoff findings of a "slavery-to-kinship" continuum, wherein the statuses of slave and kin member merge into one another and where neat definitions become blurred and ambiguous. The family members who enslaved these children did so with motives that had little or nothing to do with the children's welfare. They sold them into the local slave system or even, in some cases, directly into the external slave trade.

Few of the children, therefore, were enslaved directly by foreign forces. Menelik may have enlisted the support of local people and their leaders, but he did not use his military to enslave any of this group of children directly, though he had a substantial material interest in the slave trade terminating in the coastal entrepôts through his dual taxation system. A tax was levied on every slave passing through his kingdom of Shewa, and an additional tax was exacted on every slave sold within his kingdom.

For the abduction of children for the purposes of slavery, slave raiders needed to effect a successful and rapid escape. The terrain in much of Oromoland was rocky, mountainous, and rugged. In such circumstances, it was logical for at least some of the captors to use horses to carry off their prey. Consistent with this information, an aggregated total of 34.9 percent of the children indicated either that their captors were on "horseback" (7.09 percent) or that they were "carried away" by their captors (27.9 percent). Distinct gender differences showed up in the analysis of the mode of capture. Aggregating reports of "seizure," in which violence was implicit with those captured using a range of violent measures, many more boys (36 percent) than girls (20.9

percent) were subjected to violent treatment at the moment of their enslavement. By contrast, the majority of the girls were enslaved through barter, negotiation, and nonviolent theft. Almost twice as many girls (2.3 percent) were born into slavery as boys, only 1.2 percent of whom were born into slavery (i.e., their families were already enslaved). Though slave capture as a consequence of birth is the most passive of all the modes of capture, slave catching was generally violent.

Eight of the Oromo children were sold for money or were bartered for food or goods at the moment of capture. Cash prices, transacted in the contemporary unit of currency in world trade of Maria Theresa dollars (MT), ranged from MT$5 to MT$16, with a mean of MT$10. Not included in these calculations was the rank outlier of MT$175 paid to effect the sole manumission in the database in 1890. The principal commodity for which the children were exchanged was *amole*, or salt bars, then regarded across the Horn of Africa as an alternative currency. Trade items also included livestock, grain, and other agricultural produce, all of whose value was enhanced by the incipient drought and famine conditions beginning to impact the region. Thirty-nine of the children reported being sold but named no price, while the remaining seventeen were acquired by other means, for example, theft by kidnapping or being slave-born.

Almost two-thirds (64 percent) of the children were adamant that domestic slavery in Oromoland and Abyssinia was their primary experience, while only 36 percent were sold directly into the external slave trade network. These findings, together with the identity of the captors, point to a thriving local slave system. Almost two-thirds of the children were enslaved locally, for periods ranging from a few weeks to nine years, before being sold into the maritime slave trade network headed for the Red Sea entrepôts. Once again, there were marked gender differences in what the children experienced. Young Oromo girls, with their reputation of great beauty, were valued most highly of all slaves in the Horn of Africa trade. This would probably account for the higher percentage of girls (25.6 percent) than boys (10.5 percent) being captured specifically for the external slave trade network. The higher number of boys (38.4 percent) than girls (25.6 percent) enslaved locally may also have been a reflection of their greater usefulness for manual and agricultural labor. It was customary for boys and men to work in the fields and with livestock. Young girls and women were limited, in the main, to indoor domestic work, reproduction, and, in a few cases, the harem. Claude Meillassoux posited the notion that women were more likely to be enslaved for their labor than for their beauty or fecundity. We have photographic evidence that many of these young Oromo girls were indeed beautiful, and there is no hint in their accounts that they were selected for their capacity to do manual labor. So we may need to regard Meillassoux's theory with some caution in dealing with this aspect of the Red Sea slave trade.

On the Road

The children were clear that they were enslaved one at a time, never as part of a group. There were no instances of any of the children coming from the same place within the same period, but six routes can be discerned, identified, and clustered as such by a congruence in the last three or four destinations on the children's journeys. The closest the journeys came to consistency lay in their destination entrepôts. The thirteen children from the later 1889 dhows all headed for Tadjoura, whereas all but one of the clustered routes of the 1888 group terminated in Araito (Rahayta).

Regardless of the destination entrepôt, all but one of the routes converged in Aussa, the major slave market governing the external trade and the seat of the powerful and wealthy Aussan Sultanate. Aussa was laid out expressly for the slave trade—one part being occupied by buyers and the other part by sellers, similar to the town called Offersdorp ("bidders or sacrifice village") on the west coast of Africa—and was effectively instrumental in controlling all external trade. What has emerged clearly from this study is that despite the disparate nature of the routes, Aussa was where the power of the commercial operators of the external trade resided. None of these aggregated routes matched any of the established routes listed in the contemporary travel literature. In one exceptional experience, one of the Oromo princesses was shipped separately aboard a slave dhow and landed on the Arabian coast. William Grant, a prominent British East Africa Company administrator, discovered her in a slave market in Hodeidah, manumitted her, and took her to Aden to join the other Oromo children at Sheikh Othman.

Neither the circumstances of enslavement nor the routes taken by the children indicate a concerted plan to enslave a particular group. What emerged from the analysis was that sixty-four children, who were brought together by force of circumstance, largely shared a common heritage and a broad, common area of origin roughly occupying the area of modern Oromia. Only their Oromo identity, whether by birth or consolidated by their later association, and their shared locale in the south and southwest of Abyssinia, bound this group together. For the most part, they met shortly before they boarded the dhows as strangers, but ultimately they cohered socially as a unified Oromo group, united against the vicissitudes of the middle passage and exile in a foreign land. Over time, being together on board ship and at the mission would have strengthened the idea of a common ethnicity.

The children's eyewitness accounts have allowed for a much closer analysis of slave experience traveling on the road to the maritime slave trade depots than has been possible using the available travel accounts, or indeed any other sources. From their accounts we know, inter alia, how many segments there were to their routes, the time spent on the road, the time spent in domestic enslavement, how many times they were sold, and the identity of the slave traders transporting them. The average total first-passage time from their capture to the coast—which included travel time and periods of domestic enslavement—was just over thirteen months (394 days), and the median was three months (ninety days). The children spent between one week and eighteen months on the road, with an average of seventy-eight days for their total traveling time. The routes were mostly complex. The number of legs en route ranged from three to twenty-three, with an average of 7.00 and a median of 7.25. The children were sold, or otherwise changed hands, between two and ten times along the way. Analysts and commentators have been able only to make assumptions about such aspects of the first passage, and there is nothing in the existing literature to suggest the full extent—or impact—of the extended time on the road, or the trauma of being traded so many times along the way.

Whereas the people who originally enslaved the children were largely local or neighboring, the slave traders along the routes were more diverse, particularly farther north toward the coastal regions. Aggregating traders and merchants across all segments of the journeys, the majority (20.78 percent) were from the Adal region. The Adal merchants dominated the littoral Ethiopian slave trade at the point of influence of the coastal entrepôts and controlled the export of human cargoes across the Red Sea to the Arabian mainlands. They were not slave raiders themselves but relied on the inland abduction forays of the Gudru (12.95 percent); Atari (10.84 percent); Sidama (8.73 percent); and others from whom they purchased child slaves close to the points of embarkation. Local traders the children mentioned were the Leka (5.12 percent); Jimma (4.22 percent); Tigre (3.92 percent); and "Mohammedan Gallas" (1.81 percent). Other local traders were mentioned once only; such miscellaneous traders constituted 21.99 percent of the whole. Traders from farther afield were rare. The children mentioned only one Abyssinian, one Arab, and one Sudanese among the slave traders.

Two of the boys endured unidentified but severe illnesses for protracted periods during their travels, while a third boy said he had fallen ill with "*finno*," a form of smallpox. One boy suffered profound brain damage, his mobility was severely compromised, and he had an ear partially bitten off by a camel during his first passage. The cause of this mental and physical impairment remains uncertain, but medical opinion suggests that bubonic plague, one of the epidemics sweeping the country at the time of the Great Famine and Great Drought along with smallpox, could have precipitated his condition.

The incidence and severity of ill-treatment experienced during the first passage has also emerged from our analysis of the young Oromo slaves. Nine children (all but one boys) recounted specific acts of cruelty meted out to them. Two boys and one girl said they were kept in chains—the boys' feet were chained, while the girl's hands were chained together. A further boy reported that he was included in a group of slave children who were chained together for a week. Others were tied rather than chained. One boy described how his hands were tied, and another boy was tied and locked up in a room. Yet another had a piece of leather stuffed into his mouth, was both tied and chained, and then was forced beneath a bed, where he was kept for a week. In the only instance of branding, a boy had three marks scarred into each cheek. The final child described how he was kept in a house in a forest with his feet in stocks for two days. Fewer than half of these instances of harsh treatment were consequences of attempting to escape, and the degree of harshness of the treatment was not determined by whether a child had attempted to escape or not. Nor was cruelty the province of one particular group of traders—they ranged from kin to black Arabs, Atari, Sidama, and traders from Entotto and Gombu.

The Middle Passage

The Red Sea slave trade presented a different picture from that of the West African/Atlantic trades. Perhaps most marked was the difference in the middle-passage experiences of slaves from the two areas. In the Red Sea trade, the sea voyage was seldom more than a day. It was usually a matter of six to twelve hours for a dhow to cross from the Abyssinian coast to the Arabian ports on the opposite shores. Mortality rates were commensurately lower in most cases—the deaths caused by the *Osprey*'s Gardner guns being the exception in this period, rather than the norm. The official record shows that there were five deaths during the children's brief middle passage in September 1888, and all five deaths took place aboard one dhow, the *Alkathora*. The captain, Ali Kira Mahomed, was one of the five who died, along with four slaves, victims of the firepower used by the *Osprey* in its interventions with the three dhows.

Whereas the daily mortality rate (DMR: the number of deaths per slaves embarked, divided by voyage length, multiplied by 1,000) aboard the *Alkathora* was 60.61, the DMR for the full slave contingent of 208 who boarded all three dhows was 19.23. Economic historian David Eltis has calculated that for ships embarking from regions along the west coast of Africa for the years 1811 to 1863, the DMR ranged from a low of 1.2 (Congo North including Cape Lopez, 1811–1836) to a high of 9.49 (South East Africa, 1837–1863).[8] According to the official British inventory tabled in Parliament, there were 1,423 slaves on board dhows intercepted by ships of the Royal Navy between 1 July 1887 and 31 December 1889, and a total of thirteen slaves died aboard those dhows (including the four killed in the course of the *Osprey* interventions), giving a DMR of 9.14, assuming all the voyages across the narrow sliver of Red Sea took no more than a single day. This rate accords with the Eltis range given above, but ranking the Oromo children's mortality rates against these figures underlines the irregularity of their experiences: these deaths were not a legacy of the first passage, nor were they caused by the conditions aboard the dhows of the middle passage, but rather the deaths were the result of external agencies.

The interventions of the British Navy changed the demographic profile of the Oromo children's middle passage in a matter of a few short but violent minutes, with tragic consequences for four of the children and the captain aboard that dhow. And the cumulated effects of an emotionally harrowing and physically damaging first passage would take a hefty toll in the lives of these children within the year at Sheikh Othman and within the first decade of their liberation at Lovedale Institution.

From the Red Sea to Lovedale

The interception of the slave dhows by the Royal Navy in September 1888 and August 1889, with the rescue of the slaves on board and their liberation, signaled the start of the next major phase in the lives of the Oromo children. Uprooted abruptly from their homes, subjected to journeys of hundreds of kilometers to the entrepôts on the Red Sea, enduring and surviving an armed sea battle in the course of their rescue, and finding themselves in the temporary care of strangers in Aden was traumatic enough. They were then exposed to a harsh and unhealthy climate at the Keith-Falconer Mission, where one-fifth of them died within months.

Significantly, the sex ratio of the group was shaped artificially at different moments in the course of their enslavement by the interventions of human agency and circumstance. Their survival of the first passage (taking into account the four slave deaths) resulted in a sex ratio of 99. Thereafter, the sex ratio changed in part as a result of religious selection in Aden, which excluded all the Muslim children in the group disembarked by the *Osprey* (i.e., approximately half). Colonel Edward Stace, British administrator in Aden, and the Keith-Falconer missionaries demonstrated their respect for the Islamic faith by ensuring that the liberated Muslim slave children were placed with established Muslim families. This sensitivity respected the Muslim children's needs to be raised in Muslim homes and again indicated an absence of anti-Islamic bias on the part of the missionaries.

Missionary selection at Sheikh Othman skewed the gender balance in favor of the boys. After deaths at Sheikh Othman and the addition of new arrivals in 1889 and 1890, the sex ratio for the group that set out for Lovedale was 191, vastly different from the original shipboard ratio at the point of their rescue. Instead of the original slight excess of girls, the group that sailed for Mauritius en route to South Africa had twice the number of boys as girls.

About the voyage from Aden to Mauritius aboard the French steamship *Rio Grande* we know nothing, except that all of the children survived. We do know that they were treated kindly aboard their next ship, *Conway Castle*, which met them in Port Louis to carry them on the final leg of their seaboard journey to East London. For example, Captain Warden and his crew even included a group trip to the Fillis Circus, undoubtedly the first such treat they had experienced in their young lives as slaves. Did the children comprehend that the landmass they saw from the deck of the *Conway* that August morning in 1890 was once again their own continent of Africa, albeit so far south?

Life and Death at Lovedale

Although the Oromo children's arrival at Lovedale brought its own set of cultural jolts and unfamiliarities, there was perhaps some comfort in knowing they were in a stable environment, with a kinder climate and a diet with which they were, at least in part, familiar. There would be no more unexpected dislocations and no more terror of the intensity they had experienced in slavery. However unfamiliar their new surroundings, they were at least on the African continent. This did not prevent them from pining for home, and many of them expressly planned to return. By the time the children arrived at Lovedale, they had coalesced into a unitary group, no doubt strengthened by their common shipboard ordeals, defined by their primary identity of Oromo, by their language, and differentiated only by their gender. Whatever nuances of clan or ethnic differences there might have been in the microcosm of their homeland were submerged when confronted by their common sense of foreignness at Lovedale.

Death once again became part of their lives and took thirteen of their companions in the first ten years. The Oromo mortality rate was markedly higher than that of their South African fellow students at Lovedale. The deleterious impact of their enslavement experience was to have enduring effects. It impacted the physical, psychological, mental, and emotional health of some of the children, compromised the quality of life of many, and demonstrably shortened nearly all of their lives. Two thirds (65.71 percent) died before reaching their thirtieth birthday. Only four are known to have survived beyond seventy years of age. Like the AIDS pandemic of the twentieth and twenty-first centuries, slavery turned their population pyramid on its head by attacking the young. Of those whose dates of death are known both at Lovedale and beyond, only 14 percent survived beyond fifty years of age.

Going Home

The call of their homeland was insistent. Between early 1900 and September 1902, eight young Oromo men sailed from South Africa independently. By early 1900, the first young Oromo man, Galgal Dikko, was ready to set off for Ethiopia on his own, and he died there circa 1902. He was followed shortly thereafter by Nagaro Chali, who became a colporteur in Harar, Ethiopia. Early in 1901, Gamaches Garba sailed for Ethiopia but died en route shortly after arriving at the Keith-Falconer Mission. Another sad return was that of Amanu Figgo, who died at Sheikh Othman circa 1904. The fifth, Tolassa Wayessa, sailed for India aboard the SS *Kaiser* on 9 January 1902. Fayissa Umbe, the sixth, returned home shortly after his Oromo wife, Ayantu Said, died in 1903. The seventh, Daba Tobo, took himself home in 1906; and Fayissa Hora, the eighth and final independent repatriate, returned to Ethiopia sometime between 1903 and 1908.

Though Lovedale asked the surviving Oromo in South Africa in 1903 if they would return home if offered an assisted passage, the mission station failed to follow through on the tantalizing promise of sending them home. Frustrated with the missionaries' inertia, the Oromo, under the leadership of Liban Bultum in Port Elizabeth, approached the German consul in 1908 to ask for assistance in returning to Ethiopia. This resulted in a flurry of correspondence between the governments of the Cape, Britain, and Germany, and the court of Menelik II. With their return passage subsidized by the emperor in Addis Ababa, a group of seventeen Oromo finally sailed for Aden on 9 June 1909 aboard Germany's *Kronprinz*. Their dramatic return to Ethiopia came, ironically, on the back of the scramble for Africa. Almost all of the Oromo who remained in South Africa found work, forged new relationships, and put down roots. Two ventured north across the Limpopo River and settled temporarily in Bulawayo—one returned to South Africa; the other repatriated. One became a sailor and ended up in America.

In Sum

Given the dearth of first-passage narratives in slave historiography, including the historiography of the Horn of Africa slave trade, the narratives of the sixty-four Oromo children in this study have presented the writer with the rare opportunity to analyze their lives and enslavement experiences in detail, using the technique of prosopography, the preeminent tool for group analysis. Accordingly, this book represents a longitudinal analytical study of a group of Oromo slave children from capture, through their first and middle passages, to liberation and their eventual arrival at Lovedale. In the general scarcity of Oromo first-passage narratives, no other such studies have been possible.

The findings conform to the broad contours of the secondary literature, but go beyond those contours in complexity and variegated specificity. The prosopographical technique used here allowed for a fully dimensioned analysis of the first passage and its effects not only on the middle passage but on the children's subsequent lives into adulthood. While some commentators might cavil at the small size of the sample of sixty-four slaves and others might pose questions of typicality, the researcher can only argue that these are the first full records of the first passage. Over and above these unique first-passage narratives, the comprehensive record-keeping of the Scottish missionaries allowed for a comprehensive longitudinal analysis of the children's lives from cradle to grave, assuredly unique in the slave literature.

The family structure of the captured slaves revealed in the narratives showed several significant results: First, the group included a higher than normal proportion of orphans, a psychological condition that had profound implications for familial incorporation—it is conjectured—into continuous enslavement, a process analogous to the Stockholm syndrome. Full and paternal orphans also had to suffer the enduring stigma in the region attached to children reared without a father.

Second, although the extended family Africa enjoys a favorable—even legendary—reputation in the secondary literature, one must note, regrettably, that immediate family members sometimes not only ushered their relatives (like the biblical Joseph) into Abyssinia's domestic slave system, but even propelled them into the slave export trade. Perhaps it is not surprising that some of the Oromo slave children could not, or would not, remember their parents' names, despite the fact that parental contact is the most significant human contact of any child's life. The captors fractured the integrity of the child's family and violated the child's sense of security. The sudden loss of their parents left a significant gap and triggered in some the need for substitute parent figures. On their first morning at Lovedale some of the Oromo girls wept, calling for their "father," that is, Dr. Alexander Paterson. Two years later, after Paterson had left Lovedale, several boys wrote letters referring to Dr. James Stewart and his wife, Mina, as their father and mother.

A wide range of experiences characterized the capture. This ranged from violent seizure on horseback to the transitioning of females, without violence, into the export trade through bartering and, on occasion, familial arrangement. At the point of capture, males and females also displayed differences. Not surprisingly, slave raiders used violence more frequently in the capture of boys than girls. Not only was the length of the total time from family hearth to dhow a surprise—ranging from a speedy one week to a staggering nine years on the road, there were significant gender differences. Generally, the traders hurried the girls into the slave trade network much faster than the boys. Of great interest was the finding that both boys and girls spent time as slaves en route. However, almost three times as many boys as girls were retained as domestic slaves. The periods of domestic enslavement also revealed a gender divide. On average the boys were enslaved locally for 462 days, or 1.3 years, compared with the girls, who averaged 288 days, or 0.8 years, in the local slave system.

The maximum period any of the boys were enslaved domestically was nine years, compared with a three-year total for any of the girls. In other words, the findings suggest that females, transported expeditiously toward the coast, were the preferred human exports in comparison to the males. A further surprise was the number of times the children changed hands. The secondary literature does not even hint at this phenomenon. The children passed from hand to hand between two and ten times—beyond even the abolitionists' imaginations.

In short, the first passage emerged as a much longer, more complex and varied ordeal, with differing physiological and variform psychological implications for the captured slaves. These hitherto undisclosed experiences must complicate any subsequent description of the slaves' ordeal. They were to cast a long shadow over the children's following captivity including, most shockingly, a foreshortened life expectancy, despite the unquestionably benign—even ideal—day-to-day living conditions of the famous Lovedale Institution. Lovedale afforded an environment that included a ready-made autochthonous and mixed cohort of South African children of similar ages who provided the researcher with a handy point of comparison. Their abbreviated lives—two-thirds did not live to celebrate their thirtieth birthdays—were unquestionably the result of the trauma of the first passage.

The yield derived from the prosopographic technique used in this study has resulted in a profoundly different and complex picture of the first passage. These findings shine a bright light on the first passage and have implications for a revision of the middle passage and subsequent life of the enslaved person. This places the middle passage, the universal target of the well-meaning abolitionists, into the penumbra of the first passage.

APPENDICES

APPENDIX A

The Variables and Authentication of the Data

The Variables

There are three types of variables used in this prosopography: (1) Core variables: The children's narratives generated each of these. They are used extensively throughout this study, for example, the ages of the children at time of interview, gender, their names, their places of origin, and so on (see, in particular, the sections "Age Structure" and "Family Composition" in chapter 2); (2) extraneous variables: The 1903 repatriation questionnaire, death registers, and other vital records provide the database with additional biographical information. For example, the death records lodged in the Western Cape Archives and Records Service list the deaths of many of the Oromo children in South Africa; and (3) derived variables: Either one or both of the preceding variables have enabled the generation of new variables. For example, the single categorical variable[1] of place generated three ratio or scale variables:[2] the coordinate values of latitude and longitude, and altitude—a progressive data transformation (see especially chapter 4, "Topography, Domicile, and Ethnicity of the Oromo Captives").

Why use systematic analysis of this sort, for example, in dealing with the narratives of these sixty-four children? Robert Fogel and Stanley Engerman warned scholars about the dangers of imputing a trend from an anecdote: "The real question is whether such cases [of whipping] were common events that were rarely reported, or whether they were rare events that were frequently reported."[3] Historians relying on anecdotal evidence have no way of answering that question. For example, what is the social historian to infer from an account such as that of Charles Tilston Beke, the English traveler who wrote of his encounter with an Abyssinian slave coffle between Gondar and Massawa in 1844: "The slaves go along without the least restraint, singing and chatting, and apparently perfectly happy. They are generally treated with attention, stopping frequently on the road to rest and feed"?[4] Can the historian assume anything from this observation about

```
names|                                                        |age=12
gender=1|  Males 1. Aguchello Chabani (age about 12 years) son
           of Chabani and Gurden was born in a village called
origin= Enge|  Enge, in the district of Barsinge in the Shan Galla
           country. The village of Enge seems to have been
           scattered over the northern slope of a mountain called
           Belchori. His father was the owner of a piece of land
           about six acres in extent, in company with another
           man. When playing about his father's hut one
           afternoon three men whom he calls black Arabs - came
           to his father's house; after some high words with his
           father they came towards him and carried him off by
           force notwithstanding the entreaties of his father and |father=1
mother=2|  mother    ...
```

FIGURE A.1. Extract from Aguchello Chabani's personal narrative (source: Sandra Rowoldt Shell).

the nature of the slave trade in Ethiopia? Can a momentary glimpse such as this imply that the trade in this area was benign? The systematic analysis of group data allows the historian to establish representivity more accurately.

From Narratives to Numbers

Each captive child is listed on a single row in a spreadsheet. What follows is an extract from the first of the verbatim personal narratives showing how the data for the spreadsheet were identified and coded (fig. A.1). The coding is in the margins.

The following figure (A.2) illustrates a portion of this extract in the child's row in the SPSS data form. The order of the variables in the database is not necessarily the same as the order presented in the narrative. The first row consists of the variable names.

ID	Firstname	Secondname	Concatenatedname	Alt_name	Bio_sex	Bio_age	Bio_birthdate	Ethnicity
1	Aguchello	Chabani	Aguchello Chabani		1	12	1878	Shangalla

FIGURE A.2. Extract from Aguchello Chabani's entry in SPSS data form (source: Sandra Rowoldt Shell).

This figure shows the first nine of 276 variables in the database. Aguchello Chabani was not known by any alternative name; so, in his case, the Alt_name variable is blank.

Words in **bold** font in the narrative extract indicate which words have been coded. A straight line with a bulb at one end (—o) indicates where the new variable resides; at the other end of the line, in the margin, is the variable name in sans serif font, thus "names—o Aguchello." The variable names and their values are shown in the marginalia. The first variable records the child's unique identifier (Aguchello Chabani was the first child listed and so is number 1) followed by gender (coded 1 = **male**, as in this example). The next two variables record the child's first name and second name (in this example, **Aguchello** and **Chabani**, respectively). As surnames were not used by the Oromo, the second name was invariably the name of the father, or, where the name of the father was not known, a matronym or toponym. The next variable records the estimated age (in this case, **12 years**), followed by the names of the father (**Chabani**) and the mother (**Gurdenfi**). The next variable, origin, records the name of the child's village (**Enge**). Whether or not the father or mother was present at moment of capture is then recorded with the binary value of **1** (**yes**), as in this example; or **0** (**no**).

The entire database is a matrix of 70,912 values, a minimal estimate calculated using a low average of four values per variable. The 276 variables may be aggregated and classified into a number of categories:

- Identification (fourteen variables: e.g., identification number, system numbers, first name, second name, names of mother and father, source locations). Some of these identification variables, particularly the children's personal names and the names of their parents, feature throughout the book. See, for example, chapter 2, "The Family Structure of the Oromo Captives."
- Biographical (nine variables: e.g., gender, age, date of birth, date of death, ethnicity). Age is a particularly significant variable that informs every section of the book. See, for example, the discussion of age in chapter 2 under the sub-heading "Age Structure." See the discussion on ethnicity and the note on the derivation of this variable under the subheading "Ethnicity" in chapter 4.
- Family reconstitution (eleven variables: e.g., number of siblings, orphans, family size, marriage, spouse, children). See, for example, the section titled "Orphanhood" in chapter 2.
- Life sequence (sixty-eight variables: e.g., date of capture, identity of captor[s], identity of owner[s], mode of capture, price/barter, date of baptism, date of repatriation). See two examples of these variables under the sections "Mode of Capture" in chapter 5; and graph 5.1, "Places of Origin of the Children's Captors."
- Cadastral (eight variables: e.g., land tenure, livestock). See the variables informing these cadastral measures of immovable and movable property under the sections "Measures of Land" and "Livestock" in chapter 3.
- Status (seven variables: e.g., parental occupation, occupations of the former Oromo captives in adulthood). Parental occupation is one of the variables acting as an indicator of wealth and status. For details, see the section titled "Parental Occupation" in chapter 3.
- Spatial (eighty-seven variables: e.g., place-names, latitudes, longitudes, altitudes, distances of journeys, addresses). There is a multiplicity of spatial variables in the dataset. Many of the children were taken to numerous places during their enslavement, and each of these places is defined by its topographical identifiers of latitude, longitude, and altitude. See the section titled "The Topography" in chapter 4.
- Chronological (sixty-six variables: e.g., duration of slave journey, length of domestic enslavement, total duration of first-passage experience). These variables inform the entirety of chapter 6, "On the Road."

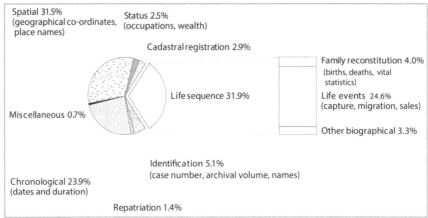

Graph A.1. Bird's-eye view of the classification of variables (source: Sandra Rowoldt Shell).

- Repatriation (four variables: e.g., numbers of repatriates). The variables relating to the repatriation of approximately half of the surviving former captives feature in chapter 11, "Going Home."
- Miscellaneous (two variables: e.g., general notes and the weighting of the sample). The final category of miscellaneous includes the WVAR, or weighting variable. See the notes on the weighting of the sample in the section titled "The Weighting Process" in this appendix (page 210–211).

The pie chart below (graph A.1) illustrates the proportion of the classification of different variables.

Not surprisingly, the life sequence, spatial, and chronological variables dominate the diagram, charting as they do the events that shaped each child's life as well as his or her first-passage experience.

Description and Authentication of Data

Coded data cannot be trusted unless the originals are checked and rechecked. All primary sources to be coded must be rigorously scrutinized for every type of bias. Reverend Matthew Lochhead, a teacher and missionary of the Free Church of Scotland, transcribed the personal narratives of the Oromo children. There is no published attribution for the compilation of the narratives. However, in a handwritten headnote on the first page of a Cory Library copy of "The Gallas and Their Country," Reverend W. J. B. Moir wrote:

> The following account of the Gallas and their country and of the capture of those who are now at Lovedale, has been drawn up by Mr M Lochhead, who assisted Dr Paterson in bringing the party from Aden to South Africa. He has also ascertained the facts of each individual's history and prepared them for this record.[5]

Lochhead's authorship was further authenticated later by one of the boys, Bayan Liliso, who wrote the following in a letter to Mrs. Mina Stewart, wife of Reverend James Stewart, then principal of Lovedale:

> It is very pity that we are very far from each other that we cannot see each other nor talk to each other about things passed during our journeys. But I think most of the people have read our Biography which was written by Mr Lochhead when he was still with us here. If not perhaps Mr Moir has got the copy of it perhaps he will give it to you.[6]

The data are flawed in that the children did not pen their own biographies. Lochhead interviewed each child, recorded the bio-narratives as he heard and understood them, and then prepared these accounts for publication. At each of these three stages of the interview process, there was room for error and misinterpretation.

The Language of the Sources

The children clearly all understood and spoke their mother tongue, Oromo. Some of them were likely to have been able to understand Amharic, the language of the ruling Abyssinian elite; and it is even possible that some may have been able to communicate in Arabic. But it is safe to assume that prior to their contact with the crew of the *Osprey*, the British gunship that intercepted the dhows on which they were being carried to the slave markets of Jeddah, Mocca, or Hodeidah, few if any of the children had any experience of English. Lochhead began to learn Oromo soon after the children arrived in September 1888 and became fluent in the language, later conducting services in Oromo at Lovedale.[7] He and his fellow missionary, the Reverend Alexander Paterson, were soon joined at the mission by the Reverend William Gardner, who also devoted his time over a period of several months to the acquisition of the Oromo language.

In early 1889, two interpreters from Ethiopia arrived at the Keith-Falconer Mission. Their first language was Amharic, but they were also fluent in Arabic and "the Galla language of the children (Oromo, or Afaan Oromoo)." One of the two also spoke English "with ease and readiness."[8] Furthermore, Lochhead and the other missionaries had an unexpected but welcomed visitor to the mission early in 1889 in the form of Gebru (Gobaw) Desta, formerly a colporteur for the Free Church of Scotland in their Egyptian agency.[9] A highly educated man, Gebru Desta was initially tutored by Theophilus Waldmeier, a Swiss missionary, and was later sent to the Samuel Gobat Missionary School in Jerusalem where he studied for three years.

Thereafter, he was given the opportunity to study at St. Chrischona, near Basel in Switzerland, where he graduated with a diploma in theology in 1876. On his return to Ethiopia, he opened a school at Azezo for Ethiopian Jews living in Gondar. Shortly thereafter, he became acutely aware of the plight of the many Oromo enslaved at the hands of the ruling elite and switched his missionary attention to their needs, establishing an Oromo school in Gudru. He is widely recognized as the first evangelist to the Oromo, but when all missionaries were expelled from Ethiopia in 1886, he had to abandon this commitment. He once again traveled to Jerusalem, then to Syria, and, on his return journey to Ethiopia, arrived in Aden. There he became aware of the group of Oromo slave children who had been rescued by the crew of the *Osprey* and placed in the care of the Keith-Falconer Mission. He offered his services to the missionaries, using "his teaching skills to help the missions organisation."[10] Gebru Desta undoubtedly helped Lochhead and William Gardner hone their Oromo language skills during his time at Sheikh Othman.

Filters and Unknowns

Matthew Lochhead unquestionably recorded the Oromo children's stories through the filter of his Christian missionary perspective.[11] The data in the narratives, therefore, are not entirely primary, and there are certainly many unknowns. There is also a shadow over Lochhead himself (see discussion in chapter 10).

Researchers would be justified in interrogating levels of perceived bias where Christian missionaries were involved in documenting Islamic involvement in the Red Sea slave trade. Missionary records would have been likely to exaggerate any Arab influence or involvement. However, Colonel Edward Stace, British administrator in Aden, and the Keith-Falconer missionaries at Sheikh Othman displayed their respect for the Islamic faith when they ensured that the liberated Muslim slave children disembarked by the *Osprey* were placed with established Muslim families.

Later, the Keith-Falconer missionaries recorded the children's accounts of their captures and journeys to the sea. A critical task was to establish the identity of the captors, merchants, and traders, a process fundamental to understanding the operations of the trade. Secondary sources invariably implicate external Arab agencies. However, the children pointed emphatically to the role of the Sidama, and also the local Sayo, Kaffa, Leka, and Jimma slave raider agencies. One boy named his captors as "a party of Mahommedan raiders," another as "three men—whom he calls black Arabs." So it was neighboring people, not outsiders, who were the principal slave raiders. Only once the children approached the coast, primarily at Aussa, did they fall into the hands of Adal traders, the most active of all slave traders in the littoral regions. That the Christian missionaries demonstrated their sensitivity to the Muslim children's needs to be raised in Muslim homes at Aden and later faithfully recorded such limited Muslim involvement in the raiding and trading suggests that these sources are innocent of anti-Muslim bias.

As sociologist and Oromo scholar Mekuria Bulcha tells us, both slave hunting and slave trafficking in the area were violent businesses and included the rape of small children.[12] English traveler and geographer Charles Beke, commenting on the coffles that he observed on their way to the Red Sea in 1844, wrote that without exception, all the female slaves, however young, were kept as concubines throughout their journey and by successive owners.[13]

Almost certainly, then, at least some of the Oromo girl captives would have been subjected to similar abuse while in captivity.

Arguing from Silence?

Other travelers reported a general but brutal disregard of female dignity.[14] The literature also suggests that many young Oromo slave boys headed for Arabian royal households were sold as eunuchs in the markets and were much sought after. According to Bulcha, there was a high demand for castrated boys in most of the slave markets of the Arab world and northeast Africa, pointing out that Ethiopia had acquired a reputation as a major source of eunuchs throughout the world from ancient times.[15] With this secondary evidence in mind, the absence of any reference to any form of sexual aberration in the data may be regarded as a little curious.

Core of the Dataset

In this critique of the dataset, we must remember that the respondents were all children. They had suffered the trauma of being forcibly separated from their parents and families, and we know from the data that many had been subjected to extensive hardships during their first passage. The data also tell us that many were small children at the time of their capture. All these factors help explain omissions. The data nonetheless allow for the creation of a comprehensive prosopography, using the less contentious and more authentic attributes of their journey.

Weighting the Cargo

The sex ratio of the liberated Oromo slave children who arrived at Lovedale was not the sex ratio of the children's first passage landed at Aden. We know the sex composition of the first passage from the evidence documenting the situation aboard the three dhows when they were intercepted in the Red Sea near Mocha. Commander Gissing wrote down his observations, and from his official reports tabled in the House of Commons, we know that there were 204 slaves aboard the three dhows. Of the total cargo of 204 slaves on these dhows, 91 were boys and 92 were girls, resulting in a sex ratio of 99.[16] There are no details of the dhows intercepted in August 1889 beyond the total number of Oromo children taken to the Keith-Falconer Mission (14) and the gender breakdown of 9 boys and 5 girls—a sex ratio of 160.

Factors That Shaped the Sex Composition

The sex ratios of intercepted Red Sea dhow traffic during this period are consistent with the ratios depicted by scholars of the Indian Ocean slave trade. Historian Patrick Manning, for example, claims the ratios were nearly equal.[17] However, six factors shaped the sex ratio of the children who would eventually arrive at Lovedale. The first factor was survival during the first passage, that is, from the moment of capture to embarkation aboard the slave dhows at Rahayta.

The second factor was survival of the passage across the Red Sea to Aden. We know from the official report that one of the dhow captains and four slaves were killed when the HMS *Osprey* opened fire on one of the dhows that refused to heave to. According to Gissing's report, there were no further deaths between interception and Aden, nor during the interception of the 1889 dhows.[18]

The third factor was one of religious selection. On arrival at Aden, the Oromo children fell under the care of Colonel Edward Vincent Stace, the assistant political resident in Aden, who was charged with finding appropriate destinations for them. Local Muslim families applied to adopt the Muslim children, who, according to Gissing, accounted for about half the group.[19] As the other half were believed to be Christian, Colonel Stace approached two Christian missionaries, the Reverend Matthew Lochhead and Dr. Alexander Paterson, asking if they could take all or at least some of these children.

The fourth factor was the result of missionary selection. Dr. Paterson selected a total of 62 children: 23 girls and 39 boys. This changed the sex ratio to 170.

Mortality was the fifth factor changing the sex ratio of the group to 200. The health of the children at the mission deteriorated. Many succumbed to ill-health. By the end of 1888, 11 of the group of 62 children taken to the mission had died, dwindling their number to 51—33 boys and 18 girls.

An adventitious sixth factor came in August 1889, when the additional 14 Oromo children, who had been rescued from various other slave dhows in the Red Sea, joined the survivors at the mission. The group of 14 comprised 9 boys and 5 girls—a sex ratio of 160. The group then totaled 64: 42 boys and 22 girls, giving a sex ratio of 191.

The following table summarizes these changes in the sex ratio:

Table A.1. Changing sex ratios

Date	Factor	Boys	Girls	Total	Sex ratio
16 Sept 1888	First passage survival (4 unidentified slaves died)	91	92	183	99
16 Sept 1888	Red Sea survival	91	92	183	99
19 Sept 1888	Religious selection ("quite half" Muslim/Christian)	46	47	93	93
30 Sept 1888	Missionary selection	39	23	62	170
31 Dec 1888	Mission mortality	34	17	51	200
5 August 1889	Additional 1889 dhow children/ Lovedale group	42	22	64	191

(Source: Sandra Rowoldt Shell.)

The missionaries had to find an alternative destination for the children and eventually decided on another Free Church of Scotland Mission in Africa, namely, Lovedale Institution in South Africa. The sex ratio of the group sent from Aden to Lovedale (191) was clearly different from that of the dhow group landed at Aden (99). We can safely conclude that the boys were oversampled, thanks to the factors cited above. The girls were therefore weighted to get the sex ratio back to the ratio at point of capture.

The Weighting Process

The statistical technique of weighting is used to obtain adjusted population estimates when a sample from a population contains a subgroup that has been over- or undersampled.[20] Using the weight command in SPSS to create a virtual doubling of the girls restored the ratio to a close fit with that of the original cargo of slave children landed at Aden in September 1888. Every girl in the group effectively has a statistical or a virtual twin.

The required weighting was achieved by computing the new blank WVAR variable representing "weighted variable," with a numeric expression of 1. The next step was to select "BIO_SEX" from the drop-down list of variables ("What was the child's gender?"), followed by the IF option:

IF (BIO_SEX EQ 2) WVAR = 2

WEIGHT BY WVAR

The syntax of the weighting process was:

COMPUTE WVAR = 1

IF (BIO_SEX EQ 2) WVAR = 2

WEIGHT BY WVAR

The weighted dataset results in 42 boys and 44 girls, giving a sex ratio of 95. This is clearly more consistent with the sex ratio of 99, or as close as we can arrive to the point of capture without creating a continuous variable (i.e., 2.15 girls).

Geographic Information Systems (GIS)

The children gave the missionaries the names of their villages, towns, regions, and countries of domicile. Not all the children were able to respond comprehensively when asked for all these details, but most had a reasonable memory of their homesteads and homelands. Situating every one of the 126 different place-names the children supplied the missionaries on either a contemporary or a modern map of Ethiopia proved a considerable challenge. Place-names frequently vary by language or new orthographies, or have been modified over time under different political dispensations. Even locating some of the place-names in old or new gazetteers proved frustrating. Moderate but welcome relief came in the form of various online tools. The tools that use a system of clustered alternative spellings based on toponymical whims and modifications, as well as linguistic swings and translations, have proved invaluable in determining the location of the most elusive places.[21]

The categorical variable of place-names generated three ratio variables: the coordinate values of latitude and longitude, and altitude—a progressive exchange. These ratio data, informing GIS technology, generated maps linking with the children's unique numeric identifiers as well as their first and second names. Using the coordinates, the maps indicate the place of origin and domicile and plot each child's slave route to the coast. These are presented in one combination route map, which shows all sixty-four journeys, as well as an individual route map for each child. The altitude variable allowed for a third-dimensional, cross-section spatial view showing the altitude range from which the children came. This technology and its graphic output have allowed new insights into Ethiopian slave trade patterns and routes of that period.

Missionary Censorship?

One possible explanation for the fact that there is no mention of rape, sexual abuse, or castration in the children's narratives recorded by Lochhead is that perhaps none of the children suffered any form of sexual interference. But we know, from the records of contemporary observers and more recent scholars like Mekuria Bulcha, such interference was common if not inevitable.[22]

This gap raises one further possibility. Perhaps the children did tell Lochhead intimate details of sexual abuse during their first passage. Perhaps Lochhead did record these details faithfully. And perhaps the Lovedale authorities regarded the document that Lochhead presented to them as salacious and scandalous. Perhaps this was what they regarded as sufficiently worthy of "a serious charge of immorality" to warrant Lochhead's immediate dismissal. Perhaps we have only the expurgated narratives, victims of a censorship borne of Victorian missionary sensibilities. Or could it be that the doctored photo carries the real clue (see figure 10.2 on page 138)?

These possibilities are only speculations at this stage, but they might explain why none of the children, writing to Mrs. Stewart between 1892 and 1894, expressed any animosity toward Lochhead. Those who mentioned him in their letters seemed only puzzled and regretful that he had left them, certainly not affronted, as we would expect had Lovedale found him guilty of any form of "immorality" involving any one of their group.[23]

Hints from Secondary Sources

Mekuria Bulcha assured his readers that both slave hunting and slave trafficking in the area were violent businesses and included the rape of small children.[24] English traveler and geographer Charles Beke, commenting on the coffles that he observed on their way to the Red Sea in 1844, wrote:

> All the female slaves, however, without exception, whatever their number, and however tender their age—and many are children of eight or nine years at most—are the concubines of their master and his servants during the journey; the same continuing through the various changes of ownership until they are disposed of to their ultimate possessors.[25]

Other travelers reported a general but brutal disregard of female dignity.[26]

The literature also suggests that many young Oromo slave boys headed for Arabian royal households were sold as eunuchs in the markets and were much sought after. According to Bulcha, there was a high demand for castrated boys in most of the slave markets of the Arab world and northeast Africa, pointing out that Ethiopia had a reputation as a major source of eunuchs throughout the world from ancient times.[27] With this secondary evidence in mind, the absence of any reference to any form of sexual aberration in the data may be regarded as a little curious.

There is at this stage only suggestive evidence that some of the Oromo boys may have been castrated. The commander of the HMS *Osprey*, Charles Gissing, recorded that three of the boys among the slave children they rescued and liberated in the Red Sea were eunuchs, but there is no way of knowing if any of these three were counted among those sent to the Keith Falconer Mission and ultimately to Lovedale.[28] According to Lovedale records, ten of the young Oromo males had died by 1900. Of the remaining thirty-two boys, only six are known to have fathered children—about 19 percent of the survivors. Perhaps there was a subset of eunuchs. We do not yet know. It is always difficult to argue from silence.

The Oromo Narratives
Males

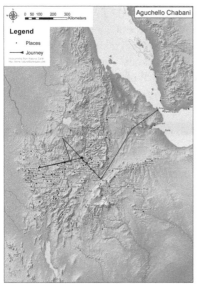

MAP B.1. Aguchello Chabani (source: Sandra Rowoldt Shell and GIS Laboratory, University of Cape Town).

Aguchello Chabani

Birthdate circa 1878. Age about 12 years. Son of Chabani and Gurdenfi. Was born in a village called Enge, in the district of Barsinge in the Shan Galla country. The village of Enge seems to have been scattered over the northern slope of a mountain called Belchori. His father was the owner of a piece of land about six acres in extent, in company with another man. When playing about his father's hut one afternoon three men—whom he calls black Arabs—came to his father's house; after some high words with his father they came towards him and carried him off by force notwithstanding the entreaties of his father and mother. They offered to return him if the parents would bring all their cattle, but after they had done so, the Arabs carried off both him and the cattle. He was taken to a village quite near, where there seems to have been a depot for collecting slaves; and here he was branded with three marks on each cheek, as he attempted to run away. After three days he was taken a day's journey to the village of his captors. He was here for two months, herding cattle, when he was sold to Mahommedan Gallas, who again sold him in their own country at a place called Gulisso. The buyer took him to Gudru, one week's journey, when he was again sold and taken to Gojam, where he met another of our boys—Fayissa Umbe. Both were again sold to another merchant—a Soudanese who took them to a place called Bofa, where they were bought by the Adal slave merchants and marched with many other children fourteen days' journey to another slave centre called Aussa—apparently laid out expressly for the slave trade—one part being occupied by buyers and the other by sellers. From this place they were taken five days' journey east to Araito (Rahayta) at the head of the Bay of Tajurrah, when they were put on board the slave dhow on which they were captured.

MAP B.2. Amanu Bulcha (source: Sandra Rowoldt Shell and GIS Laboratory, University of Cape Town).

Amanu Bulcha

Birthdate circa 1878. Age about 12 years. Son of Bulcha and Sanbate. His parents lived in a village called Chonge in the Wallaga district, and tilled a piece of land for the Chumi (chief) of the village, to whom they gave one fourth of the produce of the land. His father possessed several cows and sheep. While he was herding these, three black men pounced upon him out of the forest and, gagging him with a piece of cloth, carried him off into the forest, taking him by night about eight hours' journey to a village where they sold him to a man called Banda. Banda took him to his home at Leka nine days' journey. He says that Banda's wife was very unkind to him. A party of slave merchants coming round, he was again sold for a horse and one dollar, and taken to Gudru. At Gudru he

was bought by the chief's son, who sold him to a Galla Mahommedan at a place called Sakal—where he fell in with some of the other boys now with us. After this he was sold four times,—at the towns of Ancharro, Warakallo, Bofa and lastly at Aussa where he was bought by the Adal slave merchants and taken with many others to Araito where they were shipped on board the slave dhows.

Amanu Figgo

Birthdate circa 1877. Age about 13 years. Son of Figgo and Zaida. He was born in a village called Agam, in the Urbarage country, the king of which was called Lallego. Here his father possessed a few acres of land, on which he cultivated barley, beans and lentils. He had a few ploughing oxen, milk cows and goats.

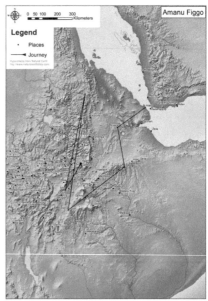

MAP B.3. Amanu Figgo (source: Sandra Rowoldt Shell and GIS Laboratory, University of Cape Town).

The people of Silte in the Gurage country, (a day's journey west from his village) finding an excuse for a quarrel, came down in large numbers upon his village, and all the people fled. He and his feeble mother were overtaken. His mother was left but he was carried off and taken to Silte. After staying here two days, he was sold to a merchant from Tigre, who took him to that place and from there after two months he was taken to Sidama and again sold. From Sidama he was taken three weeks' journey east to a town called Dawe—a large centre for the traffic in slaves—and here he was bought by those iniquitous dealers, the Adal merchants. With them he went fifteen days' journey east to Aussa, where he first met many of the other boys now with us, and from there was taken five or six days' journey to Araito and embarked on board the slave dhows. According to his account, he was treated with greater kindness as he came near the coast, where his value was increasing.

MAP B.4. Amaye Tiksa (source: Sandra Rowoldt Shell and GIS Laboratory, University of Cape Town).

Amaye Tiksa

Birthdate circa 1877. Age about 13 years. Son of Tiksa and Gabai. The name of the village in which he was born was Badda, in a country called Yassa. The presumptuous being who called himself king bore the remarkable title of Abba Wakayo, the Father of God. His father was a small crofter possessing about two acres of land and some cows and ploughing oxen. He cultivated wheat, maize, barley, durra, and beans. A dispute with a neighbouring tribe led to a battle, and he was taken and carried off by the victorious tribe about two days' journey to their own country. Here he was sent to herd cattle, but after a few days was sold. He was taken to a place called Majo, and sold in the market there. He was sold several times after this at Kau, Billo, Gudru, Ajubi. In the latter place he was bought by the Sidama merchants, and taken via Bofa, to Aussa.

Here the Adal merchants bought him and he was taken by them to Araito, where was put on board the slave dhow.

Map B.5. Badassa Nonno (source: Sandra Rowoldt Shell and GIS Laboratory, University of Cape Town).

Badassa Nonno

Birthdate circa 1879. Age about 11 years. Son of _____ and Ganne. He forgets the name of his father, who died when he was young, and so he has been called by the other boys after the name of the district from which he was taken—Nonno. His mother stayed with her brother who had a piece of land which he cultivated. The people of Leka fought against those of Nonno and defeated them. He and his mother, with two brothers and a sister, hid in a forest, but were discovered by their enemies and taken by them to their own country. He and his mother were sold to a merchant from Gudru, one week's journey from Leka. In Gudru he stayed for two years herding cattle, and here his mother died. After his mother's death he was sold at a slave market a day and a half's journey

north from Gudru, and taken by his new master to Gamoji (the cool country). He was again sold and taken to Ajuba where he met several of the boys now with us. He was only in Ajuba five days, when, a caravan of Sidama merchants coming along, he was sold to them and taken to Dawe—passing through Ancharro. In Dawe he met three of our girls and with them was sold to the Adal merchants, who bought them via Aussa to Araito, where with the others he was put on board the slave dhow.

Badassa Wulli

Birthdate 1876. Age about 14 years. Son of Wulli and Gawe. His home was in a district called Badda, in the Kaffa country, where his father assisted his grandfather in cultivating a few acres of land. They had a few cattle, sheep and

Map B.6. Badassa Wulli (source: Sandra Rowoldt Shell and GIS Laboratory, University of Cape Town).

goats. When he was tending the flocks one afternoon, two men came out of the forest and asked him to go with them to another very beautiful country. He began to cry, but they gagged his mouth with a piece of cloth and concealed him in the forest [and] took him, when it grew dark, to a house near by. In the morning he was taken to the Jimma country, two days' journey east where he was sold for six pieces of salt to a Mahommedan Galla. He stayed one year with this man, but was again sold to a man from his native district, Badda. He was with this man two years and a half, and at the end of that time was again sold to a Tekur merchant. Merchants from Gojam next bought him for seven and a half pieces of salt. He was taken by them to the Sidama country, and from there to Dawe where he fell into the hands of the Adal merchants, with whom were many of the children now with us. From Dawe they journeyed to a place called Bofa and thence to Aussa, and there joined a large slave caravan to Araito, where they embarked.

MAP B.7. Baki Malakka (source: Sandra Rowoldt Shell and GIS Laboratory, University of Cape Town).

Baki Malakka

Birthdate circa 1872. Age about 18 years. Son of Malakka and Muja. His father had been a slave with the king of the country for a long time. Having served faithfully, he received a few acres of land to cultivate and support himself. Baki, on his father's death was taken by the king to work in his household. On one occasion, the king was absent and his wife sold Baki to a party of Atari merchants who came through the country. They took him to a slave market, and sold him to a man called Chirpi, who took him to Seka. Here he stayed for two months when he was taken to [a] place called Billo, where he was again sold and then taken to Gojam. In Gojam he was sold for ten pieces of silver and a handful of peppers. After passing through the hands of [an]other three masters he was at length sold at a place called Ajubi to Atari merchants, who took him to Araito and sold him to the Adal merchants. He was shipped from there with the others.

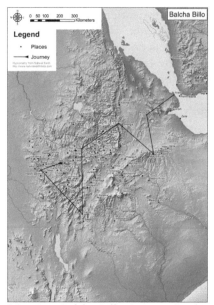

MAP B.8. Balcha Billo (source: Sandra Rowoldt Shell and GIS Laboratory, University of Cape Town).

Balcha Billo

Birthdate circa 1877. Age about 13 years. Son of Billo and Ashani. His father, mother, six brothers and two sisters were alive when he was taken from his home. His father stayed in a village called Wachali, in a district called Dapo, north of Walagga, and owned a small piece of land, but had a great many cattle. Balcha was one day herding the cattle, at some distance from his home, when three men on horseback came up to him, and, gagging him, carried him off. They took him to Walagga, where he was kept for three months and then taken to a place called Sayo. After staying here for one month, he was being taken to a market to be sold, when, passing near his father's home, he tried to run away, but was overtaken at a river which he was unable to ford. He was more effectively secured after this, and taken to the slave market at Danu where he was sold and taken to Gudru. From Gudru he was taken about fourteen days east to Ancharro, where he was sold to the Adal merchants and taken via Dawe and Aussa to Araito. Here he joined the others.

Bayan Liliso

Birthdate circa 1876. Age about 14 years. Son of Liliso and Bushere. His father is dead, but his mother, two brothers, and two sisters, were alive when he was captured. His home was called Chefita, in the Kambatta country, N.W. of Gurage. When his father died, his uncle took charge of the piece of land which they cultivated. Early one morning they were surprised by a party of Mahommedan raiders, coming down upon them. The people, being unarmed,

MAP B.9. Bayan Liliso (source: Sandra Rowoldt Shell and GIS Laboratory, University of Cape Town).

fled in all directions. His uncle and he managed to conceal themselves in a tree, and thus escaped the notice of the attacking party. But the looters who usually follow up the attacking force discovered them, and threatened that if they did not come down they would shoot them. Their captors took him, with a number of his playmates, to a slave-market in Gurage three days' journey from his home, and there sold them all to different individuals. Bayan was sold several times within the next eighteen months, when he was taken to Ancharro, where he stayed for three years with a man who at the end of that time sold him for sixteen dollars to an Atari merchant, who took him via Warakallo to Dawe. Here he was sold to the Adal merchants and taken via Aussa to Araito where he was put on board the slave dhow.

MAP B.10. Daba Tobo (source: Sandra Rowoldt Shell and GIS Laboratory, University of Cape Town).

Daba Tobo

Birthdate circa 1878. Age about 12 years. Son of Tobo and Ibbi. His home was in Leka, the country east of Jimma, in a village called Lalo. His father had a piece of land which he cultivated, but when he died, the ground being uncultivated, they could not pay the tax, so the chief of the village took their cattle, and made the family his slaves. Daba's duty was to herd the cattle, and one day, as he was doing so, a man came up to him, and gagging his mouth, carried him away one day's journey to Jimma. After staying in Jimma one week, he was sold to an Atari merchant, who took him to a place the name of which he forgets, where he was again sold. His statement is rather confused between this time and his falling into the hands of the Adal merchants at Aussa, by whom he was taken to Tajurrah. At Tajurrah he was put on board a slave dhow with about twenty other boys and girls. Seven dhows left Tajurrah together, but on sighting a gunboat two of the dhows, the one in which he was and another, put back. They stayed in Tajurrah for two months and then started again. This time, there were three dhows. They were not long out when they were becalmed, and sighted by a gunboat. One of the dhows was captured, one got away, and the third was found empty, (see Isho's story, No. 23), all the slaves and sailors having thrown themselves into the sea rather than allow themselves to be captured. These were, of course, a different lot from those captured by the Osprey.

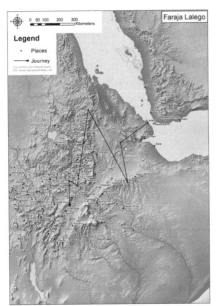

MAP B.11. Faraja Lalego (source: Sandra Rowoldt Shell and GIS Laboratory, University of Cape Town).

Faraja Lalego

Birthdate circa 1874. Age about 16 years. Son of Lalego and Uligge. His parents were both dead when he left home, but he had seven brothers and six sisters alive. He stayed in a village called Silte, in Gurage, which lies S.W. of Shoa. His father owned a small piece of land which he cultivated, but on his death it was neglected, and the family were unable to pay the yearly tax to the Sidama, or King. Some soldiers were sent to seize them or their cattle, in lieu of the tax. On their approach, he and his brothers ran away, but he was overtaken and captured. He accompanied this band of soldiers to another village, called Ulbarag, which they also plundered, capturing a large number of slaves. Returning to their own district, he was, with a large number of other slaves, sold at Entotto in Shoa. They all remained here chained together for one week, when they were taken to Tigre, where he stayed two months, when he was again sold and taken to Dawe. Here the Adal merchants brought him and he was taken via Aussa to Araito where he was put on board the slave dhow.

Faraja Jimma

Birthdate: circa 1872. Age about 18 years. Son of _____ and _____. He was so young when taken from home that he does not remember the name of his father or mother. His first recollections are of a man, whose slave he was, in a village called Horro, near Gudru. This man's name was Jimma and so he came to be called Faraja Jimma. He was with Jimma about four years, when, on account of a famine in the land, Jimma

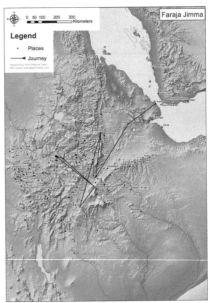

MAP B.12. Faraja Jimma (source: Sandra Rowoldt Shell and GIS Laboratory, University of Cape Town).

had to remove his cattle and household to another part of the country. On the way, the caravan was pillaged, and he was taken by the pillagers to the king of a place called Badda. He stayed here for one week herding cattle, when, the king going to fight another tribe, he ran away and got back to his old home, only to find the place forsaken. He made his way to the house of a sister of his late master. She took him to Gudru, and gave him to another brother with whom he stayed one month. He was again taken to Badda where he stayed two months, and from here he was taken to the Sidama country (Shoa). Here a merchant bought him and took him to Ancharro about three weeks' journey east, when he was again sold. From Ancharro he was taken to Bofa and sold to Adal merchants. They took him to Araito via Aussa.

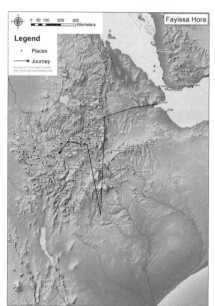

MAP B.13. Fayissa Hora (source: Sandra Rowoldt Shell and GIS Laboratory, University of Cape Town).

Fayissa Hora

Birthdate circa 1875. Age about 15 years. Son of Hora and Soye. He lived in a village called Billo in a district called Leka. A large river, called the Gibbi, was a little south of his village. On the death of his father and mother, he and a younger sister were adopted by a neighbour, who employed him in herding cattle. One day, on enquiring for his sister, he found that she had been sold to some passing merchants. Not long after this he was sent with a friend of his foster-parents to another village. On the way, he discovered that they were going to sell him, and escaping into a field through which they were passing, he found his way to the house of the chief, who sent him back to his old master. He was not long back however, when he was taken to Gudru and sold.

After being two weeks with his new master, he was again sold at a place called Ajubi to Atari merchants. From here he was taken to Warakallo—about one month's journey east—and from Warakallo to Ancharro. In Ancharro the Atari sold him to the Adal merchants, who took him via Aussa to Tajurrah. He is one of those more recently rescued.

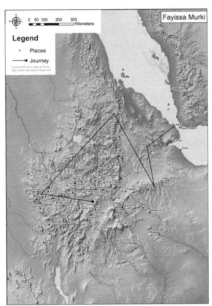

Map B.14. Fayissa Murki (source: Sandra Rowoldt Shell and GIS Laboratory, University of Cape Town).

Fayissa Murki

Birthdate circa 1873. Age about 17 years. Son of Murki and Shonte. His parents are both alive and also two sisters. The name of his native village was Alle, in the country called Danno. His father possessed a small piece of land, also about twenty head of cattle and a few goats. One afternoon, he was playing near his home, when a neighbour of his father's came up to him and asked him to go to his house not far off. He accompanied this man, and was detained by him. At night he was taken to a slave market near, and sold to Atari merchants who took him about two weeks' journey to a place called Dalotti which he says is in the Tigre country. Here he was sold to other merchants who took him to a town called Tigre. From here he was taken to Dawe, where he was sold to the Adal merchants. The Adal merchants took him via Aussa to Araito, where he joined the others.

Fayissa Umbe

Birthdate circa 1875. Age about 15 years. Son of Umbe and Asseti. He stayed with his parents, one sister, and one brother, in a village called Mangera, in a country called Sayo, which was governed by a king called Burayo. Two towns were near his home, Dappo to the S.E. and Afillo to the N.W. The river Birbir was one day's journey south and flowed east. On the death of his father, one year before he left his home, his uncle took charge of the piece of land that belonged to the family. One day while he was herding the cattle, two men came up to him, and gagging him carried him off. They took him across the river Birbir to Dappo one

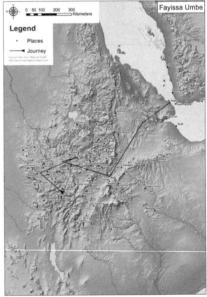

Map B.15. Fayissa Umbe (source: Sandra Rowoldt Shell and GIS Laboratory, University of Cape Town).

full day's journey. Here he was sold, and taken to Gudru, about four days' journey north. From Gudru he was taken to Kau in the Leka country, and again sold. He was bought by an Abyssinian merchant called Amanu, and taken to Bofa. Here he met Faraja Jimma and several of the other boys, and after staying two weeks was, with them, sold to an Adal merchant and taken via Aussa to Araito where he was put on board the slave dhow.

MAP B.16. Gaite Goshe (source: Sandra Rowoldt Shell and GIS Laboratory, University of Cape Town).

Gaite Goshe

Birthdate circa 1877. Age about 13 years. Son of Goshe and Haiven. He comes from a village called Gualla, near the river Gojob, in the Kaffa Country. His father cultivated a piece of land from which he supported himself, his wife, and a family of four boys. One day, his father went to pay a visit to a brother of his, and when he returned he left Gaita with his uncle. After he had been with him for one year, while he was herding cattle, a party of Sidama—whom he describes as the emissaries of the king— came upon him and carried him away. They took him to a house in a forest at some distance, and kept him there for two days, with his feet in the stocks. At the end of the second day, he was loosed, and told to go and bring some water, when he attempted to run away, but a woman, seeing him, gave the alarm, and he was overtaken by a man who dragged him back. Next day, he was taken to a slave market and sold to a Mohammed Galla who took him to his home. He was there for one month, when he was taken, along with a number of boys and girls, six weeks' journey east to Jimma. Here, he and the others were sold to a Tigre merchant, for a few pieces of salt. From Tigre, he was taken to Entotto in Shoa, and there sold to Sidama merchants who took him to Dawe. In Dawe he stayed three days, when he was again sold to Adal merchants who took him via Bofa and Aussa to Araito, where he joined the others.

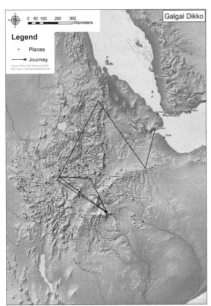

MAP B.17. Galgal Dikko (source: Sandra Rowoldt Shell and GIS Laboratory, University of Cape Town).

Galgal Dikko

Birthdate circa 1873. Age about 17 years. Son of Dikko and Hudo. He was very young when he left his home, but old enough to remember that he had five brothers and one sister, and that his mother was dead. He remembers a party of men on horseback, with guns, coming down upon his village, and, after a fierce fight, carrying himself and one of his brothers away. He became very ill as they were taking him away, and he was left by them on the wayside, near a place called Gobbu. Here he was found by a man who took him to his house. The chief of the country hearing the circumstances of this man's finding Galgal, claimed him as his property, and promised to allow him to return to his own country when he grew up. In a battle, however, the chief was killed, and the Sidama making

a raid on the village carried off all the guns they could find. They returned soon after, this time for slaves, and he was carried off by them to a place called Tibbe. He stayed two weeks in Tibbe, when he was taken to Shoa. Here he stayed for six weeks, when he ran away. He found his way to the house of a chief whom he did not know. This chief gave him to another man to sell, and he was taken by way of Gobbu to Billo, and sold in the market there to a Gudru merchant. He was taken by this man to Tigre, and there sold to the Atari, and taken via the Adal country to Tajurrah.

Gamaches Garba

Birthdate circa 1872. Age about 18 years. Son of Garba and Badani. His home was in a village called Kilerito, in a country called Liban, west of the river Abaye. His

MAP B.18. Gamaches Garba (source: Sandra Rowoldt Shell and GIS Laboratory, University of Cape Town).

father possessed a piece of land of his own, and seems to have been among the well to do people. Father and mother, one brother and one sister, were alive when he was taken away from home. The circumstances were these. He was herding his father's cattle, his father being away from home at the time when four men from a country called Rafiso came up to him and carried him away. They stayed in a forest near by over night, and in the morning he was taken to Gudru and kept in the house of one of his captors for two days. He was then taken to Ajubi and sold privately to the Atari merchants. They were evidently afraid to sell him in the open market, in case any one from Liban might be there who would recognise him. From Ajubi, he was taken by the Atari to a place the name of which he does not remember, but he recollects being kept with chains on his feet every night, as he several times attempted to run away by night. He was afterwards taken to Warakallo. He was then taken to Ancharro, where he was very ill with what he calls finno (probably smallpox) for nearly two months. On his recovery, he was taken by his Atari owner to Bofa and from thence via Aussa to Araito.

MAP B.19. Gilo Kashe (source: Sandra Rowoldt Shell and GIS Laboratory, University of Cape Town).

Gilo Kashe

Birthdate circa 1874. Age about 16 years. Son of Kashe and _____. This boy is mentally defective, and it is impossible to get any accurate information from him. He gives his father's name as Kashe every time he is asked, so we may consider that correct. Milko says he saw Gilo in Tigre and he was then employed, by a man named Butta, in going round from house to house gathering up cow dung which when dried was used as fuel. Gilo corroborates this when reminded of it. He was among those more recently rescued, and therefore was put on board the slave dhows at Tajurrah.

MAP B.20. Gutama Tarafo (source: Sandra Rowoldt Shell and GIS Laboratory, University of Cape Town).

neighbouring slave market for five dollars. His purchaser took him to Leka where he stayed for one year, employed as a herd boy. At the end of this time, he went with his master to Hochocha to sell coffee, but the Sidama would not allow a slave to be taken back from there to Leka, so his master sold him to the chief of Hochocha. At Hochocha, Gutama was sick for two months. On his recovery, he was sold at two different places, the Adal merchants buying him at Dalatti and taking him via Aussa to Tajurrah. Here he was very ill again, and on convalescence was taken back to a village in Adal to regain strength. Afterwards, he was taken to Araito where he was shipped.

Guyo Tiki

Birthdate circa 1874. Age about 16 years. Son of Tiki and Obse. His parents were both alive and two brothers when he left

Gutama Tarafo

Birthdate circa 1874. Age about 16 years. Son of Tarafo and Guro. His father cultivated a small piece of land near a village called Gamoje, in the Gera country. He had two brothers and six sisters. His father was discovered selling honey to a neighbouring tribe. The chief of the village reported this—which seems to have been an offence against the King of the country,—with the result that his father's land and possessions were seized and the family given as slaves to the chief of the village. Shortly after this, his father became sick and died. Some dispute arising between the king and the Sidama, the latter came upon the country and carried the king away captive. They offered him to ransom for a certain amount, and to raise this ransom money all the chiefs were asked to contribute. To assist in this object, Gutama was taken and sold in a

MAP B.21. Guyo Tiki (source: Sandra Rowoldt Shell and GIS Laboratory, University of Cape Town).

his home. He stayed in a village called Gella in the Guma Country which lies west of Gibbe and Gombota. His father possessed a few cows, sheep, and goats. He was herding these one day, when a man came up to him, and carried him away. He was taken to Gomma and from there to Jimma. In Jimma he was sold for a horse, to a merchant from Limmu who took him to that place. His master was taking him to Nonno to sell him there, when he ran away. On the road a woman caught him and took him to her house. This woman's husband took him next day to a place called Halelu where he was sold and remained for six months. He was then taken to Chora and sold again to a man called Dinki Harbu. After he had served this man for one year the Sidama made a raid on the country, and he was caught by them and taken via Kasalu to Leka, and after staying at Leka for a short time he was taken through Sayo, Dappo Gacho, Walagga, Billo, and Ilu, to a place called Nollekabba. Here he stayed for one year, when he again ran away. He was however recaptured and taken via Dappo Gumbi to Leka-tocho. He was ultimately sold in Nonno and taken via Gudru and Ajubi to Dawe where the Adal merchants bought him. He was taken by them via Aussa to Araito where he joined the others.

MAP B.22. Hora Bulcha (source: Sandra Rowoldt Shell and GIS Laboratory, University of Cape Town).

Hora Bulcha

Birthdate circa 1877. Age about 13 years. Son of Bulcha and Asa. He was born in a village called Kosher in the Kaffa country. His father cultivated a large piece of land which was rented by the king of the country to him. The king's son, having borrowed a slave boy from a merchant, and wishing to return his loan, took Hora and gave him instead. He was taken to a place called Angisho, one day's journey off; but one morning when his master went to market he slipped away, and got back to his home. He was, however, sought for by his master and again carried off. A second time he ran away, this time to a brother's house in a place called Chara, but he was once more discovered, and soon afterwards sold to a Mahommedan Galla. He was taken by him to a market in Jimma and there sold to a Gurage merchant. He was sold four times after this, and ultimately fell into the hands of the Adal merchants, who shipped him with the others at Araito.

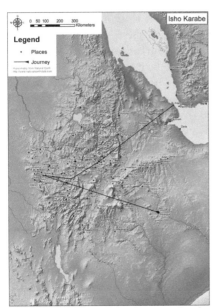

MAP B.23. Isho Karabe (source: Sandra Rowoldt Shell and GIS Laboratory, University of Cape Town).

Isho Karabe

Birthdate circa 1876. Age about 14 years. Son of Karabe and Harbe. His parents are both dead. He lived with his uncle in a village called Imo in the Malagga country. One day going with his uncle to a market near his village, he was asked by a stranger to take a sheep down to a river close by. He did so, but the owner quickly followed, and when no one was near took him and tied his hands behind his back. His cries were heard by a passer by, who interfered, and the two men began to fight. While they were fighting, the king came along, and, finding the cause of the quarrel, sent the thief to prison. Isho was taken away by the king, and given as a present to one of the chiefs. Taking a spear one evening, he tried to run away to his home, but he was overtaken and brought back. After a few weeks, he was one day sent with the reapers to the fields. A party of merchants from Nopa coming round, he was sold and taken by them to their country. He was here for two weeks, when he was taken to a village called Koma—a slave centre—where he was sold to Limu merchants, who took him to Jimma and sold him. He was sold and resold four or five times, and ultimately fell into the hands of the Adal merchants at Aussa, and taken by them to Araito, where he was put on board a slave dhow. He is the only one saved from a whole dhow full of slaves. When the dhow was pursued by the English gun-boat, the Arabs, seeing they were likely to be captured, took all the slaves forty-one in number,—and threw them into the water, jumping in themselves also. Isho hid below some planks at the bottom of the boat. He was not discovered until the evening, when one of the English officers went on board the dhow to inspect her.

Katshi Wolamo

Birthdate circa 1880. Age about 10 years. Son of Walamo and _____. He is the

MAP B.24. Katshi Wolamo (source: Sandra Rowoldt Shell and GIS Laboratory, University of Cape Town).

youngest of the boys, and must have been a mere child when he left his home, as he remembers little or nothing about it. He had one brother and one sister. He was attending to a few cows one day when a man came and took him away to a place, the name of which he forgets. He has a dim recollection of men called Atari, and two places called Dawe and Aussa. He was put on board the slave dhow at Araito. More than this it is impossible to get from him, as events since his arrival in Aden and transference to Lovedale have taken exclusive possession of his mind and seem to have driven out almost all memory of anything preceding.

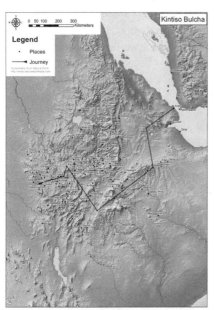

MAP B.25. Kintiso Bulcha (source: Sandra Rowoldt Shell and GIS Laboratory, University of Cape Town).

Kintiso Bulcha

Birthdate circa 1876. Age about 14 years. Son of Bulcha and Lucha. He had four brothers and three sisters all of whom with this father and mother were alive when he was taken from his home. His father owned a few cattle and sheep, and cultivated a piece of land in the country called Sayo. The Sidama came to fight against the chief of the country, and he and his brothers ran away. He was caught hiding in a forest, and taken by his captors to Leka, where he was given to a man who took him to his house. He stayed here for six weeks, when he was sold in the market to a merchant who took him to Kau. At Kau he was bought by a Gudru merchant for three dollars and four pieces of salt. This man again sold him to Sidama merchants who took him to their country. Here the Adal merchants bought him and took him via Dawe and Aussa to Araito where he joined the others and was put on board the slave dhows.

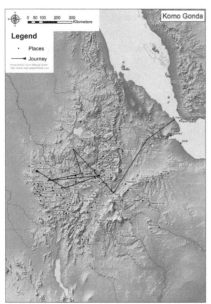

MAP B.26. Komo Gonda (source: Sandra Rowoldt Shell and GIS Laboratory, University of Cape Town).

via Aussa to Araito, where with the others he was put on board the slave dhow.

Liban Bultum

Birthdate circa 1877. Age about 13 years. Son of Bultum and Sumburi. His father was the owner of a large piece of land in the Ilu country, possessing a number of oxen sheep and goats, and also two horses. A brother and sister were alive when he left his home. The Sidama came to collect tribute money from his father but for some reason or other he refused to give it. The Sidama thereupon laid hold of Liban and carried him to a slave market one day's journey from his home. His purchaser took him to a market another day's journey off, and sold him to Dagadi merchants who took him to

Komo Gonda

Birthdate circa 1872. Age about 18 years. Son of Gonda and Golo. The name of the district where his father lived was Bambasse. His father was a slave in the house of the chief; he ploughed the land and attended to the cattle. Having borrowed some cattle from a neighbouring tribe and not being able to return them on demand, a raid was made upon their village, and all their cattle with the women and children taken away. Komo was sold at the slave market in Leka, and stayed with his purchaser for three years, when he was sold to merchants from Jimma. He was afterwards sold in the markets of Gulisso, Gudru, and Gojam. At Gojam, he was bought by the Atari merchants who took him to Bofa, where he was sold to the Adal merchants, and taken

MAP B.27. Liban Bultum (source: Sandra Rowoldt Shell and GIS Laboratory, University of Cape Town).

Dappo. From Dappo he was taken to Leka and again sold, and from Leka to Gudru where he was bought by a Gudru merchant. His next master kept him six months herding cattle, but he was again sold in the market to a man who took him to Yajubi, about three day's [*sic*] journey east. From Yajubi he was taken to Dawe where he was bought by the Adal merchants and taken to Bofa. Here he joined some of the other boys and girls now with us, and was taken with them via Aussa and Araito.

MAP B.28. Milko Guyo (source: Sandra Rowoldt Shell and GIS Laboratory, University of Cape Town).

Milko Guyo

Birthdate circa 1878. Age about 12 years. Son of Guyo and Jorbo. He had two brothers and four sisters, who with their father and mother were alive when he left home. His father possessed a piece of land which he cultivated; he had also sixteen oxen and some sheep. His village was in Gomma. He was carried off after a fierce fight between his countrymen and the people of Jimma, in which the latter were victorious. Milko was taken three days' journey east into the Jimma country. When he had been here nearly six months, his father quite unexpectedly came upon him. He at once offered to ransom him, but asked leave to return home to get money. While he was away his master sold him to the chief of the district, and the chief's wife shortly after this sold him to the Sidama merchants for thirty pieces of salt. The Sidama merchants again sold him to a man from a place called Sodo, for nine dollars and two pieces of salt. This Sodo merchant took him to Tigre, and from thence to Dawe, a very long journey of over two months. In Dawe he was sold to the Adal merchants who took him via Aussa to Araito, where he joined the others.

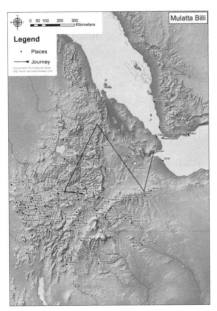

MAP B.29. Mulatta Billi (source: Sandra Rowoldt Shell and GIS Laboratory, University of Cape Town).

Mulatta Billi

Birthdate circa 1879. Age about 11 years. Son of Billi and Jorge. He had five brothers and one sister, some of whom were kidnapped like himself. He was too young to remember the name of the village or district from which he was taken. The facts regarding his capture are these. He was tending his father's cattle, and had gone away a little distance, in company with another boy, when he was stolen by a man and taken to his house. Next morning this man sold him to a merchant who was passing, who took him with other slaves to Jimma. He attempted to run away from Jimma, but was captured and sold soon after to a merchant from Gudru. In Gudru he was sold and taken by his new master to Tigre. After staying about one month

in Tigre he was sold in the market there to the Sidama merchants, and taken by them to the Adal country, when he was again sold to the Adal merchants and taken to Tajurrah, where he was put on board the slave dhow. He is one of those more recently captured.

Nagaro Chali

Birthdate circa 1877. Age about 13 years. Son of Chali and _____. He does not remember his mother's name, but says, he was born while she was a slave in the house of a man called Safo. He had two brothers and one sister. They stayed in a village called Deko in the Dappo country. His master sold him to a merchant who took him to another place in the Dappo country. He stayed here for two years when his master took him

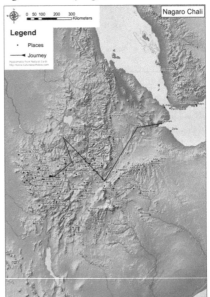

MAP B.30. Nagaro Chali (source: Sandra Rowoldt Shell and GIS Laboratory, University of Cape Town).

one week's journey to Leka and sold him there. From Leka he was taken to Gudru and again sold to a man belonging to the place. He says he was there for two years, so that he must have been very young when he left his home. He was next taken to Gojam and sold to Atari merchants, who brought him to Bofa. In Bofa he was sold to the Adal merchants, and taken via Aussa to Tajurrah where he joined the rest of those who were more recently captured.

Map B.31. Nuro Chabse (source: Sandra Rowoldt Shell and GIS Laboratory, University of Cape Town).

Nuro Chabse

Birthdate circa 1878. Age about 12 years. Son of Chabse and Shokachi. His home was in a village called Bita in the Kaffa country. His father had a large piece of land, also several oxen and sheep. He had one brother and two sisters. Nuro's duties were to look after the cattle in the fields. As he was doing so one day, four men came up to him and asked him to go with them to the Shonga country. He refused to do this and tried to run away, but they seized him and took him away with them. He was about six weeks in Shonga, when he tried to get away, but he was caught on the road by a man who took him back to his master. He was locked up in a room for several days and not allowed to go out. A party of merchants coming along, he was sold to them and taken to a place called Chaga where he was bought by a man residing in the place. Here he again tried to run away but he did not know in which direction to go, and soon found that he had gone the wrong road. He met a man who asked him to come and stay with him. He was here two days when his master found him, and, after beating him cruelly, tied his hands behind his back, and kept him bound all night. In the morning he was taken to a market near and sold to a man called Abba Ismael, a Mahommedan Galla—who took him to Tigre. Here another merchant bought him and he was taken to Gojam where he fell into the hands of the Adal merchants, and was taken by them via Aussa to Araito.

MAP B.32. Rufo Gangila (source: Sandra Rowoldt Shell and GIS Laboratory, University of Cape Town).

Rufo Gangila

Birthdate ca. 1873. Age about 17 years. Son of Gangila and Jorbo. His father died when he was young, and his mother with two brothers and three sisters stayed in a village called Tosa, in the district of Gera, between Jimma and Kaffa. He stayed with an elder brother for some time, then he was hired to a neighbouring crofter with whom he stayed one year. Difficulties arising between this man and the Sidama slave merchants, his brother sent for him, but on his way home he was caught by the Sidama, and taken by them a long journey to their own home. After staying one year with them, he found an opportunity to run away, but, at the end of five days, he was again captured by the Ilu tribe. He contrived to escape from them after one week, but had not

gone far when he was recognised by a friend of his master and taken back. He was soon afterwards sold to the Atari merchants. From Ajubi he was taken to Bofa and sold to the Adal merchants, who took him via Aussa to Araito, where he joined the others.

Sego Oria

Age about 14 years. Son of Oria and Galgali. He had one brother and three sisters. His father was a farmer in a small way. According to his story, he was given away by his father to a neighbour, who had no child of his own and offered to adopt him. This man took him to the Sidama country, and after staying there one year, he was stolen by a man who came out of a forest near to which he was playing. They both stayed in

MAP B.33. Sego Oria (source: Sandra Rowoldt Shell and GIS Laboratory, University of Cape Town).

the forest over night and next morning he was taken to a place called Kelem. After staying here for one week, he was taken to Leka and sold in the market there. His new master did not keep him long and he was soon after sold at Gulisso. He then passed from one merchant to another, being sold at the markets in Gudru, Luma, and Yajubi. He ultimately fell into the hands of the Atari merchants, and taken via Warakallu to Bofa where he was sold to the Adal merchants and taken to Araito.

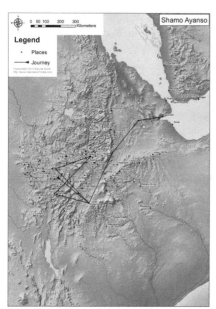

Map B.34. Shamo Ayanso (source: Sandra Rowoldt Shell and GIS Laboratory, University of Cape Town).

Shamo Ayanso

Age about 16 years. Son of Ayanso and Sakuri. He stayed with his parents, two brothers, and two sisters in a village called Yanfa in the Guma country. His father had a piece of land which he leased from another man, giving him a certain return of the produce of the land. The chief of his village was asked to send some of his people to help the Sidama to build some houses at a place about one day's journey from his home. Shamo was sent with them and when he was returning, a Sidama caught him and carried him to his home. He kept him in his house for two days when he took him to a market called Chara. When near the place, Shamo ran away. Meeting a man on the road, he asked him to show him the way. This man at once offered to take him to his father's home, but instead of that he took him to his own house. He kept him for one week, when he sold him to another man for a donkey. This man took him by night to Jimma, and from thence to Leka, where he was sold in the market, along with a little girl, for one hundred and six pieces of salt. He stayed for one month with his new master when he was again sold for four dollars to a Sidama merchant. This merchant took him to his home, one month's journey east; and after staying there for two weeks, he was taken to Ifat. At Ifat he was bought by a Sidama merchant, and taken to a market where he was sold to the Adal merchants, who took him via Aussa to Tajurrah. He is one of those more recently rescued.

MAP B.35. Tola Abaye (source: Sandra Rowoldt Shell and GIS Laboratory, University of Cape Town).

Tola Abaye

Birthdate circa 1878. Age about 12 years. Son of Abaye and Ganne. He was very young when taken from his home and so remembers very little about it. He had two brothers, and one sister who died before he left. The people of Leka came to fight with his country-men, and after defeating them carried off all the children. He was taken with many others to the Leka country where he stayed for a few months, and then he was sold in a slave market at Billo to a Gudru merchant. This man resold him in the same town. He was taken next to Kau, and sold in the market there to Sidama merchants. They took him to Dawe and there the Adal merchants bought him, and took him via Aussa to Araito, where he was put on board the slave dhow.

Tola Lual

Birthdate circa 1872. Age about 18 years. Son of Lual and Nawor. His father possessed a large piece of land which he cultivated, having about twenty ploughing oxen, and several sheep and goats. He had two brothers and two sisters. His grandfather was the chief of a country called Yambo, where Tola's home was. The chief of a place near, called Shechak, invited Tola's grandfather to a feast, he says, to drink something resembling brandy, and while there poison was put into his food and he died. Another chief was appointed in Yambo, called Todal. Todal very soon found a cause of quarrel with a neighbouring tribe—the Obojote. They fought a battle which lasted three days, in which the Yambo people were defeated, the victors carrying off all the

MAP B.36. Tola Lual (source: Sandra Rowoldt Shell and GIS Laboratory, University of Cape Town).

cattle and slaves they could find. Tola and his father escaped to a forest near and hid there. One year after this Tola's father sent him to the Obojote country to try and find his mother who had been carried away in the raid of the previous year. He went under the care of a man who said he knew where his mother was. This man however, did not take him to Obojote at all, but to his own house, and kept him there as a slave. The chief of Obojote raiding some of the villages near his territory, came to this house, and found Tola and a girl, who was also a slave. He was taken by the chief to his own house, and given to one of his servant[s] as a present. He stayed with this man for three years, and during that time discovered his mother, but was not allowed to return with her to their old home. Soon after this he was sold to a Gulisso merchant for five cows, and taken to the Gulisso country. He was sold there again to a Gudaya merchant with whom he stayed for six years, herding cattle. At the end of this time he was sold for twelve pieces of salt in the Nakante slave market. A Gudru merchant bought him, and took him to Yajubi, where he was sold to the Atari, and taken via Aussa to Araito.

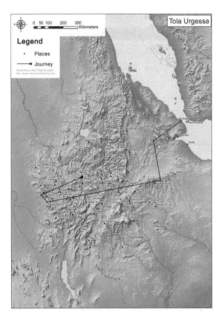

Map B.37. Tola Urgessa (source: Sandra Rowoldt Shell and GIS Laboratory, University of Cape Town).

Tola Urgessa

Birthdate circa 1874. Age about 16 years. Son of Urgessa and Badatu. He had four brothers and four sisters who, with his parents, were all alive when he left home. His father had a large piece of land of his own, with about sixty oxen and a few sheep and goats. He also possessed four horses. His village was called Windi, and was in the Sayo country, near to the river Birbir. The Sidama attacked their country, and he was captured and taken to a place called Afillo. Here he ran away and was captured again by another Afillo man. He stayed for about a week with this man, when he was sold at a place called Dappo Gacho, for a hundred pieces of salt, to a Gudru merchant. This man sold him to the Atari who took him to Dawe and sold him there. The Adal merchants were the purchasers and they took him via Aussa to Araito.

MAP B.38. Tolassa Wayessa (source: Sandra Rowoldt Shell and GIS Laboratory, University of Cape Town).

Tolassa Wayessa

Birthdate circa 1877. Age about 13 years. Son of Wayessa and Hatatu. He lived in a village called Jimma in the Tibbe country. His father possessed a large piece of land and about twenty oxen and fifteen sheep, also a horse. He was playing at a little distance from his home, when three men came up to him and asked him if he had seen a stray horse. He replied in the affirmative, telling them in what direction the horse had gone. Suspecting them, he immediately threw away his skin covering, and ran towards his home; but he was soon overtaken, and covering his mouth with their hands, they carried him off into the forest. He was taken by these men to a place called Godawarabessa, and there sold to slave merchants. These merchants took him to the market at Billo, about two weeks' journey. A disturbance between the neighbouring tribes paralysed the

slave market, and being unable to sell him there, he was taken to Kau, and sold to a man from Gudru. This man took him to Ajubi on the other side of the Abayi River (Blue Nile) and sold him to the Atari slave merchants. He tried to run away from them as they threatened to sell him to a tribe called the Bulgu (the men eaters). He was however recaptured, and kept with chains on his feet for six days. He was taken by these Atari merchants a long journey to Ancharro, where he joined some of the other boys with us, and from thence to Bofa where the Adal merchants bought him. With them he went to Aussa and from there to Araito where he was put on board the dhow.

Wakinne Nagesso

Birthdate circa 1874. Age about 16 years. Son of Nagesso and Dingisse. He had two brothers and two sisters. His father

MAP B.39. Wakinne Nagesso (source: Sandra Rowoldt Shell and GIS Laboratory, University of Cape Town).

died when he was a child. On his death Wakinne's eldest brother supported the family by cultivating their land. The village was called Humbe and was in the Bunno country. He was playing near his home, when two men came up and spoke to him. They asked him to go with them and shew them the cattle, and, when they had got some distance from the house, they laid hold on him and dragged him to their own house. He was kept there, closely watched, for three days, and then taken to a place called Doranni, and sold in the market to a Leka merchant. He was afterwards taken to Gudru and again sold. He was with the man who bought him for a year and a half, when he was sold to another man in the same place. This man took him to Ajubi, and sold him to an Arab called Mahommed, who took him to Bofa and sold him to the Adal merchants. He was then taken to Aussa, where he joined some of the other boys, and was with them taken to Araito.

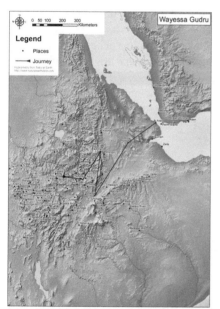

MAP B.40. Wayessa Gudru (source: Sandra Rowoldt Shell and GIS Laboratory, University of Cape Town).

Wayessa Gudru

Birthdate circa 1878. Age about 12 years. Son of _____ and Mune. He does not remember his father's name, and has been called by the other boys, Gudru, after the name of the country from which he came. He had one brother and two sisters. He and his mother were carried off as slaves to another town in Gudru, and bought by a man named Galata. They were with this man for a considerable time. One day a slave who had run away from his master took refuge in Galata's house. Galata kept him, but he died shortly after this. This slave's master, hearing that the fugitive had been staying in Galata's house, came, and demanded his property. He was not satisfied on being told that he had died, and demanded compensation. Wayessa was therefore given to him, and taken to Yajubi, about three days' journey off, and there sold him to the Sidama merchants. They brought him to Ancharro, and sold him to the Atari merchants, who took him to Bofa. Here he fell into the hands of the Adal merchants and was taken via Aussa to Araito.

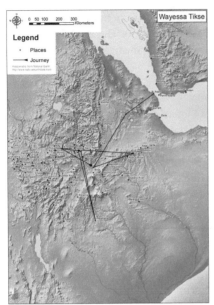

MAP B.41. Wayessa Tikse (source: Sandra Rowoldt Shell and GIS Laboratory, University of Cape Town).

Wayessa Tikse

Birthdate circa 1872. Age about 18 years. Son of Tikse and Jibbe. He was born in a village called Geddo in the Rafisso district. Near his village were Wagedi and Adeya, to the east, Tibbe south, Gudru, and west, Liban. The river Abaye lay to the west of his home. He had three brothers and one sister. His father owned a large piece of land, had several oxen, two horses, and a few sheep and goats. He employed men to plough for him. He had gone to pay a visit to a cousin of his, when one day his cousin's cousin proposed that they should go down to the market. They went off together, and afterwards they both went to a house to visit a friend. They stayed there all night, and, in the morning, when it was time to go away, they caught hold of Wayessa and stopped his mouth

with a piece of leather, so that he could not cry for help. He tried to tear this away, but they beat him, and tied ropes around him. He was kept thus, and with chains on his legs and arms, beneath a bed, for a week. At the end of this time he was taken to Gudru and sold there. From Gudru he came to Ajubi, then to Warakalla. Passing through Dibdibbe, Dawe, and Bofa, he was brought to Aussa where he fell into the hands of the Adal merchants, and by them was taken to Araito.

Wayessa Tonki

Birthdate circa 1879. Age about 11 years. Son of Tonki and Meti. He stayed with his father in a village called Nama, in a district called Boniya. He was sent

MAP B.42. Wayessa Tonki (source: Sandra Rowoldt Shell and GIS Laboratory, University of Cape Town).

one day by his mother to his aunt's house, with one of his brothers. On the way his brother died, and his aunt kept him to watch her cattle. One day he allowed the cattle to stray into the fields of standing grain. His aunt was very angry and sent him away. He tried to find his way home, but was benighted, and sought shelter in a house on the road. He thus put himself into the hands of Sidama merchants, who took him by night to a village near by and sold him there for a donkey. From there he was taken to Tigre about three months' journey. Here he was again sold, and taken to some place near the Hawash river—he forgets the name. He was only three days here when he was sold to the Atari merchants and taken by them via Aussa to Tajurrah. He is one of those rescued more recently.

Females

Map B.43. Agude Bulcha (source: Sandra Rowoldt Shell and GIS Laboratory, University of Cape Town).

Agude Bulcha

Birthdate circa 1875. Age about 15 years. Daughter of Bulcha and _____. She forgets the name of her mother. She had three brothers and one sister. Her father cultivated a piece of land for the chief of a district, called Dange, in which he lived. Her aunt paid a visit to her father, and on returning to her own village asked for Agude to accompany her. She did so and stayed for some time with her aunt. One day her aunt went on a visit to a friend; and she went to the field to eat sugar-cane; while doing so, two men pounced upon her, and, gagging her mouth with a piece of cloth, carried her away. These men took her to a house not far distant. During the evening, the owner of this house found out who Agude was, and, being a relation, he waited till night, and when all was quiet took her on horseback to her father's house. Her father reported the matter to the chief, who tried to find out the thieves, but without success. Her father suspected two men, but when he had gone out one day to look for them, they came to his house by another way, and, finding Agude playing about, again carried her away. She cried for help, but they silenced her by putting a piece of cloth in her mouth. She was taken by them over a large river, called Jabalu, to their own country near a high mountain, called Guma. She was here four days without food, having refused to eat the first day. Her captors then took her to the slave market of Gulisso, but, being unable to sell her, took her over the River Birbir, to a market at Kotche, where she was sold to a Gudru merchant. She was sold three times after this, before being brought to the coast by the Adal merchants via Aussa to Araito.

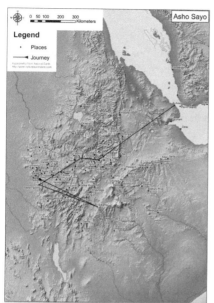

MAP B.44. Asho Sayo (source: Sandra Rowoldt Shell and GIS Laboratory, University of Cape Town).

Ayantu Said

Birthdate circa 1874. Age about 16 years. Daughter of Said and Fatto. She had one brother and one sister. Her father cultivated a piece of land for the chief of the village which was in the Ulbaragga country, and called Tode. The ground formerly belonged to her father, but he left the district for some time, and on his return the chief gave him his land back only on condition that he would give the chief half of the produce. Her village was attacked by a neighbouring tribe, and all the people ran away; but passing through a district called Shashoga she was caught by a man and taken to his home. This man took her to a slave market near and sold her, and she was taken a long journey to Tigre, where she was again sold. From Tigre she was taken to Dibdibbi. In Dibdibbi she was bought by the Adal merchants and taken via Aussa to Araito.

Asho Sayo

Birthdate circa 1879. Age about 11 years. Daughter of _____ and Adoye. She does not remember her father's name. Her mother and she, and also a younger brother, were slaves in the house of a man called Abba Urgessa. She has been called after the name, of the country from which she came, Sayo. Abba Urgessa was the owner of a piece of land, several cows and some goats. Failing to pay tribute, the Sidama came down upon the village. Abba Urgessa ran away, and she and her mother were taken by the raiders to the Sidama country, and from thence to Dappo-Gacho. At Dappo, she saw her mother for the last time, and she was taken from there to Gudru and sold to the Atari merchants. She was then taken to Dibdibbi where the Adal merchants bought her and took her via Aussa to Araito.

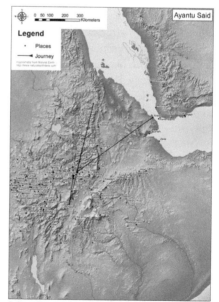

MAP B.45. Ayantu Said (source: Sandra Rowoldt Shell and GIS Laboratory, University of Cape Town).

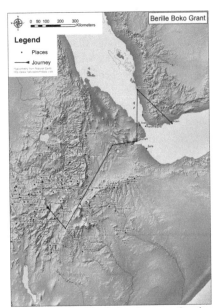

MAP B.46. Berille Boko (source: Sandra Rowoldt Shell and GIS Laboratory, University of Cape Town).

large dhow which was full sailed at the same time. They were near the Arabian coast when they were pursued by an English gunboat, but they ran the dhows ashore and escaped into a forest. After two days hiding they were put on camels and brought to the town of Hodeidah. Here they were all exposed for sale in a fondak, a native caravanserai—and she was bought by a Scotch gentlemen, Mr. Grant, for the sum of one hundred and seventy five dollars. He brought her to our mission in Aden and put her into our hands to be educated at his expense. He is himself now one of the pioneering party of the British East Africa Company in Uganda.

Berille Nehor

Birthdate circa 1877. Age about 13 years. Daughter of Nehor and Bushaseche. Her

Berille Boko

Birthdate circa 1875. Age about 15 years. Daughter of Boko and Turungi. She had two brothers and one sister. She does not remember the name of her village or the country in which it was, but says it was near the Gibbe River. Her father was the chief of the village and possessed land which it would take a whole day to go round. He had many oxen and sheep and had one slave staying in his house. She was a very little girl when the Sidama made a raid on her village, and captured the whole family. They were taken to the house of one of the Sidama, and kept there about a month, when she was sold in a slave market to a Gudru merchant who had a number of other slaves with him. This man took her to Tajurrah via Aussa and sold her there to the Adal merchants. Here she was put on board a dhow with twenty-two other girls and twenty-eight boys. Another

MAP B.47. Berille Nehor (source: Sandra Rowoldt Shell and GIS Laboratory, University of Cape Town).

home was in Ishete in the Kaffa country. She had several brothers and sisters. Her father was a slave, and held a piece of land from his master which he cultivated. She was employed by her mistress in nursing her child for sometime. On one occasion her master after returning from a skirmish with a neighbouring tribe, in which he had lost his goga (kaross), sold her to buy a new one. He did it in this way. He told her to go to a neighbouring hut, and bring his sword. When she got there, she found a man who gagged her and carried her off. She was taken to Jimma and there sold. Her new master took her to Tigre. In Tigre she was sold to the Adal merchants and taken to Araito via Aussa.

MAP B.48. Bisho Jarsa (source: Sandra Rowoldt Shell and GIS Laboratory, University of Cape Town).

Bisho Jarsa

Birthdate circa 1874. Age about 16 years. Daughter of Jarsa and Dingati. Her father and mother were dead when she was first taken away from her own country. They both died at the same time, during the prevalence of a sickness which carried away a great many people. The cattle also died in large numbers. She had two brothers. On the death of her parents, she was taken care of by one of her father's slaves. A famine was over all the land at the time, and she was sent with a man to buy food in another county called Gobu. When they arrived there, she was told that she must be sold for corn. She was therefore sold here to a merchant in that place. The Atari merchants coming round to buy up slaves, she was sold to them and taken to Ancharro in the Warakalla country, where she was sold again to another slave merchant who had a great many other children. This merchant sold her to merchants in Adal, who took her via Dawe to Tajurrah. She was here put on board a dhow, which sailed with five other dhows. They were not long out, when they saw a gunboat, and two of the dhows put back. All the captives were taken ashore and kept for six weeks. Then they started again. This time a gunboat captured the two dhows, one of them being the one in which Isho was found—the only survivor of a whole dhow full of slaves. They were taken to Aden.

MAP B.49. Damuli Diso (source: Sandra Rowoldt Shell and GIS Laboratory, University of Cape Town).

Damuli Diso

Birthdate circa 1875. Age about 15 years. Daughter of Damara and Bushu. She was named Damuli by one of her masters who had two girls of the same name. Diso was the name given to her by her parents. She had two brothers and two sisters. Her father and mother died before she left home. Her father was a ploughman, who worked for any one who wished to hire him. On her father's death, her mother supported the family by cutting wood and selling it to men who made earthenware. Her country was called Gobbu. When her mother died, she went to stay with her uncle. After she had been about a year with her uncle, a party of Sidama came upon the location, and she was carried away by them and sold to a merchant in Gombu. Here her hands were chained, to prevent her

running away, as her own village was not far off. She was kept in Gombu for two months and then taken to Kau, one day's journey, where she was sold to a Gudru merchant and taken to Ajubi. Here she was sold to other Sidama merchants and taken to Bofa. From Bofa she was taken to Dawe, and thence via Aussa to Araito, where she was put on board the slave dhow.

Damuli Dunge

Birthdate circa 1876. Age about 14 years. Daughter of _____ and Dunge. She does not remember her father's name, so has been called after her mother. She had one brother and one sister. Her home was called Ginjo, in Jimma. Her mother supported the family, on their father's death, by buying in the market, and

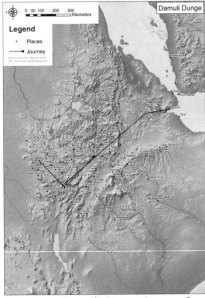

MAP B.50. Damuli Dunge (source: Sandra Rowoldt Shell and GIS Laboratory, University of Cape Town).

selling retail. One day, her mother having gone to the market, a man came to the house, and told her that her mother wanted her in the market. She went, but instead of being taken to the market, she was taken away from the village and sold. The man who bought her took her to a place called Adiya where she was again sold and taken to Dalate. In Dalate, a Tigre merchant bought her and took her to Arguba where she was sold, and taken via Aussa to Tajurrah. She was put on board the same slave dhow with Bisho (No. 6 [Bisho Jarsa was sixth in the list of girls but the fiftieth child in the sequence of the full group]), and from this point their stories coincide.

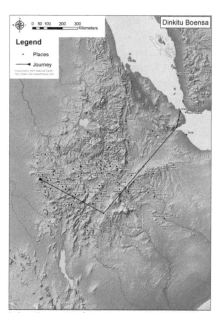

MAP B.51. Dinkitu Boensa (source: Sandra Rowoldt Shell and GIS Laboratory, University of Cape Town).

Dinkitu Boensa

Birthdate circa 1873. Age about 17 years. Daughter of Boensa and Kurni. Her home was in a village called Garjeda in the Gindo country. She had one sister and two brothers. Her father was the chief of the village. He had large lands and some hundreds of cattle. She was about eight years old when she left home. The Sidama came upon their village because they could not pay tribute, and sacked and burned it. She and her mother fled but they were captured by a Sidama merchant. Her mother was sold, but she stayed with this man for several years as his child. At the end of this time a stranger came and said he wished to take Dinkitu back to her home. He gave eight dollars as a ransom, but instead of taking her home he took her to Tajurrah and sold her there as a slave. From Tajurrah she was taken to Araito, where she stayed for one month, before being, with the others, shipped on board the slave dhows.

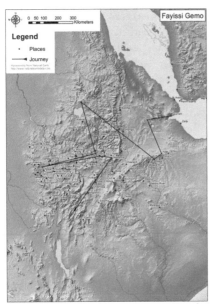

MAP B.52. Fayissi Gemo (source: Sandra Rowoldt Shell and GIS Laboratory, University of Cape Town).

Fayissi Gemo

Birthdate circa 1877. Age about 13 years. Daughter of Gemo and Yarachi. She stayed in a village called Upa in the Kaffa country. Her father was dead when she left home, but her mother and two sisters remained behind. Her father owned a piece of land which he ploughed. He had several oxen, and a few sheep and goats. On her father's death, two years before she left home, her mother supported the family, employing labourers to plough the land. Her mother had gone away to her native place, when one day the chief of Upa took Fayissi and sold her for a horse to merchants who were passing. These merchants took her to a place called Galegoda, and sold her to a man called Abba Ismael who took her to Jimma. Ismael had bought her for another man

who stayed in Jimma, and when she was given over to her new master, he took her, with a number of other girls, to Dalatte, and sold her. This time a Tigre merchant bought her and took her to Totosse, and then to Gondar, the chief town of Abyssinia. Here she was sold to Adal merchants, and taken a long journey to Dawe. From Dawe she was taken to the Adal country, probably Aussa, and there another man bought her, and took her to Tajurrah. Here she was put on board a slave dhow with those who were more recently rescued.

Galani Warabu

Birthdate circa 1876. Age about 14 years. Daughter of Warabu and Diribe. Her father was dead, but her mother was alive when she left home. She had five

MAP B.53. Galani Warabu (source: Sandra Rowoldt Shell and GIS Laboratory, University of Cape Town).

brothers and four sisters. Her father was the chief of a village. On her father's death, her uncle claimed all his cattle and property; and, a short time after this, the Sidama made a raid upon their country, killing her two eldest brothers. She and her sisters hid in a forest, and when the Sidama left they came back to their home. A short time after this, a cousin came to visit them, and she was asked to return with him to his home. She did so, but on asking to get back one day, her cousin took her to a place called Macharro and sold her. She was then taken to Dappo-Gacho and again sold. From here she was taken to Leka via Dappo-Gumbe. She was sold in the market here to a merchant who took her to Gudru. From Gudru she was taken to Ajubi. Here she was bought by the Atari merchants, and taken to Dawe, and thence to Tajurrah. She was rescued from the same dhow as Bisho and Damuli Dunge.

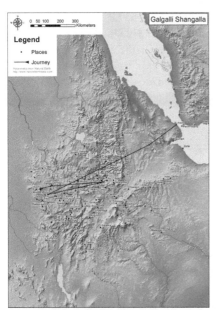

MAP B.54. Galgalli Shangalla (source: Sandra Rowoldt Shell and GIS Laboratory, University of Cape Town).

Galgalli Shangalla

Birthdate circa 1872. Age about 18 years. Daughter of _____ and _____. She does not remember the names of her parents, and does not know of having any brothers or sisters. She is called Shangalla after the name of the first country she remembers. It would seem as though she were so young when she was taken from her parents that she has no recollection of home. Her first recollections are of staying with a man who had a piece of land which he ploughed in a place called Kilema, in the Shangalla country. This man sold her to a Gudru merchant who brought her to a market at Guliso and there sold her again. Her new master took her to Ajubi. Here she was again sold and taken to Dappo, where the Adal merchants bought her. She was then taken via Aussa to Araito, where she was put on board the slave dhow.

MAP B.55. Halko Danko (source: Sandra Rowoldt Shell and GIS Laboratory, University of Cape Town).

merchants. The Adal merchants took her via Aussa to Araito where she joined the others and was put on board the slave dhows.

Hawe Sukute

Birthdate circa 1874. Age about 16 years. Daughter of Sukute and Ibse. She had two brothers and one sister. Her father died when she was very young. Her mother was taken as a slave by the people of Sayo, who were at feud with her country. Her village was called Gani in the Garjeja country. When her mother died, she and her brothers stayed with their uncle. Another uncle, on her father's side, claimed them as his property and took them to his house where they worked for him. This uncle was in debt to the king of the country, so

Halko Danko

Birthdate circa 1877. Age about 13 years. Daughter of Danko and Balale. She had five sisters and two brothers who, with her father and mother, were alive when she left home. Her father possessed a small piece of land which he ploughed. He had a few oxen, and four donkeys. Her country was called Limamu. The chief of her village having refused to pay tribute, for some reason or other, the Sidama came upon the village, killed many of the men, and carried the women and children away as slaves. She stayed with the man who captured her for one year, when she was sold in a slave market to a man called Ali, another Sidama merchant. This man sold her again shortly after this at Dawe, where she fell, with Wakenne [Wakinne] Nagesso, into the hands of the Adal

MAP B.56. Hawe Sukute (source: Sandra Rowoldt Shell and GIS Laboratory, University of Cape Town).

he sold Hawe to pay the debt. A Leka merchant bought her and took her to a slave market in Gudru and sold her there, to a Gudru merchant. From Gudru she was taken to Ajubi where a Sidama merchant bought her and took her to their country, Aussa. From Aussa she was taken to Araito, where she joined the others.

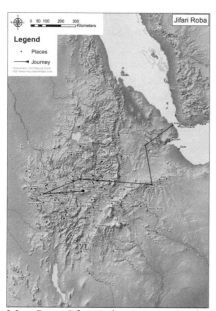

MAP B.57. Jifari Roba (source: Sandra Rowoldt Shell and GIS Laboratory, University of Cape Town).

Jifari Roba

Birthdate circa 1877. Age about 13 years. Daughter of Roba and Dongoshe. Her home was in a village called Galani, in the Sayo country. She had three brothers and four sisters. Her father had died about one year before she left home. She has also heard that her mother died after she left. Her father supported the family by hiring himself out as a ploughman. On her father's death, her mother went out to work in the fields, reaping, etc. Another woman, in a village near, offered to keep Jifari, but, shortly after she went to stay with her, this woman sold her for ten pieces of salt to some people called Nagadi, who were passing. They took her to Dappo. She stayed here about one year, with a man who bought her from the Nagadi. At the end of this time she was sold to a man called Gumbi and taken to a slave market in Gudru. Here a Gudru man bought her and sold her to the Atari merchants. The Atari sold her to the Adal merchants who took her to Dawe. From Dawe she was taken to Aussa, and from there to Araito.

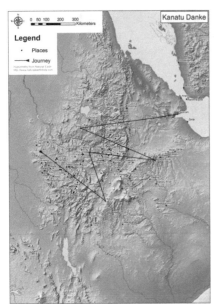

MAP B.58. Kanatu Danke (source: Sandra Rowoldt Shell and GIS Laboratory, University of Cape Town).

Kanatu Danke

Birthdate circa 1871. Age about 19 years. Daughter of Danke and Angatu. She had five brothers and four sisters who were all alive with their father and mother when she left home. Her village was called Lalo, in the Sayo country. Her father possessed a piece of land on which he employed many labourers. He was the chief of the village. The Sidama came and fought with their country, and she was taken away by them. They were all in the house when the fight was going on, but she happened to go outside, and a man on horseback came up to her and carried her off. She stayed in the Sidama country for about two years. One day she was told to take horses to the water, and after doing so she tried to run away but was captured by another man who took her to Gudru. Here she was sold and taken to a place near the Abaye river, where she was again sold to a man called Wage. This man took her to a slave market in Gojam, where she was sold to the Atari merchants. From here she was taken to Aussa and sold to the Adal merchants who took her to Tajurrah, where she joined those of the party who were last captured.

Meshinge Salban

Birthdate circa 1874. Age about 16 years. Daughter of Salban and Dadi. The name of the village in which she stayed was Abbo in the Sayo country. She had no brothers or sisters. Her mother died when she was quite young, and her father also died about two years before she left her home. Her mother was a secondary wife of Salban's. She stayed

MAP B.59. Meshinge Salban (source: Sandra Rowoldt Shell and GIS Laboratory, University of Cape Town).

with Salban's chief wife for some time, until one day the people of Gojam came to fight with Sayo. Salban's son was then the chief of the village. The Gojam people asked the Sajo country to pay tribute to them, and they did so but not enough to satisfy them. They demanded slaves, and a great number of boys and girls were given to them. Meshinge's foster-mother hid her and so she escaped. The victorious Gojam people passed on to another country, but on their return demanded more slaves. Meshinge this time was taken by the chief and given to the Gojam people. They took her to Dappo-Gacho and sold her there. Here a Leka merchant bought her and took her to his home, where, after staying a short time, she was sold to a man from Gudru. From Gudru she was taken to Ajubi, and here the Atari bought her. The Atari took her to Ancharro, and from there to Arguba, where the Adal merchants bought her and took her to Aussa and thence to Araito, where she joined the others.

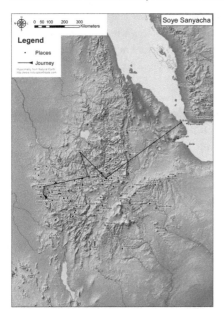

MAP B.60. Soye Sanyacha (source: Sandra Rowoldt Shell and GIS Laboratory, University of Cape Town).

Soye Sanyacha

Birthdate circa 1874. Age about 16 years. Daughter of Sanyacha and Magartu. She had three brothers but no sisters. Her village was in the Sayo country. Her father cultivated a piece of land for the chief of the country, who was called Abba Gimbe. The king's wife asked Soye to come and nurse her child, and, after she had stayed in the king's house for two weeks, her mistress sent her to a village to buy tobacco. At the same time, the king's son was told to be at this place and to sell her, which he did. She was sold for an ox, to a Leka merchant, who took her to a place called Kilema. Here a Gudru merchant called Dingu bought her, and took her to his own country and sold her in the market there. She was taken by the new purchaser to the town of Gojam, and sold in the market to the Atari. They brought her to Dibdibbe where the Adal merchants bought her, and took her via Aussa to Araito, where she joined the others.

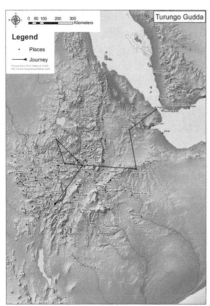

Map B.61. Turungo Gudda (source: Sandra Rowoldt Shell and GIS Laboratory, University of Cape Town).

Turungo Gudda

Birthdate circa 1876. Age about 14 years. Daughter of _____ and Dabeche. She stayed in a village called Shuter in the Kaffa country. She has no recollection of her father. Her mother supported the family, consisting of two sons and two daughters, by going into the fields to sow or reap or work in any other way for an uncle. She is called Turungo Gudda—which means "big Turungo,"—to distinguish her from another girl of the same name who is called "little Turungo." Before her father's death he had borrowed some things from her uncle, and as the family were unable to return the loan, Turungo was taken by the uncle. He sold her to a man in the country, called Agadi, who took her to a market near, and sold her to Jimma merchants, who took her to their own country. She was then taken to Gudru and sold there to a merchant in that place. She stayed for a short time in Gudru when she was taken to Gojam, where she was sold again to a Nagadi. This Nagadi took her to Dibdibbe and sold her there to the Atari. From Dibdibbe she was taken to Dawe where she met some of the other boys and girls, and was taken with them via Aussa to Araito.

Turungo Tinno

Birthdate circa 1877. Age about 13 years. Daughter of _____ and Nibiashe. She had five brothers and two sisters. She does not remember her father's name or whether he was alive when she left her home, as she was very young. Her village was called Saate in the Kaffa

Map B.62. Turungo Tinno (source: Sandra Rowoldt Shell and GIS Laboratory, University of Cape Town).

country. She is called Turungo Tinno—"little Turungo"—to distinguish her from Turungo Gudda. When she was playing about her home, a man came up to her, and, gagging her, carried her away to a slave market not far distant, where she stayed for a fortnight. She was then sold to a Kulo merchant. This man took her to a place, the name of which she does not remember, and sold her there. She was then taken to Gudru, and thence to Ajubi. From Ajubi she was taken to Dibdibbe where the Adal merchants bought her and took her via Aussa to Araito.

MAP B.63. Wakinni Ugga (source: Sandra Rowoldt Shell and GIS Laboratory, University of Cape Town).

Wakinni Ugga

Birthdate circa 1879. Age about 11 years. Daughter of Ugga and Desta. She is the youngest of the girls. She had two brothers but no sisters. She stayed in a village in the Guma country. Her father was a tailor. (This is the only instance of the parents of any of the children following any other pursuit than farming.) The people of a neighbouring tribe, called Hawu, came to fight with her tribe, and they all ran away, her mother carrying her. When her mother saw there was a likelihood of her being overtaken, she laid Wakinni down among some bushes where another child, a boy, was hiding. The enemies saw this boy as they passed, and killed him, but Wakinni escaped their notice. On their return, however, they found her, and she was taken away on horseback by a man, who, when he was galloping away with her, dropped her, and did not come back to lift her up. She got up and tried to find her way back to her village, but night came on and she slept under a tree. She stayed here for two days without food, and in the evening of the second day two men found her and took her to a house at some distance. She was then taken on horseback to another place, where she was sold to a man who took her to a market, the name of which she does not remember. When she was being taken away by this man, they met some of the Atari on the road, and he sold her to them. Gamaches was with them at this time. She was then taken to Aussa and thence to Araito where she joined the others.

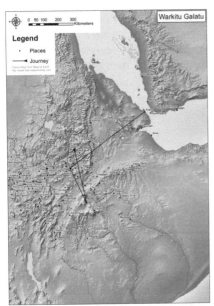

MAP B.64. Warkitu Galatu (source: Sandra Rowoldt Shell and GIS Laboratory, University of Cape Town).

Warkitu Galatu

Birthdate circa 1874. Age about 16 years. Daughter of Galatu and Sanbate. She had three brothers and one sister. She was the second of the family. Her father died many years before she left home. She stayed in a village called Godeti in the Chaja country. They had a piece of land from the king, which they cultivated, hiring a man to do the ploughing. She had gone with her mother to the home of her grandmother, and from there she was sent to stay with her uncle. She was sent out one day to get firewood along with a woman, who begged Warkitu to come and stay with her, as her husband was going out to fight and she had no children of her own. This woman took her to Gomoji and she stayed with her for one month. At the end of this time, the woman proposed to take her to her mother, but instead of this she took her to a brother's house, and left her there, promising to return shortly. Some merchants came along and she was sold to them. She was taken by them to Dibdibbe, where they sold her to Tigre merchants. She was afterwards sold to the Adal merchants and taken by them via Aussa to Araito.

Gazetteer of Place-Names
Mentioned in the Narratives

TABLE C.1. Place-names and alternatives mentioned by the Oromo children

Place-name	Alternative or modern name(s)	Latitude	Longitude
Abbo	Abbo	8.533	34.800
Adal Country	Adal	9.583	42.300
Aden	Aden	12.800	45.033
Afillo (Afillu)	Afillu	8.417	34.650
Agam	Agam	9.500	39.270
Ajuba	Ajuba	9.400	38.700
Ajubi	Ajuba, Yajubi	9.400	38.700
Alle		8.367	38.233
Ancharro		11.050	39.783
Angisho		7.333	37.850
Araito	Rahayta, Roheita	12.727	43.084
Arguba		7.400	36.433
Aussa	Awsa, Awusa	11.564	41.433
Badda	Bada	7.917	39.383
Bambasse	Bambesi	9.750	34.733
Barsinge	Bassibe	8.500	35.967
Billo		8.900	37.000
Bita		10.383	39.133
Bofa		8.467	39.450
Boniya	Boneya	9.600	38.267
Bunno		8.217	36.417

TABLE C.1. Place-names and alternatives mentioned by Oromo children (*continued*)

Place-name	Alternative or modern name(s)	Latitude	Longitude
Chaga	Chaja	10.183	35.000
Chefita		11.317	39.900
Chonge	Ch'Ange	8.167	39.433
Chora		8.333	36.250
Dalate	Dalatte, Dalatti, Dalotti	8.850	35.050
Dange	Dango	9.200	35.567
Danno	Dano, Danu	5.767	37.550
Dappo		8.683	35.317
Dappo-Gacho		8.000	35.000
Dappo Gumbi	Dappo-Gumbe	8.767	36.283
Dawe		9.267	41.850
Deko		8.750	36.150
Dibdibbe		9.483	38.533
Doranni		9.683	38.850
Enge	Ch'Enge	9.800	38.283
Entotto in Shoa	Entotta	9.100	38.800
Galani	Gelan	8.867	37.783
Gamoje	Gamoji, Gomoji	0.000	0.000
Gani	Agani	10.017	34.317
Garjeda	Gerjeda	8.767	34.650
Geddo	Gedo	8.567	39.333
Gella		9.617	42.717
Gera		7.500	36.667
Gindo		9.467	38.900
Ginjo		9.117	38.367
Gobbu		7.000	39.983
Godawarabessa		9.750	38.767
Godeti		10.600	38.817
Gojam		11.000	37.000
Gombu	Gombo	8.833	35.533
Gomma		7.767	36.633
Gondar		12.600	37.467
Gualla		7.333	37.350
Gudru		9.583	37.500
Guduya	Gudaya	9.117	37.167
Gulisso		9.167	35.467
Guma		8.167	36.200
Gurage		8.400	38.400

Table C.1. Place-names and alternatives mentioned by Oromo children (*continued*)

Place-name	Alternative or modern name(s)	Latitude	Longitude
Halelu	Oda Halelu	8.000	41.183
Hawash River		8.983	40.167
Hochocha		8.033	39.983
Hodeidah		14.783	42.117
Humbe		8.467	36.100
Ifat		9.733	39.900
Ilu		9.483	38.883
Imo		6.467	42.167
Ishete	Ijeta	9.983	38.567
Jimma		9.467	38.600
Kaffa		7.000	36.500
Kambatta		7.833	37.750
Kasalu		9.333	42.333
Kau		9.333	36.667
Kilema	Kelem	9.000	34.833
Kilerito	Koreta	11.483	37.533
Koma		8.450	36.867
Kosher		8.000	38.533
Kotche		12.133	39.833
Lalo		9.667	34.517
Leka		8.750	36.467
Leka-Tocho		8.750	36.467
Limamu	Zulimamu	6.017	35.200
Limmu		7.850	36.800
Luma		8.333	36.817
Majo	Amajo	10.550	39.333
Malagga		6.467	42.167
Mangera		7.500	36.667
Nakante		9.000	35.500
Nama	Mama	9.350	38.483
Nollekabba	Nole Kaba	8.750	35.750
Nonno		8.300	39.783
Nopa		8.667	35.150
Obojote		8.983	34.617
Abaye River		9.100	41.517
Hawash River		8.983	40.167
Rafisso		9.000	37.500
Saate	Saarte	5.350	37.633

TABLE C.1. Place-names and alternatives mentioned by Oromo children (*continued*)

Place-name	Alternative or modern name(s)	Latitude	Longitude
Sakal	Sakala	11.050	37.150
Sayo		8.333	35.000
Seka		7.600	36.733
Shangalla	Shan Galla	9.000	34.833
Shashoga		7.617	38.100
Shewa	Shoa	9.000	39.000
Shonga		10.883	40.000
Shuter	Shuda	7.183	36.900
Sidama		6.750	38.500
Silte		7.917	38.333
Sodo		8.583	35.817
Tajurrah	Tadjoura, Tadjourah, Tajoura	11.783	42.883
Tibbe		9.067	37.150
Tigre		13.500	39.500
Tode	Dode	9.317	38.333
Totosse	Tatecha	9.600	38.300
Ulbaragga	Ula Āwara	9.400	38.283
Upa	Uba	6.300	37.000
Urbaraga	Urbarag	7.767	38.183
Adal		9.583	42.300
Wachali	Wichalē	8.750	36.283
Walagga	Welega, Wallaga, Wallega	8.600	35.733
Warakalla	Warakallu, Warrakallo	5.383	39.533
Windi	Wendi	9.467	37.167
Yajubi	Ajubi	9.400	38.700
Yambo Country		8.333	36.017
Yanfa		8.250	36.600
Yassa	Yasa	9.567	38.667

(Source: Sandra Rowoldt Shell.)

My Essay Is upon Gallaland[1]

by Gutama Tarafo

Mr Chairman and Members,

In Gallaland many things are different from South African things. The people are different, and the country itself is different from this country.

First of all, I want to speak about the climate of the country. Perhaps many of you won't believe about the climate, because none of you have been there, except those that came from there. But you read in the books of Geography, and those books say the climate is very hot. I can tell you the climate is not all very hot. But it is quite true that the southern part of the country is exceedingly hot, because there are no mountains there. The upper country is much cooler than Cape Colony, although it is near the Equator, because there are many high mountains near Abyssinia. There are no lakes in Gallaland. But there are many small rivers. The largest river is the River Abaye, that is, I think, the Blue Nile. Also the Hawash River runs through the north of Gallaland and falls into the Blue Nile, at the West of Abyssinia. There are many other rivers, whose names I forget.

Now I shall tell you about the marriage customs. I heard George Tyamzashe's paper about Kaffir marriages.[2] He said when the Kaffirs are going to get married, they buy their wives. I think you remember when Jacob wanted to marry, he worked for fourteen years, and then he got those two wives. Well, that is not the way of marrying people in our country. When a man wants to marry a girl, first he goes and speaks with her parents, and then if her parents agree with him, he will take her, but if not he will leave her.

The Galla people are quite different from the people of South Africa. They are different in dressing. The Galla people never wear red blankets, as the Kaffirs do. Rich people wear short trousers and a fine mantle of cloth, and poor people wear the same clothes as the Arabs. The women wear a fine skin dress and no one of you could tell the difference between that skin and cloth.

The houses are not the same as those here. The Galla huts are four or five times bigger than these Kaffir huts. I may say the Galla house has got two storeys. In the upper storey they keep corn and other things; but in the lower one the people sleep. There are two rooms in the lower storey, one is where the mother of the house does her work and the other one is for sleeping and eating.

There are many kinds of grain, as wheat, barley, maize, and bishinga, that is Kaffir-corn, also pumpkins, potatoes, and other things like potatoes, beans, coffee, peas, bananas, also cabbages and tobacco and many other things which I can't name in English. There is plenty of honey. The people don't keep bees as in this country. They hang a kind of basket made of reeds high on a tree. When the honey is ready, the people climb the tree, and get the honey. They sell it in the markets, of these there are many. Gallas never eat wild animals. They don't eat pigs in northern Gallaland; and they don't eat any kind of birds; and few people eat fowls or eggs. But there are some tribes that live among the Gallas, that eat nearly everything. The Galla people are rich in cattle and corn. Some of them have farms for cattle, and some for corn.

The Gallas are not lazy people. The men never allow their wives to go and build the house for them, and they won't allow them to go and labour in the fields all day for food, while they sit down in their huts and smoke their long pipes. The women there do not work like that but they only work in the house while their husbands till the ground. The Gallas are not lazy people in working. Don't think because you saw these boys, that all the Gallas are like them. If you go there, then you will know what work is. The Gallas do not waste their money on tobacco and in buying pipes about one foot long. They won't do that. What they do is this. They get up early in the morning, and they take their breakfast without washing their face, and then they take their bullocks and their yokes, and go to plough the ground. They never return again till the sunset.

The bullocks in Gallaland are very big, much bigger than those in South Africa, as high as a horse. The yokes are nearly like those used in this country. It is a custom to train one of the oxen to guard the Kraal and they sharpen its horns to fight. It does no work but just keeps the kraal. The kraals in Gallaland are bigger than those here, but are made of bushes too. Many people's cattle go into one kraal. Nearly every cow or ox has a name, and they like very much to eat salt. There are blacksmiths who make the ploughs, long narrow ploughs, and only two oxen draw them.

There are many forests in Gallaland. In these forests there are many dangerous things, worst of all are robbers that hunt for small boys and girls, and also for big people to kill them, and when they kill anyone, there is a great feast, because he has killed a man or a beast.

There are lots of wild animals in Gallaland, such as elephants, lions, leopards, wild bucks or antelopes and many others too. There are many snakes, a very big hairy one, the boa constrictor, the python, the egg-eater, the horned snake, water snakes, and others. Especially the pythons are troublesome. The Galla horses are just the same as the Arab horses; they all look like race horses.

The Gallas are heathens in religion. They worship a big tree, and in the mountains. They obey just as the king tells them, and the rule is if a person breaks the king's commandment, he is taken to the market and punished, by being beaten, or sold as a slave.

Each part of the country has got a king or a chief of its own. For instance, let us take the Jimma country. That country has got a king or a cheif [sic] of its own. These Kings are always wanting to fight each other, and everyone wants to be the greatest of all the kings. If he conquers one of these kings, first of all he asks for a tax; and if that king won't pay it, he just comes and destroys him. Sometime that king wants about 200 oxen or he wants some horses, and the other king has to give, because if he won't he knows that his life will be taken from him, and what he has too.

Repatriation Questionnaire, 1903[1]

Lovedale, Cape Colony
26th August, 1903

As there is some possibility of a way being found for the Lovedale Gallas returning to Abyssinia, it is desirable that the present addresses and occupations of each one be sent to Lovedale.

Will you, therefore, please fill in the information asked for below, and return this paper in the enclosed envelope without delay.

It is only right to add that, judging from the reports which come from Abyssinia, the life there is likely to be much harder than it is in this country. Civilisation is not so advanced and neither life, property nor personal freedom are so well guarded as here.

Name, _____

Address, _____

Present occupation, _____

_____

If the opportunity does occur of returning to Abyssinia, would you wish to go, or would you rather remain in South Africa?

Reply, _____

_____

Date, _____   Signed _____

NOTES

Archival Source Abbreviations Used

CL	Cory Library for Humanities Research, Rhodes University
CL MS	Cory Library manuscript series
CL PIC	Cory Library photographic and illustrative series
CO	Colonial Office series
GH	Government House
MOOC	Master of the Orphan Chamber
NLS	National Library of Scotland
NLSA	National Library of South Africa
PMO	Prime Minister's Office
RU	Rhodes University
UCT	University of Cape Town
UCTM&A	University of Cape Town Libraries, Manuscripts and Archives
WCARS	Western Cape Archives and Records Services

Introductory Ruminations

1. "Ethiopia" has been used since antiquity to describe a range of geographic locations. In addition to the area of today's modern Ethiopia, early Western cartographers used the term to describe the entire continent of Africa. Also, in the era prior to the accession of Menelik II in 1889, the Ethiopian territory led by the Amhara or the Tigrayan elites was considerably smaller than the area we recognize today—roughly the northern half of today's Ethiopia. This smaller area was generally described on nineteenth-century Western maps as "Abyssinia" (see, for example, John Bartholomew's map of Africa dated 1885). However, in the late nineteenth century, the king of Shewa (Sahle Maryam, later Emperor Menelik II) expropriated and incorporated the lands to the south, east, and west of Abyssinia to form an empire, the area of which is defined in the modern, augmented state of Ethiopia. See, inter alia, John Young, "Regionalism and Democracy in Ethiopia," *Third World Quarterly* 19, no. 2 (June 1998): 191–204; and Ernest A. Wallis Budge, *A History of Ethiopia*, vol. 1, *Nubia and Abyssinia* (London: Methuen, 1928), vii.

2. Now the Cory Library for Humanities Research, Rhodes University, Grahamstown.

3. In earlier times, the term "Galla" was commonly used to describe the Oromo people. The term has long been considered pejorative and was declared illegal in Ethiopia in 1974.

4. Theodor Mommsen, *Prosopographia Imperii Romani Saec I. II. III* (Berlin: Georgium Reaimerum, 1897); and Matthias Gelzer, *Die Nobilität der Römischen Republik* (Leipzig: Teubner, 1912).

5. Lewis B. Namier, *The Structure of Politics at the Accession of George III* (London: Macmillan, 1929).

6. Ghada Osman, "Foreign Slaves in Mecca and Medina in the Formative Islamic Period," *Islam and Christian-Muslim Relations* 16, no. 4 (October 2005): 345–59.

7. Lawrence Stone, *The Crisis of the Aristocracy, 1558–1641* (Oxford: Clarendon, 1966).

8. Lawrence Stone, "Prosopography," *Daedalus* 100, no. 1 (Winter 1971): 46.

9. Ibid., 46–79.

10. Lawrence Stone, personal communication to Robert Shell, 1989.

11. Bruce M. Haight, "Bole and Gonja: Contributions to the History of Northern Ghana" (PhD thesis, Northwestern University, 1981).

12. Bruce M. Haight and William R. Pfeiffer II, "Computerized Handling of Oral and Written Information for Prosopography of Gonja," *History in Africa* 12 (1985): 89–99.

13. Katharine S. B. Keats-Rohan, "Prosopography and Computing: A Marriage Made in Heaven?" *History and Computing* 12, no. 1 (2000): 6.

14. Prosopography Research, Modern History Research Unit, University of Oxford, accessed 18 April 2018, http://prosopography.modhist.ox.ac.uk/prosopdefinition.htm.

15. While a synchronic database would indicate conditions at a particular moment in time, a diachronic database, drawing on data covering a span of years, reveals conditions over time.

16. Ned Alpers examined what he referred to as "the other middle passage," pointing to the differences between the iconic Atlantic Ocean and the lesser documented Indian Ocean middle passages to "bring a measure of balance to this historiography." Alpers contended that it is a mistake to restrict analyses of the middle passage to oceanic passages alone, adding that "enslaved Africans embarked from the African coast as though they were leaving their native country, when in fact their passage from freedom into slavery actually began with the moment in which they were swept up by the economic forces that drove the slave trade deep into the African interior." That journey, from capture to coast, which Alpers regards as "another middle passage," is more logically regarded in slave historiography as the "first passage" of the slave trade. Edward A. Alpers, "The Other Middle Passage: The African Slave Trade in the Indian Ocean," in *Many Middle Passages: Forced Migration and the Making of the Modern World*, ed. Emma Christopher, Cassandra Pybus, and Marcus Rediker (Berkeley: University of California Press, 2007), 20–38. See, for example, Walter Johnson's chapter, "Time and Revolution in African America: Temporality and the History of Atlantic Slavery," in *A New Imperial History: Culture, Identity, and Modernity in Britain and the Empire, 1660–1840*, ed. Kathleen Wilson (Cambridge: Cambridge University Press, 2004), 200.

17. The rarity of first-passage narratives has prompted some historians to regard them as virtually nonexistent. See, for example, the views of David Henige, "Measuring the Immeasurable: The Atlantic Slave Trade, West African Population and the Pyrrhonian Critic," *Journal of African History* 27, no. 2 (July 1986): 295–313. The Oromo narratives stand as modest evidence to the contrary.

18. Ships captured during a wartime engagement were regarded as "prizes." Similarly, slaves captured and liberated after the abolition of the British slave trade in 1807 were termed "Prize Slaves" or "Prize Negroes." Captors received monetary rewards for both captured ships and liberated slaves.

19. His own life-narrative, a multiedition autobiography first published in 1789, has been examined, edited, and interpreted by several scholars. Publications in more recent years include most notably Olaudah Equiano, *Equiano's Travels: The Interesting Narrative of the Life of Olaudah Equiano or Gustavus Vassa the African*, ed. Paul G. Edwards (Oxford: Heinemann, 1996); Equiano, *The Interesting Narrative and Other Writings*, ed. Vincent Carretta (New York: Penguin Books, 1995), with a fresh interpretation in the revised edition of 2003; and Paul E. Lovejoy's sequence of journal articles. See, for example, Lovejoy, "Autobiography and Memory: Gustavus Vassa, alias Olaudah Equiano, the African," *Slavery and Abolition* 27, no. 3 (2006): 317–47; Lovejoy, "Construction of Identity: Olaudah Equiano or Gustavus Vassa?" *Historically Speaking* 7, no. 3 (January–February 2006): 8–9; and Lovejoy, "Olaudah Equiano or Gustavus Vassa—What's in a Name?" *Atlantic Studies* 9, no. 2 (2012): 165–84.

20. Robin Law and Paul E. Lovejoy, eds., *The Biography of Mahommah Gardo Baquaqua: His Passage from Slavery to Freedom in Africa and America* (Princeton, NJ: Markus Wiener, 2001). This biography includes relatively little relating to his actual enslavement but focuses largely on his description of his homeland.

21. Mekuria Bulcha, *The Making of the Oromo Diaspora: A Historical Sociology of Forced Migration* (Minneapolis: Kirk House, 2002), 115–31, 116. All four—Malike Ambar (ca. 1550–1626); Onesimos Nasib (ca. 1855–1931); Bililé or Mahbuba (ca. 1825–1840); and Aster Ganno (ca. 1871–1962)—rose above their slave status to achieve intellectual and social recognition in their liberated lives.

22. Alice Bellagamba, Sandra E. Greene, and Martin A. Klein., eds., *African Voices on Slavery and the Slave Trade*, vol. 1, *The Sources* (Cambridge: Cambridge University Press, 2013); Bellagamba, Greene, and Klein, eds., *African Voices on Slavery and the Slave Trade*, vol. 2, *Essays on Sources and Methods* (Cambridge: Cambridge University Press, 2016). Sandwiched in between these two sister volumes, the same team released their study of the legacy and memory of slavery and the slave trade in Nigeria, Mali, the Bight of Biafra, Cameroon, Ghana, the Gambia, and Senegal; see Bellagamba, Greene, and Klein, eds., *The Bitter Legacy: African Slavery Past and Present* (Princeton, NJ: Markus Wiener, 2014). This volume includes two twentieth-century slave narratives from Cameroon. Another group of scholars, drawn from all points of the African slave diaspora and using a diversity of approaches and a kaleidoscope of multimedia sources, contributed to a compendium of scholarship on the history and memory of African slavery; see Ana Lucia Araujo, Mariana P. Candido, and Paul E. Lovejoy, eds., *Crossing Memories: Slavery and African Diaspora* (Trenton, NJ: Africa World Press, 2011).

23. Abdul Sheriff, *Slaves, Spices and Ivory in Zanzibar: Integration of an East African Commercial Empire into the World Economy, 1770–1873* (Athens: Ohio University Press, 1987).

24. Marcia Wright, *Strategies of Slaves and Women: Life-Stories from East/Central Africa* (New York: L. Barber Press, 1993), 23.

25. Arthur C. Madan, a missionary with the Universities Mission to Central Africa (UMCA) at Kiungani in Kenya, translated and edited *Kiungani; or, Story and History from*

Central Africa, Written by Boys in the Schools of the Universities' Mission to Central Africa (London: George Bell and Sons, 1887). Edward A. Alpers, *Ivory and Slaves in East Central Africa: Changing Patterns of International Trade in East Central Africa to the Later Nineteenth Century* (London: Heinemann, 1975), 240. Alpers, "The Story of Swema: Female Vulnerability in Nineteenth-Century East Africa," in *Women and Slavery in Africa,* ed. Claire C. Robertson and Martin A. Klein (Madison: University of Wisconsin Press, 1983), 185–99. Margery F. Perham, ed., *Ten Africans* (London: Faber, 1936), especially Rashid bin Hassani's account on pages 81–119. The narratives express, inter alia, African observations of internal slavery and the slave trade, with only one of the ten being a personal experience as a slave. Edward A. Alpers, "Representation of Children in the East African Slave Trade" *Slavery and Abolition* 30, no. 1 (2009): 27–40. Fred Morton, "Small Change: Children in the Nineteenth-Century East African Slave Trade," in *Children in Slavery through the Ages,* ed. Gwyn Campbell, Suzanne Miers, and Joseph C. Miller (Athens: Ohio University Press, 2009), 55–70.

26. Paul Bohannan, "The Impact of Money on an African Subsistence Economy," *Journal of Economic History* 19, no. 4 (December 1959): 494.

27. Suzanne Miers and Igor Kopytoff, eds., *Slavery in Africa: Historical and Anthropological Perspectives* (Madison: University of Wisconsin Press, 1977), 3–4.

28. Alpers, *Ivory and Slaves in East Central Africa,* 240–41. Richard B. Allen, "Children and European Slave Trading in the Indian Ocean during the Eighteenth and Early Nineteenth Centuries," in Campbell, Miers, and Miller, *Children in Slavery through the Ages,* 42–43.

29. Timothy D. Fernyhough, "Serfs, Slaves and 'Shefta': Modes of Production in Southern Ethiopia from the Late Nineteenth Century to 1941" (PhD thesis, University of Illinois at Urbana-Champaign, 1986). Regrettably, Fernyhough died before he could complete the editing of his thesis for publication. Fortunately, his widow, Anna Fernyhough, completed the editing of the text and this was released in 2010: Timothy Fernyhough. *Serfs, Slaves and Shifta: Modes of Production and Resistance in Pre-Revolutionary Ethiopia* (Addis Ababa: Shama Books, 2010).

30. Ayalew Duressa, "*Guddifachaa*: Adoption Practice in Oromo Society with Particular Reference to the Borana Oromo" (master's thesis, University of Addis Ababa University, 2002), 66 passim.

31. Major Henry Darley, a former British army officer, spent seven years in southern Ethiopia, from 1907 until the outbreak of the First World War, observing slave raiding and trading practices among the Oromo. Darley's detailed and forthright observations offer insights into Oromo society at the end of Menelik's reign and beyond. Major Lawrence Athill, who accompanied Major Henry Darley on a return trip to southern Ethiopia in 1919, commented in detail in a paper delivered to the Royal Geographical Society in 1920. Lawrence Athill, "Extracts from a Paper Read by . . . at a Meeting of the Royal Geographical Society [1920]," in Henry Darley, *Slaves and Ivory: A Record of Adventure and Exploration among the Abyssinian Slave-Raiders* (London: Witherby, 1926, repr. 1935), 191–209.

32. Philip D. Curtin, *Economic Change in Precolonial Africa: Senegambia in the Era of the Slave Trade* (Madison: University of Wisconsin Press, 1975).

33. See, for example, Mordechai Abir, *Ethiopia: The Era of the Princes; The Challenge of Islam and the Re-Unification of the Christian Empire, 1769–1855* (London: Longmans, 1968), 54. See also Fernyhough, "Serfs, Slaves and 'Shefta,'" 105–208; and Fernyhough, "Slavery

and the Slave Trade in Southern Ethiopia in the 19th Century," *Slavery and Abolition* 9, no. 3 (1988): 103–30. Fernyhough's journal article immediately preceding here also appears as a chapter in *The Economics of the Indian Ocean Slave Trade in the Nineteenth Century*, ed. William Gervase Clarence-Smith (Totowa, NJ: Frank Cass, 1989), 103–30; Abdussamad H. Ahmad, "Trading in Slaves in Bela-Shangul and Gumuz, Ethiopia: Border Enclaves in History, 1897–1938," *Journal of African History* 40, no. 3 (1999): 433–46; Herbert S. Lewis, *Jimma Abba Jifar: An Oromo Monarchy: Ethiopia, 1830–1932* (Lawrenceville, NJ: Red Sea Press, 2001), 66–67; Bulcha, *Making of the Oromo Diaspora*, 48–85; Mekuria Bulcha, "The Red Sea Slave Trade: Captives' Treatment in the Slave Markets of North-East Africa and the Islamic Societies of the Middle East," in *Reflections on Arab-Led Slavery of Africans*, ed. Kwesi Kwaa Prah (Cape Town: Centre for Advanced Studies of African Society, 2005), 109–15.

34. Morton, "Small Change," 58.

35. Philip D. Curtin, *The Atlantic Slave Trade: A Census* (Madison: University of Wisconsin Press, 1969); Curtin, *Economic Change*, 272.

36. Fred Cooper detailed an empirical model for area studies within East Africa in his *Plantation Slavery on the East Coast of Africa* (New Haven, CT: Yale University Press, 1977). Jon R. Edwards contributed a significant study of the slave trade and economic reorganization in Ethiopia in his article "Slavery, the Slave Trade and the Economic Reorganization of Ethiopia, 1916–1935," *African Economic History*, no. 11 (1982): 3–14. Abdussamad H. Ahmad explored slave exports in several Red Sea entrepôts, primarily in "Ethiopian Slave Exports at Matamma, Massawa and Tajura, c. 1830 to 1885," *Slavery and Abolition* 9, no. 3 (1988): 93–102. William Gervase Clarence-Smith compiled a notable anthology of essays on the economics of the nineteenth-century Indian Ocean slave trade in *Economics of the Indian Ocean Slave Trade*, which included Timothy Fernyhough's analysis of prices and routes, "Slavery and the Slave Trade in Southern Ethiopia in the 19th Century," 103–30. And Patrick Manning's work *Slavery and African Life: Occidental, Oriental, and African Slave Trades* (Cambridge: Cambridge University Press, 1990) provided an important normative analysis of the sex ratios of the Red Sea slave trade.

37. Lindsay Doulton, "The Royal Navy's Anti-Slavery Campaign in the Western Indian Ocean, c. 1860–1890: Race, Empire and Identity" (PhD thesis, University of Hull, 2010).

38. Official reports and associated documents later tabled in United Kingdom, Parliament, Correspondence Relative to the Slave Trade, 1888–1889, C.5821, 1889, 34–35; the Aden-based records of the India Office in the British Library, IOR/R/20/A/667: 1888 (vol. 1037, Slave Trade); and further material published verbatim (including the naval commander's account of the events surrounding the capture of the dhows carrying one group of the Oromo in 1888) by Raymond W. Beachey, ed., in *A Collection of Documents on the Slave Trade of Eastern Africa* (London: Collings, 1976), a companion volume to the editor's *The Slave Trade of Eastern Africa* (London: Collings, 1976).

39. Christopher C. Saunders, "Between Slavery and Freedom: The Importation of Prize Negroes to the Cape in the Aftermath of Emancipation," *Kronos* 9 (1984): 36–43; Saunders, "Liberated Africans in Cape Colony in the First Half of the Nineteenth Century," *International Journal of African Historical Studies* 18, no. 2 (1985): 223–39; Saunders, "'Free, Yet Slaves': Prize Negroes at the Cape Revisited," in *Breaking the Chains: Slavery and Its Legacy in the Nineteenth-Century Cape Colony*, ed. Nigel Worden and Clifton C. Crais (Johannesburg: Witwatersrand University Press, 1994), 99–115; and Saunders, "Liberated Africans in

the Western Cape: My Work and After," *Bulletin of the National Library of South Africa* 70, no. 1 (June 2016): 21–34. Richard L. Watson, *Slave Emancipation and Racial Attitudes in Nineteenth-Century South Africa* (Cambridge: Cambridge University Press, 2012); Watson, "'Prize Negroes' and the Development of Racial Attitudes in the Cape Colony, South Africa" (paper presented at the Southeastern Regional Seminar in African Studies [SERSAS], 14–15 April 2000), http://www.ecu.edu/african/sersas/Watson400.htm. Patrick Harries, "Culture and Classification: A History of the Mozbieker Community at the Cape," *Social Dynamics* 26, no. 2 (2000): 29–54.

40. Dora Taylor, using the pseudonym of Nosipho Majeke, published an influential polemic on missionaries in 1952, the tercentenary of the occupation of the Cape: *The Role of the Missionaries in Conquest* (Cape Town: Society of Young Africa, 1952). Jean Comaroff and John L. Comaroff, *Of Revelation and Revolution*, vol. 1, *Christianity, Colonialism, and Consciousness in South Africa* (Chicago: University of Chicago Press, 1991), 1, 310.

41. These publications range from Norman Etherington, "The Rise of the Kholwa in Southeast Africa: African Christian Communities in Natal, Pondoland and Zululand, 1835–1880" (PhD thesis, Yale University, 1971), published by Ann Arbor, MI: University Microfilms International, 1974; and later under the title *Preachers, Peasants, and Politics in Southeast Africa, 1835–1880: African Christian Communities in Natal, Pondoland, and Zululand* (London: Royal Historical Society, 1978); to his edited volume *Missions and Empire* (Oxford: Oxford University Press, 2005). Also see Etherington, "Mission Station Melting Pots as a Factor in the Rise of South African Black Nationalism," *International Journal of African Historical Studies* 9, no. 4 (1976): 592–605; Donovan Williams, "African Nationalism in South Africa: Origins and Problems," *Journal of African History* 11, no. 3 (1970): 371–83. Rick Watson's recent book, *Slave Emancipation and Racial Attitudes in Nineteenth-Century South Africa*, has contributed new insights into postabolition missions and racial attitudes, and has helped elucidate the South African context.

42. Tim Keegan, *Dr. Philip's Empire: One Man's Struggle for Justice in Nineteenth-Century South Africa* (Cape Town: Zebra Press, 2016).

43. Donovan Williams, *Umfundisi: A Biography of Tiyo Soga, 1829–1871* (Lovedale: Lovedale Press, 1978), 3–8; Tiyo Soga, *The Journal and Selected Writings of the Reverend Tiyo Soga*, ed. Donovan Williams (Cape Town: Balkema for Rhodes University, 1985), 7.

44. Sheila M. Brock, "James Stewart and Lovedale: A Reappraisal of Missionary Attitudes and African Response in the Eastern Cape, 1870–1905" (PhD thesis, University of Edinburgh, 1974), [i-ii], 99–114.

45. Leon de Kock, *Civilising Barbarians: Missionary Narrative and African Textual Response in Nineteenth-Century South Africa* (Johannesburg: Witwatersrand University Press, 1996), 88.

46. Deborah Gaitskell, "Race, Gender and Imperialism: A Century of Black Girls' Education in South Africa" (working paper presented to the African Studies Institute, University of the Witwatersrand, August 1988), 1–19, http://hdl.handle.net/10539/8726.

47. See Fiona Vernal, *The Farmerfield Mission: A Christian Community in South Africa, 1838–2008* (Oxford: Oxford University Press, 2013), 112–15.

48. Ethiopia has a unique historiography. It is alone on the continent in never having been colonized.

49. Richard Pankhurst, *Economic History of Ethiopia, 1800–1935* (Addis Ababa: Haile Sellassie I University Press, 1968); Pankhurst, "Ethiopian Slave Reminiscences of the Nine-

teenth Century," *Transafrican Journal of History* 5, no. 1 (1976): 98–110; Pankhurst, "The Role of Fire-Arms in Ethiopian Culture (16th to 20th Centuries)," *Journal des africanistes* 47, no. 2 (1977): 131–44; and Pankhurst, *A Social History of Ethiopia: The Northern and Central Highlands from Early Medieval Times to the Rise of Emperor Téwodros II* (Trenton, NJ: Red Sea Press, 1992). Harold G. Marcus, *A History of Ethiopia* (Berkeley: University of California Press, 1994); and Marcus, *The Life and Times of Menelik II: Ethiopia, 1844–1913* (Lawrenceville, NJ: Red Sea Press, 1975).

50. Mekuria Bulcha, "Historical, Political and Social Causes of Mass Flight from Ethiopia," in *Refugees and Development in Africa*, ed. Peter Nobel (Uppsala: Scandinavian Institute of African Studies, 1987), 19–36. See also Bulcha, *Flight and Integration: Causes of Mass Exodus from Ethiopia and Problems of Integration in the Sudan* (Uppsala: Scandinavian Institute of African Studies, 1988); and Bulcha, *Contours of the Emergent and Ancient Oromo Nation: Dilemmas in the Ethiopian Politics of State and Nation-Building* (Cape Town: Centre for Advanced Studies of African Society, 2011). In addition, Professor Bulcha has published countless articles and chapters in books on the history and present status of the Oromo people. See also Donald Crummey, "Society, State and Nationality in the Recent Historiography of Ethiopia," *Journal of African History* 31, no. 1 (1990): 103–19; and Mohammed Hassen, *The Oromo of Ethiopia: A History, 1570–1860* (Cambridge: Cambridge University Press, 1990); and Asafa Jalata, *Oromia and Ethiopia: State Formation and Ethnonational Conflict, 1868–1992* (Boulder, CO: Rienner, 1993). See also, as examples drawn from his prolific output, titles such as Jalata, ed., *Oromo Nationalism and the Ethiopian Discourse: The Search for Freedom and Democracy* (Lawrenceville, NJ: Red Sea Press, 1998); Jalata, *Oromia and Ethiopia: State Formation and Ethnonational Conflict, 1868–2004* (Trenton, NJ: Red Sea Press, 2005); Jalata, *Contending Nationalisms of Oromia and Ethiopia: Struggling for Statehood, Sovereignty, and Multinational Democracy* (Binghamton, NY: Global Academic, 2010); and Jalata, *Fighting against the Injustice of the State and Globalization: Comparing the African American and Oromo Movements* (Basingstoke: Palgrave Macmillan, 2012).

51. Bahru Zewde and Siegfried Pausewang, eds., *Ethiopia: The Challenge of Democracy from Below* (Uppsala: Nordiska Afrikainstitutet, 2003).

52. Seyoum Y. Hameso and Mohammed Hassen, eds., *Arrested Development in Ethiopia: Essays on Underdevelopment, Democracy, and Self-Determination* (Trenton, NJ: Red Sea Press, 2006).

53. Bulcha, *Contours of the Emergent and Ancient Oromo Nation*.

54. Ludger Schadomsky, "Ethiopia: Who Is the New Prime Minister Abiy Ahmed Ali?," AllAfrica, 29 March 2018, http://allafrica.com/stories/201803310066.html.

55. When Ethiopia declared a state of emergency on 8 October 2016, the simple, peaceful gesture of raising one's hands and crossing them at the wrists was banned and became a criminal offense in Ethiopia. As simple as it was (and remains), that gesture drew more international attention to the plight of the Oromo people than any well-intentioned human rights report hitherto, and has become a potent symbol of protest, recognized worldwide.

56. Simon Allison, "Ethiopia's Feyisa Lilesa Gets a Silver for Running—and a Gold for Bravery," *Daily Maverick*, 22 August 2016, http://www.dailymaverick.co.za/article/2016-08-22-rio-2016-ethiopias-feyisa-lilesa-gets-a-silver-for-running-and-a-gold-for-bravery-/#.V-zcbfl967o.

Chapter 1. Ethiopia: The Lie of the Land

1. Central Intelligence Agency, *The World Factbook*, accessed 3 August 2017, https://www.cia.gov/library/publications/the-world-factbook/geos/et.html.

2. United States Census Bureau, International Data Base, Ethiopia, accessed 3 August 2017, http://www.census.gov/population/international/data/idb/region.php?N=%20Results%20&T=13&A=separate&RT=0&Y=2016&R=-1&C=ET.

3. Mekuria Bulcha, *Contours of the Emergent and Ancient Oromo Nation: Dilemmas in the Ethiopian Politics of State and Nation-Building* (Cape Town: Centre for Advanced Studies of African Society, 2011), 11. James E. Kiefer, "Biographical Sketches of Memorable Christians of the Past: Onesimus Nesib, Translator and Missionary," accessed 18 April 2018, http://justus.anglican.org/resources/bio/190.html; Chris Prouty and Eugene Rosenfeld, *Historical Dictionary of Ethiopia and Eritrea* (Metuchen, NJ: Scarecrow Press, 1993), s.v. "Oromo."

4. Bulcha, *Contours of the Emergent and Ancient Oromo Nation*, 71.

5. Sahle Mariam, spelled variously Sahlé Maryam and Sahlé Miriam, was born in Ankober, Shewa, on 17 August 1844; was king of Shewa from 1865 to 1889; and reigned as Menelik II, emperor of Ethiopia, from 1889 until his death on 12 December 1913. He achieved international recognition for his victory against the Italians in the battle of Adwa (1896). He is also regarded as the great modernizer of Ethiopia, which was by the 1890s much expanded from the old area of Abyssinia through his seizure and incorporation of adjacent lands. He was known as "Menelik" throughout his life, including during his reign as king of Shewa prior to his imperial accession, and this is the name that will be used for him throughout this study. This decision is informed by this usage and by the example set by leading Oromo scholars such as Mekuria Bulcha; Menelik's biographer, Harold Marcus; Timothy Fernyhough; Donald Donham; and Wendy James.

6. It is ironic that, as Herbert S. Lewis has written, "while keeping Ethiopia free of European domination and creating the 'unusually powerful discourse of nationhood,' Emperors Johannis IV, Tewodros II, Menelik II, and Haile Selassie I subjugated many other peoples." The majority of the Oromo people today regard their lands as having been colonized. Lewis, "Ethnicity in Ethiopia: The View from Below (and from the South, East and West)," in *The Rising Tide of Cultural Pluralism: The Nation-State at Bay?*, ed. Crawford Young (Madison: University of Wisconsin Press, 1993), 161.

7. Bulcha, *Contours of the Emergent and Ancient Oromo Nation*, 563–64.

8. Elisée Reclus, *Nouvelle géographie universelle: La terre et les hommes*, vol. 10 (Paris: Hachette, 1885), as cited in Rawson W. Rawson, "European Territorial Claims on the Coasts of the Red Sea, and Its Southern Approaches," *Proceedings of the Royal Geographical Society and Monthly Record of Geography*, n.s. 7, no. 2 (February 1885): 103–4. Volumes 10–13 of the *Nouvelle géographie universelle* were devoted to Africa.

9. A standard outline map of modern Ethiopia provided the base on which to represent Reclus's tabular population data graphically using proportional population circles. Reclus's population table may be found in Rawson, "European Territorial Claims on the Coasts of the Red Sea," 104.

10. Ibid.

11. Leonard Bloomfield, *Language* (London: Allen and Unwin, 1935), 51. Oromo is a *dialect continuum*: there are minor differences in dialect between contiguous regions, but,

over increased time and distance, the dialects can modify and become mutually incomprehensible.

12. Ioan M. Lewis, "Sufism in Somaliland: A Study in Tribal Islam," in *Islam in Tribal Societies: From the Atlas to the Indus*, ed. Akbar S. Ahmed and David M. Hart (London: Routledge and Kegan Paul, 1983), 152.

13. Asebe Regassa Debelo, "Contesting Views on a Protected Area Conservation and Development in Ethiopia," *Social Science* 1, no. 1 (2012): 24–46.

14. Carl Wilhelm Isenberg, "The Gallas of Abyssinia," *Church of England Magazine*, 1841, 264.

15. Mekuria Bulcha, *The Making of the Oromo Diaspora: A Historical Sociology of Forced Migration* (Minneapolis: Kirk House, 2002), 46.

16. Asma Giyorgis and Bairu Tafla, *Asma Giyorgis and His Work: History of the Galla and the Kingdom of Sawa*, ed. Bairu Tafla (Stuttgart: Franz Steiner, 1987), 135.

17. Mordechai Abir, *Ethiopia and the Red Sea: The Rise and Decline of the Solomonic Dynasty and Muslim-European Rivalry in the Region* (London: Frank Cass, 1980), 59, quoted in Bulcha, *Making of the Oromo Diaspora*, 46–47.

18. Bulcha, *Making of the Oromo Diaspora*, 47.

19. Abbas Haji Gnamo, "Islam, the Orthodox Church and Oromo Nationalism (Ethiopia)," *Cahiers d'études africaines* 165, no. 1 (2002): 99–120, http://etudesafricaines.revues.org/137.

20. Steven Kaplan, "Themes and Methods in the Study of Conversion in Ethiopia: A Review Essay," *Journal of Religion in Africa* 34, no. 3 (August 2004): 379.

21. Mohammed Hassen, *The Oromo of Ethiopia: A History, 1570–1860* (Cambridge: Cambridge University Press, 1990), 150.

22. Ibid., 161.

23. Ibid., 152.

24. Ibid., 153.

25. Ibid., 152.

26. Ibid., xiii.

27. Ibid., alluding to Darrell Bates, *The Abyssinian Difficulty: The Emperor Theodorus and the Magdala Campaign, 1867–68* (Oxford: Oxford University Press, 1979), 7.

28. Ibid.

29. Hassen, *Oromo of Ethiopia*, xiii.

30. Yohannes K. Mekonnen, ed., *Ethiopia: The Land, Its People, History and Culture* (Dar es Salaam: New Africa Press, 2013), 263.

31. Richard A. Caulk, "Firearms and Princely Power in Ethiopia in the Nineteenth Century," *Journal of African History* 13, no. 4 (1972): 611.

32. Donald Donham and Wendy James, eds., *The Southern Marches of Imperial Ethiopia: Essays in History and Social Anthropology* (New York: Cambridge University Press, 1986), 21–24.

33. Bahru Zewde, *A History of Modern Ethiopia, 1855–1991*, 2nd ed. (Athens: Ohio University Press, 2001), 47.

34. Bulcha, *Making of the Oromo Diaspora*, 55.

35. Harold Marcus, *The Life and Times of Menelik II: Ethiopia, 1844–1913* (Lawrenceville, NJ: Red Sea Press, 1975), 73.

36. Ibid.; Bulcha, *Making of the Oromo Diaspora*, 55.

37. Marcus, *Life and Times of Menelik II*, 47.

38. "Les Français sont mes amis, c'est sur eux que je fonde l'espoir de mon règne. Je vous donne toute ma confiance et mon amitié; mon pays est le vôtre, et vous êtes au milieu d'un peuple qui vous aimera aussi." L. Louis-Lande, "Un voyageur français dans l'Ethiopie méridionale," *Revue des deux mondes* 30, no. 6 (1878): 888.

39. Charles Nicholl, *Somebody Else: Arthur Rimbaud in Africa 1880–91* (London: Jonathan Cape, 1997), 183ff.

40. Jon R. Edwards, "Slavery, the Slave Trade and the Economic Reorganization of Ethiopia, 1916–1935," *African Economic History*, no. 11 (1982): 4–5.

41. Senait Fesseha, "The Rinderpest Factor in the Great Famine of Ethiopia," University of Massachusetts, Boston, Critical and Creative Thinking Program, http://faculty.umb .edu/peter_taylor/640-02SF.doc. There is an extensive body of literature on this epizootic disease, which killed up to 90 percent of the cattle, first in Ethiopia (see, e.g., Sven Rubenson, "Environmental Stress and Conflict in Ethiopian History: Looking for Correlations," *Ambio* 20, no. 5 [August 1991]: 179–82); and then in successive countries across the continent between 1888 and 1898. Writers such as Alan L. Olmstead, "The First Line of Defense: Inventing the Infrastructure to Combat Animal Diseases," *Journal of Economic History* 69, no. 2 (June 2009): 327–57, have looked at the impact of rinderpest globally and in Africa. Others have examined the effects of the disease in other African countries, for example, Holger Weiss, "Dying Cattle: Some Remarks on the Impact of Cattle Epizootics in the Central Sudan during the Nineteenth Century," *African Economic History* 26 (1998): 173–99; Daniel Gilfoyle, "Veterinary Research and the African Rinderpest Epizootic: The Cape Colony, 1896–1898," *Journal of Southern African Studies* 29, no. 1 (March 2003): 133–54; and Benedict Carton's "The Forgotten Compass of Death: Apocalypse Then and Now in the Social History of South Africa," *Journal of Social History* 37, no. 1 (Fall 2003): 199–218.

42. Tsegay Wolde-Georgis, "The Use of El Niño Information as Drought Early Warning in Ethiopia," *Internet Journal of African Studies* 2 (March 1997): paragraph 1, http://ccb. colorado.edu/ijas/ijasno2/georgis.html.

43. Ibid., table 1 (no pagination).

44. Chris Prouty Rosenfeld, *A Chronology of Menelik II of Ethiopia, 1844–1913* (East Lansing, MI: African Studies Center, 1976), 129 (see date of 2 April 1888).

45. Translated from the French by the present author. *Les missions Catholiques: Bulletin hebdomadaire de l'oeuvre de la propagation de la foi* 20 (1888): 557, http://gallica.bnf.fr /ark:/12148/bpt6k1056284.

46. Mike Davis, *Late Victorian Holocausts: El Niño Famines and the Making of the Third World* (London: Verso, 2001), 128; Donald Crummey, "Explaining Famines in Ethiopian History: The Case of the Kefu Qan, 1888–1981" (Interdisciplinary Seminar, Center for African Studies, University of Illinois at Urbana-Champaign, 2002), 23.

47. Richard Pankhurst, "The Great Ethiopian Famine of 1888–1892: A New Assessment, Part One," *Journal of the History of Medicine and Allied Sciences* 21, no. 2 (April 1966): 95–124; and as cited in the African Union, InterAfrican Bureau for Animal Resources (AU-IBAR), *The Eradication of Rinderpest from Africa: A Great Milestone* (Nairobi: African Union, 2012), 4–5.

48. Rosenfeld, *Chronology of Menelik II*, 129 (see date of 2 April 1888).

49. See the account of the rinderpest in southern Africa by Pule Phoofolo, "Epidemics and Revolutions: The Rinderpest Epidemic in Late Nineteenth-Century Southern Africa,"

Past and Present 138 (February 1993): 112–43; S. W. Vogel and H. Heyne, "Rinderpest in South Africa—100 Years Ago," *Journal of the South African Veterinary Association* 67, no. 4 (1996): 164–70; Charles van Onselen, "Reactions to Rinderpest in Southern Africa 1896–97," *Journal of African History* 13, no. 3 (1972): 473–88. Crummey, "Explaining Famines in Ethiopian History," 15–24.

50. Davis, *Late Victorian Holocausts*, 6.

Chapter 2. The Family Structure of the Oromo Captives

1. Fred Morton, "Small Change: Children in the Nineteenth-Century East African Slave Trade," in *Children in Slavery through the Ages*, ed. Gwyn Campbell, Suzanne Miers, and Joseph C. Miller (Athens: Ohio University Press, 2009), 55–70.

2. Mike Davis, *Late Victorian Holocausts: El Niño Famines and the Making of the Third World* (London: Verso, 2001), 11.

3. Richard Pankhurst, "The Great Ethiopian Famine of 1888–1892: A New Assessment, Part Two," *Journal of the History of Medicine and Allied Sciences* 21, no. 3 (July 1966): 271.

4. Christopher Grant, "Stones, Slabs, and Stelae: The Origins and Symbolism of Contemporary Oromo Burial Practice and Grave Art" (Independent Study Project, ISP Collection, paper 263, 2006), http://digitalcollections.sit.edu/isp_collection/263.

5. Suzanne Miers and Igor Kopytoff, eds., *Slavery in Africa: Historical and Anthropological Perspectives* (Madison: University of Wisconsin Press, 1977), 3–4.

6. Ibid., 7.

7. Paul Bohannan, "The Impact of Money on an African Subsistence Economy," *Journal of Economic History* 19, no. 4 (December 1959): 494.

8. Edward A. Alpers, *Ivory and Slaves in East Central Africa: Changing Pattern of International Trade in East Central Africa to the Later Nineteenth Century* (London: Heinemann, 1975), 240–41.

9. Richard B. Allen, "Children and European Slave Trading in the Indian Ocean during the Eighteenth and Early Nineteenth Centuries," in Campbell, Miers, and Miller, *Children in Slavery through the Ages*, 42–43.

10. Miers and Kopytoff, *Slavery in Africa*, 8–9.

11. Ibid., 23–24.

12. Ibid.

13. Mekuria Bulcha, *Contours of the Emergent and Ancient Oromo Nation: Dilemmas in the Ethiopian Politics of State and Nation-Building* (Cape Town: Centre for Advanced Studies of African Society, 2011), 135–42.

14. Ayalew Duressa, "*Guddifachaa*: Adoption Practice in Oromo Society with Particular Reference to the Borana Oromo" (master's thesis, University of Addis Ababa, 2002), 1–2, 8, 23.

15. Dessalegn Negeri, "*Guddifachaa* Practice as Child Problem Intervention in Oromo Society: The Case of Ada'a Liban District" (master's thesis, Addis Ababa University, 2006), 54.

16. The sex ratio is the number of males to every 100 females in the population. The normal human sex ratio at birth is 105 or 106 males per 100 females. Given the higher mortality of males, the slightly higher number of males at birth could be nature's corrective mechanism to keep the human population in balance. The average sex ratio of the slaves in

the Atlantic slave trade was around 180:100. Philip D. Curtin, *The Atlantic Slave Trade: A Census* (Madison: University of Wisconsin Press, 1968), 19, 141; David Geggus, "Sex Ratio, Age and Ethnicity in the Atlantic Slave Trade: Data from French Shipping and Plantation Records," *Journal of African History* 30, no. 1 (March 1989): 25.

17. Mekuria Bulcha, *The Making of the Oromo Diaspora: A Historical Sociology of Forced Migration* (Minneapolis: Kirk House, 2002), 92.

18. Ibid., 92–93.

19. Morton, "Small Change," 58.

20. Timothy Fernyhough, "'Serfs, Slaves and 'Shefta': Modes of Production in Southern Ethiopia from the Late Nineteenth-Century to 1941" (PhD thesis, University of Illinois at Urbana-Champaign, 1986), 120.

21. The children gave the length of time they spent in domestic servitude as well as the length of the journey to the external slave trade entrepôts of Raheita and Tadjoura. Calculating the years of capture meant the creation of a derived variable rooted in the constants of the two dates of liberation by the Royal Navy, minus the combined lengths of domestic servitude and journey from capture to the coast for each child. See full discussion of the drought, famine, and rinderpest in chapter 1 under the section titled "The Famine Days."

22. Miers and Kopytoff, *Slavery in Africa*, 11.

23. For the entries relating to "Sidama," see *A Galla-English, English-Galla Dictionary*, compiled by Edwin C. Foot, assisted by Liban Bultum (Cambridge: Cambridge University Press, 1913), 50 and 59. This dictionary (with the title modified to reflect the correct name of the language) is now available online: Oromo Studies Collection, http://gadaa .com/OromoStudies/wp-content/uploads/2012/11/An_AfanOromo_English_English _AfanOromo_dictionary.pdf. The first multilingual dictionary on record was trilingual: *Dictionary of the Galla Language*, Part 1, *Galla-English-German*, composed by Charles Tutschek (Munich: Lawrence Tutschek, 1844). See also discussion in Seyoum Y. Hameso and Mohammed Hassen, eds., *Arrested Development in Ethiopia: Essays on Underdevelopment, Democracy, and Self-Determination* (Trenton, NJ: Red Sea Press, 2006), 58.

24. Gwyn Campbell, "The State and Pre-Colonial Demographic History: The Case of Nineteenth-Century Madagascar," *Journal of African History* 32, no. 3 (1991): 426.

25. Elisée Reclus, *Nouvelle géographie universelle: La terre et les hommes*, vol. 10 (Paris: Hachette, 1885), as cited in Rawson W. Rawson, "European Territorial Claims on the Coasts of the Red Sea, and Its Southern Approaches, in 1885," *Proceedings of the Royal Geographical Society and Monthly Record of Geography*, n.s. 7, no. 2 (February 1885): 103–4.

26. R. T. Jackson, "Periodic Markets in Southern Ethiopia," *Transactions of the Institute of British Geographers* 53 (July 1971): 33.

27. The mean (or average) family size across both genders was 5.690, with a median of 5.000 and a standard deviation of 2.995.

28. UNICEF, Eastern and Southern Africa, "Orphans," accessed 4 August 2017, http:// www.unicef.org/esaro/5440_ orphans.html.

29. "Full" or "double" orphans refers to those children whose mothers and fathers have both died. These figures compare negatively when ranked against the 2.7 percent of children estimated to be double orphans in South Africa in 2005. This figure, considered to be high in global terms and a near doubling from 1.4 percent in 1995, reflects the impact of the HIV/AIDS pandemic sweeping the subcontinent over that period of ten years (1995–2005). Yet the South African figure is less than a quarter of that for the Oromo children in this study. According to

the 2007 Ethiopian census, the prevalence of total orphanhood nationwide was 9.93 percent. Graph 2.4 compares the percentages of orphanhood in Ethiopia nationally (2007), for Oromia specifically and South Africa (2005), against those of the Oromo children.

A recent Ethiopian demographic survey indicates that in 2005, the prevalence of total orphanhood nationwide (measuring the percentage of children under age eighteen whose mother, father, or both parents had died) was 11.9 percent. Two years later the Ethiopian national census produced comparable, but slightly lower figures across the entire population. Of this figure, 6.44 percent were paternal orphans, 2.09 percent were maternal orphans, and 1.40 percent were full or double orphans. The Oromia figure correlates closely with the contemporary national figure. The prevalence of orphans in the Oromia region was 9.61 percent, of which 6.30 percent were paternal orphans, 1.98 percent were maternal orphans, and 1.34 percent were full or double orphans. The 2007 census gives the numeric population data for children in Ethiopia nationally and for Oromia specifically. In 2007, the prevalence of paternal orphans in the region of Oromia was 6.30 percent, of maternal orphans 1.98 percent, and of full or double orphans, 1.34 percent. This meant a total of 9.61 percent of the children below eighteen years of age in modern Oromia were either maternal, paternal, or full orphans (see graph 2.4).

30. International Household Survey Network, "Ethiopia—Population and Housing Census, 2007," http://catalog.ihsn.org/index.php/ catalog/3583; World Bank, "Population and Housing Census 2007 Report, Oromiya, Part I: Population Size and Characteristics," http://microdata.worldbank.org/index.php/catalog/2747; HIV/AIDS Survey Indicators Database, "Country Report: Ethiopia," accessed 31 July 2017, http://hivdata.dhsprogram .com/reports/; DHS Program, "Ethiopia Demographic and Health Survey of 2005," https://www.dhsprogram.com/pubs/pdf/FR179/ FR179%5B23June2011%5D.pdf.

31. Morton, "Small Change," 59.

32. Laura Camfield, "Outcomes of Orphanhood in Ethiopia: A Mixed Methods Study," *Social Indicators Research* 104, no. 1 (2011): 87–102.

33. Abbi Kedir and Lul Admasachew, "Violence against Women in Ethiopia," *Gender, Place and Culture* 17, no. 4 (2010): 449.

34. Joseph, the youngest of Jacob and Rachel's twelve children, was his father's favorite son. The well-known story of the rainbow-colored coat that Jacob fashioned for Joseph focuses on the sale of Joseph by his jealous half brothers. When Joseph was seventeen years old, sibling resentment peaked, and his half brothers threw him into a pit, leaving him to die. They then decided not to kill him, but rather to spare him, and ultimately sold him into slavery for twenty pieces of silver.

35. Miers and Kopytoff, *Slavery in Africa*, 3–4.

Chapter 3. Wealth and Status of the Oromo Captives' Families

1. Mekuria Bulcha, "The Red Sea Slave Trade: Captives' Treatment in the Slave Markets of North-East Africa and the Islamic Societies of the Middle East," in *Reflections on Arab-Led Slavery of Africans*, ed. Kwesi Kwaa Prah (Cape Town: Centre for Advanced Studies of African Society, 2005), 118–20; see also Fred Cooper, *Plantation Slavery on the East Coast of Africa* (New Haven, CT: Yale University Press, 1977), 242.

2. For example, Liban Bultum, excerpt from letter to Lovedale in "Lovedale News," *Christian Express*, 1 October 1910, 171.

3. Philip D. Curtin, *Economic Change in Precolonial Africa: Senegambia in the Era of the Slave Trade* (Madison: University of Wisconsin Press, 1975), 29–37.

4. Ibid., 156.

5. Kassaye Ayalew, "Beekeeping Extension in Ethiopia" (unpublished paper, Holeta Bee Research Center, 1978), cited in Gidey Yirga and Kibrom Ftwi, "Beekeeping for Rural Development: Its Potentiality and Constraints in Eastern Tigray, Northern Ethiopia," *Agricultural Journal* 5, no. 3 (2010): 201.

6. Liban Bultum, excerpt from letter to Lovedale in "Lovedale News," *Christian Express*, 1 October 1910, 171.

7. James C. McCann, *People of the Plow: An Agricultural History of Ethiopia, 1800–1990* (Madison: University of Wisconsin Press, 1995).

8. In collating the information given in the narratives, the term "cattle" includes all references to "cattle," "cows," and "oxen."

9. The breed is known as the Oromo or the Abyssinian horse.

10. Nathan Nunn and Diego Puga, "Ruggedness: The Blessing of Bad Geography in Africa," *Review of Economics and Statistics* 94, no. 1 (February 2012): 20–36.

11. Only 1.2 percent of the boys had "many," while 11.6 percent had "several sheep." By comparison, 2.3 percent of the girls had "many" sheep, and the same percentage had "several."

12. "The maize and Kaffir corn and pumpkins and sour milk [*amasi*], reminds them of the native land they left so long ago, and has given them quite a home feeling." Extract from a report on the Oromo children shortly after reaching Lovedale by Dr. Alexander Paterson, "Galla Reports," *Christian Express*, 1 January 1891, 4, 13.

13. See, for example, Emily Ruete, *Memoirs of an Arabian Princess from Zanzibar* (New York: Markus Wiener, 1989); Randy J. Sparks, *The Two Princes of Calabar: An Eighteenth-Century Atlantic Odyssey* (Cambridge, MA: Harvard University Press, 2004); Emma Christopher, Cassandra Pybus, and Marcus Rediker, eds., *Many Middle Passages: Forced Migration and the Making of the Modern World* (Berkeley: University of California Press, 2007); Terry Alford, *Prince among Slaves* (Oxford: Oxford University Press, 2007); Olaudah Equiano, *The Interesting Narrative of the Life of Olaudah Equiano; or, Gustavus Vassa, the African* (Radford, VA: Wilder, 2008); and the story of Massavana van Madagaskar in Dan Sleigh, *Die Aanslag op die Slaweskip "Meermin," 1766* (Kaapstad: Africana Uitgewers, 2012), 128–35. Massavana van Madagaskar, a wealthy rancher in Madagascar, visited the king of Tulear on diplomatic business, carrying gold, silver, and jewelry on his person. In the course of conversation, the king suggested that Massavana accompany him aboard the *Meermin*, then at anchor in the bay. Once aboard, the king promptly sold Massavana into slavery. Needless to say, the slavers also seized Massavana's gold, silver, and jewelry.

Chapter 4. Topography, Domicile, and Ethnicity of the Oromo Captives

1. See, for example, Mekuria Bulcha, *The Making of the Oromo Diaspora: A Historical Sociology of Forced Migration* (Minneapolis: Kirk House, 2002), 48–85; Bulcha, "The Red Sea Slave Trade: Captives' Treatment in the Slave Markets of North-East Africa and the Islamic Societies of the Middle East," in *Reflections on Arab-Led Slavery of Africans*, ed. Kwesi Kwaa Prah (Cape Town: Centre for Advanced Studies of African Society, 2005),

109–15; Timothy Fernyhough, "Serfs, Slaves and 'Shefta': Modes of Production in Southern Ethiopia from the Late Nineteenth Century to 1941" (PhD thesis, University of Illinois at Urbana-Champaign, 1986), 105–208; and Fernyhough, "Slavery and the Slave Trade in Southern Ethiopia in the 19th Century," *Slavery and Abolition* 9, no. 3 (1988): 103–30. Fernyhough's journal article immediately preceding here also appears as a chapter in *The Economics of the Indian Ocean Slave Trade in the Nineteenth Century*, ed. William Gervase Clarence-Smith (Totowa, NJ: Frank Cass, 1989), 103–30. Abdussamad H. Ahmad, "Trading in Slaves in Bela-Shangul and Gumuz, Ethiopia: Border Enclaves in History, 1897–1938," *Journal of African History* 40, no. 3 (1999): 433–46; Herbert S. Lewis, *Jimma Abba Jifar, An Oromo Monarchy: Ethiopia, 1830–1932* (Lawrenceville, NJ: Red Sea Press, 2001), 66–67.

2. See the discussion on page 211 regarding the challenges experienced in the process of identifying and locating some of the lesser known places, including some no longer in existence.

3. The current name for Araito is Rahayta (in Eritrea); and Tajurrah is now Tadjoura (in Djibouti).

4. I am grateful to Oromo sociologist and scholar Mekuria Bulcha for his generous assistance and guidance in ascribing each child's identity using the children's first and second names, the names of both parents, and the names of their villages, towns, districts, and countries of domicile. Mekuria Bulcha, e-mail correspondence with author, 2010. W. T. Lerebo, an Ethiopian student in the statistics department of the University of the Western Cape (2003), also offered advice and corrections.

5. Immanuel M. Wallerstein, *The Modern World-System: Capitalist Agriculture and the Origins of the European World-Economy in the Sixteenth Century* (New York: Academic Press, 1974).

6. Ibid., 356.

7. Jack Goody, *Technology, Tradition, and the State in Africa* (Oxford: Oxford University Press, 1971), 31.

8. Ibid., 30–31.

9. Solomon Gashaw, "Nationalism and Ethnic Conflict in Ethiopia," in *The Rising Tide of Cultural Pluralism: The Nation-State at Bay?*, ed. Crawford Young (Madison: University of Wisconsin Press, 1993), 139–41.

10. Bulcha, *Making of the Oromo Diaspora*, 61–69.

11. Ibid., 67.

12. Pietro Antonelli, "Scioa e scioani, lettera del Conte P. Antonelli," *Bollettino della società geografica italiana* 19 (1882), 86, cited in Harold G. Marcus, *The Life and Times of Menelik II: Ethiopia, 1844–1913* (Lawrenceville, NJ: Red Sea Press, 1975), 64.

13. Wallerstein, *Modern World-System*, 357.

Chapter 5. The Moment of Capture

1. See, for example, Mekuria Bulcha, *The Making of the Oromo Diaspora: A Historical Sociology of Forced Migration* (Minneapolis: Kirk House, 2002), 42; Mordechai Abir, *The Era of the Princes; The Challenge of Islam and the Re-Unification of the Christian Empire, 1769–1855* (London: Longmans, 1968), 54; Timothy Fernyhough, "Serfs, Slaves and 'Shefta': Modes of Production in Southern Ethiopia from the Late Nineteenth Century to 1941" (PhD thesis, University of Illinois at Urbana-Champaign, 1986), 118–19.

2. Fernyhough, "Serfs, Slaves and 'Shefta,'" 119–20; Lawrence Athill, "Extracts from a Paper Read by . . . at a Meeting of the Royal Geographical Society [1920]," in Henry Darley, *Slaves and Ivory: A Record of Adventure and Exploration among the Abyssinian Slave-Raiders* (London: Witherby, 1926, repr. 1935), 134.

3. Abir, *Era of the Princes*, 55; Fernyhough, "Serfs, Slaves and 'Shefta,'" 119.

4. Fred Morton, "Small Change: Children in the Nineteenth-Century East African Slave Trade," in *Children in Slavery through the Ages*, ed. Gwyn Campbell, Suzanne Miers, and Joseph C. Miller (Athens: Ohio University Press, 2009), 58.

5. See, for example, Mekuria Bulcha, "The Red Sea Slave Trade: Captives' Treatment in the Slave Markets of North-East Africa and the Islamic Societies of the Middle East," in *Reflections on Arab-Led Slavery of Africans*, ed. Kwesi Kwaa Prah (Cape Town: Centre for Advanced Studies of African Society, 2005), 108.

6. The word *Sidama* means "Abyssinian" (or "Amhara") in Afaan Oromoo. While "Sidama" here could theoretically refer to the neighboring people in the area south of old Abyssinia, in the context of the people who were seizing the Oromo children, the term almost certainly refers to the Abyssinians.

7. Menelik II expropriated the Sidama lands as part of his strategy to amplify his sphere of influence, wealth, and power. The Sidama were, like the Oromo, beleaguered people at that time. It is highly unlikely they would have been the major aggressors as reflected in the children's responses.

8. Abir, *Era of the Princes*, 55; Fernyhough, "Serfs, Slaves and 'Shefta,'" 119.

9. These figures, particularly those for the females, are probably higher than the "few" Fred Morton maintains were born into slavery on the East African coast and adjoining islands. Morton, "Small Change," 66.

10. Bulcha, *Making of the Oromo Diaspora*, 95; Fernyhough, "Serfs, Slaves and 'Shefta,'" 136.

11. Fernyhough, "Serfs, Slaves and 'Shefta,'" 126–27.

Chapter 6. On the Road

1. David Henige, "Measuring the Immeasurable: The Atlantic Slave Trade, West African Population and the Pyrrhonian Critic," *Journal of African History* 27, no. 2 (July 1986): 295–313.

2. Fred Morton, in his examination of the narratives of a group of East African slave children, confirms the dearth of evidence recording the experiences of children enslaved after 1873 or the impact of slavery on their lives. Fred Morton, "Small Change: Children in the Nineteenth-Century East African Slave Trade," in *Children in Slavery through the Ages*, ed. Gwyn Campbell, Suzanne Miers, and Joseph C. Miller (Athens: Ohio University Press, 2009), 65.

3. The first sketch, captioned by the *Graphic* as "The Raid," was annotated by Billy King (W. B. King): "The Arab often go out, travelling about in the mountain, to get the slaves & if one interrupt to ran they fire the gun with them." *Graphic*, 25 November 1893, 656.

4. Ibid. The *Graphic* captioned the second sketch as "The March to the Coast," and Billy annotated it: "When they had gathere[d] many, so they carr[i]ed all down, home, see they tight [tied] their hand, the little one as well, & woman too."

5. Ibid. The *Graphic* captioned the third sketch "Tied up for the night," and Billy added the annotation "This is the wood [yoke]. And at night when they sleeps, all the wood [yokes] are tight [tied] up to the cros bare, one man always go up to tight [tie] the end."

6. Ibid. The *Graphic* captioned the fourth sketch "Embarking in the Slave Dhow," and Billy added the annotation "All the slaves are un landing [?] and r[e]ady to [be] rec[e]ived on board (Daue) [dhow]."

7. Ibid. The *Graphic* captioned the fifth sketch "Pursued by a British Man-of-war," and Billy added the annotation "Now the rober [robbers] are caught, they shout [shoot] her, once to stat [start] with, but they wouldn't stop, some time fire again, and burn their sails, un till they get near."

8. Ibid. The *Graphic* captioned the sixth sketch "Burning the Dhow after Rescuing the Slaves," and Billy added the annotation "After having all out, they put daue [dhow] a far off, & light it with fire & burn it, and ship go her way, to Seychelles."

9. James Mbotela's 1934 historical novel, *Uhuru wa Watumwa* (London: Sheldon Press, 1934).

10. Morton, "Small Change," 57.

11. Mekuria Bulcha, *The Making of the Oromo Diaspora: A Historical Sociology of Forced Migration* (Minneapolis: Kirk House, 2002), 88, 94–95; Timothy D. Fernyhough, "Serfs, Slaves and 'Shefta': Modes of Production in Southern Ethiopia from the Late Nineteenth Century to 1941" (PhD thesis, University of Illinois at Urbana-Champaign, 1986), 126–27.

12. "Gilo: The Last of the Galla Slaves," *South African Outlook*, 1 May 1926, 119.

13. Dr. Louis Botha, Cape Town, personal communication with the author; "Gilo: The Last of the Galla Slaves," *South African Outlook*, 1 May 1926, 119.

14. British Library, India Office Records and Private Papers, Records of the British Administrations in Aden, 1837–1967, vol. 1037, Slave Trade, IOR /R/20/A/667, 1888.

15. *Nelson's Textbook of Pediatrics*, 20th ed., vol. 1 (Philadelphia, PA: Elsevier, 2016), 297.

16. This information is drawn from Sandra Rowoldt Shell, "Trauma and Slavery: Gilo and the Soft, Subtle Shackles of Lovedale," *Bulletin of the National Library of South Africa* 71, no. 2 (December 2017): 149–64.

17. See chapter 5, "The Moment of Capture." Raiders often scooped up several siblings, whole families, or even whole villages at moment of capture but separated the families at first sale.

18. Also known by the alternative names of Asaita and Asayita.

19. Matthew Lochhead, *Short Biographies of the Galla Rescued Slaves, Now at Lovedale: With an Account of Their Country and Their Capture* (Lovedale: Lovedale Press, 1891), 11. Aussa is similar in nature to the town that was known as "Offersdorp" (bidders or sacrifice village). The town, also named Whydah or Ouidah, is an old coastal slaving port in Benin (formerly Dahomey) on the west coast of Africa. The Arabic for the word's root means "sacrifice," for which the Dutch term is "offer." Archibald Dalzel, *The History of Dahomy, an Inland Kingdom of Africa* (London: Spilsbury and Son, 1793), xii; André Marthinus van Rensburg, "The Secret Modus Operandi Used to Obtain Slaves from Guinea for the Cape: The Ship *Hasselt*, 1658," *Familia* 38, no. 2 (2001): 78–92. See also Robin Law, *Ouidah: The Social History of a West African Slaving "Port," 1727–1892* (Athens: Ohio University Press, 2004).

20. Richard Pankhurst, *Economic History of Ethiopia, 1800–1935* (Addis Ababa: Haile Sellassie I University Press, 1968), 429. See also Stephen L. Pastner, "Lords of the Desert Border: Frontier Feudalism in Southern Baluchistan and Eastern Ethiopia," *International Journal of Middle East Studies* 10, no. 1 (February 1979): 101.

21. Commander Gissing to Rear-Admiral Fremantle, *Osprey*, at Aden, 1 January 1889. Enclosure 5 in No. 25, United Kingdon, Parliament, Correspondence relative to the Slave Trade, 1888–1889, C.5821, 1889, 36.

22. Abir, *Era of the Princes*, 25.

23. Mekuria Bulcha, "The Red Sea Slave Trade: Captives' Treatment in the Slave Markets of North-East Africa and the Islamic Societies of the Middle East," in *Reflections on Arab-Led Slavery of Africans*, ed. Kwesi Kwaa Prah (Cape Town: Centre for Advanced Studies of African Society, 2005): 111.

24. Creating a Cost Distance Surface chart would entail covering the area of interest with a grid. The next step would be to assign each grid cell a "cost to cross" based on various factors such as steepness of slope, roughness of terrain, the presence of a river or road, soil type, and so on. The cost could be a unit—for example, time or energy—but would usually be just an abstract, relative value. The model would then be used to find the "best" route between two points by following the route (contiguous cells) of lowest summed cost between them. Paul Doherty (Esri Public Safety Technology), "Cost Surface," ArcGIS, accessed 3 August 2017, https://www.arcgis.com/; Thomas Slingsby, University of Cape Town GIS Laboratory, e-mail correspondence with author, 23 August 2016.

25. See, in particular, Fred Morton, who remarks on the complexity of routes and extended length of time on the road of the thirty-nine East African slave children documented by the Church Missionary Society. Morton, "Small Change," 57; see also Bulcha, "Red Sea Slave Trade," 110–11; Bulcha, *Making of the Oromo Diaspora*, 88, 94–95; and Fernyhough, "Serfs, Slaves and 'Shefta,'" 126–27.

26. Philip D. Curtin, *Economic Change in Precolonial Africa: Senegambia in the Era of the Slave Trade* (Madison: University of Wisconsin Press, 1975), 272.

27. Ibid.

28. Fernyhough, "Serfs, Slaves and 'Shefta,'" 126–27.

29. Ibid.

30. Richard Pankhurst, "Ethiopian Slave Reminiscences of the Nineteenth Century," *Transafrican Journal of History* 5, no. 1 (1976): 102, cited in Bulcha, "Red Sea Slave Trade," 110–11.

31. Ibid.

32. Fred Morton's study of thirty-nine East African slave children, in which all but three were male, confirms this, saying that "weeks, sometimes months or more" went by between capture and the coast. Morton, "Small Change," 60.

33. John Grace, *Domestic Slavery in West Africa, with Particular Reference to the Sierra Leone Protectorate, 1896–1927* (New York: Barnes and Noble, 1975), 7.

34. Bulcha, *Making of the Oromo Diaspora*, 48–49.

35. Alpers alludes to East African slaves being held for periods of one to two years locally before heading for the coast. Edward A. Alpers, *Ivory and Slaves in East Central Africa: Changing Pattern of International Trade in East Central Africa to the Later Nineteenth Century* (London: Heinemann, 1975), 241.

36. See, for example, accounts such as that of Samuel W. Baker, *The Nile Tributaries of Abyssinia, and the Sword Hunters of the Hamran Arabs* (London: Macmillan, 1867), 516–17. Bulcha, *Making of the Oromo Diaspora*, 95–107.

37. Claude Meillassoux, "Female Slavery," in *Women and Slavery in Africa*, ed. Claire C. Robertson and Martin A. Klein (Madison: University of Wisconsin Press, 1983), 49–65.

38. Timothy Fernyhough, "Slavery and the Slave Trade in Southern Ethiopia in the 19th Century," in *The Economics of the Indian Ocean Slave Trade in the Nineteenth-Century*, ed. William Gervase Clarence-Smith (Totowa, NJ: Frank Cass, 1989), 113.

39. Charles Edward Gissing to Fremantle, 1 January 1889, BPP, C.5821, 37.

40. These relatives were not among the sixty-four Oromo children who eventually reached Lovedale but rather were among the larger group of 204 Oromo slaves rescued and liberated aboard the *Osprey*, Gissing's ship, in September 1888. Margaret Muirhead, "Arrival of Our Sixty-Four Galla Girls and Boys at Lovedale: Another Picture," *Free Church of Scotland Monthly*, 1 November 1890, 334; *Anti-Slavery Reporter* 3, 1 May 1890, 108.

41. Some of Lochhead's and Hunter's photographs feature in this study, showing the Oromo girls either in groups or in solo portraits. One or two of the group photographs are too distant to show personal features, but others clearly demonstrate the beauty of some of the Oromo girls, as do their individual portraits. See, for example, pages 114, 119, 143, 151 and 152.

42. The word *Sidama* means "Abyssinian" in Afaan Oromoo. While "Sidama" here could refer to the neighboring people in the area south of old Abyssinia, in the context of the Oromo children, the term is more likely to refer to the Abyssinians. See the discussion on page 36.

43. This was not a uniquely Oromo practice nor even only an African one. Fred Morton notes that of thirty-nine East African children whose accounts were recorded by the Church Missionary Society around the same time as the Oromo narratives, all but one were pawned or sold by parents or relatives. Morton, "Small Change," 68. The practice of selling one's own children was also common in areas like Bali in southern Asia. Richard B. Allen, "Children and European Slave Trading in the Indian Ocean during the Eighteenth and Early Nineteenth Centuries," in Campbell, Miers, and Miller, *Children in Slavery through the Ages*, 42.

44. Henry Salt, *A Voyage to Abyssinia, and Travels into the Interior of That Country, Executed under the Orders of the British Government, in the Years 1809 and 1810* (London: Frank Cass, 1967; facsimile of 1st ed., London, 1814), 311; W. Cornwallis Harris, *The Highlands of Ethiopia*, vol. 3 (Farnborough: Gregg, 1968; republication of 1st ed.; London: Longman, Brown, Green and Longmans, 1844), 76, 303–8; Johann Ludwig Krapf, *Travels, Researches, and Missionary Labours, during Eighteen Years' Residence in Eastern Africa* (London: Trübner, 1860), 50–53, 74; George A. Mountnorris, *Voyages and Travels to India, Ceylon, the Red Sea, Abyssinia, and Egypt, in the Years 1802, 1803, 1804, 1805, and 1806*, vol. 2 (London: Printed for W. Miller, 1809), 62; Baker, *Nile Tributaries of Abyssinia*, 517.

45. A year later, the young Scotsman William Grant joined a British East India Company party led by Captain Frederick Lugard to Uganda. They arrived in October 1890, and, in September 1893, Grant was appointed as officer-in-charge of Basoga affairs in the kingdom of Busoga. He remained in senior positions in Uganda until at least 1908. According to Isaac Mufumba writing in the Ugandan *Observer*, Grant was appointed governor, established the Busoga Lukiika (Parliament), and was eventually knighted.

See George Wilson, "The Progress of Uganda," *Journal of the Royal African Society* 6, no. 22 (January 1907): 113–35; John E. Flint, "Frederick Lugard: The Making of an Autocrat (1858–1943)," in *African Proconsuls: European Governors in Africa*, ed. Lewis H. Gann and Peter Duignan (New York: Free Press, 1978), webAfriqa/Libraryhttp://www.webafriqa.net/library/african_proconsuls/lugard_autocrat.html. Secretariat Minute Paper, 966/1908, William Grant, "Busoga District Annual Report for 1908–09," May 1908, cited in Peter F. B. Nayenga, "Commercial Cotton Growing in Busoga District, Uganda, 1905–1923," *African Economic History* 10 (1981): 179; Isaac Mufumba, "Basoga Struggle to Right a Wrong Made 400 Years Ago," *Observer*, 24 September 2008, http://

www.observer.ug/index.php?option=com_content&view=article&id=1172:isaac-mufum-
ba&catid=34:news&Itemid=114.

46. There were several methods for linking and securing slaves en route. Forked branches lashed together and fastened around the slaves' necks were the norm in Northeast Africa. None of the Oromo children mentioned being forced into any method of coffling.

47. Morton, "Small Change," 58.

48. Margaret Muirhead, "Arrival of our Sixty-Four Galla Girls and Boys at Lovedale: Another Picture," *Free Church of Scotland Monthly*, 1 November 1890, 334.

Chapter 7. Interception to Aden

1. Great Britain, *An Act for the Abolition of the Slave Trade*, 47, George III, Session 1, cap. XXXVI.

2. The full list of European powers subscribing to the terms agreed at the conference were Britain, France, Austria, Germany, Russia, Spain, Portugal (which was not included after 1807), Holland, Belgium, and Italy. "Appendix—Chronology of Measures against Slavery," in Paul E. Lovejoy, *Transformations in Slavery: A History of Slavery in Africa*, 3rd ed. (Cambridge: Cambridge University Press, 2012): 285–92, doi: http://dx.doi.org/10.1017/CBO9781139014946.018

3. Lindsay Doulton, "The Royal Navy's Anti-Slavery Campaign in the Western Indian Ocean, c. 1860–1890: Race, Empire and Identity" (PhD thesis, University of Hull, 2010), 25; Christopher C. Saunders, "Between Slavery and Freedom: The Importation of Prize Negroes to the Cape in the Aftermath of Emancipation," *Kronos* 9 (1984): 36–43; Saunders, "'Free, Yet Slaves': Prize Negroes at the Cape Revisited," in *Breaking the Chains: Slavery and Its Legacy in the Nineteenth-Century Cape Colony* (Johannesburg: Witwatersrand University Press, 1994), 99–115; Saunders, "Liberated Africans in Cape Colony in the First Half of the Nineteenth-Century," *International Journal of African Historical Studies* 18, no. 2 (1985): 223–39.

4. Gerridae (or water-skaters) can move over a water surface at a rate of more than one meter per second. Nils Møller Andersen and Lanna Cheng, "The Marine Insect *Halobates* (Heteroptera: Gerridae): Biology, Adaptations, Distribution, and Phylogeny," *Oceanography and Marine Biology* 42 (2004): 119, 126. Two-masted dhows were also in use. Gissing's description of the action in his report to Rear-Admiral Fremantle is ambiguous: "I then, feeling sure they must be slavers, went to quarters, firing from the 7-pounder and 64-pounders at their masts. Several shots went through their sails, but none striking the masts or halyards," and "Unless I had made use of the Gardner guns no capture would have been made. The big guns were never fired at the dhows, but only at their masts, and the crews, when brought on board, stated that: they did not mind the big guns, but it was the bullets from the guns up the masts which made them lower their sails." Gissing to Fremantle, 18 September 1888, BPP, C.5578, 81. The plural use of "masts" here could imply either single- or two-masted slave dhows.

5. Captain Purvis to the Admiralty, 19 May 1866, Great Britain, Parliament, S.P. LXXIII, No. 84, cited in Raymond W. Beachey, *The Slave Trade of Eastern Africa* (London: Collings, 1976), 68, 278.

6. Philip H. Colomb, *Slave-Catching in the Indian Ocean: A Record of Naval Experiences* (London: Dawsons, 1873; repr. 1968), 38.

7. The Gardner gun was an early mechanical machine gun invented in 1874, known for its lightness, strength, simplicity, and durability. Consisting of two parallel breech-loading barrels, the gun was "loaded, fired, and ejected alternately by one complete revolution of the hand crank." Rejected by the US Navy, the British acquired the rights to manufacture it in Britain, where it was deployed in action by both the British Army and the Navy. "Anti-Torpedo Boat and Machine Guns of the Victorian Era (1862–1900)," http://www.victorianshipmodels.com/antitorpedoboatguns/Gardner/.

8. United Kingdom, Parliament, Correspondence with British Representatives and Agents Abroad, and Reports from Naval Offices and the Treasury Relative to the Slave Trade 1883–1884, C.3849, *Slave Trade*, no. 1 (1884): 124–25.

9. The HMS *Osprey*, launched on 5 August 1876, was an *Osprey*-class screw composite sloop, with a displacement of 1,130 long tons (1,150 tonnes). Her maximum speed was 11 knots (20 km/h or 13 mph). She was sold for scrap on 29 April 1890. David Lyon and Rif Winfield, *The Sail and Steam Navy List: All the Ships of the Royal Navy 1815–1889* (London: Chatham, 2004), 291–92. "Naval and Military Intelligence," *Times*, 6 June 1889, 7, col. 6.

10. Christopher Lloyd, *The Navy and the Slave Trade: The Suppression of the African Slave Trade in the Nineteenth Century* (London: Frank Cass, 1968), 81–84, as explained in Doulton, "Royal Navy's Anti-Slavery Campaign," 180.

11. Doulton, "Royal Navy's Anti-Slavery Campaign," 186.

12. Charles Edward Gissing, Obokh, to Colonel Edward Vincent Stace, Aden, 6 September 1888, United Kingdom, Parliament, Reports on Slave Trade on the East Coast of Africa, 1887–1888, C.5578: Enclosure 2 in No. 64, p. 79.

13. Rahayta, today situated in Eritrea, lies between modern landlocked Ethiopia and the Red Sea. While the colony of Italian Eritrea was established only in 1890, strategic groupings of Italians began settling in Massawa and elsewhere some ten years earlier. Tajurrah is now known as Tadjoura in Djibouti.

14. Commander Gissing to Rear-Admiral Fremantle, *Osprey*, at Aden, 1 January 1889, Enclosure 5 in No. 25, United Kingdom, Parliament, Correspondence Relative to the Slave Trade, 1888–89, C.5821, 1889, 36. "Mahommed Kumfereh" almost certainly refers to Mahammad ibn Hanfadhe (also known as Mahammad "Illalta" ibn Hanfere, the sultan of Aussa from 1862 to 1902). See earlier discussion on the dominance of the Aussa sultanate in the final stages of the Red Sea slave trade supply chain, pages 77–78.

15. Gissing to Fremantle, 1 January 1889, BPP, C.5821, 36–37.

16. The Red Sea slave trade was clearly flourishing, and, despite the fact that at the time the French flag was flying over Tadjoura, Gissing complained that the French authorities made no effort to prevent or control this trade.

17. Matthew Lochhead, "The Gallas and Their Country," 1890; CL, PR 1468, 6.

18. Gissing to Fremantle, 1 January 1889, BPP, C.5821, 37.

19. Abu Bakr, an Afar from Tadjoura, was a powerful figure who dominated trade through the kingdom of Shewa, particularly the trade of slaves. He was *Pasha* (or governor) of Zeila, and after his death in 1885 his sons carried on the tradition of Abu Bakr family dominance within the slave trade. Richard A. Caulk, *"Between the Jaws of Hyenas": A Diplomatic History of Ethiopia (1876–1896)*, ed. Bahru Zewde (Wiesbaden: Harrassowitz, 2002), 21, 452.

20. Gissing to Fremantle, 1 January 1889, BPP, C.5821, 37.

21. Commander Gissing to Colonel Stace, Enclosure 2 in No. 54, Obokh, 6 September 1888, BPP, C.5578, 69.

22. BPP, C.5821, 34–35.

23. Mr. Wright's recall of the precise dates of the engagement was shaky: 17 September 1888 and 18 September 1888 were a Monday and a Tuesday, respectively. All official records date the interception as Sunday, 16 September 1888. Infoplease Perpetual Calendar, http://www.infoplease.com/.

24. A. T. V. Wright, "The Galla Slaves: Death of Gilo Kashe," *South African Outlook*, 1 April 1948, 60.

25. Commander Gissing aboard the *Osprey* at Aden, to Rear-Admiral E. R. Fremantle, 18 September 1888, BPP, C.5578, 81.

26. Ibid.

27. Putting slaves and traders ashore was common, as, unlike the masters of dhows found to be carrying slaves, they would not be prosecuted.

28. Gissing to Fremantle, 18 September 1888, BPP, C.5578, 81.

29. National Archives, Kew (UK), Ships' Logs, *Osprey*, ADM 53/14847, 16 September 1888, Records of the Admiralty, Naval Forces, Royal Marines, Coastguard, and related bodies.

30. Ibid.; Gissing to Fremantle, 18 September 1888, BPP, C.5578, 81–82.

31. "List of Dhows captured during the period 21st April to 31st December 1888," BPP, C.5821, 34–35.

32. Gissing to Fremantle, 18 September 1888, BPP, C.5578, 82.

33. National Archives, Kew (UK), Ships' Logs, *Osprey*, ADM 53/14847, 16 September 1888.

34. Wright, "Galla Slaves," 60.

35. Gissing to Fremantle, 18 September 1888, BPP, C.5578, 82.

36. Wright, "Galla Slaves," 60.

37. Margaret Muirhead, "Arrival of Our Sixty-Four Galla Girls and Boys at Lovedale," *Scotland Monthly*, 1 November 1890, 334.

38. Ibid.; Robert H. W. Shepherd, "Bantu Vignettes: The Strangers," *South African Outlook*, 1 September 1939, 201–2.

39. For one such example emanating from the probably mythical Nabee people, see Gubirmans Publishing, "Hillu and Dhugaasaa," http://www.gubirmans.com/Hillu_Dhugaasaa.htm.

40. Doulton, "Royal Navy's Anti-Slavery Campaign," 186.

41. Lochhead, "Gallas and Their Country," 8.

42. In this report to Rear-Admiral Fremantle after the *Osprey* incident, written from Aden on 1 January 1889, Gissing was giving background information on the slave trade in the region. BPP, C.5821, 37. His information, as he acknowledges, was gleaned from "Europeans [who] have travelled with these caravans," not from any statistical count. Pankhurst estimated deaths as high as 60 percent (see page 83).

43. Margaret Muirhead, "Arrival of Our Sixty-Four Galla Girls and Boys at Lovedale," *Free Church of Scotland Monthly*, 1 November 1890, 334. Fred Morton cites a comparable glimpse of life aboard a slave dhow, where the slaves were "wasted to skeletons," in his exploration of the narratives of thirty-nine East African slave children. Morton, "Small Change: Children in the Nineteenth-Century East African Slave Trade," in *Children in*

Slavery through the Ages, ed. Gwyn Campbell, Suzanne Miers, and Joseph C. Miller (Athens: Ohio University Press, 2009), 64.

44. Lists of Dhows captured during the period 1 July 1887 to 20 April 1888 and 21 April 1888 to 31 December 1888. BPP, C.5821, 1889, 33–35.

45. Margaret Muirhead, "Arrival of Our Sixty-Four Galla Girls and Boys at Lovedale," *Free Church of Scotland Monthly*, 1 November 1890, 334. The official number of slaves aboard the dhows was 204.

46. BPP, C.5578, 82.

47. Wright, "Galla Slaves," 60.

48. A. T. V. Wright, Benoni, letter to Rev. R. H. W. Shepherd, Lovedale, 11 April 1948. CL MS 8753.

49. Ibid.

50. Wright, "Galla Slaves," 60.

51. Great Britain, An Act for the Abolition of the Slave Trade, 47, George III, Session 1, cap. XXXVI, 1807.

52. BPP, C.5578, 81.

53. Wright to Shepherd, 11 April 1948, CL MS 8753; Robert H. W. Shepherd, "Bantu Vignettes: The Strangers," *South African Outlook*, 1 September 1939, 201–2.

54. Doulton, "Royal Navy's Anti-Slavery Campaign," 207.

55. Sir Evan MacGregor, Permanent Secretary to the Admiralty, to the Foreign Office, November 2, 1888, Received by the Admiralty, 7 November 1888. BPP, C.5578, 81.

56. "Another Capture of Galla Slaves," *Free Church of Scotland Monthly*, 1 October 1889, 305.

57. There is no record of whether or not any of the slaves and crew survived the swim for the shore.

58. Hodeidah (now known as Al Hudaydah and also called Hudaida) is today the fourth-largest city in Yemen with a population of nearly half a million people. It is also the center of the Al Hudaydah *muhafazah*, or governorate (the designation of a first-level administrative division in many Arab countries). An important trading center for slaves, coffee, cotton, dates, and hides, it was developed as a seaport by the Ottoman Turks during the mid-nineteenth century.

59. Consider at Caravanserai, Tom Schutyser, "What Is a Caravanserai?," accessed 4 August 2017, http://www.consideratcaravanserai.net/Caravanserai/Caravanserai.

60. "The Red Sea Slave Trade: By Eye-Witnesses," *Anti-Slavery Reporter* 3, 1 May 1890, 108.

61. Matthew Lochhead, *Short Biographies of the Galla Rescued Slaves, Now at Lovedale: With an Account of Their Country and Their Capture* (Lovedale: Lovedale Press, 1891), 41. Soon afterward, he accompanied Captain Frederick D. Lugard on an expedition into Uganda and went on to become a leading pioneer figure attached to the British East African Company. See George Wilson, "The Progress of Uganda," *Journal of the Royal African Society* 6, no. 22 (January 1907): 113–35; John E. Flint, "Frederick Lugard: The Making of an Autocrat (1858–1943)," in *African Proconsuls: European Governors in Africa*, ed. Lewis H. Gann and Peter Duignan (New York: Free Press, 1978), 290–312, http://www.webafriqa.net/library/african_proconsuls/lugard_autocrat.html. Isaac Mufumba, "Basoga Struggle to Right a Wrong Made 400 Years Ago," *Observer* (Kampala), 24 September 2008.

Chapter 8. Sojourn in the Desert and the Onward Voyage

1. The oasis of Sheikh Othman, where the Keith-Falconer Mission stood, drew its name from a shrine to honor Sheikh Othman Al-Zubairi Al-Wahki in the territory of the sultan of Lahej. Today it is a city district in Aden with an estimated 2009 population of 117,803. Situated eleven and a half kilometers northwest of Aden, its deep wells supplied—and continue to supply—the whole of the city with water. In 1882 the British purchased Sheikh Othman from the sultan and set about developing the area for public settlement, building schools, markets, and other facilities. Columbia University Press, *Columbia Lippincott Gazetteer of the World*, ed. Leon E. Seltzer (New York: Columbia University Press, 1952; repr. 1962), 1748.

2. Dr. Alexander Paterson, medical missionary, writing from the Keith-Falconer Mission, Sheikh Othman, 26 September 1888. "Rescued Slaves at Aden," *Christian Express*, 1 January 1889, 1.

3. United Kingdom, Parliament, Reports on Slave Trade on the East Coast of Africa, 1887–1888, C.5578, 82.

4. "Rescued Slaves at Aden," *Christian Express*, 1 January 1889, 1.

5. Ibid. The records of the India Office include the names of the Oromo landed in Aden, as recorded by Stace. British Library, India Office Records, vol. 1037, Slave Trade, IOR/R/20/A/667, 1888.

6. "Rescued Slaves at Aden," *Christian Express*, 1 January 1889, 1.

7. Ibid.

8. Lochhead, *Short Biographies of the Galla Rescued Slaves*, 10.

9. Ibid., 1.

10. Robert H. W. Shepherd, "Bantu Vignettes: The Strangers," *South African Outlook*, 1 September 1939, 201–2.

11. John Fairley Daly, "A Mid-Night Visit to Shaikh Othman," *Free Church of Scotland Monthly*, 1 May 1889, 134.

12. Reverend Dr. Gulian Lansing was a missionary in Cairo from 1856 until his death on 12 September 1892. USGenWeb Archives, "Records of the American Cemetery, Cairo, Egypt," accessed 1 August 2017, http://files.usgwarchives.net/foreign/egypt/cemeteries /egypt.txt; John Fairley Daly, "A Mid-Night Visit to Shaikh Othman," *Free Church of Scotland Monthly*, 1 May 1889, 134.

13. Ibid.

14. The Foreign Missions Committee selected William R. W. Gardner, a promising young Semitic scholar, to succeed Keith-Falconer. He arrived at the mission in October 1888.

15. William R. W. Gardner, "The Keith-Falconer Mission: A Year's Work," *Free Church of Scotland Monthly*, 1 May 1889, 140, http://www.dacb.org/stories/ethiopia/ gebru_desta .html.

16. John Fairley Daly, "A Mid-Night Visit to Shaikh Othman," *Free Church of Scotland Monthly*, 1 May 1889, 134.

17. Ibid.

18. Ibid.

19. Ibid. Daly reported that he was glad to hear Lochhead and Gardner speak well of their new home and Sheikh Othman in general. Daly continued, "It promises to be a comfortable home, and is a marvel of cheapness."

20. "Another Capture of Galla Slaves," *Free Church of Scotland Monthly*, 1 October 1889, 305.

21. George Smith, letter written from Edinburgh on 4 July 1890 to the *Free Church of Scotland Monthly*, 1 October 1890, 302. Earlier, Paterson had insisted that despite their appeals for one hundred children, Stace refused to give the Roman Catholic Mission even one. "Rescued Slaves at Aden," *Christian Express*, 1 January 1889, 1. While the apostolic vicariate of southern Arabia was established only in 1888 (as the apostolic vicariate of Aden), there has been a Roman Catholic presence in Aden since 1841, when Father Serafini of the Servites of Mary was installed as vice-prefect. Over the years other priests joined him, and together they built a school and an orphanage (presumably where the Oromo slave children who landed in Aden were housed). In 1855 they built a large church dedicated to the Holy Family, and later appointees added a church and a burial ground for the Catholics at Steamer Point. In June 1886 Rome appointed the French Capuchin, Monsignor Louis Lasserre, to be the prefect apostolic. He reorganized the girls' school and built another school for boys, to be run by the Marist Brothers. When Rome raised the prefecture to an apostolic vicariate entrusted to the Capuchins of Lyons in 1888, Monsignor Lasserre was installed as the first apostolic vicar. The vicariate of Aden became the vicariate apostolic of Arabia in 1889, entrusted with the care of about fifteen thousand Catholics. The Apostolic Vicariate of Southern Arabia, accessed 1 August 2017, http://stfrancisjebelali.ae/ccsarabia/vicariate.php.

22. Christopher C. Saunders, "Liberated Africans in Cape Colony in the First Half of the Nineteenth-Century," *International Journal of African Historical Studies* 18, no. 2 (1985): 226.

23. William J. B. Moir, Lovedale, Letter to James Stewart, 5 September 1890, BC106, C254.14, James Stewart Papers, UCTM&A.

24. "Rescued Slaves at Aden," *Christian Express*, 1 January 1889, 11.

25. The Reverend James Stewart (1831–1905, MD, DD, FRGS) was the second principal of Lovedale, taking over the mantle of responsibility from the Reverend William Govan, principal at Lovedale Institution's founding in 1841. Stewart's educational plan for Lovedale differed markedly from Govan's and led to a serious rift among the missionaries when Stewart took over the reins in 1870.

26. T. M. Lindsay, Letter to James Stewart, Christmas 1889, UCTM&A, James Stewart Collection, BC106, 254.15.

27. Sandra Rowoldt Shell, "A Missionary Life among the amaXhosa: The Eastern Cape Journals of James Laing, 1830–1836" (master's thesis, University of Cape Town, 2006), 213; Robert H. W. Shepherd, *Lovedale, South Africa: The Story of a Century, 1841–1941* (Lovedale: Lovedale Press, 1941), 64–102.

28. James Stewart (1831–1905) was born in Edinburgh, Scotland, and educated at the University of Edinburgh and Friedrich-Alexander University Erlangen-Nürnberg in Germany. Inspired by David Livingstone's account in his *Missionary Travels and Researches in South Africa*, Stewart was determined to pursue missionary work in Africa. In 1863, after spending more than a year accompanying Livingstone in his explorations of Central Africa, Stewart traveled to the Free Church of Scotland missions in the Eastern Cape of South Africa. There he met the Reverend William Govan, first principal of Lovedale Institution, established in 1841. Stewart returned to Scotland where he was ordained for missionary service in 1865, graduated in medicine, and married Wilhelmina ("Mina") Stephen. During his visit, Govan

had offered him a post at Lovedale Institution. Stewart finally felt he was ready to accept. He and Govan argued on points of educational principle, Govan resigned, and Stewart took over as principal at the beginning of 1867, a post he held till his death in 1905.

Chapter 9: By Sea and Land to Lovedale

1. "Castle Line," *Graham's Town Journal*, 26 June 1890, p. 2, col. 6.

2. "Arrival of the Galla Rescued Slaves," *Christian Express*, 1 September 1890, 129; Margaret Muirhead, "Arrival of Our Sixty-Four Galla Girls and Boys at Lovedale," *Free Church of Scotland Monthly*, 1 November 1890, 334.

3. "Arrival of the Galla Rescued Slaves," *Christian Express*, 1 September 1890, 129.

4. Margaret Muirhead, "Arrival of Our Sixty-Four Galla Girls and Boys at Lovedale," *Free Church of Scotland Monthly*, 1 November 1890, 334.

5. "In circuses of the 19th and early 20th centuries, the horse dominated the scene. Frank Fillis was the founder of a British circus which toured throughout the western world, and presented sophisticated horse routines." Rosemary Dixon-Smith, "A Visit to the Circus," http://www.fad.co.za/Resources/contribs/rose/circus.asp.

6. W. J. B. Moir, "Lovedale and the Galla Children," *Free Church of Scotland Monthly*, 1 October 1890, 302.

7. Margaret Muirhead, "Arrival of Our Sixty-Four Galla Girls and Boys at Lovedale," *Free Church of Scotland Monthly*, 1 November 1890, 334.

8. Robert H. W. Shepherd, "Bantu Vignettes: The Strangers," *South African Outlook*, 1 September 1939, 201–2.

9. Moir to Stewart, 5 September 1890, BC106, C254.14, UCTM&A.

10. The contract for the construction of a railway line linking Djibouti and Addis Ababa was awarded only in 1896. Aden's railway came even later, when the military laid a line linking Aden with Sheikh Othman in 1915–1916—and then for military purposes only.

11. Moir to Stewart, 5 September 1890, BC106, C254.14, UCTM&A.

12. Ibid.

13. Amathole Museum, "The Xiniwe Family and the Temperance Hotel," accessed 1 August 2017, http://www.museum.za.net/index.php/imvubu-newsletter/106-the-xini-we-family-and-the-temperance-hotel.

14. Moir to Stewart, 5 September 1890, BC106, C254.14, UCTM&A.

15. Ibid.

16. Ibid.

17. Ibid.

18. "Lovedale 1887–1889: A Student Looks Back through Childish Eyes," *South African Outlook*, 1 March 1948, 44–45.

19. W. J. B. Moir, "Lovedale and the Galla Children," *Free Church of Scotland Monthly*, 1 October 1890, 302.

20. William J. B. Moir, 5 September 1890, Letter to James Stewart, UCTM&A, James Stewart Collection, BC106, C254.14. This letter was subsequently published as William J. B. Moir to Rev. Dr. Stewart. Margaret Muirhead, "Arrival of Our Sixty-Four Galla Girls and Boys at Lovedale," *Free Church of Scotland Monthly*, 1 November 1890, 333–34.

21. Margaret Christina Muirhead née Potter (27 August 1841–3 April 1891) was lady superintendent of the Lovedale Girls' School from 1881 to 1891.

22. Margaret (May) Muirhead (2 July 1861–1946) married former Keith-Falconer medical missionary Dr. Alexander Paterson (1863–1940) on 30 June 1891 at Lovedale. She was an assistant teacher at Lovedale from 1881 to 1891.

23. W. J. B. Moir, "Lovedale and the Galla Children," *Free Church of Scotland Monthly*, 1 October 1890, 302.

24. This was Mr. Odendaal and his wagon with twenty of the smaller boys.

25. Margaret Muirhead, "Arrival of Our Sixty-Four Galla Girls and Boys at Lovedale," *Free Church of Scotland Monthly*, 1 November 1890, 334.

26. Ibid.

27. Either *umkrayo* (crushed maize) or the more common *umngqusho* (stamped maize or samp cooked with sugar beans, sometimes with a variety of spices and other ingredients). Umkrayo is more usually prepared in rural areas and is normally eaten with a cooked vegetable like spinach. Isaac Ntabankulu, Manuscripts and Archives, UCT Libraries, personal e-mail correspondence with author, 2 July 2012.

28. Margaret Muirhead, "Arrival of Our Sixty-Four Galla Girls and Boys at Lovedale," *Free Church of Scotland Monthly*, 1 November 1890, 334.

29. Moir to James Stewart, 5 September 1890, UCTM&A, BC106, C254.14.

30. Margaret Muirhead, "Arrival of Our Sixty-Four Galla Girls and Boys," *Free Church of Scotland Monthly*, 1 November 1890, 334.

31. Moir to James Stewart, 5 September 1890, UCTM&A, BC106, C254.14.

32. Dominick LaCapra, *Writing History, Writing Trauma* (Baltimore, MD: Johns Hopkins University Press, 2001), 1, 39.

Chapter 10. Education at Lovedale

1. The 1890 annual report for Lovedale Institution listed a total of 666 students excluding the 64 Oromo children. "Lovedale Missionary Institution: Report for 1890," *Christian Express*, 1 January 1891, 3.

2. The reports enabled the creation of a database of 1,053 class marks across the Oromos' core Lovedale years of 1892–1894.

3. Nosipho Majeke (pseud. Dora Taylor), *The Role of the Missionaries in Conquest* (Cape Town: Society of Young Africa, 1952).

4. "Galla Reports," *Christian Express*, 1 January 1891, 13.

5. Ibid., 4.

6. Lovedale Institution, "Our Complete Curriculum," *Annual Report* (1892), 11.

7. That is, the teacher-training class.

8. Lovedale Institution, "Detailed Reports: Higher Educational Departments," *Annual Report* (1892), 29–30.

9. Lovedale Institution, "Our Complete Curriculum," *Annual Report* (1892), 11; Lovedale Institution, "The University Examination," *Annual Report* (1897), 73.

10. Lovedale Institution, "The University Examination," *Annual Report* (1897), 73.

11. Lovedale Institution, *Arrangements for Classes and Subjects, and Other Information: First Session, 1896* (Lovedale: Lovedale Press, 1896), 9.

12. Ibid., 9–10.

13. The class books for the different levels are listed in brief, inter alia, in "Class Books Required," in Lovedale Institution, *Arrangements for Classes and Subjects*, 37–39. Thomas W. Harvey, *The Graded-School Fourth Reader* (Cincinnati: Wilson, Hinckle, 1875).

14. For example, Joseph Whiteside, *A New School History of South Africa* (Cape Town: Juta, [189–]).

15. Lovedale Institution, *Arrangements for Classes and Subjects*, 10–11.

16. *Royal Readers no. V* (London: Thomas Nelson and Sons, 1881); William Davidson and Joseph Crosby Alcock, *English Grammar and Analysis* (London: Allman, 1889).

17. William Lawson, *Class-Book of Geography* (Edinburgh: Oliver and Boyd, 1875); *The World at Home: A New Series of Geographical Readers Adapted to the Latest Code* (London: Thomas Nelson and Sons, 1891).

18. *The Primary History of England in Reading Lessons: . . . Adapted to the Latest Requirements of the Education Department* (London: Thomas Nelson and Sons, 1884).

19. Whiteside, *New School History of South Africa*, 11–12.

20. Lovedale Institution, *Arrangements for Classes and Subjects*, 12–13.

21. Rural men would be driven into the fields to do the essential and heavily manual work themselves. This movement began with the Watson Institute, established at Farmerfield in the Eastern Cape after 1838. See Fiona Vernal, *The Farmerfield Mission: A Christian Community in South Africa, 1838–2008* (Oxford: Oxford University Press, 2013), 112–15. See also the discussion on page 10, and the section in the essay by Gutama Tarafo on the contrast between the Eastern Cape and the Oromo divisions of labor along gender lines in appendix D.

22. Natasha Erlank, "Sexual Misconduct and Church Power on Scottish Mission Stations in Xhosaland, South Africa, in the 1840s," *Gender and History* 15, no. 1 (April 2003): 78.

23. "Lovedale 1887–1889: A Student Looks Back through Childish Eyes," *South African Outlook*, 1 March 1948, 44–45.

24. André Germond, "The Lower Classes," Lovedale Institution, *Annual Report* (1892), 34.

25. This separation was based on linguistic considerations only. Through this temporary arrangement, the Oromo children were able to learn in their own language—thanks to the interventions of missionaries Lochhead and Paterson—while improving their proficiency in English. Thereafter they were absorbed into the mainstream classes. The Galla Trade classes paralleled the mainstream industrial department.

26. William J. B. Moir to James Stewart, 5 September 1890, UCTM&A, BC106, C254.14.

27. Thomas M. Lindsay, letter to Alexander Paterson, 24 January 1891, MS 7774, 522/204, folio 407, Archive of the Church of Scotland Foreign Mission Committee, NLS.

28. "Lovedale Institution: Report for 1891," *Christian Express*, 1 January 1892, 3.

29. Thomas M. Lindsay, letter to Matthew Lochhead, 13 January 1892, MS 7774, 404, folio 740, Archive of the Church of Scotland Foreign Mission Committee, NLS.

30. "A Sad Admission," *Christian Express*, 1 October 1892, 1.

31. Robert H. W. Shepherd, *Lovedale, South Africa: The Story of a Century, 1841–1941* (Lovedale: Lovedale Press, 1941), 232.

32. Gamaches Garba, Lovedale, Letter to Mrs Stewart, 20 October 1892, UCTM&A, BC 106, C.254.

33. Fayissa Hora, Lovedale, Letter to Mrs Stewart, 20 October 1892, UCTM&A, BC 106, C.254.1.

34. Bayan Liliso, Letter to [Mrs. Mina Stewart], 3 September 1894, UCTM&A, BC 106, C.254.

35. These exercises were not uncommon. Fred Morton alludes to those written by a group of liberated East African slave children (see Morton, "Small Change," 56–57).

36. Robert Young, *African Wastes Reclaimed: Illustrated in the Story of the Lovedale Mission* (London: Dent, 1902), facing page 198.

37. Shepherd, *Lovedale, South Africa*, 270.

38. Moir to James Stewart, 5 September 1890, UCTM&A, BC106, C254.14.

39. "Galla Reports," *Christian Express*, 1 January 1891, 13.

40. Margaret Muirhead, "Arrival of our Sixty-Four Galla Girls and Boys at Lovedale," *Free Church of Scotland Monthly*, 1 November 1890, 334.

41. "Galla Reports," *Christian Express*, 1 January 1891, 13.

42. Ibid., 4.

43. Ibid.

44. Ibid., 4, 13.

45. Ibid., 13.

46. Lovedale Institution, "The Gallas," *Annual Report* (1892), 34.

47. André Germond, "The Lower Classes," Lovedale Institution, *Annual Report* (1892), 34.

48. Lovedale Institution, "New Centres," *Annual Report* (1892), 18.

49. Erlank, "Sexual Misconduct," 77.

50. Lovedale Institution, *Results of Examinations and Work for Session Ending December 1894* (Lovedale: Lovedale Press, 1894), 6.

51. These family names are historically renowned in South Africa with distinguished progenitors including the composers John Knox Bokwe and Benjamin Tyamzashe; celebrated author Samuel Edward Krune Mqhayi; educationist, political and social commentator, poet, and churchman, the Reverand Isaac Wauchope, who rallied the troops of the South African Native Labour Corps (SANLC) aboard the sinking *Mendi* in 1917; Sekgoma II, son of Khama III and later king of the Bamangwato people; the Reverend Daniel D. Tywakadi of the Congregational Union and prominent community leader; Pambani Jeremiah Mzimba, ordained as the first South African–trained black Presbyterian Church minister on 2 December 1875 and a pioneer of the African independent church movement; the hereditary line of Chief Mbovane Mabandla, leader of the amaBhele near Alice, and his descendants Justice Thandatha Jongilizwe Mabandla (appointed first president of the apartheid-era Ciskei), and former parliamentary minister and now member of the African National Congress National Executive Council, Bridgitte Mabandla; Robert Balfour of Burnshill and his descendants, including former South African politician Ngconde Balfour; and the family of musicians Samuel Bokwe Matshikiza and Grace Ngqoyi Matshikiza, including Todd Matshikiza, who composed the music (and penned some of the lyrics) of the internationally acclaimed musical *King Kong*, as well as being a *Drum* journalist and author of *Chocolates for My Wife*; and his son, the late John Matshikiza, well-known actor, theater director, journalist, and poet.

52. Meshinge Salban, Death notice, MOOC, 6/9/312, reference 209, part 1, 1893, WCARS; Lovedale Missionary Institution, Report, 1892, 19.

53. Gamaches Garba, letter to Mrs Stewart, BC 106, C.254.

54. Amanu Bulcha, Lovedale Institution, Class records, Standard 6, Second session, 1894, CL MS 16,291/C, 1894, no. 31, page 95; Amanu Buetcha [sic], death notice, MOOC, 6/9/335, reference 2800, part 1, 1894, WCARS.

55. Wayessa Tikse, letter to James Stewart, James Stewart Collection, BC106, C254, UCTM&A.

56. "Departed," *Lovedale News* 11, 16, 12 June 1895, 1.

57. "Lovedale Post," *Christian Express*, 1 January 1892, p. 15, col. 2.

58. "The Death of a Galla Boy," *Christian Express*, 1 November 1895, 162.

59. Guyo Tiki, letter to Mina Stewart, 20 October 1892, BC106, C254.6, James Stewart Papers, UCTM&A.

60. Fayissa Murki died on Christmas Day, 1892, not long after Badassa wrote his letter.

61. Badassa Nonno, letter to Mina Stewart, 20 October 1892, James Stewart Papers, BC106, C254.2, UCTM&A.

62. "Lovedale Report," *Christian Express*, 1 January 1897, 14.

63. Katshi Wolamo, letter to Mina Stewart, 20 October 1892, James Stewart Papers, BC106, C254.8, UCTM&A.

64. Lovedale Institution, "Distribution of Gallas Outside Lovedale," 15 January 1898 (Boys), CL MS 17,125.

65. "Health," *Christian Express*, 1 February 1899, p. 7, col. 6; p. 8, col. 1.

66. Lovedale Institution, "The Rescued Gallas," 15 January 1898, CL MS 17,125.

67. I am grateful to Dr. Stephen Craven, who has a strong research interest in medical history, for agreeing to assess Asho's condition on the evidence of the surviving records. He has posited a tentative diagnosis of multiple sclerosis: "Although multiple sclerosis is rare in those of African stock, it is not absent. Its aetiology has not been fully established—it involves both environment and heredity, being commonest in those of northern European stock and their descendants who have emigrated. It is said not to exist in South African blacks, and to be not uncommon in Caribbeans. One very rare disease which features increasing paralysis, blindness and deafness is *Friedrich's ataxia*. This is hereditary, and presents during childhood. There is no mention of these symptoms in the account of Asho's mother. And, if Asho were suffering from *Friedrich's ataxia*, the slave merchants would not have wasted their time and money on her. Therefore I believe that multiple sclerosis is the most likely diagnosis." Stephen Craven, e-mail correspondence with author, 1 September 2012.

68. David Alexander Hunter (1864–1949) was a Scottish lay missionary who joined the staff of Lovedale Institution in 1895. He was editor of the institution's journal when it was named the *Christian Express* and also later when its title was changed to the *South African Outlook*.

69. "Asho Sayo," *Christian Express*, 1 May 1899, 166–67.

70. The last Oromo left Lovedale in 1900.

71. Charles Simkins and Elizabeth van Heyningen, "Fertility, Mortality, and Migration in the Cape Colony, 1891–1904," *International Journal of African Historical Studies* 22, no. 1 (1989): 79–111.

72. Those admitted to full membership in the church were Faraja Jimma, Rufo Gangila, Wayessa Tikse, Galani Warabu, and Bisho Jarsa (all in 1895); Damuli Dunge, Damuli Diso, Berille Grant, Warkitu Galatu, and Ayantu Said (all in 1897); and Liban Bultum, Gutama Tarafo, and Bayan Liliso (all in 1898). Lovedale Institution, "The Gallas: Statement Shewing Address Occupation etc., on 10th of March 1900," CL MS 17,125, p. 2.

73. Aguchello Chabani (King William's Town); Amanu Figgo (East London); Balcha Billo (King William's Town); Galgal Dikko (Port Elizabeth); Gamaches Garba (Pietermaritzburg); Kintiso Bulcha (East London); Mulatta Billi (Port Elizabeth); Nuro Chabse (Bulawayo); Shamo Ayanso (King William's Town); and Wayessa Gudru (Debe Nek). "Lovedale Report," *Christian Express*, 1 January 1897, 18.

74. Fred Morton, "Small Change: Children in the Nineteenth-Century East African Slave Trade," in *Children in Slavery through the Ages*, ed. Gwyn Campbell, Suzanne Miers, and Joseph C. Miller (Athens: Ohio University Press, 2009), 66.

75. Lovedale Institution, "The Gallas: Statement Statement Shewing Address Occupation etc., on 10th of March 1900," CL MS 17,125, p. 6.

76. An extended version of Bisho's life history is scheduled for publication elsewhere.

77. In the context of the nineteenth-century Eastern Cape, domestic work for women was, in fact, not a demotion but an emancipation from agricultural labor. See discussion on page 10.

78. Berille Boko married Liban Bultum and moved to Port Elizabeth with him. They both returned to Ethiopia in 1909 (see chapter 11, "Going Home"). Warkitu Galatu, the only other Oromo woman to train as a teacher, took up a teaching post at the Free Church Mission School at Macfarlan, close to Lovedale.

79. Bisho Jarsa, completed questionnaire and letter to the principal, Lovedale, regarding her possible return to Ethiopia. Cradock, 15 March 1903, CL MS 8796.

80. Neville Alexander, personal communication to the author, 2008.

81. Nelson Rolihlahla Mandela (1918–2013) was installed as the newly free and democratic South Africa's first president in 1994. In 1963 he had been tried and convicted on charges of sabotage and conspiracy to overthrow the government and sentenced to imprisonment on Robben Island. In 1988 he was removed from the island and hospitalized for tuberculosis in Cape Town. On his release from hospital, he was transferred to a house on the grounds of the Victor Verster Prison near Paarl (a town close to Cape Town), and finally released on 11 February 1990.

82. Na-iem Dollie, Salim Vally, Crain Soudien et al., "Tribute to Neville Alexander (22 October 1936–27 August 2012)," South African History Online, accessed 4 August 2017, http://www.sahistory.org.za/ archive/tribute-neville-alexander.

83. Francis Wilson, "Neville Alexander 1936–2012: A Prophet Rather than a Politician," *Cape Times*, 30 August 2012; and *The Frantz Fanon Blog: Reading Frantz Fanon in Grahamstown, South Africa*, accessed 4 August 2017, http://readingfanon.blogspot.co.za/2014/01 /reading-frantz-fanon-in-grahamstown.html; Brian Ramadiro, Jane Duncan, and Salim Vally, "Neville Alexander: Revolutionary Who Changed Many Lives," *Mail and Guardian*, 30 August 2012, http://mg.co.za/article/2012-08-30-neville-alexander-revolutionary-who-changed-many-lives.

84. Sandra Rowoldt Shell, "How an Ethiopian Slave Became a South African Teacher," BBC News: Africa, 25 August 2011, http://www.bbc.co.uk/news/world-africa-14357121.

Chapter 11. Going Home

1. Lovedale Institution, "The Gallas: Statement Shewing Address Occupation etc., on 10th of March 1900," CL MS 17,125, p. 4. In 1907 George Clerk, the chargé d'affaires of the British legation in Addis Ababa, wrote to inform Liban Bultum that Galgal had died

at Harar "about four or five years ago." Letter from George Clerk, H. B. M. Chargé d'Affaires, Addis Ababa to Liban Bultum, 28 February 1907, CL MS 8814.

2. "Lovedale News," *Christian Express*, 11 January 1901, 4.

3. Lovedale Institution, "The Gallas: Statement Shewing Address Occupation etc., on 10th of March 1900," CL MS 17,125, p. 5.

4. "Lovedale News," *Christian Express*, 1 November 1901, 164.

5. "Letters from the Natal Front," *Christian Express*, 2 July 1900, 99. The *Koenig* (*König*), built by the Hamburg company Reiherstieg Schiffswerfte & Maschinenfabrik Ag in 1896, was a liner operating in the Intermediate Line of the Deutsche Ost Afrika Linie. *Deutsche Ost-Afrika-Linie, Hamburg: Handbook* (Hamburg: DOAL, 1911), 7–11. The *König* was scuttled on the East African coast on 3 December 1914, shortly after the outbreak of World War I. Wreck Site, accessed 2 August 2017, http://www.wrecksite.eu/wreck.aspx?122060.

6. "Lovedale News," *Christian Express*, 1 April 1901, 52.

7. "Lovedale News" *Christian Express*, 1 May 1901, 68.

8. Lovedale Institution, "The Gallas: Statement Shewing Address Occupation etc., on 10th of March 1900," CL MS 17,125, p. 4.

9. Shamo was almost certainly suffering from advanced tuberculosis.

10. "Lovedale News," *Christian Express*, 1 November 1901, 164.

11. "Lovedale News," *Christian Express*, 11 January 1901, 4.

12. Letter from George Clerk, H. B. M. Chargé d'Affaires, Addis Ababa, to Liban Bultum, 28 February 1907, CL MS 8814.

13. "Lovedale News," *Christian Express*, 1 January 1901, 4. The superintendent general of education, in his report for 1894, pointed to the "serious deficiency of adequate knowledge or of the training necessary for the difficult work of teaching." He hoped that "the three years' Normal course proposed for those yet to be trained may be expected to raise the standard of attainment and proficiency in the future." Editorial comment on the "Report of the Superintendent-General of Education for 1894," "Education in This Country," *Christian Express*, 1 June 1895, 82.

14. "Lovedale News," *Christian Express*, 1 January 1901, 4.

15. The term "colporteur" was in common use in missionary and religious circles and literature, particularly during the eighteenth, nineteenth, and early twentieth centuries. The *Oxford English Dictionary* defines the term as "A hawker of books, newspapers, etc. esp. (in English use) one employed by a society [to travel about and sell or distribute Bibles and religious writings]." *The Shorter Oxford English Dictionary on Historical Principles*, 3rd ed., s.v. "colporteur."

16. "Lovedale Notes," *Christian Express*, 1 January 1903, 4.

17. Letter from George Clerk, H. B. M. Chargé d'Affaires, Addis Ababa, to Liban Bultum, 28 February 1907, CL MS 8814.

18. "Lovedale News," *South African Outlook*, 2 February 1925, 48.

19. "The Gallas," *Christian Express*, 1 May 1899, 67.

20. Lovedale Institution, "The Gallas: Statement Shewing Address Occupation etc., on 10th of March 1900," CL MS 17,125, p. 6.

21. "Letter from a Galla Boy, 22 January 1900," *Christian Express*, 1 March 1900, 35; "Letters from the Natal Front," *Christian Express*, 2 July 1900, 99.

22. "Letter from a Galla Boy, 22 January 1900," *Christian Express*, 1 March 1900, 35.

23. "Letters from the Natal Front," *Christian Express*, 2 July 1900, 99.

24. Established more than eight thousand years ago, Bharuch is not only the oldest city in Gujarat, it is also the second-oldest continuously inhabited city in India. Christian missionary efforts began in Bharuch as early as AD 45, and Catholicism consolidated its influence there in the thirteenth century. Protestant missionaries followed in the late nineteenth century, led by members of the Church of the Brethren, a movement with German roots. G. Abraham, "Impact of Christianity on Varlis in Gujarat" (PhD thesis, Manonmaniam Sundaranar University, 2008), 117–30.

25. "Lovedale News," *Christian Express*, 1 January 1902, 4.

26. Ibid.; "Lovedale News," *Christian Express*, 1 April 1902, 52.

27. "Lovedale News," *Christian Express*, 1 September 1903, 132.

28. Berouk Terefe, personal e-mail to the author, 23 September 2011.

29. Unlike the East African slave children in Fred Morton's study—few of whom married or had children—the Oromo seem to have experienced no problem forming long-term relationships. Some married within the Oromo group in South Africa, some chose South Africans as spouses, and some, like Tolassa, married on their return home. Morton, "Small Change: Children in the Nineteenth-Century East African Slave Trade," in *Children in Slavery through the Ages*, ed. Gwyn Campbell, Suzanne Miers, and Joseph C. Miller (Athens: Ohio University Press, 2009), 67.

30. An extended version of Tolassa's life history is scheduled for publication elsewhere.

31. "Lovedale News," *Christian Express*, 2 November 1903, 164.

32. "Lovedale News," *Christian Express*, 1 December 1903, 180.

33. Letter from George Clerk, H. B. M. Chargé d'Affaires, Addis Ababa, to Liban Bultum, 28 February 1907, CL MS 8814.

34. "The Gallas: Statement Shewing Address Occupation etc., on 10th of March 1900," CL MS 17,125, 5.

35. Daba Tobo, repatriation questionnaire response, 1903, CL MS 8804. David Hunter, a lay missionary at Lovedale since 1894, distributed a questionnaire to all living and traceable Oromo in 1903 posing the question "If the opportunity does occur of returning to Abyssinia, would you wish to go, or would you rather remain in South Africa?" Hunter took a particular interest in the Oromo children during their time at Lovedale.

36. Lovedale Institution, "The Gallas: Statement Shewing Address Occupation etc., on 10th of March 1900," CL MS 17,125.

37. Fayissa Hora presumably married a South African woman.

38. Fayissa Hora, repatriation questionnaire response, 1903, CL MS 8795.

39. Fayissa is implying that, as a gentleman, he would need his wife and child to be funded as well, as he would not abandon them to return home alone. Fayissa Hora, Cape Town, letter to [David Hunter], Lovedale, 18 September 1903, CL MS 8808.

40. Fayissa Hora, repatriation questionnaire response, 1903, CL MS 8795.

41. Lovedale Institution, *Annual Report* (1892), 35.

42. "M. Billi," in *San Diego City Directory 1912*, Ancestry.com, http://search.ancestry.com/; "M. Billi," in *St. Louis, Missouri, City Directory, 1930*, Ancestry.com, http://search.ancestry.com/.

43. Kentiba Ghebrau ze Gondar [Gebru Desta], to David Hunter, 3 October 1903, CL MS 8809.

44. "Lovedale News," *Christian Express*, 2 November 1903, 164.

45. Kentiba Ghebrau ze Gondar [Gebru Desta], to David Hunter, 3 October 1903, CL MS 8809.

46. Extract from a formal letter written by Lieutenant Colonel John Harrington, British diplomatic agent and consul general in Addis Ababa to Lovedale, May 1903, cited by James Henderson, Lovedale, Letter to High Commissioner, Pretoria, 12 May 1909, WCARS, PMO 240, reference 100/09, part 1.

47. John Harrington, confidential covering letter, May 1903, cited by Henderson, 12 May 1909, WCARS, PMO 240, reference 100/09, part 1.

48. Guluma Gemeda, "Conquest and Resistance in the Gibe Region, 1881–1900," *Journal of Oromo Studies* 3, nos. 1–2 (Winter–Summer 1996): 59.

49. Menelik's desire for territorial hegemony, money, and weapons to boost his bid for the imperial throne led to his expropriation of the Oromo lands (and therefore the Oromo people's means of subsistence) and the enslavement of their children (which brought him additional wealth through taxes on their passage through and their sale within his kingdom of Shewa). See chapter 1, "Ethiopia: The Lie of the Land," for full details of the impact of Menelik's actions on the Oromo people.

50. One of the earliest questionnaires distributed in South Africa, the core question read: "If the opportunity does occur of returning to Abyssinia, would you wish to go, or would you rather remain in South Africa?"

51. Bisho Jarsa, repatriation questionnaire response, 1903, CL MS 8796.

52. Dinkitu Boensa, repatriation questionnaire response, 1903, CL MS 8783.

53. There are frequent, common variations on the spelling of Addis Ababa and other places in Ethiopia. I have corrected these silently for ease of reading.

54. John C. Young, Sheikh Othman, Letter to David Hunter, Lovedale, 12 July 1904, CL MS 8812.

55. Herbert Hervey, British Legation, Addis Ababa, to Sir Edward Grey, Foreign Office, London, 18 August 1909, WCARS, PMO 240, Reference 100/09; Harold G. Marcus, *The Life and Times of Menelik II: Ethiopia, 1844–1913* (Lawrenceville, NJ: Red Sea Press, 1975), 225–26.

56. Robert H. W. Shepherd, *Lovedale, South Africa: The Story of a Century, 1841–1941* (Lovedale: Lovedale Press, 1941), 264.

57. Stewart, second principal of Lovedale, introduced a radically different educational plan for Lovedale from that put in place by his predecessor and first principal, the Reverend William Govan. Stewart advocated a practical education for black scholars instead of the classical education received by both black and white children under Govan. Stewart's racially discriminatory system sadly foreshadowed South Africa's iniquitous Bantu Education program that was legalized under apartheid, the legacy of which still impacts the majority of South Africans. This was, arguably, apartheid's most heinous infliction on the nation. That said, from the time he assumed the principalship in 1870, Stewart had worked hard and with great energy and determination to consolidate and advance Lovedale Institution. By 1904 he was seventy-three years of age and tiring.

58. Liban A. Bultum, Port Elizabeth, Letter to Dr James Stewart, Lovedale, 14 November 1905, UCTM&A, BC 106, C254.12.

59. Shepherd, *Lovedale, South Africa*, 266–67.

60. Henderson, 12 May 1909, WCARS, PMO 240, Reference 100/09, part 1.

61. Letter from George Clerk, H. B. M. Chargé d'Affaires, Addis Ababa, to Liban Bultum, 28 February 1907, CL MS 8814.

62. Liban S. Bultum, Port Elizabeth, Letter to A. Geddes, Lovedale, 11 April 1907, CL MS 8813.

63. David A. Hunter, Lovedale, Letter to Chargé d'Affaires, Addis Ababa, WCARS, GH. 35/224, volume 320, 29 May 1908.

64. Ibid.; James Henderson repeated these sentiments in his letter to the high commissioner, Pretoria, 12 May 1909, WCARS, PMO 240 100/09, part 1.

65. David Hunter, Lovedale, Letter to Chargé d'Affaires, Addis Ababa, WCARS, GH. 35/224, volume 320, 29 May 1908.

66. Ibid.

67. Sven Rubenson, "The Protectorate Paragraph of the Wichalē Treaty," *Journal of African History* 5, no. 2 (1964): 243–83.

68. Ethiopia is the only African country to have defeated a colonizing power, but the country never capitalized on its gains at Adwa in 1896. Throughout the twentieth century, the rest of colonized Africa looked in vain to independent Ethiopia to lead its countries out of colonial domination. The second Italian invasion in 1936 put paid to that dream. Nonetheless, Ethiopia's defeat of Italy's troops in 1896 was a milestone in Ethiopian history, and a rallying point for future African nationalism and Pan Africanism. It is no accident that the headquarters of the African Union is situated in Addis Ababa.

69. Friedrich Rosen, the son of Dr. Georg Rosen, the former Prussian consul in Jerusalem, was born in Leipzig in 1856. Rosen was an Orientalist, politician, and diplomat, representing his country at Beirut, Tehran, Baghdad, and then Addis Ababa from 1904 to 1905, establishing what came to be known as the Rosengesandtschaft ("the Rosen Embassy"). During 1921 he served briefly as German foreign minister, but, with the rise of Nazism, his Jewish descent caused a fall from favor. He died while on a visit to Beijing in 1935. Ernest A. Wallis Budge, *By Nile and Tigris: A Narrative of Journeys in Egypt and Mesopotamia on Behalf of the British Museum between the Years 1886 and 1913*, vol. 2 (London: John Murray, 1920), 158–59.

70. Chris Prouty Rosenfeld, *A Chronology of Menelik II of Ethiopia, 1844–1913* (East Lansing, MI: African Studies Center, 1976), 219.

71. Edward Ullendorff, a historian specializing in Ethiopian studies, regarded Gebru Desta as a major figure of the Menelik II, Regency, and Haile Selassie eras. Desta had the ear of and undoubtedly held considerable sway in Menelik's court at that time. Edward Ullendorff, "Some Amharic and Other Documents from the Eugen Mittwoch *Nachlass*," *Bulletin of the School of Oriental and African Studies* 43, no. 3 (October 1980): 429–52. See further information on Gebru Desta on pages 114, 116, as well as in "Kentiba Gebru (Gobaw) Desta," in *Dictionary of African Christian Biography*, http://www.dacb.org/stories/ethiopia/gebru_desta.html.

72. Chris Prouty, *Empress Taytu and Menelik II, Ethiopia 1883–1910* (Trenton, NJ: Red Sea Press, 1986), 273.

73. Rosenfeld, *Chronology of Menelik II of Ethiopia*, 222.

74. Ibid., 222–23. Enno Littmann, who headed the expedition, was a German linguist. His small team comprised Daniel Krencker, an architect; Erich Kaschke, a medical doctor; and Theodor von Lüpke, an architect and photographer. Strangely, there

was no archaeologist on the expedition team. Enno Littmann, *Publications of the Princeton Expedition to Abyssinia* (Leiden: Brill, 1913).

75. Robert Gellately and Ben Kiernan, eds., *The Specter of Genocide: Mass Murder in Historical Perspective* (Cambridge: Cambridge University Press, 2003), 161; Sara Friedrichsmeyer, Sara Lennox, and Susanne Zantop, eds., *The Imperialist Imagination: German Colonialism and Its Legacy* (Ann Arbor: University of Michigan Press, 1999), 87.

76. Princeton professor William Patch, personal e-mail communication with the author, 29 April 2013.

77. Bernhard Dernburg was born in Darmstadt, Hesse, on 17 July 1865. He died on 14 October 1937.

78. Princeton professor William Patch, personal e-mail communication with the author, 29 April 2013.

79. "Bernhard Durnberg," in *Historical Dictionary of European Imperialism*, ed. James S. Olson (New York: Greenwood Press, 1991), 169–70.

80. "The Month," *Christian Express*, 1 May 1909, 74.

81. "The Morocco Crisis of 1911," Mount Holyoke College, https://www.mtholyoke .edu/acad/intrel/boshtml/bos137.htm.

82. "The Expansion of Germany," *Christian Express*, 1 June 1909, 97.

83. Rosenfeld, *Chronology of Menelik II of Ethiopia*, 220 (see date of March 1905).

84. James Henderson, Lovedale, letter to the High Commissioner, Pretoria, 12 May 1909, WCARS, PMO 240, Reference 100/09, part 1.

85. Ibid.

86. Ibid.

87. James Henderson, Lovedale, letter to Walter Francis Hely-Hutchinson, Cape Town, 24 May 1909, WCARS, GH 35/224, volume 320.

88. James Henderson, Lovedale, telegram to Walter Francis Hely-Hutchinson, Cape Town, 29 May 1909, WCARS, GH 35/224, volume 320.

89. "Pendriver" [Government House], Cape Town, telegram to "Gravido" [Imperial Secretary], Johannesburg, 29 May 1909, WCARS, GH 35/224, volume 320.

90. Walter Francis Hely-Hutchinson, Minute 373, WCARS, GH 35/224, volume 320, 29 May 1909.

91. "Gravido" [Imperial Secretary], Johannesburg, telegram to "Pendriver" [Private Secretary, Government House], Cape Town, 29 May 1909, WCARS, GH 35/224, volume 320.

92. Ibid.

93. "Chiltonite" [High Commissioner], Johannesburg, Telegram to Governor, 31 May 1909, WCARS, GH 35/224, volume 320.

94. Walter Hely-Hutchinson, Cape Town, Despatch to the High Commissioner, Johannesburg, 4 June 1909, GH 35/224, volume 320.

95. W. P. Minckley, Private Secretary, Cape Town, Postscript to James Henderson, Lovedale, 4 June 1909, WCARS, GH 35/224, volume 320.

96. Edward Dower, Native Affairs, Letter to the Prime Minister [John Xavier Merriman], 1 June 1909, WCARS, PMO, 240, reference 100/09, part 5.

97. Edward Dower, Cape Town, Letter to John X. Merriman, Cape Town, 1 June 1909, WCARS, PMO 240, 100/09.

98. Despite his avowed opposition to slavery and the slave trade, Menelik II was one of the most prolific slavers in Ethiopia, leading Harold Marcus to dub him "Ethiopia's greatest slave entrepreneur." Marcus, *Life and Times of Menelik II*, 73.

99. John X. Merriman, Cape Town, minute 1/206, H.C. 200, 4 June 1909, WCARS, GH 35/224, volume 320.

100. James Henderson, Lovedale, letter to Government House, 08 June 1909, WCARS, PMO 240, reference 100/09, part 6.

101. E. Schnoster to James Henderson, Cape Town, 5 July 1909, CL MS 8820.

102. Liban emerged early in the Lovedale records as a talented scholar and debater and a natural leader. A number of the Oromo followed him to Port Elizabeth when they left Lovedale (for example, eight gave their address as Butler Street where Bultum lived).

103. Built in 1900 by Blohm and Voss, Hamburg, for the Deutsche Ost-Afrika Linie, the *Kronprinz* commenced her Hamburg-round Africa voyages on 30 June 1900. In August 1914, on the outbreak of war, she was laid up at Lourenco Marques. On 23 February 1916 she was seized by Portuguese authorities and renamed *Quelimane*. Thereafter she was managed by Transportes Maritimos do Estado in Lisbon until 1927, when she was scrapped. Specifications: 5,645 gross tons, length 125.3m x beam 14.6m, one funnel, two masts, twin screw, speed 12½ knots, accommodation for 72-1st, 56-2nd, and 60-3rd class passengers. The Ships List, accessed 2 August 2017, http://www.theshipslist.com/ships/descriptions/ShipsK.shtml.

104. I am grateful to Eberhard Stoetzner, archivist of the Deutsche Ost-Afrika Linie in Hamburg, for this information. Eberhard Stoetzner, personal e-mail to author, 6 November 2008.

105. "Shipping," *Beira Post*, 21 July 1909, 2.

106. John X. Merriman, minute, WCARS, PMO 240, 100/09, Confidential no. 2, 20 October 1909.

107. On 6 December 1906, Sir John Harrington, British agent at Menelik's Court and British consul general (later minister plenipotentiary) in Abyssinia, left the British legation in the charge of Lord Herbert Hervey. He did not return until January 1908, only to leave the country permanently eight months later on 30 September 1908, leaving Hervey to step into his shoes. Rosenfeld, *Chronology of Menelik II of Ethiopia*, 227.

108. Herbert Hervey, British Legation, Addis Ababa, to Sir Edward Grey, Foreign Office, 18 August 1909, WCARS, PMO 240; reference 100/09.

109. Ibid.

110. Ibid.

111. Ibid.

112. Liban himself soon found good employment assisting missionary and lexicologist Edwin C. Foot, who collected and compiled an early Afaan Oromoo–English/English–Afaan Oromoo dictionary. *A Galla-English, English-Galla Dictionary*, compiled by Edwin C. Foot, assisted by Liban Bultum (Cambridge: Cambridge University Press, 1913). The Gress Press, Farnborough, published a facsimile edition of this dictionary in1968. A digitized version is now downloadable from Oromo Studies Collection, http://gadaa.com/OromoStudies/restored-1913-afan-oromo-english-english-afan-oromo-dictionary/.

113. "Lovedale News," *Christian Express*, 1 October 1910, 171.

114. Wayessa Tonki, who had initially worked as an assistant to Mr. J. Knibbs, a photographer in King William's Town earning thirty shillings a month plus board, left for

Kimberley to branch out on his own. During the Anglo-Boer War, he was in charge of a body of special police, holding the rank of sergeant. "The Gallas: Statement Shewing Address Occupation etc., on 10th of March 1900," CL MS 17, 125, 5–6; "The Gallas," *Christian Express*, 1 June 1900, 95.

115. When the city of Port Elizabeth was settled by the British in 1820, the white population clustered round the little town, while the black population lived on the adjacent hill. This area became known as Stranger's Location (now Richmond Park).

116. Sarah Stein, *Plumes: Ostrich Feathers, Jews, and a Lost World of Global Commerce* (New Haven, CT: Yale University Press, 2008); Arthur Douglass, *Ostrich Farming in South Africa* (London: Cassell, Petter, Galpin, 1881), 67–93; Julius de Mosenthal and James E. Harting, *Ostriches and Ostrich Farming* (London: Trübner, 1877), 187–239; "Game Tourism: Oudtshoorn's Ostriches Charm Tourists," *Farmers' Weekly*, 13 October 2006, http://www.farmersweekly.co.za/bottomline/game-tourism-oudtshoorns-ostriches-charm-tourists/.

117. South Africa's dried, cured meat, similar to American "jerky."

118. "The Gallas: Statement Shewing Address Occupation etc., on 10th of March 1900," CL MS 17,125.

Part V. Reflections

1. Ruth Scodel, "The Captive's Dilemma: Sexual Acquiescence in Euripides Hecuba and Troades," *Harvard Studies in Classical Philology* 98 (1998): 140.

2. Claudia Card, "Women, Evil and Grey Zones," *Metaphilosophy* 31, no. 5 (October 2000): 509–28.

3. Barbara A. Huddleston-Mattai and P. Rudy Mattai, "The Sambo Mentality and the Stockholm Syndrome Revisited: Another Dimension to an Examination of the Plight of the African-American," *Journal of Black Studies* 23, no. 3 (March 1993): 344–57.

4. "The Church's Abyssinian Family," *Free Church of Scotland Monthly*, 1 December 1888, 365–66.

5. Sandra Rowoldt Shell, "Trauma and Slavery: Gilo and the Soft, Subtle Shackles of Lovedale," *Bulletin of the National Library of South Africa* 71, no. 2 (December 2017): 163.

6. The French satire *Candide; ou l'Optimisme*, by Voltaire, was first published in 1759.

7. Today, Yambo territory is situated in the administrative region of Illubabor in modern Oromia. The country of the Gurage is now an administrative zone in the Southern Nations, Nationalities, and People's Region (SNNPR), which borders on modern Oromia.

8. David Eltis, "Mortality and Voyage Length in the Middle Passage: New Evidence from the Nineteenth Century," *Journal of Economic History* 44, no. 2 (June 1984): 303.

Appendix A. The Variables and Authentication of the Data

1. Categorical variables describe nonnumerical attributes. Robert Carl Heinz Shell, and Sandra Rowoldt Shell, *The Island of Research: A Practical Guide and E-Toolkit For the Information Age*, vol. 1, *Data and Graphics* (Cape Town: NagsPro Multimedia, 2011), 34.

2. Ratio variables are numerical variables distinguished by their zero intercept. Ibid., 40.

3. Robert W. Fogel and Stanley L. Engerman, *Time on the Cross: The Economics of American Negro Slavery* (Boston: Little, Brown, 1974), 131–32.

4. Charles T. Beke, "Abyssinia: Being a Continuation of Routes in That Country," *Journal of the Royal Geographical Society of London* 14 (1844): 20.

5. W. J. B. Moir, in Matthew Lochhead, "The Gallas and Their Country," 1890, CL, PR 1468.

6. Bayan Liliso, Letter to [Mrs. Mina Stewart], Lovedale, 3 September 1894, UCT-M&A, BC106, C254, 3–4.

7. Matthew Lochhead, "Galla Reports: Boys . . . Our Galla service on Sabbath Morning Has Not Been without Results," *Christian Express*, 1 January 1891, 8.

8. John Fairley Daly, "A Mid-Night Visit to Shaikh Othman," *Free Church of Scotland Monthly*, 1 May 1889, 134.

9. Ibid.

10. "Kentiba Gebru (Gobaw) Desta," in *Dictionary of African Christian Biography*, http://www.dacb.org/stories/ethiopia/gebru_desta.html.

11. Edward A. Alpers and Matthew S. Hopper examine the linguistic and other challenges of interpretation and representation in their article on the narratives of freed slaves of the Western Indian Ocean area recorded in British Admiralty, consular, and court records. Alpers and Hopper, "Parler en son nom? Comprendre les témoignages d'esclaves africains originaires de l'océan Indien (1850–1930)," *Annales* 63, no. 4 (2008): 799–828. Despite the caveats they raise in this study, the authors contend that they remain the most significant sources for the articulation of authentic African voices in our understanding of the Indian Ocean slave trade.

12. Mekuria Bulcha, "The Red Sea Slave Trade: Captives' Treatment in the Slave Markets of North-East Africa and the Islamic Societies of the Middle East," in *Reflections on Arab-Led Slavery of Africans*, ed. Kwesi Kwaa Prah (Cape Town: Centre for Advanced Studies of African Society, 2005), 116.

13. Beke, "Abyssinia," 21.

14. Bulcha, "Red Sea Slave Trade," 117.

15. Ibid., 115–16.

16. BPP, Correspondence Relative to the Slave Trade, 1888–1889, C.5821, 1889, 34–35.

17. Patrick Manning, *Slavery and African Life: Occidental, Oriental, and African Slave Trades* (Cambridge: Cambridge University Press, 1990), 52.

18. BPP Reports on Slave Trade on the East Coast of Africa, 1887–1888, *Africa*, no. 7 (1888), C.5578, 1888, 81–82.

19. Ibid., 82.

20. "Weight," in *SPSS 6.1 Syntax Reference Guide* (Chicago: SPSS, 1994), 819.

21. Particularly useful online tools include the Fuzzy Gazetteer, which was developed by Christian Kohlschütter for the Interoperable Services for Data Products (ISODP) Project and claims that it searches 7,205,433 place-names worldwide. Fuzzy Gazetteer, accessed 4 May 2013, http://isodp.hof-university.de/fuzzyg/query/. Its particular advantage lies in suggesting close name matches based mostly on toponymical whims and changes, linguistic swings, and translations. Thus the Fuzzy Gazetteer leads the researcher from Urbaragga (in the text) to Urbarag or Urbaragh (identical coordinates). One of the most authoritative and useful websites is GeoNames, an online resource containing over 10 million geographical names (7.5 million unique features of 2.8 million populated places and 5.5 million alternate names). Developed by Marc Wick, a self-employed software engineer, GeoNames lists a host of sources for its information, the most significant and

authoritative being the National Geospatial-Intelligence Agency (NGA) and the United States Board on Geographic Names, the US Geological Survey Geographic Names Information and the Ordnance Survey OpenData gazetteer. GeoNames, accessed 4 May 2013, http://www.geonames.org/search.html?q= Genjo&country=ET. The Ethiopian pages of City Population are useful for regions and larger cities and towns. This international website, conceived and managed by Professor Thomas Brinkhoff of the Institut für Angewandte Photogrammetrie und Geoinformatik (IAPG) in Oldenburg, Germany, provides population statistics for all countries and major agglomerations of the world, with interactive maps and diagrams. Brinkhoff names his major source as *The International Atlas* (Chicago: Rand McNally, 1977). City Population, accessed 4 May 2013, http://www.citypopulation.de/Ethiopia.html.

22. For example, the observations of traveler Charles T. Beke, in "Abyssinia," 21; Bulcha, "Red Sea Slave Trade," 110–17; Mordechai Abir, *Ethiopia: The Era of the Princes: The Challenge of Islam and the Re-Unification of the Christian Empire, 1769–1855* (London: Longmans, 1968), 56–59.

23. See letters to Mrs. Stewart by Gamaches Garba, Lovedale, 20 October 1892; Fayissa Hora, Lovedale, 20 October 1892; and Bayan Liliso, Lovedale, 3 September 1894. UCT-M&A, BC106, C254.

24. Bulcha, "Red Sea Slave Trade," 116.

25. Beke, "Abyssinia," 21.

26. Bulcha, "Red Sea Slave Trade," 117.

27. Ibid., 115–16.

28. BPP, Reports on Slave Trade on the East Coast of Africa, 1887–1888, *Africa*, no. 7 (1888), C.5578, 1888, 82.

Appendix D. "My Essay Is upon Gallaland," by Gutama Tarafo

1. This essay was not signed but, from internal evidence, was almost certainly written by Gutama Tarafo and delivered to the Lovedale Literary Society after 15 October 1897. BC 106, James Stewart Collection, C254.16, UCTM&A.

2. Possibly a paper delivered by George Tyamzashe on 15 October 1897 to the Lovedale Literary Society. See Lovedale Institution, Annual report, Lovedale Literary Society syllabus, 2nd session, 1897.

Appendix E. Repatriation Questionnaire, 1903

1. Repatriation questionnaires, CL, MS 8781–MS 8821.

SELECTED BIBLIOGRAPHY

Archival Sources

South Africa

Cory Library for Humanities Research, Rhodes University, Grahamstown
   Lovedale Collection
   Presbytery of Kaffraria archival records
   Photographs
PIC/A 1319–PIC/A 1320: Two albums including photographs of the Galla [Oromo] slaves
PIC/M 1093: Photograph of Gallas [Oromo] rescued from slavery
Western Cape Provincial Archives and Records Service
GH archival series
MOOC archival series
PMO archival series
University of Cape Town, Manuscripts and Archives
James Stewart Papers, BC 106
Monica and Godfrey Wilson Papers, BC 880

British Library

British Library, India Office Records and Private Papers, Records of the British Administrations in Aden, 1837–1967
National Archives, Kew
Records of the Admiralty, Naval Forces, Royal Marines, Coastguard, and related bodies. ADM 53/14847, Ships' Logs. *Osprey*, 19 July 1887–08 October 1888
National Library of Scotland
Archive of the Church of Scotland Foreign Mission Committee. Ms. 7548, Mss.7530–8022, Mss. 8942–89
Photographs of Keith-Falconer Mission, Sheikh Othman, Yemen. Acc.10023/417 (packet 3); BSC 21.12.38

Published Official Records (Non–South African)
United Kingdom
Act for the Abolition of the Slave Trade, 1807
Parliament. Correspondence Relative to the Slave Trade: 1888–1889. C.5821, 1889
Parliament. Reports on Slave Trade on the East Coast of Africa, 1887–1888. *Africa, no. 7 (1888)*. C.5578, 1888, 81–82
Parliament. Reports from H.M. Diplomatic and Consular Officers Abroad on Trade and Finance. C.5252, 1888
Parliament. Correspondence with British Representatives and Agents Abroad, and Reports from Naval Offices and the Treasury Relative to the Slave Trade: 1883–1884. C.3849, Slave Trade, no. 1 (1884)
Newspapers and Periodicals
Beira Post
Christian Express
Daily Maverick
Free Church of Scotland Monthly
Graham's Town Journal
Lovedale Institution Annual Report, 1888–1920
South African Outlook
The Times (London)

Other Sources

Abir, Mordechai. *Ethiopia and the Red Sea: The Rise and Decline of the Solomonic Dynasty and Muslim-European Rivalry in the Region.* London: Frank Cass, 1980.
———. *Ethiopia: The Era of the Princes; The Challenge of Islam and the Re-Unification of the Christian Empire, 1769–1855.* London: Longmans, 1968.
Abraham, G. "Impact of Christianity on Varlis in Gujarat." PhD thesis, Manonmaniam Sundaranar University, 2008.
Ahmad, Abdussamad H. "Ethiopian Slave Exports at Matamma, Massawa and Tajura, c. 1830 to 1885." *Slavery and Abolition* 9, no. 3 (1988): 93–102.
———. "Trading in Slaves in Bela-Shangul and Gumuz, Ethiopia: Border Enclaves in History, 1897–1938." *Journal of African History* 40, no. 3 (1999): 433–46.
Ahmed, Hussein. *Islam in Nineteenth-Century Wallo, Ethiopia: Revival, Reform, and Reaction.* Leiden: Brill, 2001.
Alford, Terry. *Prince among Slaves.* Oxford: Oxford University Press, 2007.
Allen, Richard B. "Children and European Slave Trading in the Indian Ocean during the Eighteenth and Early Nineteenth Centuries." In Campbell, Miers, and Miller, *Children in Slavery through the Ages*, 34–54.
Alpers, Edward A. *Ivory and Slaves in East Central Africa: Changing Pattern of International Trade in East Central Africa to the Later Nineteenth Century.* London: Heinemann, 1975.
———. "The Other Middle Passage: The African Slave Trade in the Indian Ocean." In Christopher, Pybus, and Rediker, *Many Middle Passages*, 20–38.

———. "Representations of Children in the East African Slave Trade." *Slavery and Abolition* 30, no. 1 (2009): 27–40.

———. "The Story of Swema: Female Vulnerability in Nineteenth-Century East Africa." In Robertson and Klein, *Women and Slavery in Africa*, 185–200.

Alpers, Edward A., and Matthew S. Hopper. "Parler en son nom? Comprendre les *témoignages* d'esclaves africains originaires de l'océan Indien (1850–1930)." *Annales* 63, no. 4 (2008): 799–828.

Amathole Museum. "The Xiniwe Family and the Temperance Hotel." http://www.museum.za.net/index.php/imvubu-newsletter/106-the-xiniwe-family-and-the-temperance-hotel.

Andersen, Nils Møller, and Lanna Cheng. "The Marine Insect *Halobates* (Heteroptera: Gerridae): Biology, Adaptations, Distribution, and Phylogeny." *Oceanography and Marine Biology* 42 (2004): 119–80.

Araujo, Ana Lucia, Mariana P. Candido, and Paul E. Lovejoy, eds. *Crossing Memories: Slavery and African Diaspora*. Trenton, NJ: Africa World Press, 2011.

Athill, Lawrence. "Extracts from a Paper Read by . . . at a Meeting of the Royal Geographical Society [1920]." In Henry Darley, *Slaves and Ivory: A Record of Adventure and Exploration among the Abyssinian Slave-Raiders*, 191–209. London: Witherby, 1926, repr. 1935.

Ayalew, Kassaye. "Beekeeping Extension in Ethiopia." Unpublished manuscript, Holeta Bee Research Center, 1978. Cited in Yirga and Ftwi, "Beekeeping for Rural Development," 201–4.

Baker, Samuel W. *The Nile Tributaries of Abyssinia, and the Sword Hunters of the Hamran Arabs*. London: Macmillan, 1867.

Bates, Darrell. *The Abyssinian Difficulty: The Emperor Theodorus and the Magdala Campaign, 1867–68*. Oxford: Oxford University Press, 1979.

Baxter, P. T. W., Jan Hultin, and Alessandro Triulzi, eds. *Being and Becoming Oromo: Historical and Anthropological Enquiries*. Uppsala: Nordiska Afrikainstitutet, 1996.

Beachey, Raymond W. *A Collection of Documents on the Slave Trade of Eastern Africa*. Edited by Raymond W. Beachey. London: Collings, 1976.

———. *The Slave Trade of Eastern Africa*. London: Collings, 1976.

Beke, Charles T. "Abyssinia: Being a Continuation of Routes in That Country." *Journal of the Royal Geographical Society of London* 14 (1844): 1–76.

Bellagamba, Alice, Sandra E. Greene, and Martin A. Klein, eds. *African Voices on Slavery and the Slave Trade*. Vol. 1, *The Sources*. Cambridge: Cambridge University Press, 2013.

———, eds. *African Voices on Slavery and the Slave Trade*. Vol. 2, *Essays on Sources and Methods*. Cambridge: Cambridge University Press, 2016.

———, eds. *The Bitter Legacy: African Slavery Past and Present*. Princeton, NJ: Markus Wiener, 2014.

Bloomfield, Leonard. *Language*. London: Allen and Unwin, 1935.

Bohannan, Paul. "The Impact of Money on an African Subsistence Economy." *Journal of Economic History* 19, no. 4 (December 1959): 491–503.

Brock, Sheila M. "James Stewart and Lovedale: A Reappraisal of Missionary Attitudes and African Response in the Eastern Cape, 1870–1905." PhD thesis, University of Edinburgh, 1974.

Budge, Ernest A. Wallis. *By Nile and Tigris: A Narrative of Journeys in Egypt and Mesopotamia on Behalf of the British Museum between the Years 1886 and 1913*. Vol. 2. London: John Murray, 1920.

———. *A History of Ethiopia*. Vol. 1, *Nubia and Abyssinia*. London: Methuen, 1928.

Bulatovich, Alexander. *Ethiopia through Russian Eyes: An Eye-witness Account of the End of an Era, 1896–1898; Consisting of Two Books: From Entotto to the River Baro* (1897) and *With the Armies of Menelik II* (1900), translated by Richard Seltzer. http://www.samizdat.com/entotto.html.

Bulcha, Mekuria. *Contours of the Emergent and Ancient Oromo Nation: Dilemmas in the Ethiopian Politics of State and Nation-Building*. Cape Town: Centre for Advanced Studies of African Society, 2011.

———. *Flight and Integration: Causes of Mass Exodus from Ethiopia and Problems of Integration in the Sudan*. Uppsala: Scandinavian Institute of African Studies, 1988.

———. "Historical, Political and Social Causes of Mass Flight from Ethiopia." In *Refugees and Development in Africa*, edited by Peter Nobel, 19–36. Uppsala: Scandinavian Institute of African Studies, 1987.

———. *The Making of the Oromo Diaspora: A Historical Sociology of Forced Migration*. Minneapolis: Kirk House, 2002.

———. "The Red Sea Slave Trade: Captives' Treatment in the Slave Markets of North-East Africa and the Islamic Societies of the Middle East." In Prah, *Reflections on Arab-Led Slavery of Africans*, 107–31.

Burton, Richard F. *First Footsteps in East Africa; or, An Exploration of Harar*. London: Longman, Brown, Green, and Longmans, 1856.

Camfield, Laura. "Outcomes of Orphanhood in Ethiopia: A Mixed Methods Study." *Social Indicators Research* 104, no. 1 (October 2011): 87–102.

Campbell, Gwyn. "The State and Pre-Colonial Demographic History: The Case of Nineteenth-Century Madagascar." *Journal of African History* 32, no. 3 (1991): 415–45.

Campbell, Gwyn, Suzanne Miers, and Joseph C. Miller, eds. *Children in Slavery through the Ages*. Athens: Ohio University Press, 2009.

Card, Claudia. "Women, Evil and Grey Zones." *Metaphilosophy* 31, no. 5 (October 2000): 509–28.

Carton, Benedict. "The Forgotten Compass of Death: Apocalypse Then and Now in the Social History of South Africa." *Journal of Social History* 37, no. 1 (Fall 2003): 199–218.

Caulk, Richard A. *"Between the Jaws of Hyenas": A Diplomatic History of Ethiopia (1876–1896)*. Edited by Bahru Zewde. Wiesbaden: Harrassowitz, 2002.

———. "Firearms and Princely Power in Ethiopia in the Nineteenth Century." *Journal of African History* 13, no. 4 (October 1972): 609–30.

Christopher, Emma, Cassandra Pybus, and Marcus Rediker, eds. *Many Middle Passages: Forced Migration and the Making of the Modern World*. Berkeley: University of California Press, 2007.

Clarence-Smith, William Gervase, ed. *The Economics of the Indian Ocean Slave Trade in the Nineteenth Century*. Totowa, NJ: Frank Cass, 1989.

Colomb, Philip H. *Slave-Catching in the Indian Ocean: A Record of Naval Experiences*. London: Dawsons, 1873; repr. 1968.

Columbia University Press. *Columbia Lippincott Gazetteer of the World*. Edited by Leon E. Seltzer. New York: Columbia University Press, 1952; repr. 1962.

Comaroff, Jean, and John L. Comaroff. *Of Revelation and Revolution*. Vol. 1, *Christianity, Colonialism, and Consciousness in South Africa*. Chicago: University of Chicago Press, 1991.

Cooper, Frederick. *Plantation Slavery on the East Coast of Africa*. New Haven, CT: Yale University Press, 1977.

Crummey, Donald. "Explaining Famines in Ethiopian History: The Case of the Kefu Qan, 1888–1981." Paper presented at Interdisciplinary Seminar, Center for African Studies, University of Illinois at Urbana-Champaign, 2002.

———. "Society, State and Nationality in the Recent Historiography of Ethiopia." *Journal of African History* 31, no. 1 (1990): 103–19.

Curtin, Philip D. *The Atlantic Slave Trade: A Census*. Madison: University of Wisconsin Press, 1969.

———. *Economic Change in Precolonial Africa: Senegambia in the Era of the Slave Trade*. Madison: University of Wisconsin Press, 1975.

Cutler, H. G., and L. W. Yaggy. *Panorama of Nations; or, Journeys among the Families of Men: A Description of Their Homes, Customs, Habits, Employments and Beliefs; Their Cities, Temples, Monuments, Literature and Fine Arts*. Chicago: Star Publishing, 1892.

Dalzel, Archibald. *The History of Dahomy, an Inland Kingdom of Africa*. London: Spilsbury and Son, 1793.

Davis, Mike. *Late Victorian Holocausts: El Niño Famines and the Making of the Third World*. London: Verso, 2001.

Debelo, Asebe Regassa. "Contesting Views on a Protected Area Conservation and Development in Ethiopia." *Social Science* 1, no. 1 (2012): 24–46.

De Kock, Leon. *Civilising Barbarians: Missionary Narrative and African Textual Response in Nineteenth-Century South Africa*. Johannesburg: Witwatersrand University Press, 1996.

DHS Program. "Ethiopia Demographic and Health Survey of 2005." https://www.dhsprogram.com/pubs/pdf/FR179/FR179%5B23June2011%5D.pdf.

Dictionary of African Christian Biography. Center for Global Christianity and Mission at Boston University School of Theology. http://www.dacb.org/stories/ethiopia/gebru_desta.html.

Dictionary of South African Biography. Edited by W. J. de Kock and Daniel Wilhelmus Krüger. Pretoria: Nasionale Boekhandel for the National Council for Social Research, Dept. of Higher Education, 1968.

Dixon-Smith, Rosemary. "A Visit to the Circus." 2 May 2005. http://www.fad.co.za/Resources/contribs/rose/circus.asp.

DOAL. *Deutsche Ost-Afrika-Linie, Hamburg: Handbook*. Hamburg: DOAL, 1911.

Dollie, Na-iem, Salim Vally, Crain Soudien et al. "Tribute to Neville Alexander (22 October 1936–27 August 2012)." South African History Online. http://www.sahistory.org.za/archive/tribute-neville-alexander.

Donham, Donald, and Wendy James, eds. *The Southern Marches of Imperial Ethiopia: Essays in History and Social Anthropology*. New York: Cambridge University Press, 1986.

Douglass, Arthur. *Ostrich Farming in South Africa*. London: Cassell, Petter, Galpin, 1881.

Doulton, Lindsay. "The Royal Navy's Anti-Slavery Campaign in the Western Indian Ocean, c. 1860–1890: Race, Empire and Identity." PhD thesis, University of Hull, 2010.

Duressa, Ayalew. "*Guddifachaa*: Adoption Practice in Oromo Society with Particular Reference to the Borana Oromo." Master's thesis, Addis Ababa University, 2002.

Edwards, Jon R. "Slavery, the Slave Trade and the Economic Reorganization of Ethiopia, 1916–1935." *African Economic History*, no. 11 (1982): 3–14.

Eltis, David. "Mortality and Voyage Length in the Middle Passage: New Evidence from the Nineteenth Century." *Journal of Economic History* 44, no. 2 (June 1984): 301–8.

Equiano, Olaudah. *Equiano's Travels: The Interesting Narrative of the Life of Olaudah Equiano or Gustavus Vassa the African*. Edited by Paul G. Edwards. Oxford: Heinemann, 1996.

———. *The Interesting Narrative and Other Writings*. Edited by Vincent Carretta. New York: Penguin Books, 1995.

Erlank, Natasha. "Sexual Misconduct and Church Power on Scottish Mission Stations in Xhosaland, South Africa, in the 1840s." *Gender and History* 15, no. 1 (April 2003): 69–84.

Etherington, Norman, ed. *Missions and Empire*. Oxford: Oxford University Press, 2005.

———. "Mission Station Melting Pots as a Factor in the Rise of South African Black Nationalism." *International Journal of African Historical Studies* 9, no. 4 (1976): 592–605.

———. *Preachers, Peasants, and Politics in Southeast Africa, 1835–1880: African Christian Communities in Natal, Pondoland, and Zululand*. London: Royal Historical Society, 1978.

———. "The Rise of the Kholwa in Southeast Africa: African Christian Communities in Natal, Pondoland and Zululand, 1835–1880." PhD thesis, Yale University, 1971.

Fernyhough, Timothy D. "Serfs, Slaves and 'Shefta': Modes of Production in Southern Ethiopia from the Late Nineteenth Century to 1941." PhD thesis, University of Illinois at Urbana-Champaign, 1986.

———. *Serfs, Slaves, and Shifta: Modes of Production and Resistance in Pre-Revolutionary Ethiopia.* Addis Ababa: Shama Books, 2010.

———. "Slavery and the Slave Trade in Southern Ethiopia in the 19th Century." *Slavery and Abolition* 9, no. 3 (1988): 103–30.

———. "Slavery and the Slave Trade in Southern Ethiopia in the 19th Century." In Clarence-Smith, *Economics of the Indian Ocean Slave Trade in the Nineteenth Century,* 103–130.

Flint, John E. "Frederick Lugard: The Making of an Autocrat (1858–1943)." In *African Proconsuls: European Governors in Africa,* edited by Lewis H. Gann and Peter Duignan, 290–312. New York: Free Press, 1978. http://www.webafriqa.net/library/african_proconsuls/lugard_autocrat.html.

Fogel, Robert W., and Stanley L. Engerman. *Time on the Cross: Evidence and Methods; a Supplement.* Boston, MA: Little, Brown, 1974.

———. *Time on the Cross: The Economics of American Negro Slavery.* Boston, MA: Little, Brown, 1974.

Friedrichsmeyer, Sara, Sara Lennox, and Susanne Zantop, eds. *The Imperialist Imagination: German Colonialism and Its Legacy.* Ann Arbor: University of Michigan Press, 1999.

Gaitskell, Deborah. "Race, Gender and Imperialism: A Century of Black Girls' Education in South Africa." Working paper presented to the African Studies Institute, University of the Witwatersrand, August 1988. http://wiredspace.wits.ac.za/handle/10539/8726.

A Galla-English, English-Galla Dictionary. Compiled by Edwin C. Foot, assisted by Liban Bultum. Cambridge: Cambridge University Press, 1913. Now accessible electronically via Oromo Studies Collection. http://gadaa.com/OromoStudies/restored-1913-afan-oromo-english-english-afan-oromo-dictionary/.

Gashaw, Solomon. "Nationalism and Ethnic Conflict in Ethiopia." In Young, *Rising Tide of Cultural Pluralism,* 138–57.

Geggus, David. "Sex Ratio, Age and Ethnicity in the Atlantic Slave Trade: Data from French Shipping and Plantation Records." *Journal of African History* 30, no. 1 (March 1989): 23–44.

Gellately, Robert, and Ben Kiernan, eds. *The Specter of Genocide: Mass Murder in Historical Perspective.* Cambridge: Cambridge University Press, 2003.

Gemeda, Guluma. "Conquest and Resistance in the Gibe Region, 1881–1900." *Journal of Oromo Studies* 3, nos. 1–2 (Winter–Summer 1996): 53–61.

Gilfoyle, Daniel. "Veterinary Research and the African Rinderpest Epizootic: The Cape Colony, 1896–1898." *Journal of Southern African Studies* 29, no. 1 (2003): 133–54.

Giyorgis, Asma, and Bairu Tafla. *Asma Giyorgis and His Work: History of the Galla and the Kingdom of Sawa.* Edited by Bairu Tafla. Stuttgart: Franz Steiner, 1987.

Gnamo, Abbas Haji. "Islam, the Orthodox Church and Oromo Nationalism (Ethiopia)." *Cahiers d'études africaines* 165, no. 1 (2002): 99–120. http://etudesafricaines.revues.org/137.

Gobat, Samuel. *Journal of Three Years' Residence in Abyssinia: In Furtherance of the Objects of the Church Missionary Society.* London: Hatchard and Son, 1834.

Goody, Jack. *Technology, Tradition, and the State in Africa.* Oxford: Oxford University Press, 1971.

Grace, John. *Domestic Slavery in West Africa, with Particular Reference to the Sierra Leone Protectorate, 1896–1927.* New York: Barnes and Noble, 1975.

Grant, Christopher. "Stones, Slabs, and Stelae: The Origins and Symbolism of Contemporary Oromo Burial Practice and Grave Art." Independent Study Project (ISP) Collection. Paper 263, 2006. http://digitalcollections.sit.edu/isp_collection /263.

Haight, Bruce M. "Bole and Gonja: Contributions to the History of Northern Ghana." PhD thesis, Northwestern University, 1981.

Hameso, Seyoum Y., and Mohammed Hassen, eds. *Arrested Development in Ethiopia: Essays on Underdevelopment, Democracy, and Self-Determination.* Trenton, NJ: Red Sea Press, 2006.

Harries, Patrick. "Culture and Classification: A History of the Mozbieker Community at the Cape." *Social Dynamics* 26, no. 2 (2000): 29–54.

Harris, W. Cornwallis. *The Highlands of Ethiopia.* Vol. 3. Farnborough: Gregg, 1968; reprint of 1st ed., London: Longman, Brown, Green and Longmans, 1844.

Hassen, Mohammed. *The Oromo of Ethiopia: A History, 1570–1860.* Cambridge: Cambridge University Press, 1990.

Henige, David. "Measuring the Immeasurable: The Atlantic Slave Trade, West African Population and the Pyrrhonian Critic." *Journal of African History* 27, no. 2 (July 1986): 295–313.

Historical Dictionary of European Imperialism. Edited by James S. Olson. New York: Greenwood Press, 1991.

Huddleston-Mattai, Barbara A., and P. Rudy Mattai. "The Sambo Mentality and the Stockholm Syndrome Revisited: Another Dimension to an Examination of the Plight of the African-American." *Journal of Black Studies* 23, no. 3 (March 1993): 344–57.

International Household Survey Network. "Ethiopia—Population and Housing Census, 2007." http://catalog.ihsn.org/index.php/catalog/3583.

Isenberg, Charles William, and Johann Ludwig Krapf. *Journals of the Rev. Messrs. Isenberg and Krapf, Missionaries of the Church Missionary Society: Detailing Their Proceedings in the Kingdom of Shoa, and Journeys in Other Parts of Abyssinia, in the Years 1839, 1840, 1841, and 1842.* London: Seeley, Burnside, and Seeley, 1843.

Jackson, R. T. "Periodic Markets in Southern Ethiopia." *Transactions of the Institute of British Geographers* 53 (July 1971): 31–42.

Jaenen, Cornelius J. "The Galla or Oromo of East Africa." *Southwestern Journal of Anthropology* 12, no. 2 (Summer 1956): 171–90.

Jalata, Asafa. *Contending Nationalisms of Oromia and Ethiopia: Struggling for Statehood, Sovereignty, and Multinational Democracy.* Binghamton, NY: Global Academic, 2010.

———. *Fighting against the Injustice of the State and Globalization: Comparing the African American and Oromo Movements*. Basingstoke: Palgrave Macmillan, 2012.

———. *Oromia and Ethiopia: State Formation and Ethnonational Conflict, 1868–1992*. Boulder, CO: Rienner, 1993.

———. *Oromia and Ethiopia: State Formation and Ethnonational Conflict, 1868–2004*. Trenton, NJ: Red Sea Press, 2005.

———, ed. *Oromo Nationalism and the Ethiopian Discourse: The Search for Freedom and Democracy*. Lawrenceville, NJ: Red Sea Press, 1998.

Johnson, Walter. "Time and Revolution in African America: Temporality and the History of Atlantic Slavery." In *A New Imperial History: Culture, Identity, and Modernity in Britain and the Empire, 1660–1840*, edited by Kathleen Wilson, 197–215. Cambridge: Cambridge University Press, 2004.

Kaplan, Steven. "Themes and Methods in the Study of Conversion in Ethiopia: A Review Essay." *Journal of Religion in Africa* 34, no. 3 (August 2004): 373–92.

Keats-Rohan, Katharine S. B. "Prosopography and Computing: A Marriage Made in Heaven?" *History and Computing* 12, no. 1 (2000): 1–11.

Kedir, Abbi, and Lul Admasachew. "Violence against Women in Ethiopia." *Gender, Place and Culture* 17, no. 4 (2010): 437–52.

Keegan, Tim. *Dr. Philip's Empire: One Man's Struggle for Justice in Nineteenth-Century South Africa*. Cape Town: Zebra Press, 2016.

Kiefer, James E. "Biographical Sketches of Memorable Christians of the Past: Onesimus Nesib, Translator and Missionary." Accessed 4 August 2017. http://justus .anglican.org/resources/bio/190.html.

Klein, Martin A. "Studying the History of Those Who Would Rather Forget: Oral History and the Experience of Slavery." *History in Africa* 16 (1989): 209–17.

Krapf, Johann Ludwig. *Travels, Researches, and Missionary Labours, during Eighteen Years' Residence in Eastern Africa*. London: Trübner, 1860.

Kretzmann, Paul E. *John Ludwig Krapf: The Explorer-Missionary of Northeastern Africa*. Columbus, OH: Book Concern, 1900.

LaCapra, Dominick. *Writing History, Writing Trauma*. Baltimore, MD: Johns Hopkins University Press, 2001.

Law, Robin. *Ouidah: The Social History of a West African Slaving "Port," 1727–1892*. Athens: Ohio University Press, 2004.

Law, Robin, and Paul E. Lovejoy, eds. *The Biography of Mahommah Gardo Baquaqua: His Passage from Slavery to Freedom in Africa and America*. Princeton, NJ: Markus Wiener, 2001.

Legesse, Asmarom. *Oromo Democracy: An Indigenous African Political System*. Lawrenceville, NJ: Red Sea Press, 2000.

Lewis, Herbert S. "Ethnicity in Ethiopia: The View from Below (and from the South, East and West)." In Young, *Rising Tide of Cultural Pluralism*, 158–78.

———. "Jimma Abba Jifar: A Despotic Galla Kingdom." PhD diss., Columbia University, 1963.

———. *Jimma Abba Jifar, An Oromo Monarchy: Ethiopia, 1830–1932*. Lawrenceville, NJ: Red Sea Press, 2001.

Lewis, Ioan M. "Sufism in Somaliland: A Study in Tribal Islam." In *Islam in Tribal Societies: From the Atlas to the Indus*, edited by Akbar S. Ahmed and David M. Hart, 127–168. London: Routledge and Kegan Paul, 1983.

Littmann, Enno. *Publications of the Princeton Expedition to Abyssinia*. Leiden: Brill, 1913.

Lloyd, Christopher. *The Navy and the Slave Trade: The Suppression of the African Slave Trade in the Nineteenth Century*. London: Frank Cass, 1968.

Lochhead, Matthew. *Short Biographies of the Galla Rescued Slaves, Now at Lovedale: With an Account of Their Country and Their Capture*. Lovedale: Lovedale Press, 1891.

Louis-Lande, L. "Un voyageur français dans l'Ethiopie méridionale." *Revue des deux mondes* 30, no. 6 (1878): 877–903.

Lovedale Institution. *Arrangements for Classes and Subjects, and Other Information: First Session, 1896*. Lovedale: Lovedale Press, 1896.

———. *Results of Examinations and Work for Session Ending December 1893; . . . Ending June 1894; . . . Ending December 1894*. Lovedale: Lovedale Press, 1893–1894.

Lovejoy, Paul E. "Appendix—Chronology of Measures against Slavery." In Lovejoy, *Transformations in Slavery*, 285–92. doi: http://dx.doi.org/10.1017/CBO9781139014946.018.

———. "Autobiography and Memory: Gustavus Vassa, alias Olaudah Equiano, the African." *Slavery and Abolition* 27, no. 3 (2006): 317–47.

———. "Construction of Identity: Olaudah Equiano or Gustavus Vassa?" *Historically Speaking* 7, no. 3 (January–February 2006): 8–9.

———. "Olaudah Equiano or Gustavus Vassa—What's in a Name?" *Atlantic Studies* 9, no. 2 (2012): 165–84.

———. *Transformations in Slavery: A History of Slavery in Africa*. 3rd ed. Cambridge: Cambridge University Press, 2012.

Lyon, David, and Rif Winfield. *The Sail and Steam Navy List: All the Ships of the Royal Navy, 1815–1889*. London: Chatham, 2004.

Madan, Arthur C., ed. *Kiungani; or, Story and History from Central Africa, Written by Boys in the Schools of the Universities' Mission to Central Africa*. Translated by Arthur C. Madan. London: George Bell and Sons, 1887.

Majeke, Nosipho [Dora Taylor, pseud.]. *The Role of the Missionaries in Conquest*. Cape Town: Society of Young Africa, 1952.

Manning, Patrick. *Slavery and African Life: Occidental, Oriental, and African Slave Trades*. Cambridge: Cambridge University Press, 1990.

Marcus, Harold G. *A History of Ethiopia*. Berkeley: University of California Press, 1994.

———. *The Life and Times of Menelik II: Ethiopia, 1844–1913*. Lawrenceville, NJ: Red Sea Press, 1975.

Massaia, Guglielmo. *I miei trentacinque anni di missione nell'alta Etiopia; Memorie storiche*. Rome: Società tipografica Manuzio, 1925.

McCann, James C. *People of the Plow: An Agricultural History of Ethiopia, 1800–1990*. Madison: University of Wisconsin Press, 1995.

Mekonnen, Yohannes K., ed. *Ethiopia: The Land, Its People, History and Culture*. Dar es Salaam: New Africa Press, 2013.

Miers, Suzanne, and Igor Kopytoff, eds. *Slavery in Africa: Historical and Anthropological Perspectives*. Madison: University of Wisconsin Press, 1977.

Morton, Fred. "Small Change: Children in the Nineteenth-Century East African Slave Trade." In Campbell, Miers, and Miller, *Children in Slavery through the Ages*, 55–70.

Mosenthal, Julius de, and James E. Harting. *Ostriches and Ostrich Farming*. London: Trübner, 1877.

Mountnorris, George A. *Voyages and Travels to India, Ceylon, the Red Sea, Abyssinia, and Egypt, in the years 1802, 1803, 1804, 1805, and 1806*. London: Printed for W. Miller, 1809.

Musil, Emily Kirkland McTighe. "La Marianne Noire: How Gender and Race in the Twentieth Century Atlantic World Reshaped the Debate about Human Rights." PhD thesis, University of California, 2007.

Negeri, Dessalegn. "*Guddifachaa* Practice as Child Problem Intervention in Oromo Society: The Case of Ada'a Liban District." Master's thesis, Addis Ababa University, 2006.

Nelson's Textbook of Pediatrics. 20th ed. Vol. 1. Philadelphia, PA: Elsevier, 2016.

Nicholl, Charles. *Somebody Else: Arthur Rimbaud in Africa, 1880–91*. London: Jonathan Cape, 1997.

Nunn, Nathan, and Diego Puga. "Ruggedness: The Blessing of Bad Geography in Africa." *Review of Economics and Statistics* 94, no. 1 (February 2012): 20–36.

Olmstead, Alan L. "The First Line of Defense: Inventing the Infrastructure to Combat Animal Diseases." *Journal of Economic History* 69, no. 2 (June 2009): 327–57.

Osman, Ghada. "Foreign Slaves in Mecca and Medina in the Formative Islamic Period." *Islam and Christian-Muslim Relations* 16, no. 4 (October 2005): 345–59.

Pankhurst, Richard. *Economic History of Ethiopia, 1800–1935*. Addis Ababa: Haile Sellassie I University Press, 1968.

———. "Ethiopian Slave Reminiscences of the Nineteenth Century." *Transafrican Journal of History* 5, no. 1 (1976): 98–110.

———. "The Ethiopian Slave Trade in the Nineteenth and Early Twentieth Centuries: A Statistical Inquiry." *Journal of Semitic Studies* 9, no. 1 (March 1964): 220–28.

———. "The Great Ethiopian Famine of 1888–1892: A New Assessment, Part One." *Journal of the History of Medicine and Allied Sciences* 21, no. 2 (April 1966): 95–124.

———. "The Great Ethiopian Famine of 1888–1892: A New Assessment, Part Two." *Journal of the History of Medicine and Allied Sciences* 21, no. 3 (July 1966): 271–94.

———. "The Role of Fire-Arms in Ethiopian Culture (16th to 20th Centuries)." *Journal des africanistes* 47, no. 2 (1977): 131–44.

———. *A Social History of Ethiopia: The Northern and Central Highlands from Early Medieval Times to the Rise of Emperor Téwodros II*. Trenton, NJ: Red Sea Press, 1992.

Pankhurst, Richard, and Leila Ingrams. *Ethiopia Engraved: An Illustrated Catalogue of Engravings by Foreign Travellers from 1681 to 1900*. London: Kegan Paul, 1988.

Pastner, Stephen L. "Lords of the Desert Border: Frontier Feudalism in Southern Baluchistan and Eastern Ethiopia." *International Journal of Middle East Studies* 10, no. 1 (February 1979): 93–106.

Perham, Margery F., ed. *Ten Africans*. London: Faber, 1936.

Phoofolo, Pule. "Epidemics and Revolutions: The Rinderpest Epidemic in Late Nineteenth-Century Southern Africa." *Past and Present* 138 (February 1993): 112–43.

Prah, Kwesi Kwaa, ed. *Reflections on Arab-Led Slavery of Africans*. Cape Town: Centre for Advanced Studies of African Society, 2005.

Prosopography Research. Modern History Research Unit, University of Oxford. Accessed 18 April 2018. http://prosopography.modhist.ox.ac.uk/prosopdefinition. htm.

Prouty, Chris. *Empress Taytu and Menilek II: Ethiopia, 1883–1910*. London: Ravens Educational and Development Services, 1986.

Prouty, Chris, and Eugene Rosenfeld. *Historical Dictionary of Ethiopia and Eritrea*. 2nd ed. Metuchen, NJ: Scarecrow Press, 1994.

Ravenstein, E. G., and Thomas Wakefield. "Somal and Galla Land; Embodying Information Collected by the Rev. Thomas Wakefield." *Proceedings of the Royal Geographical Society and Monthly Record of Geography* 6, no. 5 (May 1884): 255–73.

Rawson, Rawson W. "European Territorial Claims on the Coasts of the Red Sea, and Its Southern Approaches, in 1885." *Proceedings of the Royal Geographical Society and Monthly Record of Geography*, n.s. 7, no. 2 (February 1885): 93–119.

Reclus, Elisée. *Nouvelle géographie universelle: La terre et les hommes*. Vol. 10. Paris: Hachette, 1885.

Rey, C. F. "A Recent Visit to Gudru and Gojjam." *Geographical Journal* 67, no. 6 (June 1926): 481–505.

Robertson, Claire C., and Martin A. Klein, eds. *Women and Slavery in Africa*. Madison: University of Wisconsin Press, 1983.

Rosenfeld, Chris Prouty. *A Chronology of Menelik II of Ethiopia, 1844–1913*. East Lansing, MI: African Studies Center, 1976.

Ruete, Emily. *Memoirs of an Arabian Princess from Zanzibar*. New York: Markus Wiener, 1989.

Salt, Henry. *A Voyage to Abyssinia, and Travels into the Interior of That Country, Executed under the Orders of the British Government, in the Years 1809 and 1810*. London: Frank Cass, 1967 (facsimile of 1st edition, London, 1814).

Saunders, Christopher C. "Between Slavery and Freedom: The Importation of Prize Negroes to the Cape in the Aftermath of Emancipation." *Kronos* 9 (1984): 36–43.

———. "'Free, Yet Slaves': Prize Negroes at the Cape Revisited." In *Breaking the Chains: Slavery and Its Legacy in the Nineteenth-Century Cape Colony*, edited by Nigel Worden and Clifton C. Crais, 99–115. Johannesburg: Witwatersrand University Press, 1994.

———. "Liberated Africans in Cape Colony in the First Half of the Nineteenth-Century." *International Journal of African Historical Studies* 18, no. 2 (1985): 223–39.

———. "Liberated Africans in the Western Cape: My Work and After." *Bulletin of the National Library of South Africa* 70, no. 1 (June 2016): 21–34.

Scodel, Ruth. "The Captive's Dilemma: Sexual Acquiescence in Euripides Hecuba and Troades." *Harvard Studies in Classical Philology* 98 (1998): 137–54.

Senait Fesseha. "The Rinderpest Factor in the Great Famine of Ethiopia." University of Massachusetts, Boston, Critical and Creative Thinking Program. http://www.faculty.umb.edu/pjt/640-02SF.doc.

Shell, Robert Carl-Heinz, and Sandra Rowoldt Shell. *The Island of Research: A Practical Guide and E-Toolkit for the Information Age.* Vol. 1, *Data and Graphics.* Cape Town: NagsPro Multimedia, 2011.

Shell, Sandra Rowoldt. "From Slavery to Freedom: The Oromo Slave Children of Lovedale, Prosopography and Profiles." PhD thesis, University of Cape Town, 2013.

———. "How an Ethiopian Slave Became a South African Teacher." BBC News: Africa. 25 August 2011. http://www.bbc.co.uk/news/world-africa-14357121.

———. "A Missionary Life among the amaXhosa: The Eastern Cape Journals of James Laing, 1830–1836." Master's thesis, University of Cape Town, 2006.

———. "Narratives of the Oromo Slaves at Lovedale." *Quarterly Bulletin of the National Library of South Africa* 55, no. 2 (December 2000): 67–80.

———. "Trauma and Slavery: Gilo and the Soft, Subtle Shackles of Lovedale." *Bulletin of the National Library of South Africa* 71, no. 2 (December 2017): 149–64.

Shepherd, Robert H. W. *Lovedale, South Africa: The Story of a Century, 1841–1941.* Lovedale: Lovedale Press, 1941.

Sheriff, Abdul. *Slaves, Spices and Ivory in Zanzibar: Integration of an East African Commercial Empire into the World Economy, 1770–1873.* Athens: Ohio University Press, 1987.

Shinn, David H., and Thomas P. Ofcansky. *Historical Dictionary of Ethiopia.* Lanham, MD: Scarecrow Press, 2004.

Simkins, Charles, and Elizabeth van Heyningen. "Fertility, Mortality, and Migration in the Cape Colony, 1891–1904." *International Journal of African Historical Studies* 22, no. 1 (1989): 79–111.

Sleigh, Dan, and Piet Westra. *Die aanslag op die slaweskip "Meermin," 1766.* Kaapstad: Africana Uitgewers, 2012.

Soga, Tiyo. *The Journal and Selected Writings of the Reverend Tiyo Soga.* Edited by Donovan Williams. Cape Town: Balkema for Rhodes University, 1985.

Sparks, Randy J. *The Two Princes of Calabar: An Eighteenth-Century Atlantic Odyssey.* Cambridge, MA: Harvard University Press, 2004.

Stein, Sarah. *Plumes: Ostrich Feathers, Jews, and a Lost World of Global Commerce.* New Haven, CT: Yale University Press, 2008.

Stone, Lawrence. *The Crisis of the Aristocracy, 1558–1641.* Oxford: Clarendon, 1966.

———. "Prosopography." *Daedalus* 100, no. 1 (Winter 1971): 46–79.

Taylor, Dora. *See* Majeke, Nosipho.

Ullendorff, Edward. *The Ethiopians: An Introduction to Country and People.* London: Oxford University Press, 1973.

———. "Some Amharic and Other Documents from the Eugen Mittwoch *Nachlass.*" *Bulletin of the School of Oriental and African Studies* 43, no. 3 (October 1980): 429–52.

UNICEF. Eastern and Southern Africa. "Orphans." Accessed 4 August 2017. http://www.unicef.org/esaro/5440_orphans.html.

Van Onselen, Charles. "Reactions to Rinderpest in Southern Africa, 1896–97." *Journal of African History* 13, no. 3 (1972): 473–88.

Vernal, Fiona. *The Farmerfield Mission: A Christian Community in South Africa, 1838–2008*. Oxford: Oxford University Press, 2013.

Villa-Vicencio, Charles. *The Spirit of Freedom: South African Leaders on Religion and Politics*. Berkeley: University of California Press, 1996.

Vogel, S. W., and H. Heyne. "Rinderpest in South Africa—100 Years Ago." *Journal of the South African Veterinary Association* 67, no. 4 (1996): 164–70.

Waldmeier, Theophilus. *The Autobiography of Theophilus Waldmeier, Missionary: Being an Account of Ten Years' Life in Abyssinia; and Sixteen Years in Syria*. London: S. W. Partridge, 1886.

Wallerstein, Immanuel M. *The Modern World-System: Capitalist Agriculture and the Origins of the European World-Economy in the Sixteenth Century*. New York: Academic Press, 1974.

Watson, Richard L. "'Prize Negroes' and the Development of Racial Attitudes in the Cape Colony." Paper presented at the Southeastern Regional Seminar in African Studies (SERSAS), 14–15 April 2000. http://www.ecu.edu/african/sersas/Watson400.htm.

———. *Slave Emancipation and Racial Attitudes in Nineteenth-Century South Africa*. Cambridge: Cambridge University Press, 2012.

———. *The Slave Question: Liberty and Property in South Africa*. Middletown, CT: Wesleyan University Press, 1990.

Weiss, Holger. "'Dying Cattle': Some Remarks on the Impact of Cattle Epizootics in the Central Sudan during the Nineteenth Century." *African Economic History* 26 (1998): 173–99.

Williams, Donovan. "African Nationalism in South Africa: Origins and Problems." *Journal of African History* 11, no. 3 (July 1970): 371–83.

———. *Umfundisi: A Biography of Tiyo Soga, 1829–1871*. Lovedale: Lovedale Press, 1978.

Wilson, George. "The Progress of Uganda." *Journal of the Royal African Society* 6, no. 22 (January 1907): 113–35.

Wolde-Georgis, Tsegay. "The Use of El Niño Information as Drought Early Warning in Ethiopia." *Internet Journal of African Studies* 2 (March 1997): paragraph 1. http://www.bradford.ac.uk/research-old/ijas/ijasno2/Georgis.html.

World Bank. "Population and Housing Census 2007 Report, Oromiya, Part I: Population Size and Characteristics." http://microdata.worldbank.org/index.php/catalog/2747.

Wright, Marcia. *Strategies of Slaves and Women: Life-Stories from East/Central Africa*. New York: L. Barber Press, 1993.

Yirga, Gidey, and Kibrom Ftwi. "Beekeeping for Rural Development: Its Potentiality and Constraints in Eastern Tigray, Northern Ethiopia." *Agricultural Journal* 5, no. 3 (2010): 201–4.

Young, Crawford, ed. *The Rising Tide of Cultural Pluralism: The Nation-State at Bay?* Madison: University of Wisconsin Press, 1993.

Young, John. "Regionalism and Democracy in Ethiopia." *Third World Quarterly* 19, no. 2 (June 1998): 191–204.

Young, Robert. *African Wastes Reclaimed: Illustrated in the Story of the Lovedale Mission.* London: Dent, 1902.

Zewde, Bahru. *A History of Modern Ethiopia, 1855–1974.* Athens: Ohio University Press, 1991.

———. *A History of Modern Ethiopia, 1855–1991.* 2nd ed. Athens: Ohio University Press, 2001.

Zewde, Bahru, and Siegfried Pausewang, eds. *Ethiopia: The Challenge of Democracy from Below.* Uppsala: Nordiska Afrikainstitutet.

INDEX

Page numbers in italics refer to illustrations.

Abaye (father of Tola Abaye), 236
Abaye, Tola. *See* Tola Abaye
Abaye/Abayi/Abbay River (Blue Nile River), 224, 240, 252, 259, 261
Abbas Haji Gnamo, 22
Abba Tabor, 159–60, *160*
Abbay River. *See* Abaye/Abayi/Abbay River (Blue Nile River)
Abbi Kedir, 39
Abdelhafid (sultan), 172
Abdussamad H. Ahmad, 8, 269n36
Abiy Ahmed, 11–12
abolition of the slave trade (1807), 8, 25, 97, 108, 267n18, 270n41, 284n2; lack of French commitment to, 101–2
Abu Bakr (pasha of Zeila), 102, 289n19; family, 102, 289n19
Abyssinia. *See* Ethiopia
Abyssinian Orthodox Church, 21, 22, 23
Acton Homes (Natal, South Africa), *161*, 162
Adal: country, 195, 224, 226, 248, 257; slave traders, 77, 88–89, 94, 102, 105, 109, 147, 195, 208, 213–24, 226–40, 242–45, 248–53, 255–56
Addis Ababa (Ethiopia), 46, 81, 159–60, 163–71, 175, 177–79, 198, 290n10, 298n46, 298n53, 299n68; Addis Ababa Master Plan, 11; British legation in, 167–68, 177–78, 295n1, 298n46, 301n107; German legation in, 46, 163, 178; Treaty of, 170
Aden (Yemen), 1–2, 76, 99, 101–5, 109–11, *112*, 112–13, 116–18, 120, *120*, 123, 137, 141, 147, 157–59, 163, 165, 169, 176, 182, 187, 189, 191, 194, 196–98, 206–10, 229, 244–45, 257,

286n42, 288n1, 290n10; Roman Catholic Vicariate of, 289n21
Adeya (village), 240
Admiralty Courts, 101, 108, 303n11
Adoye (mother of Asho Sayo), 243
Adwa, battle of, 170, 183, 272n5, 299n68
Afaan Oromoo (language), 2, 19–20, 32, 36, 64, 91–92, 114, 116, 191, 207, 280n6, 283n42; Afaan Oromoo/English dictionaries, 36, 301n112
Afar or Danakil Depression, 15, 27, 52–53
Afar people, 285n19
Afillo (town), 222, 237, 257
African Methodist Episcopal Church, 182
African nationalism, 9, 299n68
African National Congress (South Africa), 293n51
Agam (village), 214, 257
agricultural, cadastral, or field laborers, 10, 40, 43, 49, 69–70, 86, 113, 135, 192, 193, 228, 233, 251, 254, 262, 292n21, 295n77
Aguchello Chabani, 64, 70, 92, 179, *204*, 204–5, 213, 295n73
Agude Bulcha, 179, 242
Ahmed, Abiy. *See* Abiy Ahmed
Ajuba (village), 216, 257
Ajubi/Yajubi (village), 215, 217, 221, 225–26, 231, 234–35, 237–40, 246, 249, 251, 253, 255, 257, 260
Al Heshima (dhow), 99, 103, 105
Alkathora (dhow), 99, 103, 105, 196
Alexander, David James, 151
Alexander, Neville Edward, 1, 151–52, *153*, 153, 166
Alexander von Humboldt Foundation fellowship, 151–52

Ali Kira Mahomed (master of the *Alkathora*), 99, 103, 105, 196
Alle (village), 36, 222, 257
Alpers, Edward (Ned) A., 6, 30, 266n16, 282n35, 303n11
altitude, 15–17, 49, 53–54, *54*, *56*, 59–60, 73, 203, 205, 211
Amanu Bulcha, 64, 91, 146, 214
Amanu Figgo, 159, 176, 179, 182, 198, 214, 295n73
amasi (sour milk), 50, 278
amaXhosa. *See* Xhosa people
Amaye Tiksa, 44, 53–54, 75, 180, 215
Amhara people, 18, 21–22, 59, 265n1, 280n6
Amharic (language), 18, 21–22, 116, 170, 207
amole (salt bars), 40, 70, 91, 193
Ancharro (town), 214, 216, 218–19, 221, 225, 238–39, 245, 253, 257
Andreolis, Lamberto, 27
Angatu (mother of Kanatu Danke), 252
Angisho (town), 227, 257
Anglo-Boer War (1899–1902), 149, 157–58, 162, 170, 172, 182, 302
antelopes, 262
Antonelli, Pietro, 59
Arabic language, 3, 19, 22, 207, 281
Arabs, 64–65, 70, 93, 105, 159, 192, 195, 208, 213, 228, 261
Araito. *See* Rahayta
Asa (mother of Hora Bulcha), 227
Asafa Jalata, 11
Ashani (mother of Balcha Billo), 218
Asho Sayo, 54, 148, 243, 294n67
Asma Giyorgis (or Giyorghis), 21–22
Assal, Lake, 15
Asseti (mother of Fayissa Umbe), 222
Atari (slave traders), 36, 88–89, 93–94, 105, 195, 217, 219, 221–22, 224–25, 229–30, 233–35, 237–39, 241, 243, 245, 249, 251–55
Attaway, Rev. Allen Henry, 182
Aussa (town and sultanate), 74, 77–78, 80, 101, 194, 208, 213–23, 225–31, 233–57, 281n19, 285n14
Austen, Ralph, 8
Awash River, 15
Ayanso (father of Shamo Ayanso), 235
Ayanso, Shamo. *See* Shamo Ayanso
Ayantu Said, 163, 198, 243, 294n72
Azezo (town), 207

Badani (mother of Gamaches Garba), 224
Badassa Nonno, 39, 147, 216
Badassa Wulli, 53–54, 85, 180, 216

Badatu (mother of Tola Urgessa), 237
Badda: district, 54, 215–17, 221, 257; mountain, 16, 52–53
Bakheita (dhow), 99, 103, 105
Baki Malakka, 91, 179, 217
Balale (mother of Halko Danko), 250
Balcha Billo, 48, 75, 180, 218, 295n73
Bale Mountains, 16, 52
Balfour, Ngconde, 293n51
Balfour, Robert, 293n51
Bambasse (district), 230, 257
bananas, 46, 262
Bank of Abyssinia (Addis Ababa), 179
Baquaqua, Mahommah Gardo. *See* Mahommah Gardo Baquaqua
bara beelaal bâraa balliyyaa (famine days), 26, 29
barley, 46, 214, 215, 262
Barnley, Miss F. J., 138, 141
Barsinge (district), 70, 213, 257
barter, 41, 68, 193, 205
Bartholomew, John, 18
Basel Mission in East Africa, 114
Bates, Darrell, 24
battle of Adwa. *See* Adwa, battle of
battle of Chelenko. *See* Chelenko, battle of
battle of Embabo. *See* Embabo, battle of
Bayan Liliso, 39, 64, 85, 137, 144, 180, 207, 218, 294n72
Beachey, Raymond W., 269n38
beans, 46, 214–15, 262, 291n27
Bechuanaland (today Botswana), 133, 143
bees and beekeeping, 44–45, 49, 262
Belchori Mountain, 213
Bellagamba, Alice, 5, 267n22
Bennie, Mrs. John Angell, 138, 141
Bennie, Rev. John, 121
Berille Boko, 44, 91, 109–11, 117–18, *119*, 121, 150, *151*, 179, 244, 295n73, 295n78
Berille Nehor, 69, 87, 92, 244–45
Bettembourg, Msgr. Nicolas, 27
Billi (father of Mulatta Billi), 232
Billi, Mulatta. *See* Mulatta Billi
Billo (father of Balcha Billo), 218
Billo, Balcha. *See* Balcha Billo
Billo (village/slave market), 215, 217, 221, 224, 227, 236, 238, 257
biltong, ostrich, 181
Birbir River, 222, 237, 242
bishinga (corn), 46, 262
Bisho Jarsa, 1–2, 29–30, 47, 70, 91, 108–9, 150–51, *152*, *153*, 166, 182, 242, 245, 247, 249, 294n72, 295n76
Bismarck, Otto Eduard Leopold, 169, *170*

Bita (village), 233, 257
Black nationalism, 9, 299n68
blacksmiths, 47, 262
Blue Nile River, 238, 261. *See also* Abaye/Abayi/
    Abbay River
Boensa (father of Dinkitu Boensa), 247
Boensa, Dinkitu. *See* Dinkitu Boensa
Bofa (town), 213–15, 217, 221, 223, 225, 230–31,
    233–35, 238–40, 246, 257
Bohannan, Paul, 30, 32
Boko (father of Berille Boko), 244
Boko, Berille. *See* Berille Boko
Bokwe, John Knox, 293
Bombay (India). *See* Mumbai (India)
Boniya (district), 240
branding, in treatment of Oromo children, 92,
    195
Brinkhoff, Thomas, 304n21
British and Foreign Bible Society, 159
bubonic plague, 27, 29, 76, 195
Bulcha (father of Agude Bulcha), 242
Bulcha (father of Amanu Bulcha), 214
Bulcha (father of Hora Bulcha), 227
Bulcha (father of Kintiso Bulcha), 229
Bulcha, Agude. *See* Agude Bulcha
Bulcha, Amanu. *See* Amanu Bulcha
Bulcha, Hora. *See* Hora Bulcha
Bulcha, Kintiso. *See* Kintiso Bulcha
Bulcha, Mekuria. *See* Mekuria Bulcha
Buller, Sir Redvers, 161, 162
bullocks, 47, 262
Bultum (father of Liban Bultum), 230
Bultum, Liban. *See* Liban Bultum
Bunno (country), 239, 257
Burayo (king of Sayo), 222
Bushaseche (mother of Berille Nehor), 69, 244
Bushere (mother of Bayan Liliso), 218
Bushu (mother of Damuli Diso), 246

cabbages, 46, 262
cabdrivers, 182
Candide (play by Voltaire), 190
Cape of Good Hope: censuses, 149; death/
    mortality rates, 149–50; demography,
    149–50; education system, 133; population,
    149–50; "prize slaves," 9, 267n18; slavery, 9
Cape Town (South Africa), 81, 163–64, 166, 173,
    175–76, 180, 182, 195n81
captor-bonding syndrome. *See* Stockholm
    syndrome
carpentry, timber, and woodworkers, 135, 148,
    151, 180–81
Castle Line, 123

Castle Mail Packets Company (shipping line),
    123
castration, 208, 211–12. *See also* eunuchs
cattle, 27, 29–30, 36, 39, 44, 46–48, 68, 70, 86,
    143, 213, 215–16, 218–23, 225, 229–33, 237,
    239, 241, 245, 247, 249, 262, 274n41, 278n8
Cecchi, Antonio, 63
Chabani (father of Aguchello Chabani), 70,
    205, 213
Chabani, Aguchello. *See* Aguchello Chabani
Chabse (father of Nuro Chabse), 233
Chabse, Nuro. *See* Nuro Chabse
Chaga (town), 233, 258
chains, as means of restraint, 92–93, 195, 220,
    225, 238, 240, 246. *See also* ligatures, as
    means of restraint
Chaja (country), 256, 258
Chali (father of Nagaro Chali), 232
Chali, Nagaro. *See* Nagaro Chali
Chara (village), 227, 235
chattel slavery, 6, 30–31, 157
Chefita (village), 218, 258
Chelenko, battle of, 25
Chiarini, Giovanni, 25
child slaves. *See* slave children; Oromo slave
    children
cholera, 27, 29
Chonge (village), 214, 258
Chora (district), 227, 258
Christian Express, 125, 136, 147, 157–58, 163, 172,
    177, 182
Church Missionary Society (CMS), 6, 74, 150,
    282n25, 283n43
Clarence-Smith, William Gervase, 8, 269n36
Clerk, George, 159, 160, 168, 295–96n1
climate, 15, 20, 26, 44–45, 74, 121, 134, 144, 172,
    183, 196–97, 261
cliometry and cliometric methods. *See*
    methodology, quantitative; prosopography
coffee, 46, 49, 125, 226, 262, 287
coffles, 74, 82, 91, 203, 208, 212, 284n46
colporteurs, 159, 198, 207, 296n15
Comaroff, Jean, 9
Comaroff, John, 9
concubines, 188, 208, 212
Congregational Union of South Africa
    (CUSA), 151, 293n51
Conway Castle (ship), 123, *123*, 125, 182, 197
cooks/chefs, 135, 180
corn, 30, 46, 50, 70, 91, 127, 245, 261–62, 278n12
Cory Library for Humanities (formerly
    Historical) Research, 1–2, 206
Coutts, James, 125

Cradock (South Africa), 1, 150–51, 182
Cuelebroeck, Edouard Blondeel van, 32
Curtin, Philip, 7–8, 42, 82–83

Daba Tobo, 108–9, 163, 179, 198, 219
Dabeche (mother of Turunga Gudda), 43, 69, 254
Dacche, Gobana. *See* Gobana Dacche
Dadi (mother of Meshinge Salban), 252
Dagadi (slave traders), 230
Dalatti/Dalatte/Dalotti (town), 36, 222, 226, 248, 258
Daly, Rev. John Fairley, 116–17, 288n19
Damara (father of Damuli Diso), 43, 246
Damuli Diso, 43, 85, 92, 246, 294n72
Damuli Dunge, 43, 85, 109, 246, 249, 294n72
Danakil Depression. *See* Afar or Danakil Depression
Dankali (slave traders). *See* Adal (slave traders)
Dange (district), 242, 258
Danke (father of Kanatu Danke), 252
Danke, Kanatu. *See* Kanatu Danke
Danko (father of Halko Danko), 250
Danko, Halko. *See* Halko Danko
Danno/Dano/Danu: country), 36, 222, 258; slave market, 218
Dapo (district), 218
Dappo (town), 222, 231–32, 243, 249, 251, 258
Dappo Gacho (town), 227, 237, 243, 249, 253, 258
Dappo Gumbi (town), 227, 258
Dar es Salaam (Tanzania), 81, 114
Darley, Henry, 63, 268n31
data and databases, 3–8, 19, 32, 37, 52, 73, 131, 140, 187–88, 203–12, 266n15; authentication of, 206–9; census and population, 4, 19, 149–50, 272n9, 276–77n29; quality of, 6; matrix, 205; diachronic or longitudinal, 4, 266n15; methodology, 203–12; Oromo children's data, 7, 30, 52, 73, 131, 140, 149, 187–88, 193, 203–6, 291n2; orphanhood, 38–40, 188, 205, 276–77n29; prosopographies (*see* prosopography); relational, 4; sex ratios, 209–11; sexual abuses, seeming absence in, 211–12; slavery and the slave trade, 8; synchronic, 4, 266n15; variables in, 203–6, 302nn1–2 (app. A); verification of, 303–4n21
Davis, Mike, 29
Dawe (town), 76–77, 215–20, 222–23, 227, 229, 231, 236–37, 240, 245–46, 248–51, 254, 258
deaths, 2, 4, 8, 11, 25–27, 29, 34–35, 38–40, 43–44, 69–70, 99, 101, 105–6, 111, 114, 117–18, 121, 130, 136, 144, 146–50, 158–59, 162–63,
165–66, 168, 176–77, 179–80, 183, 196–98, 200, 203, 209–10, 212, 216, 218–19, 226, 234, 236, 239, 241, 245–46, 250–52, 256, 268n29, 276–77n29, 286n42, 294n60, 295n1, 299n69, 300n77. *See also* mortality
Debelo, Asebe Regassa. *See* Asebe Regassa Debelo
Deko (village), 232, 258
Dernburg, Bernhard, 171, 300n77
Dessalegn Negeri, 31
Desta (mother of Wakinni Ugga), 255
Desta, Gebru (Gobaw, Ghebroa). *See* Gebru (Gobaw, Ghebroa) Desta
Deutsche Ost-Afrika-Linie, 176, *176*, 296n5, 301nn103–4
dhows, 1–2, 8, 35–36, 38, 87, 94, 97, *98*, 98–101, 103–6, *106*, 107–10, 187, 194, 196, 207, 209–10, 214–15, 219, 225, 229, 244–49, 269n38, 281n6, 284n4, 286n27, 286n43
diamonds, 180
Dibdibbe (town), 240, 253–56, 258
Dikko (father of Galgal Dikko), 224
Dikko, Galgal. *See* Galgal Dikko
Dingati (mother of Bisho Jarsa), 245
Dingisse (mother of Wakinne Nagesso), 238
Dinkitu Boensa, 44, 48, 85, 87, 91, 107, 166, 179, 247
Dire-Dawa (town), 160
Diribe (mother of Galani Warabu), 248
diseases and illnesses, 27, 29, 144, 146–48. *See also specific illnesses*
Diso, Damuli. *See* Damuli Diso
Dodds, M. J., 138, 141
Dongoshe (mother of Jifari Roba), 40, 43, 70, 251
Donham, Donald, 272n5
donkeys, 46, 82, 91, 235, 241, 250
Doranni (town), 239, 258
Doulton, Lindsay, 8, 106, 108
Dower, Edward, 174
drought, 15, 26–27, 29–31, 34–35, *35*, 38–39, 41, 46, 63, 76, 90, 193, 195, 276n21
Dunge (mother of Damuli Dunge), 246
Dunge, Damuli. *See* Damuli Dunge
durra (sorghum), 215
dysentery, 26, 29

Eastern Cape (South Africa), 1–2, 9–10, 50, 121, 135, 177, 289n28, 292n21, 295n77
East London (South Africa), *122*, 123, 125–26, *127*, 128, 146, 159, 162–63, 182, 197, 295n73
Edward VII (king), 159, *160*
Edwards, Jon R., 8, 26, 269n36

eggs, 50, 262

Egypt, 19, 24, 60, 120, 136, 207

elephants, 262

El Niño–Southern Oscillation (ENSO), 26

Eltis, David, 196

Embabo, battle of, 24, 58

Enarya (kingdom), 54

Enge (village), 70, 205, 213, 258

Engerman, Stanley, 203

England, R. Brian, 163

Enno Littmann Expedition to Axum (1906), 171, 299n74

ENSO. *See* El Niño–Southern Oscillation (ENSO)

Entotto (town), 93, 195, 220, 223, 258

Entotto Maryam Church, 26

Equiano, Olaudah (also known as Gustavus Vassa), 5, 267n19

Eritrea, 15, 27, 169, 279n3, 285n13

Erlank, Natasha, 135, 143

Etherington, Norman, 9

Ethiopia: delegation at the coronation of Edward VII (1902), 159–60, *160*; demography and population, 17–19, *19*; languages, 19–20; religions, 20–23; topography, 15–17, *17*

Ethiopia-Germany Commercial Treaty (1906), 171

eunuchs, 32, 68, 86, 107, 208–9, 212

famine, 15, 26–27, 29, 34–35, 38–39, 41, 46, 63, 76, 90, 166–67, 193, 195, 220, 245, 276

Faraja Jimma, 37, 85, 146, 180–81, 220, 223, 294n72

Faraja Lalego, 92, 180, 220

Farmerfield Mission, 10, 292n21

Fatto (mother of Ayantu Said), 243

Fayissa Hora, 109, 137, 163–64, 179, 198, 221, 297n37, 297n39

Fayissa Murki, 36, 48, 75, 222, 294

Fayissa Umbe, 39, 163–64, 179, 198, 213, 222

Fayissi Gemo, 40, 70, 109, 179, 248

Fernyhough, Timothy, 8, 34, 52, 63, 66, 71, 75, 82–83, 86, 90, 268n29, 269n36, 272n5

Fetha Nagast, 22

feudalism, 31, 51, 190

Feyisa Lilesa, 12

field workers. *See* agricultural, cadastral, or field laborers

Figgo (father of Amanu Figgo), 214

Figgo, Amanu. *See* Amanu Figgo

Fillis Circus, 123, *124*, 197

finno (smallpox), 91, 195, 225

first passage (slave trade), 3–4, 6, 8–9, 29, 51, 73–74, 76–77, 81, 84–85, 87–88, 91–92, 93–94, 97, 105–7, 110–11, 114, 118, 121–22, 130, 138, 149–50, 157, 183, 187–88, 194–96, 198–200, 205–6, 209, 210, 212, 266nn16–17

Fogel, Robert, 203

fondaks (fondouks or caravanserais), 86, 109, 244

Foot, Edwin C., 36, 276n23, 301n112

France, 172, 284n2

Free Church of Scotland, 1–2, 111, 116, 150, 206–7, 210, 289n28; Foreign Missions Committee, 113, 135–36

Friedrich-Alexander University Erlangen-Nürnberg (Germany), 289n28

Gabai (mother of Amaye Tiksa), 215

gabbars. *See* serfs

gadaa (Oromo system of democratic governance), 18, 27, 31, 85

Gaite Goshe, 92, 148, 223

Galani Warabu, 39, 44, 93, 109, 248, 294n72

Galatu (father of Warkitu Galatu), 256

Galatu, Warkitu. *See* Warkitu Galatu

Galgal Dikko, 40, 109, 157, 179, 198, 224, 295n73

Galgali (mother of Sego Oria), 234

Galgalli Shangalla, 37, 179, 249

Galla (pejorative term). *See* Oromo

Gamaches Garba, 68, 92–93, 137, 146, 158, 179, 198, 224, 295n73

Gamoje (village), 44, 226, 258

Gamoji (cool country), 216, 258

Gangila (father of Rufo Gangila), 234

Gangila, Rufo. *See* Rufo Gangila

Ganne (mother of Badassa Nonno), 216

Ganne (mother of Tola Abaye), 236

Garba (father of Gamaches Garba), 224

Garba, Gamaches. *See* Gamaches Garba

Gardner, Rev. William, *115*, 116–17, *118*, *120*, 121, 131, 191, 207–8, 288n14, 288n19

Gardner guns, 99, *100*, 105, 108, 196, 284n4, 285n7

Gashaw, Solomon. *See* Gashaw Solomon

Gawe (mother of Badassa Wulli), 216

Gebru (Gobaw, Ghebroa) Desta, 114, 116, *118*, *120*, 121, 159–60, *160*, 164, 171, 207–8, 299n71

Geddes, Alexander, 137, *138*, 143, 148, 168, 189

Geddes, Mrs. Alexander, 128, 137, 148

Geddes family, 148

Geddo (village), 240, 258

Geez alphabet, 19–20

Gella (village), 227, 258

Gellately, Robert, 171
Gemeda, Guluma. *See* Guluma Gemeda
Gemo (father of Fayissi Gemo), 40, 70, 248
Gemo, Fayissi. *See* Fayissi Gemo
genocide, 171; of Herero people, 171; of Maji
    Maji people, 171
Geographic Information Systems (GIS),
    52, 78, 211, 282n24, 303–4n21; City
    Population, 304n21; Fuzzy Gazetteer,
    303n21; GeoNames, 303n31; Institut
    für Angewandte Photogrammetrie und
    Geoinformatik, 304n21; *International Atlas*,
    304n21; Interoperable Services for Data
    Products (ISODP) Project, 303n21; National
    Geospatial-Intelligence Agency (NGA),
    304n21; Ordnance Survey OpenData
    Gazetteer, 304n21; United States Board on
    Geographic Names, 304n21; US Geological
    Survey Geographic Names Information,
    304n21
Gera (country/district), 44–45, 49, 226, 234, 258
German East Africa, 171
German South West Africa, 171; language,
    116; Legation of Addis Ababa, 46, 163, 167,
    178; literature, 151–52; maritime rights, 183;
    missionaries, 21; Mittelafrika, 157, 169, *170*;
    Morocco, involvement with, 172; naval
    ascendancy, 170–75; Oromo repatriates,
    169–83, 198; Port Elizabeth (South Africa)
    consulate, 169–83, 198; Princeton University,
    relationship with, 171; shipping, 158, 169, 183;
    slave trade, suppression of, 97
Germany, 97, 152, 157, 160, 171, 182, 297n24,
    299n69, 299n74, 304n21; Anglo-Boer War
    (1899–1902), 170; ascendancy, political power
    and influence, 169–78; Berlin Conference
    (1884–1885), 97, 169, 284n2; diplomacy, 157,
    167–75, 183, 198; Ethiopia, relationship with,
    170–78; Ethiopia-Germany Commercial
    Treaty (1905–1906), 171
Germond, André, 135, 138, 143, 147, 148
Germond, Paul, 138
Getenesh Woldeyes, 163
Gibbe (village), 227
Gibbe/Gibbi River, 24, 221, 244
Gibe (region), 23, 58, 71, 85
Gilo Kashe, 37, 76–77, 81, 109, 148, 182, 189, 225
GIS. *See* Geographic Information Systems
    (GIS)
Gissing, Charles Edward, 78, 87, 93, 97,
    100–108, 110, 112, 114, 209, 212, 283n40,
    284n4, 285n16, 286n42
Giyorgis (or Giyorghis), Asma, 21–22

Glasgow Missionary Society, 9, 121
Glencoe (Natal, South Africa), 162–63
goats, 36, 40, 46, 49–50, 214, 217, 222, 227, 230,
    236–37, 240, 243, 248
Gobana Dacche, 57–58
Gobbu/Gobu: country, 30, 245–46, 258; village,
    40, 224
Godawarabessa (village), 238, 258
Godeti (village), 256, 258
Gojjam/Gojam: slave market, 217, 230, 233, 252,
    254; slave raiders, 91, 93, 146, 253; town, 91,
    213, 258
Gojob River, 223
gold, 180, 278n13
Golo (mother of Komo Gonda), 230
Goma (kingdom), 54
Gombota (village), 227
Gomma (district), 23, 227, 231, 258
Gomoji/Gamoji (village), 216, 256, 258
Gonda (father of Komo Gonda), 230
Gonda, Komo. *See* Komo Gonda
Gondar (town), 159, 164, 203, 207, 248, 258
Gonja people (West Africa), 4
Goody, Jack, 57
gosa (descent group), 31
Goshe (father of Gaite Goshe), 223
Goshe, Gaite. *See* Gaite Goshe
Govan, Rev. William, 121, 289n25, 289n28,
    298n57
Grace, John, 85
Grant, William, 91, 109–10, 194, 244, 283n45
Great East African Rift, 16
Great Rift Valley, 15–16, 52
Greene, Sandra, 5, 267n22
Green River (South Africa), 126
Grey, Sir Edward, 177
Gualla (village), 223, 258
Gudaya: slave market, 258; traders, 237
Gudda, Turungo. *See* Turungo Gudda
guddifachaa (Borana Oromo system of
    adoption), 7, 31–32, 34, 41
Gudru (country), 216, 239
Gudru: slave market/traders), 88, 91–92, 109,
    213, 215, 221, 224, 229–33, 236–38, 242–44,
    246, 249, 251–54; slave raiders, 195, 237;
    town, 207, 214, 218, 220–21, 223, 225, 227,
    239–40, 249, 254–55, 258
Gudru, Wayessa. *See* Wayessa Gudru
Gulisso: country, 237; slave market/traders, 91,
    230, 235, 237, 242; town, 213, 258
Guluma Gemeda, 165
Guma: kingdom, 54, 71, 227, 235, 255, 258;
    mountain, 242

gunboat diplomacy, 172
gunrunners, 26
guns and firearms, 24, 26, 40, 59, 99, 162, 224.
  See also Gardner guns
Gurage: country, 215, 218, 220, 258, 302n7;
  people, 56, 66, 191, 256; slave market/traders,
  219, 227; slave raiders, 66
Gurdenfi (mother of Aguchello Chabani), 70,
  205, 213
Guro (mother of Gutama Tarafo), 226
Gutama Tarafo, 10, 20, 44, 48, 59, 74, 144, 166,
  179, 191, 226, 261, 292n21, 294n72, 304n1
Guyo (father of Milko Guyo), 231
Guyo, Milko. *See* Milko Guyo
Guyo Tiki, 77, 81, 91, 147, 226

Haight, Bruce M., 4
Haile Sellassie Abayneh, 160, *160*
Haiven (mother of Gaite Goshe), 223
Halelu (village), 227, 259
Halko Danko, 85, 250
Hani (ox-wagon driver), 126
Harar, 24, 25, *25*, 157, 159, *160*, 160, 198, 295n1
Harbe (mother of Isho Karabe), 228
Harries, Patrick, 9
Harrington, Sir John, 165, 167, 171–72, 177,
  301n107
Harris, William Cornwallis, 63, 90
Hassen, Mohammed. *See* Mohammed Hassen
Hatatu (mother of Tolassa Wayessa), 238
Hausa language, 19
Hawe Sukute, 35, 53, 69, 179, 250
Hawu people, 255
Hely-Hutchinson, Sir Walter Francis, 173, 175
Henderson, Rev. James, 168, 172–75, 177,
  298n46, 299n64
Henige, David, 73, 187, 266n17
Hepworth Stores, Cape Town, 181
Herero genocide (German South West Africa)
  (1904–1907), 171
Hervey, Herbert, 177–78, 301n107
historical methodology. *See* methodology,
  quantitative; prosopography
historiography: British, 3; Ethiopia, 10, 270n48;
  missions and missionaries, 9–10, 131; Oromo,
  10–12; slavery and the slave trade, 4–9, 198,
  266n16; trauma, 130
HIV/AIDS pandemic, 38, 198, 276n29
HMS *Osprey* (British Royal Navy gunship),
  34–36, 38–39, 78, 87, 93, 97–105, *106*, 106–9,
  111–13, 118, 191, 196–97, 207–9, 212, 219,
  283n40, 285n9, 285n14, 286n42
Hochocha (town), 226, 259

Hodeidah/Al-Hudaydah (Yemen), 91, 109, 194,
  207, 244, 259, 287n58
Holy Rosary Convent (Cradock, South Africa),
  151
honey, 44–45, 49, 226, 262
Hora (father of Fayissa Hora), 221
Hora, Fayissa. *See* Fayissa Hora
Hora Bulcha, 180, 227
Horro (village), 220
horses and cavalry, 36, 40, 46–50, 59, 70–71,
  91, 158, 162, 192, 199, 214, 218, 224, 227, 230,
  237–38, 240, 242, 248, 252, 255, 262, 278n9,
  290n5
Huddleston-Mattai, Barbara, 189
Hudo (mother of Galgal Dikko), 40, 224
Humbe (village), 239, 259
Hunter, David A., 87, 148, 163–69, 176–77, 180,
  183, 283n41, 294n68, 297n35
hymns, 126

Ibbi (mother of Daba Tobo), 219
Ibn Al'-Assal, 22
Ibrahim Ali (master of the *Al Heshima*), 99, 103
Ibse (mother of Hawe Sukute), 69, 250
Ifat (town), 235, 259
illnesses. *See* diseases and illnesses; *specific
  illnesses*
Illubabor (region), 16, 58, 302n7
Ilu: country, 44, 227, 230, 259; people, 234
Imo (village), 53, 228, 259
Incerha Mission (renamed Lovedale Mission),
  121
International Railway Trust and Construction
  Company, 163
interpreters: aboard HMS *Osprey*, 107–8; at
  Keith-Falconer Mission; 2, 32, 111, 114, 116,
  171, 207; for Brian England, 163
Isenberg, Carl (Charles) William, 21, 63
Isho Karabe, 37, 53, 92, 109, 146–47, 228, 245
Islam, 21–24, 27, 65
Italians, 25, 27, 169–70, 183, 272n5, 285n13,
  299n68
Italo-Ethiopian War, 170

Jabalu River, 242
Jacob (Old Testament patriarch), 261, 277n34
Jalata, Asafa. *See* Asafa Jalata
James, Wendy, 272n5
Jarsa (father of Bisho Jarsa), 245
Jarsa, Bisho. *See* Bisho Jarsa
Jeddah, 87, 99, 101, 103, 107, 207
Jerusalem, 207, 299n69
Jews in Ethiopia, 60, 207

Jibbe (mother of Wayessa Tikse), 240

Jifari Roba, 40, 43, 70, 85, 87, 180, 251

Jimma: kingdom, 54, 59, 217, 219, 231, 234–35, 262; people, 231; region, 16; slave market/ traders, 69–70, 88, 195, 223, 227–28, 230, 232, 245, 248, 254; slave raiders, 64, 72, 191, 208; village, 238, 246, 259

Jimma, Faraja. *See* Faraja Jimma

Jorbo (mother of Milko Guyo), 231

Jorbo (mother of Rufo Gangila), 234

Jorge (mother of Mulatta Billi), 232

Kaffa: country, 40, 53, 62, 70–71, 216, 223, 227, 233–34, 245, 248, 254–55, 259; people, 191; slave raiders, 64, 66, 71, 191, 208

Kafficho: people, 56, 66; slave raiders, 66

Kaiser, SS (German ship), 163, 198

Kambatta (country), 218, 259

Kanatu Danke, 44, 85, 109, 252

Kaplan, Steven, 23

Karabe (father of Isho Karabe), 228

Karabe, Isho. *See* Isho Karabe

Kasalu (town), 227, 259

Kashe (father of Gilo Kashe), 76, 225

Kashe, Gilo. *See* Gilo Kashe

Kassaye Ayalew, 45

Katshi Wolamo, 32, 147, 228

Kau (slave market), 91, 215, 223, 229, 236, 238, 246, 259

Keats-Rohan, Katharine, 4

Kedir, Abbi. *See* Abbi Kedir

Keetmanshoop (Namibia), 182

Keiskamma River, 126–27

Keith-Falconer, Ion, 114

Keith-Falconer Mission, Sheikh Othman (Yemen), 4, *34*, 110–11, 113, 116, *117*, *118*, 120–21, 141, 144, 147, 158–59, 163, 171, 187, 191, 196–98, 207–9, 288n1

Kelem (town), 235, 259

Kenya, 6–7, 15–16, 19, 267n25

kholwa (African converts), 9

Kibrom Ftwi, 45

kidnapping, 7, 49, 67–68, 191, 193

Kiernan, Ben, 171

Kilerito (village), 224, 259

Kimberley (South Africa), 157, 159, 163, 180

King Kong (musical), 293n51

King William's Town (South Africa), 125–26, 148, 295n73, 301n114

King, Billy, 74, *75*, 280nn3–5 (chap. 6)

kinship, 6–7, 29–32, 34–35, 41, 63, 192

Kintiso Bulcha, 54, 91, 182, 229, 295n73

Klein, Martin, 5, 267n22

Kohlschütter, Christian, 303n21

Koma (slave market), 228, 259

Komo Gonda, 85, 148, 230

König (German ship), 158, *158*, 296n5

Kopytoff, Igor, 6–7, 30–31, 35, 41, 192

Kosher (village), 227, 259

Kotche (slave market), 242, 259

kraals (cattle enclosures), 47, 262

Krapf, Johann Ludwig, 63, 90

Kronprinz (German ship), *175*, *176*, 176–77, 179, 183, 198, 301n103

Kumfereh, Mahommed. *See* Mahommed Kumfereh (Danakil king)

Kurni (mother of Dinkitu Boensa), 247

LaCapra, Dominick, 130

Lahej, sultan of, 288n1

Lalego (father of Faraja Lalego), 220

Lalego, Faraja. *See* Faraja Lalego

Lalo (village), 44, 219, 252, 259

Lansing, Gulian, 114, 288n12

Leka: country, 64, 72, 91, 214, 219, 221, 223, 226–27, 229, 236, 259; people, 64, 216, 236; slave markets/traders, 69, 88–89, 91, 195, 229–31, 233, 235, 239, 251, 253, 249; slave raiders, 66, 89, 191, 208

Leka-Tocho, 227, 259

leopards, 262

Lewis, Herbert S., 272n6

Lewis, Ioan M., 20–21

Liban (country), 224–25, 240

Liban Bultum, 36, 44, 46, 49, 69, 89, 144, 159, 167–68, 176–79, 183, 198, 230–31, 276n23, 294n72, 295n78, 295–96n1, 301n102, 301n112

Libya, 19

ligatures, as means of restraint, 92, 147, 195, 228, 233, 240, 280nn4–5 (chap. 6). *See also* chains, as means of restraint

Lilesa, Feyisa. *See* Feyisa Lelisa

Liliso (father of Bayan Liliso), 218

Liliso, Bayan. *See* Bayan Liliso

Limmu, slave markets/traders, 227, 259

Limmu-Ennarya, 23

Limu (slave traders), 228

Lindsay, Thomas Martin, 117, 120, 136

linguistic diversity and swings, 211, 303n21

lions, 123, 262

Livingstonia Committee (Scotland), 116

Lochhead, Matthew, 43, 76, 87, 106, 109, 111, 113–14, 116–17, *118*, *120*, 121, 123, 125–26, 129, 189, 191, 206–9, 211–12, 283n41, 288n19, 292n25

Lovedale Mission and Lovedale Institution, 1–2, 4, 9–11, 18, 20, 42, 44, 46, 50, 59, 74, 76, 107,

113–14, 117, 120–22, 125–35, *136*, 136–37, *138*, 138–42, *143*, 143–53, 157–65, *166*, 166–200, 206–7, 209–10, 212, 229, 263, 278n12, 283n40, 289n25, 289–90n28, 291nn1–2, 291n7, 291nn21–22, 291n24, 292n13, 292n21, 292n25, 293n35, 293n51, 294nn67–68, 294n70, 294n72, 295n79, 297n35, 298n57; Student Volunteer Missionary Movement, 146
Lual (father of Tola Lual), 236
Lual, Tola. *See* Tola Lual
Lucha (mother of Kintiso Bulcha), 229
Lul Admasachew, 39
Luma (slave market), 235, 259

Mabandla, Bridgitte, 293n51
Mabandla, Chief Mbovane (leader of the amaBhele), 293n51
Mabandla, Justice Thandatha Jongilizwe, 293n51
Macfarlan Free Church Mission School, 150, 182, 295n78
Macharro (slave market), 40, 249
Madagascar, 36, 123, 278n13
Madan, Arthur C., 6
Magartu (mother of Soye Sanyacha), 253
Mahammad ibn Hanfadhe, sultan of Aussa (1862–1902), 285n14
Mahammad "Illalta" ibn Hanfere. *See* Mahammad ibn Hanfadhe, sultan of Aussa, (1862–1902)
Mahomed, Ali Kira. *See* Ali Kira Mahomed
Mahomet Ali (interpreter aboard HMS *Osprey*), 107
Mahomet Sayed (interpreter aboard HMS *Osprey*), 107
Mahommah Gardo Baquaqua, 5
Mahommed Kumfereh (Danakil king and sultan of Aussa), 101. *See also* Mahammad ibn Hanfadhe, sultan of Aussa (1862–1902)
maize (corn/mealies/mielies), 46, 50, 129, 215, 262, 278n12, 291n27
Majeke, Nosipho (pseud. of Dora Taylor), 131, 270n40
Maji-Maji rebellion (German East Africa; 1905–1906), 171. *See also* genocide
Majo (slave market), 215, 259
Malagga (country), 228, 259
Malakka (father of Baki Malakka), 217
Malakka, Baki. *See* Baki Malakka
Malawi (formerly Nyasaland), 143
Malay Camp (Kimberley, South Africa), 180
Mandeb, Strait of. *See* Strait of Mandeb
Mangera (village), 222, 259

Manning, Patrick, 8, 209
Marcus, Harold G., 25, 59, 272n5, 301n98
Maria Theresa (MT) dollars (or thaler), 25, 90–91, 103, 109, 178, 193
market vendors (Oromo), 43, *43*, 190
marriages, Oromo, 261
Massawa, 27, 32, 203, 269n36, 285n13
Matabeleland (southern province in today's Zimbabwe), 143
Matshikiza: Grace Ngqoyi, 293n51; John, 293n51; Samuel Bokwe, 293n51; Todd, 293n51
Mattai, P. Rudy, 189
Mbotela, James, 75
McCann, James, 47
mealies/mielies (corn or maize). *See* corn
Mecca, 3, 101
Medina, 3
Meillassoux, Claude, 86–87, 193
Mekuria Bulcha, 5, 11, 18, 21, 31–32, 52, 59, 75, 80, 83, 85, 208, 211–12, 267n21, 272n5, 279n4
Mendi (ship), 293n51
Menelik II (Ethiopian emperor), 7, 11–12, 18, 21, 24, 26, 36, 51, 57–59, 64, 70, 72, 77, 157, 159–60, 165, 167–72, 174–75, 177–78, 190–92, 198, 265n1, 268n31, 268n71, 272nn5–6, 280n7, 298n49, 299n71, 301n98, 301n107
Merriman, John Xavier, 174–75, 177
Meshinge Salban, 37, 146–47, 252
Messageries Maritimes (French shipping line), 123
methodology, quantitative, 2–4, 203–12. *See also* prosopography
Meti (mother of Wayessa Tonki), 240
middle passage (slave trade), 5, 8, 93, 97, 107–10, 187, 194–96, 198–200, 266n16
Middledrift (South Africa), 126
Miers, Suzanne, 6–7, 30–31, 35, 41, 192
migration, 11, 38, 150, 164
Milko Guyo, 76, 91, 158, 160, 179, 231
missions and missionaries, 6, 7, 9–10, 21–23, 270n41, 296n15, 297n24; Basel Mission in East Africa, 114, 116; Church Missionary Society (CMS), 74–75, 282n25, 283n43; Free Church of Scotland/Glasgow Missionary Society (FCS/GMS), 1–2, 4–5, 10, 32–34, 36, 43–45, 64, 70, 76, 107, 110–21, 125–53, 157–200, 206–12, 244, 270n40, 288nn1–2, 288n12, 288n14, 289n25, 289n28, 291n22, 292n21, 292n25, 294n68, 295n78, 297n35; London Missionary Society, 121; Moravian, 6; Roman Catholic, 26–27, 289n21; Universities' Mission to Central Africa

missions and missionaries (*continued*)
(UMCA), 6, 267n25; Wesleyan Methodist
Missionary Society, 10
Mittelafrika, 157, 169, *170*
Mocha (Yemen), 209
Mohammed Hassen, 11, 23–24
Moir, William J. B., 125–26, 128–30, 135,
137–38, 206–7, 290n20
Mombasa (Kenya), 120, 163
morbidity, 144, 146–48. *See also* diseases and
illnesses; *specific illnesses*
Mordechai Abir, 63
Morocco, 172; sultan of, 172
mortality, 38–40, 74, 106, 118, 121, 144, *145*, *149*,
149–50, *150*, 177, 183, 196–98, 210, 275n16.
See also deaths
Morton, Fred, 6–7, 29, 33, 38, 63, 74, 92, 150,
280n9, 280n2 (chap. 6), 282n25, 282n32,
283n43, 286n43, 293n35, 297n29
mountains, 15–17, 20–21, 49, 52–53, 60, 71,
73–74, 80–81, 192, 213, 242, 261–62, 280n3
(chap. 6)
Mountnorris, George Annesley, 90
Mqhayi, Samuel Edward Krune, 144, *144*, 293n51
Muirhead, Margaret Christina (née Potter),
128–29, 136, 139, 291n21
Muirhead, Margaret (May), 128, 136, 291n22
Muja (mother of Baki Malakka), 217
Mulatta Billi, 109, 164, 180, 232, 295n73
Mumbai (formerly Bombay, India), 113, 116,
150, 163
Mune (mother of Wayessa Gudru), 239
Murki (father of Fayissa Murki), 222
Murki, Fayissa. *See* Fayissa Murki
Muslim children/families (Aden), 112–13, 197,
208–9
Muslims. *See* Islam
"My Essay Is upon Gallaland" (descriptive essay
by Gutama Turafo), 20, 191, 261–62, 304n1
Mzimba, Mr., 126, 128
Mzimba, Pambani Jeremiah, 293n51

naftanyagabbar (armed settler-serfs). *See* serfs
Nagadi (slave traders), 36, 40, 70, 251, 254
Nagaro Chali, 85, 109, 159, 164, 179, 198, 232
Nagesso (father of Wakinne Nagesso), 238
Nagesso, Wakinne. *See* Wakinne Nagesso
Nakante (slave market), 91, 237, 259
Nama: people (South West Africa now
Namibia), 171; village, 240, 259
Namier, Lewis B., 3
Nawor (mother of Tola Lual), 236
Ncerha River (Eastern Cape), 121

Negeri, Dessalegn. *See* Dessalegn Negeri
Nehor (father of Berille Nehor), 69–70, 244
Nehor, Berille. *See* Berille Nehor
Nibiashe (mother of Turungo Tinno), 254
Nigeria, 5, 30, 267n22
Nollekabba (town), 227, 259
Nonno: district, 216, 227, 259; people, 216
Nonno, Badassa. *See* Badassa Nonno
Nopa: slave markets/traders, 147, 228, 259
Noupoort (South Africa), 182
Nunn, Nathan, 49
Nuro Chabse, 68, 92, 144, 179, 233, 295n73
Nyasaland. *See* Malawi

Obojote: country, 237, 259; people, 236; slave
raiders, 66, 237
Obse (mother of Guyo Tiki), 226
Odendaal, Mr., 126, 291n24
Omo River, 15
oral history and oral tradition (Africa), 4, 5
Oria (father of Sego Oria), 234
Oria, Sego. *See* Sego Oria
Oromia region, 7, 11–12, 15–16, 18, 27–28,
37–40, 49, 52, 56, 60, 64–66, 163, 191, 194,
276–77n29, 302n7
Oromo: language (*see* Afaan Oromoo); people,
5, 10–12, 15, 18–21, 27, 31, 59, 85, 114, 162,
165, 266n3, 271n50, 271n55, 272n6, 298n49;
religions, 18, *20*, 20–23, 27–28
Oromo Liberation Front, 60
Oromo slave children: age structure, 32–33, *33*,
38, *132*, 188, 200, 203; captors, 7–8, 38–41,
51, 63–64, *65*, 65–66, 68, 70–72, 88, 91–93,
105, 118, 187–88, 191–93, 199, 205, 208, 213,
219, 225, 229, 249, 267n18; at Keith-Falconer
Mission, Sheikh Othman, 111–14, *114–15*,
115–20, *120*, 121; changing hands, 74, 88–90,
90, 91; education, Lovedale Institution,
131–38, *139*, 139–40, *140*, 141–42, *142*,
143–53; family composition, 33–37, *37*; home
countries, places of origin and ethnicity,
54–57, *57–58*, 58–60, 64–65, *65–66*, 73, 203,
205; horses and cavalry, 36, 40, 46, 48–49,
50, 59, 70–71, 90–91, 158, 162, 192, 199,
214, 218, 224, 227, 230, 237–38, 240, 242,
248, 252, 255, 262, 278n9, 290n5; ill-health
and ill-treatment, 91–94, 147, 192, 195, 213,
220, 225, 228, 233, 238, 240, 246, 280nn4–5;
itineraries, 73–94, 213–56; livestock owned,
46–47, *47*, 48–50; measures of land held,
44–45, *45*, 46; mode of capture, 66–67, *67*,
68–72; orphanhood, 29, 34–35, 37–39, *39*,
40–41, 69–70, 146–47, 165, 188–89, 199, 205,

276–77n29, 289n21; parental occupation 43, *43* (*see also individual occupations*); religion, 112–13, 150, 262; royal daughters (Berille Boko, Dinkitu Boensa, Galani Warabu, and Kanatu Danke), 44, 107, 194, 244, 247–48, 252; sales and prices, 30–31, 35, 41, 69–72, 89–90, 107; servitude within the country, 7, 43, 68, 72–73, 84–87, 93, 187, 276n21; time on the road, 82–84, 87, 195, 282n25; wealth and status, 42–51

Osprey, HMS. *See* HMS *Osprey*

ostriches and ostrich feather dressers, 181–82

oxen, 30, 36, 40, 46–48, *48*, 59, 68, 214–15, 230–31, 233, 236–38, 240, 244, 248, 250, 262, 278n8

ox-wagons, 125–28

painters (of buildings), 180

Palmer, William Waldegrave, second Earl of Selborne, 173

Pankhurst, Richard, 83, 286n42

Panther (German gunboat), 172

Patch, William, 171

Paterson, Alexander, 111–13, 118, *120*, 121, 123, 125–26, 129, 131–32, 135–39, 141–42, 199, 206–7, 209–10, 278n12, 288n2, 289n21, 291n22, 292n25

Peace of Vereeniging (1902), 170

peas, 46, 262

Perham, Margery, 6, 267–68n25

Perim Island, 102, 103, *103*, 111

Pfeiffer II, William R., 4

Philip, Rev. John, 9

photographers, 162, 180, 299n74, 301n114

Pietermaritzburg (South Africa), 137, 158, 295n73

plagues, 27, 29, 76, 166–67, 195

plows and plowing, 47–48, 214–15, 230, 236, 240, 246, 248–51, 256, 262

Poona (India), 120

Port Elizabeth (South Africa), 151, 169, 174–76, 180, 182–83, 198, 295n73, 295n78, 301n102, 302n115

Port Louis (Mauritius), 123, 197

potatoes, 46, 262

poultry, 50, 262

Presbyterian Church Sunday School (East London, South Africa), 125

Princeton University, 171, 299–300n74

prize slaves/prize money, 5, 8–9, 101, 108, 120, 267n18

Project for the Study of Alternative Education in South Africa (PRAESA), 152

prosopography and prosopographic techniques, 3–5, 187, 198, 200, 203, 209. *See also* methodology, quantitative

Puga, Diego, 49

pumpkins, 46, 262, 278n12

Qubee alphabet, 19–20

questionnaires, repatriation, 150, 157, 163–66, 180, 203, 263, 297n35, 298n50

Rafiso (country), 225

Rafisso (district), 240, 259

Rahayta/Araito, 20–23, 53, 74, 77–78, 98–99, 101–4, *104*, 147, 194, 209, 213–19, 225–31, 233–40, 242–47, 249–51, 253–57, 279n3, 285n13

railways, 125, 163–64, 166–67, 169, 182, 290n10; employees of, 157, 159, 163–64, 180

rape, 208, 211–12

Ras Makonnen (Ras Mäkonnen Wäldä-Mika'él), 159–60, *160*

Rawson, Rawson W., 18–19, 272n9

Reclus, Jacques Élisée, 18–19, *19*, 36–37, 272n9

Red Sea, 1–2, 4, 8, 15–18, 27, 32–33, 36, 41, 49, 53, 64–65, 71, 73–75, 86–87, 97, 100–106, 110, 146–47, 167, 187, 190–91, 193, 195–96, 208–10, 212, 269n36, 285n13, 285n14, 285n16

repatriation poll questionnaire (1903), 4, 150, 157, *166*, 168, 180, 203, 263, 297n35, 297n38, 298n50

Rhodes University, 1

Rhodesia Railways, 159, 163–64

rights-in-persons, 7, 30–31

Rimbaud, Arthur, 26

rinderpest, 27, 29, 35, 274n41, 274n49, 276n21

Rio Grande (French ship), 123, 197

Roba (father of Jifari Roba), 40, 70, 251

Roba, Jifari. *See* Jifari Roba

Roman Catholic Church, 21–22, 26–27, 118, 177, 289n21, 297n24; Vicariate of Aden, 289n21

Rosen, Friedrich, 170–71, 299n69

Ross, Rev. John, 121

Royal Navy. *See* United Kingdom. Royal Navy

Rubenson, Sven, 274n41

Rubusana, Rev. Walter Benson, 146

Rufo Gangila, 39, 179, 182, 234, 294n72

Russians, 101

Sahlé Mariam (king of Shewa). *See* Menelik II (emperor of Ethiopia)

Said (father of Ayantu Said), 243

Said, Ayantu. *See* Ayantu Said

Sakal (district), 214, 260

Sakuri (mother of Shamo Ayanso), 235

Saladin Ibrahim (master of the *Bakheita*), 99, 103

Salban (father of Meshinge Salban), 252

Salban, Meshinge. *See* Meshinge Salban

salt, 40, 47, 70, 90–91, 193, 217, 223, 229, 231, 235, 237, 251, 262. *See also amole* (salt bars)

Salt, Henry, 90

Samuel Gobat Missionary School (Jerusalem), 207

Sanbate (mother of Amanu Bulcha), 214

Sanbate (mother of Warkitu Galatu), 256

Sanyacha (father of Soye Sanyacha), 253

Sanyacha, Soye. *See* Soye Sanyacha

Saunders, Christopher, 9, 120

Sayo: kingdom, 40, 44, 54, 64, 70–71, 218, 222, 227, 229, 237, 243, 251–53, 260; people, 69; slave raiders, 66, 69, 72, 191, 208, 250

Sayo, Asho. *See* Asho Sayo

Scheepers, Dimbiti Bisho, 1, 151

Scheepers, Rev. Frederick, 151, 166

Schnoster, E., 175

schoolteachers, 23, 114, 117, 131–33, 138, 141, 150

Scodel, Ruth, 188

Sego Oria, 146, 234

Seka (town), 217, 260

Sekhoma/Sekgoma II (son of Khama III), 143–44, 293n51

Senegambia, 7, 42, 82

serfs, 31, 57, 190. *See also* feudalism

sex ratios, 8, 32, 113–14, 118, 196–97, 209–11, 269n36, 275n16. *See also* under data and databases

sexual abuses, seeming absence of, 130, 209, 211–12. *See also* under data and databases

Seychelles, 74, 281n8

Shamo Ayanso, 91, 109, 144, 147, 159, 182, 235, 295n73

Shangalla: country, 70, 249, 260; people, 56, 66, 191, 249

Shangalla, Galgalli. *See* Galgalli Shangalla

Sheba, queen of, 24

Shechak (district), 236

sheep, 36, 40, 46, 49, 68, 214, 216, 227–31, 233, 236–38, 240, 244, 248, 278n11

Sheikh Othman (Yemen), 1–2, 4, 32–33, 76, 111, 113, *114*,116, 118, *120*, 131, 137, 159–60, 163, 171, 177, 180, 187, 189, 191, 194, 196–98, 208, 288nn1–2, 288n19, 290n10. *See also* Keith-Falconer Mission

Shell, Robert Carl-Heinz, 2, 4

Shepherd, Robert Henry Wishart, 125, 137

Sheriff, Abdul, 5

Shewa (kingdom), 16, 18, 22, 24–26, 57, 70–71, 77–78, 102, 192, 260, 265n1, 272n5, 285n19, 298n49

Shoa. *See* Shewa

Shokachi (father of Nuro Chabse), 233

Shonga (country), 233, 260

Shonte (mother of Fayissa Murki), 222

shop assistants and storemen, 180–81

Sidama: country, 215, 217, 234–35, 243–44, 260, 280n6; meaning Abyssinian, 36, 39–40, 64, 191, 276n23, 280n6; people, 64, 91, 235, 280n7; slave traders, 88, 91–92, 215–16, 223, 226, 229, 231–32, 234–36, 239, 241, 246–47, 250–51

Sidama/Abyssinians (slave raiders), 36, 39–40, 54–55, 64–66, 71, 88–89, 93–94, 191, 195, 208, 220–21, 223–24, 226–27, 229–31, 234, 237, 243–44, 247, 249–50, 252, 280n6, 283n42

Siege of Ladysmith (30 October 1899–28 February 1900), 158, 162

Silte: slave raiders, 215; village, 215, 220, 260

Simkins, Charles, 149–50

slave children, 33, 38, 74, 92, 280n2 (chap. 6), 282n25, 282n32, 286n43, 293n35, 297n29. *See also* Oromo slave children

slave loyalty syndrome. *See* Stockholm syndrome

slave trade: first passage, 3–4, 6, 8–9, 29, 51, 73–74, 76–77, 81, 84–85, 87–88, 91–92, 93–94, 97, 105–7, 110–11, 114, 118, 121–22, 130, 138, 149–50, 157, 183, 187–88, 194–96, 198–200, 205–6, 209, 210, 212, 266nn16–17; middle passage, 8, 93, 97, 107–10, 187, 194–96, 199–200, 266n16

smallpox (*finno*), 29, 91–92, 195, 225

snakes, 262

Sodo: slave traders, 76, 231; village, 231, 260

Soga, Rev. Tiyo, 9

Solomon (king), 24

Solomon Gashaw, 59

Somalia, 15, 19

sorghum (*durra*), 215

South African Native Labour Corps (SANLC), 293n51

Southern Nations, Nationalities, and People's Region (SNNPR), 64, 302n7

South Sudan, 15

Soye (mother of Fayissa Hora), 221

Soye Sanyacha, 54–55, 253

Spain, 172, 284n2

Stace, Colonel Edward Vincent, 101, 111–13, 197, 208–9, 288n5, 289n21

St. Chrischona Pilgrim Mission (Switzerland), 207

Stewart, Mina, 137, 146–48, 199, 207, 212, 289n28

Stewart, Rev. James, 10, 120–21, 137, 146, 167–68, 199, 207, 289n25, 289n28, 298n57

Stockholm syndrome, 41, 188–89, 199

Stone, Lawrence, 3

storemen, 180

Strait of Mandeb/Bab-El-Mandeb, 102, *103*

Strangers' Location, Port Elizabeth (South Africa), 180

Sudan, 15, 19, 25

Sudanese (slave raiders), 195

Sudanese Mahdists, 25

Sukute (father of Hawe Sukute), 69, 250

Sukute, Hawe. *See* Hawe Sukute

sultan: of Aussa, 78, 285n14 (see also Aussa sultanate); of Lahej, 288n1; of Morocco, 172; of Tadjoura, 78, 108; of Zanzibar, 100

Sumburi (mother of Liban Bultum), 230

Swahili language, 19

Syria, 16, 207

Table Bay Harbour Board (Cape Town), 181

Tadjoura/Tadjourah/Tajoura/Tajurrah (port), 32, 53, 76–78, 91, 101–2, *102*, 103–4, 108–9, 194, 213, 219, 221, 224–26, 232–33, 235, 241, 244–45, 247–49, 252, 260, 276n21, 279n3, 285n13, 285n16, 285n19; sultan of, 78, 108

tailors, 43, 190, 255

Tarafo (father of Gutama Tarafo), 45, 226

Tarafo, Gutama. *See* Gutama Tarafo

Tarry & Company, engineering firm (Kimberley, South Africa), 180

Taylor, Dora (Nosipho Majeke), 270n40

Tecmessa (slave concubine of mythological Greek hero Ajax), 188

Tekur (slave traders), 217

Temperance Hotel (King William's Town, South Africa), 126

thalers. *See* Maria Theresa dollars

Tibbe (country), 40, 224, 238, 240, 260

Tigrayan people, 11, 18, 22, 28, 88, 265n1

Tigre: country, 36, 76, 220, 222, 260; slave markets/traders, 195, 215, 222–23, 232–33, 241, 243, 245, 247–48, 256; slave raiders, 88; town, 222–25, 230–33, 241, 243, 245, 260

Tiki (father of Guyo Tiki), 226

Tiki, Guyo. *See* Guyo Tiki

Tiksa (father of Amaye Tiksa), 215

Tiksa, Amaye. *See* Amaye Tiksa

Tikse (father of Wayessa Tikse), 240

Tikse, Wayessa. *See* Wayessa Tikse

Tinno, Turungo. *See* Turungo Tinno

Tiv people, 30

tobacco, 46, 253, 262

Tobo (father of Daba Tobo), 219

Tobo, Daba. *See* Daba Tobo

Todal (Yambo leader), 236

Tola Abaye, 180, 236

Tola Lual, 48, 85, 91, 146–47, 236

Tolassa Wayessa, 46, 48–49, 68, 92, 105, 133, *161*, 162–63, 166, 179, 198, 238

Tola Urgessa, 48–49, 180, 237

Tonki (father of Wayessa Tonki), 240

Tonki, Wayessa. *See* Wayessa Tonki

Tosa (village), 234

train travel, 125–26. *See also* railways; Rhodesia Railways

transport drivers (Anglo-Boer War, 1899–1902), 162, 182

Treaty of Addis Ababa (1896), 170

Treaty of Wuchale (1889), 170

trees, *20*, *21*

tribute debt, 36, 89, 230, 243, 247, 250, 253

Tsegay Wolde-Georgis, 26

Turkana, Lake, 15

Turungi (mother of Berille Boko), 244

Turungo Gudda, 43, 69, 180, 254–55

Turungo Tinno, 53, 69, 180, 254–55

Tyamzashe, Benjamin, 144, 293n51

Tyamzashe, George, 261, 304n2

Tyhume (Eastern Cape, South Africa), 121

Tyhume River, 121, 127

typhoid, 29

Tywakadi, Rev. Daniel D., 144, 293n51

Ugga (father of Wakinni Ugga), 255

Ugga, Wakinni. *See* Wakinni Ugga

Ulbarag (village), 220

Ulbaragga (country), 243, 260

Uligge (mother of Faraja Lalego), 220

Umbe (father of Fayissa Umbe), 222

Umbe, Fayissa. *See* Fayissa Umbe

UMCA. *See* Universities' Mission to Central Africa

UNICEF (United Nations Children's Fund), 38, 188

United Kingdom Royal Navy, 2, 4, 8, 74, 76, 78, 97–100, 105, 108–9, 117, 147, 172, 187, 196, 276n21, 285n7

United Nations Children's Fund. *See* UNICEF

United States Navy, 285n7

Universities' Mission to Central Africa (UMCA), 6, 267n25

University of Cape Town, 1–2, 151–52
University of Edinburgh, 289n28
University of the Cape of Good Hope, 133
University of Tübingen, 152
Urbarage country, 214
Urgessa (father of Tola Urgessa), 237
Urgessa, Tola. See Tola Urgessa

Van Heyningen, Elizabeth, 149–50
Vassa, Gustavus (also known as Olaudah
    Equiano), 5, 267n19
Vernal, Fiona, 292n21
Victoria Suspension Bridge, 127
Voltaire (French philosopher, historian, and
    satirist), 190

Waaqa (Oromo Supreme Being), 20–21, 23
Wachali (village), 218, 260
Wagedi (village), 240
wagonmakers, 128, 164, 180
Wakinne Nagesso, 39, 176, 181, 238, 250
Wakinni Ugga, 43, 76, 180, 255
Walagga/Wallaga (district, now Mirab Welega,
    Oromia), 58, 163, 214, 218, 227, 260
Waldmeier, Rev. Theophilus, 207
Wallerstein, Immanuel, 56–57, 59
Walstroom, S., 150
Warabu (father of Galani Warabu), 248
Warabu, Galani. See Galani Warabu
Warakalla/Warakallo/Warakallu (country), 214,
    219, 221, 225, 235, 240, 245, 260
Warkitu Galatu, 133, 150, 182, 256, 294n72,
    295n78
water, 21, 26, 98, 101, 128–29, 163, 223, 252;
    aerated water factory (Cape Town, South
    Africa), 163; in religion, 21; sources and
    supply, 15, 288n1
Watson Institute (Farmerfield, South Africa),
    10, 292n21
Wauchope, Rev. Isaac, 144, 293n51
Wayessa (father of Tolassa Wayessa), 238
Wayessa Gudru, 182, 239, 295n73
Wayessa Tikse, 49, 92, 146, 181, 240, 294n72
Wayessa Tonki, 91, 109, 180, 240, 301n114

Wayessa, Tolassa. See Tolassa Wayessa
Webster, Sophie Nell, 182
Weir, James W., 126
wheat, 46, 215, 262
White, Sir George, 158
Wick, Marc, 303n21
Wilhelm II (Kaiser), 170–71
Windi (village), 237, 260
Woermann Afrika Linie, 176
Wolamo (father of Katshi Wolamo), 228
Wolamo, Katshi. See Katshi Wolamo
Wolde-Georgis, Tsegay. See Tsegay Wolde-
    Georgis
Woldeyes, Getenesh. See Getenesh Woldeyes
woredas (administrative zones), 49
World War I (1914–1918), 7, 157, 172, 176, 181,
    183, 296n5
Wright, A. T. V., 97, 104–5, 107–8
Wulli (father of Badassa Wulli), 216
Wulli, Badassa. See Badassa Wulli

xenophobia, 152
Xhosa: language (isiXhosa), 132–33; people
    (amaXhosa), 9–10, 135, 143–44
Xiniwe, Paul, 126

Yajubi. See Ajubi
Yambo: country, 236, 260, 302n7; people, 56,
    66, 191, 236
Yanfa (village), 235, 260
Yao people, 30
Yarachi (mother of Fayissi Gemo), 40, 70,
    248
Yassa country, 215, 260
Yirga, Gidey. See Gidey Yirga
Yohannes IV (Ethiopian emperor), 24–26
Young, Dr. John Cameron, 158–59, 163, 166
Young, Robert, 137, 138

Zaida (mother of Amanu Figgo), 214
zamacha (predatory expeditions), 25
Zanzibar, 113, 123; slave trade, 5, 97, 100; sultan
    of, 100
Zeila/Zaila/Zayla, 101, 285n19